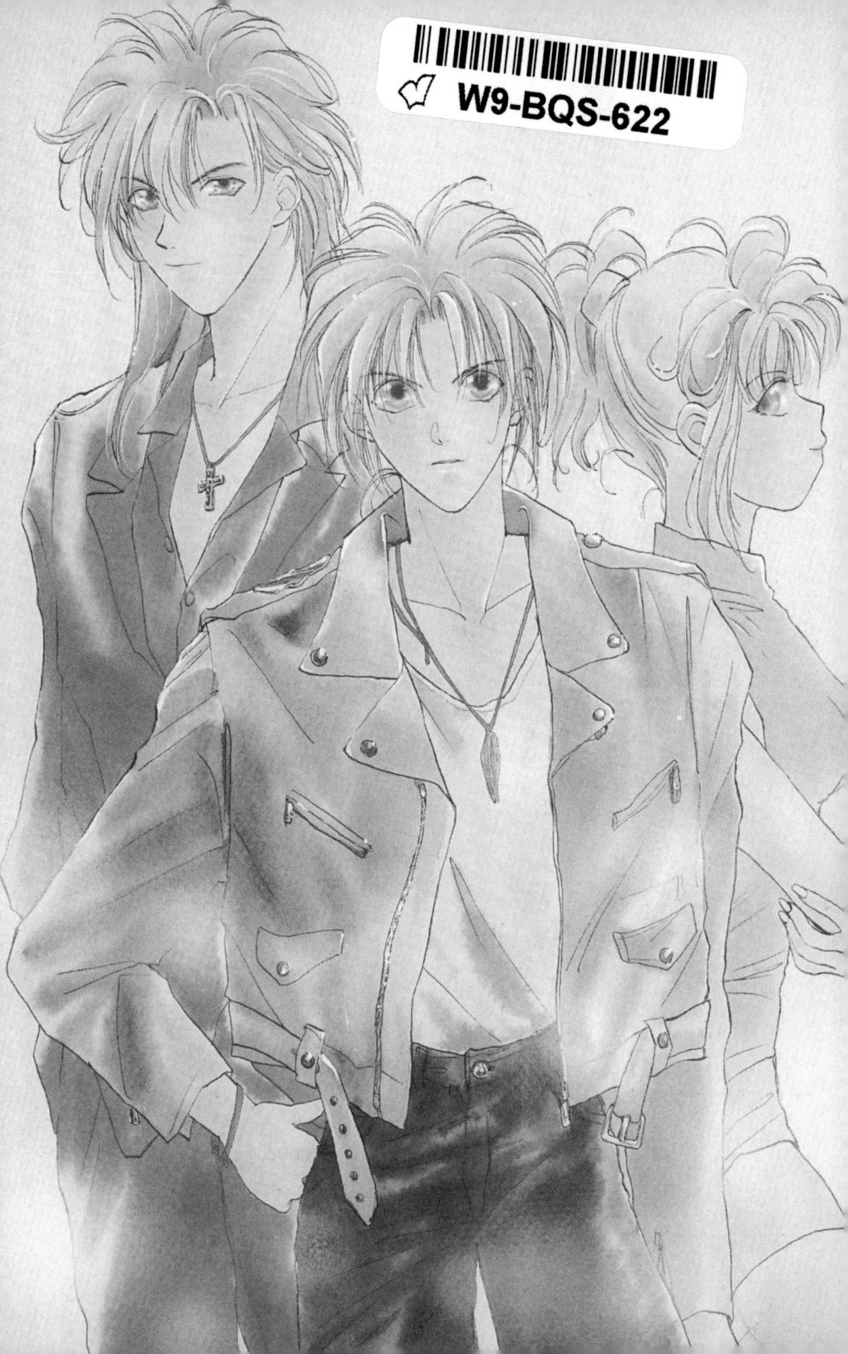

Translator - Ray Yoshimoto
English Adaptation - Jamie S. Rich
Associate Editor - Paul Morrissey
Retouch and Lettering - Miyuki Ishihara
Graphic Design - Monalisa J. de Asis
Cover Layout - Raymond Makowski
Licensing Inspiration - Kate Kiley

Editor - Jake Forbes
Managing Editor - Jill Freshney
Production Coordinator - Antonio DePietro
Production Manager - Jennifer Miller
Art Director - Matt Alford
Editorial Director - Jeremy Ross
VP of Production - Ron Klamert
President & C.O.O. - John Parker
Publisher & C.E.O. - Stuart Levy

Email: editor@TOKYOPOP.com
Come visit us online at www.TOKYOPOP.com

A  Manga

TOKYOPOP Inc.
5900 Wilshire Blvd. Suite 2000
Los Angeles, CA 90036

Gravitation Vol. 3

ISBN: 1-59182-335-8

First TOKYOPOP® printing: December 2003

10 9 8 7 6 5 4 3 2 1
Printed in the USA

Volume 3

By
Maki Murakami

TOKYOPOP®
Los Angeles • Tokyo • London

CONTENTS

GRAVITATION

THE MEMBERS OF THE GRAVITATION BAND

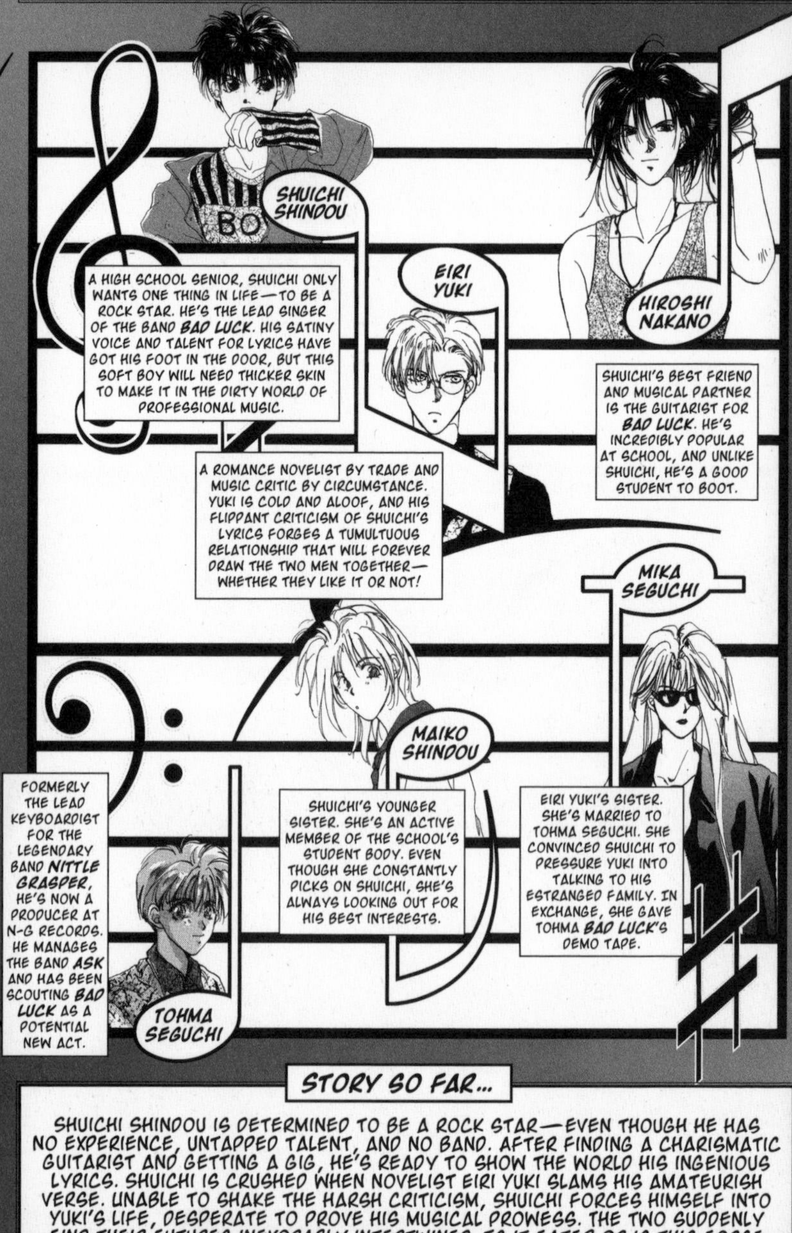
HIROSHI NAKANO
SHUICHI'S BEST FRIEND AND MUSICAL PARTNER IS THE GUITARIST FOR BAD LUCK. HE'S INCREDIBLY POPULAR AT SCHOOL, AND UNLIKE SHUICHI, HE'S A GOOD STUDENT TO BOOT.
SHUICHI SHINDOU
A HIGH SCHOOL SENIOR, SHUICHI ONLY WANTS ONE THING IN LIFE—TO BE A ROCK STAR. HE'S THE LEAD SINGER OF THE BAND BAD LUCK. HIS SATINY VOICE AND TALENT FOR LYRICS HAVE GOT HIS FOOT IN THE DOOR, BUT THIS SOFT BOY WILL NEED THICKER SKIN TO MAKE IT IN THE DIRTY WORLD OF PROFESSIONAL MUSIC.
BO
EIRI YUKI
A ROMANCE NOVELIST BY TRADE AND MUSIC CRITIC BY CIRCUMSTANCE. YUKI IS COLD AND ALOOF, AND HIS FLIPPANT CRITICISM OF SHUICHI'S LYRICS FORGES A TUMULTUOUS RELATIONSHIP THAT WILL FOREVER DRAW THE TWO MEN TOGETHER—WHETHER THEY LIKE IT OR NOT!
MIKA SEGUCHI
EIRI YUKI'S SISTER. SHE'S MARRIED TO TOHMA SEGUCHI. SHE CONVINCED SHUICHI TO PRESSURE YUKI INTO TALKING TO HIS ESTRANGED FAMILY. IN EXCHANGE, SHE GAVE TOHMA BAD LUCK'S DEMO TAPE.
MAIKO SHINDOU
SHUICHI'S YOUNGER SISTER. SHE'S AN ACTIVE MEMBER OF THE SCHOOL'S STUDENT BODY. EVEN THOUGH SHE CONSTANTLY PICKS ON SHUICHI, SHE'S ALWAYS LOOKING OUT FOR HIS BEST INTERESTS.
TOHMA SEGUCHI
FORMERLY THE LEAD KEYBOARDIST FOR THE LEGENDARY BAND NITTLE GRASPER, HE'S NOW A PRODUCER AT N-G RECORDS. HE MANAGES THE BAND ASK AND HAS BEEN SCOUTING BAD LUCK AS A POTENTIAL NEW ACT.

STORY SO FAR...

SHUICHI SHINDOU IS DETERMINED TO BE A ROCK STAR—EVEN THOUGH HE HAS NO EXPERIENCE, UNTAPPED TALENT, AND NO BAND. AFTER FINDING A CHARISMATIC GUITARIST AND GETTING A GIG, HE'S READY TO SHOW THE WORLD HIS INGENIOUS LYRICS. SHUICHI IS CRUSHED WHEN NOVELIST EIRI YUKI SLAMS HIS AMATEURISH VERSE. UNABLE TO SHAKE THE HARSH CRITICISM, SHUICHI FORCES HIMSELF INTO YUKI'S LIFE, DESPERATE TO PROVE HIS MUSICAL PROWESS. THE TWO SUDDENLY FIND THEIR FUTURES INEXORABLY INTERTWINED. IS IT FATE? OR IS THIS FORCE SOMETHING MORE PRIMAL—LIKE GRAVITY?

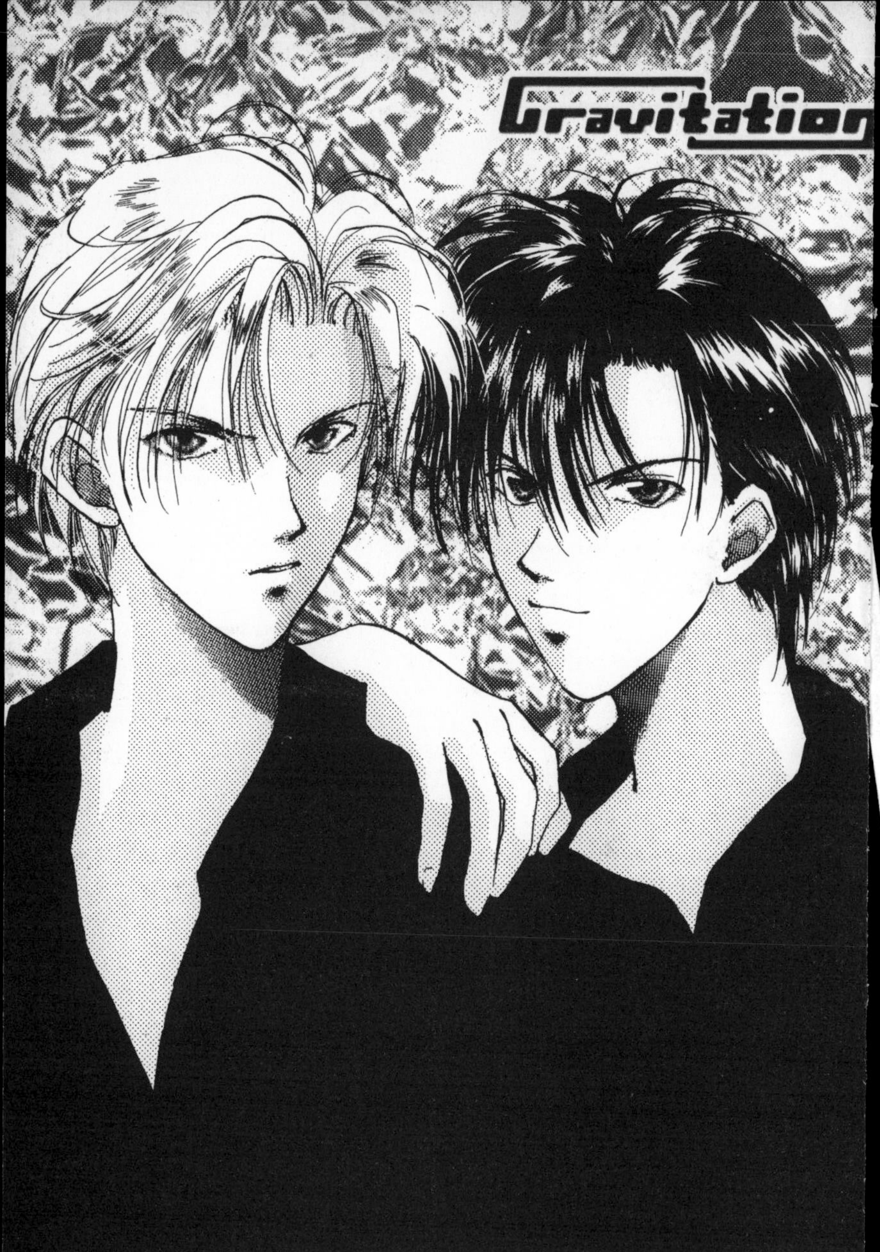
Gravitation

track 9

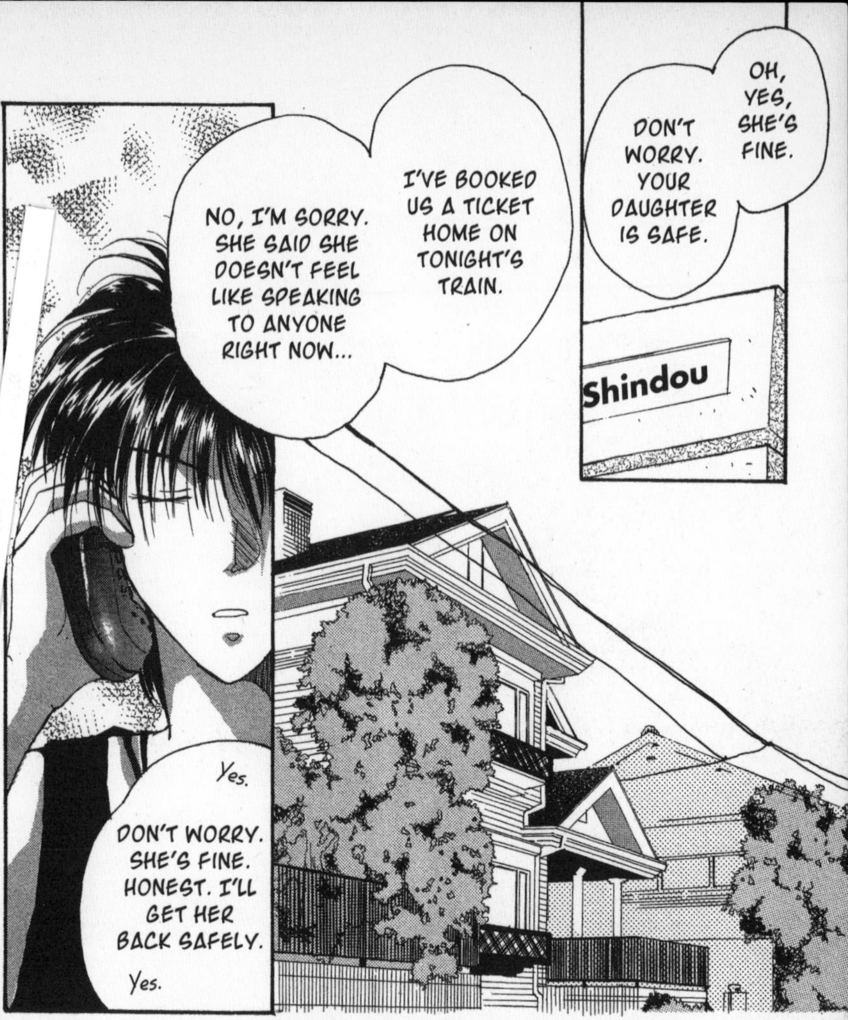
OH, YES, SHE'S FINE.
DON'T WORRY. YOUR DAUGHTER IS SAFE.
Shindou
I'VE BOOKED US A TICKET HOME ON TONIGHT'S TRAIN.
NO, I'M SORRY. SHE SAID SHE DOESN'T FEEL LIKE SPEAKING TO ANYONE RIGHT NOW...
Yes.
DON'T WORRY. SHE'S FINE. HONEST. I'LL GET HER BACK SAFELY.
Yes.

ABOUT GRAVITATION TRACK 9

Things are going nuts now. Eiri's totally lost it. Tatsuha Uesugi has turned things upside down. And he's only 16? Hey, doesn't he have school to go to? And he's bisexual, too?! So he likes guys **and** girls. I'm just taking things to the limit. I guess I'm a glutton for punishment. Big bro's got a soft side to him, but his younger brother, Tatsuha, is a complete sadist. What to do?

But really, he's a good guy...

It'd be pretty crazy if there really were 16 year olds like him running around. I wonder where I could find one? Oh, I'm getting so excited! No, I need to calm down. Guys like this are always great to watch from afar. Tatsuha is gonna play a big role in Track 9, so read on! Laugh! Cry!

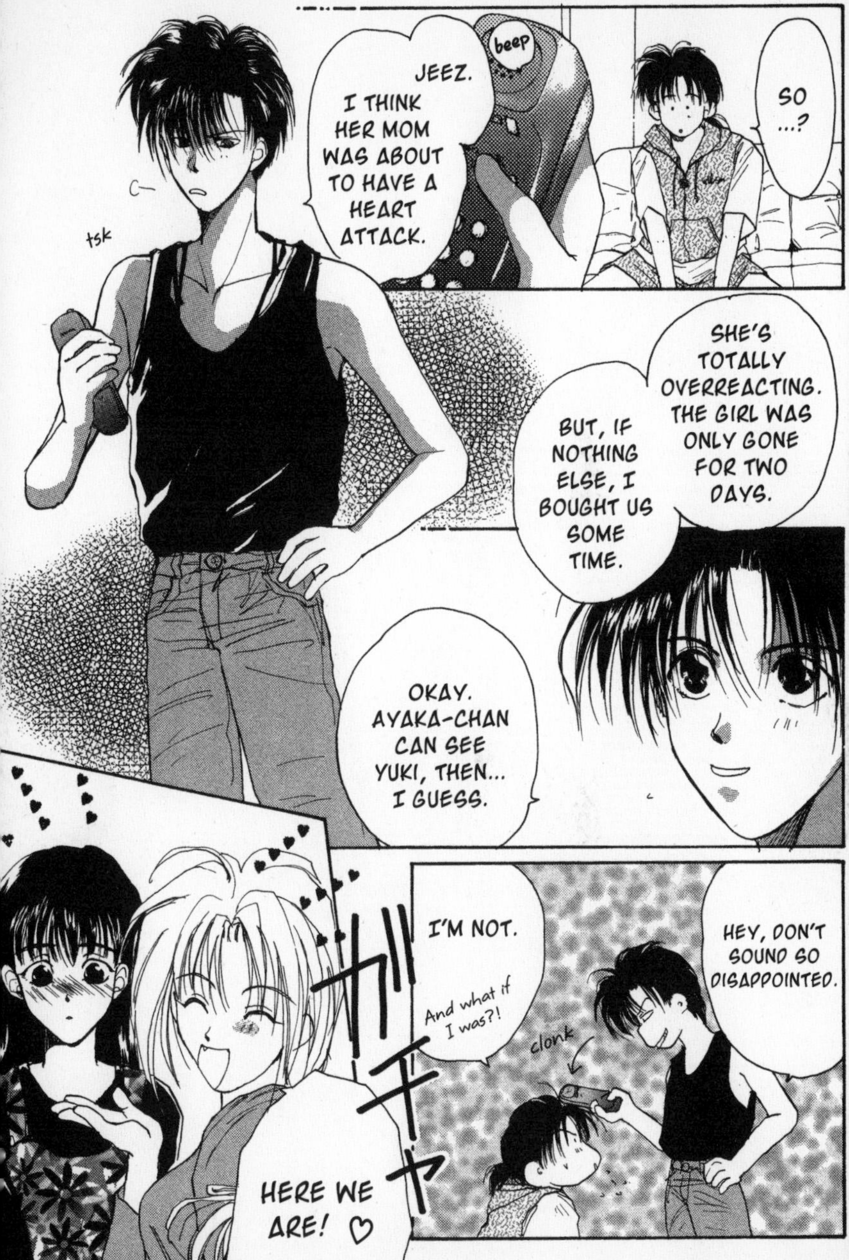
SO ...?
beep
JEEZ. I THINK HER MOM WAS ABOUT TO HAVE A HEART ATTACK.
C—
tsk
SHE'S TOTALLY OVERREACTING. THE GIRL WAS ONLY GONE FOR TWO DAYS.
BUT, IF NOTHING ELSE, I BOUGHT US SOME TIME.
OKAY. AYAKA-CHAN CAN SEE YUKI, THEN... I GUESS.
HEY, DON'T SOUND SO DISAPPOINTED.
I'M NOT.
And what if I was?!
clonk
ガチャ
HERE WE ARE! ♡

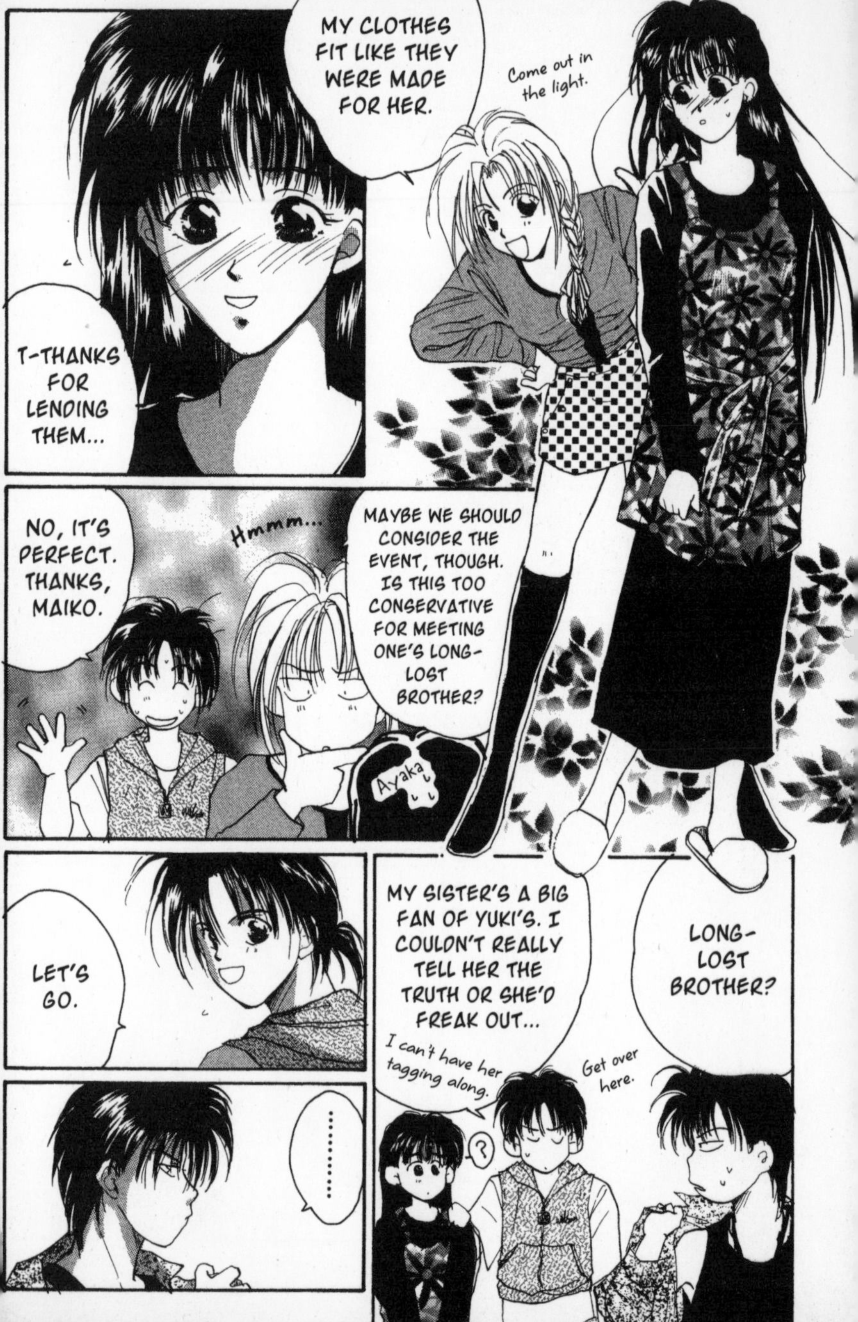
Come out in the light.
MY CLOTHES FIT LIKE THEY WERE MADE FOR HER.
T-THANKS FOR LENDING THEM...
MAYBE WE SHOULD CONSIDER THE EVENT, THOUGH. IS THIS TOO CONSERVATIVE FOR MEETING ONE'S LONG-LOST BROTHER?
Hmmm...
NO, IT'S PERFECT. THANKS, MAIKO.
Ayaka
LONG-LOST BROTHER?
Get over here.
MY SISTER'S A BIG FAN OF YUKI'S. I COULDN'T REALLY TELL HER THE TRUTH OR SHE'D FREAK OUT...
I can't have her tagging along.
?
LET'S GO.
......

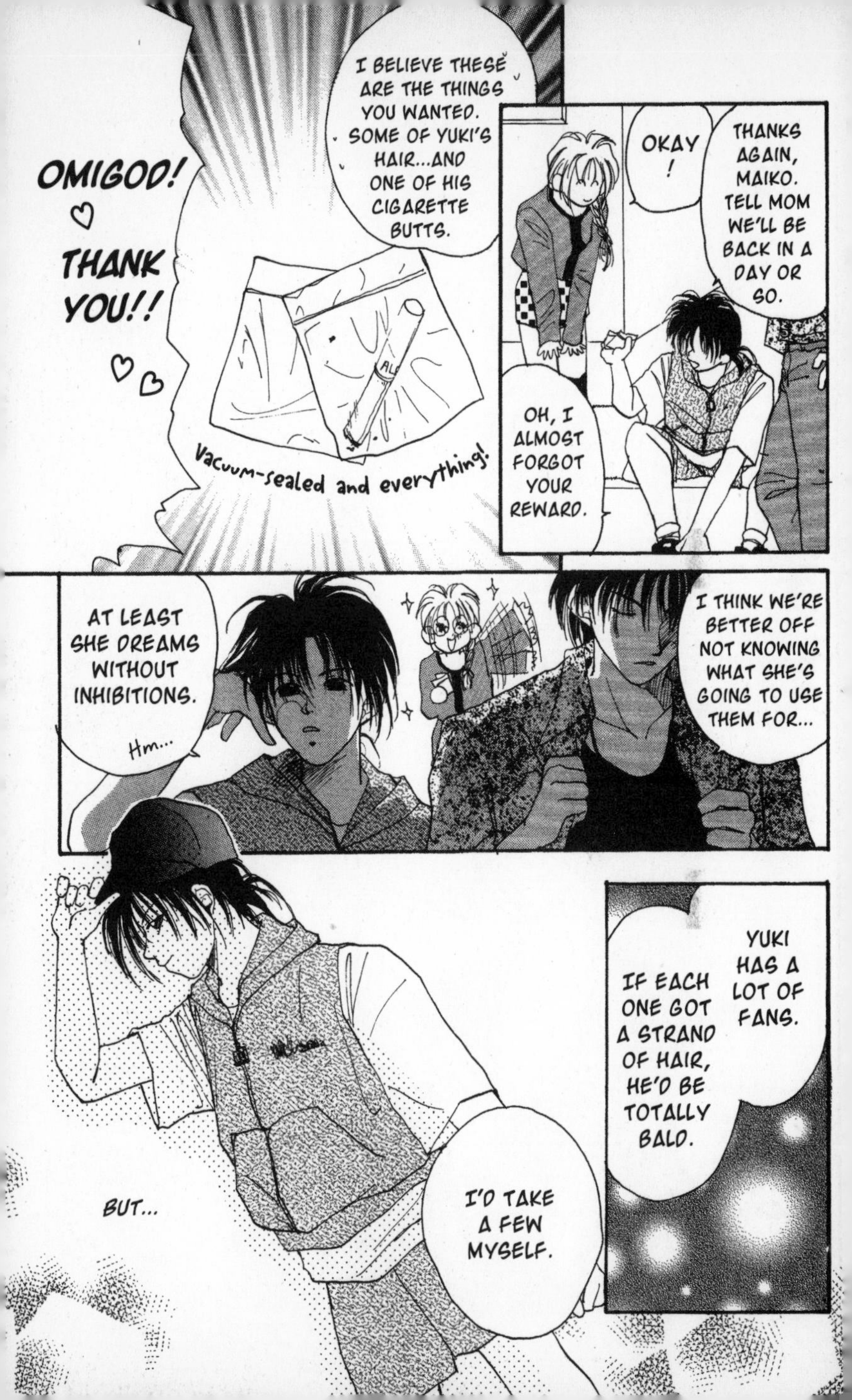
I BELIEVE THESE ARE THE THINGS YOU WANTED. SOME OF YUKI'S HAIR...AND ONE OF HIS CIGARETTE BUTTS.
OMIGOD! ♡ THANK YOU!! ♡ ♡
Vacuum-sealed and everything!
THANKS AGAIN, MAIKO. TELL MOM WE'LL BE BACK IN A DAY OR SO.
OKAY!
OH, I ALMOST FORGOT YOUR REWARD.
I THINK WE'RE BETTER OFF NOT KNOWING WHAT SHE'S GOING TO USE THEM FOR...
AT LEAST SHE DREAMS WITHOUT INHIBITIONS.
Hm...
YUKI HAS A LOT OF FANS.
IF EACH ONE GOT A STRAND OF HAIR, HE'D BE TOTALLY BALD.
BUT...
I'D TAKE A FEW MYSELF.

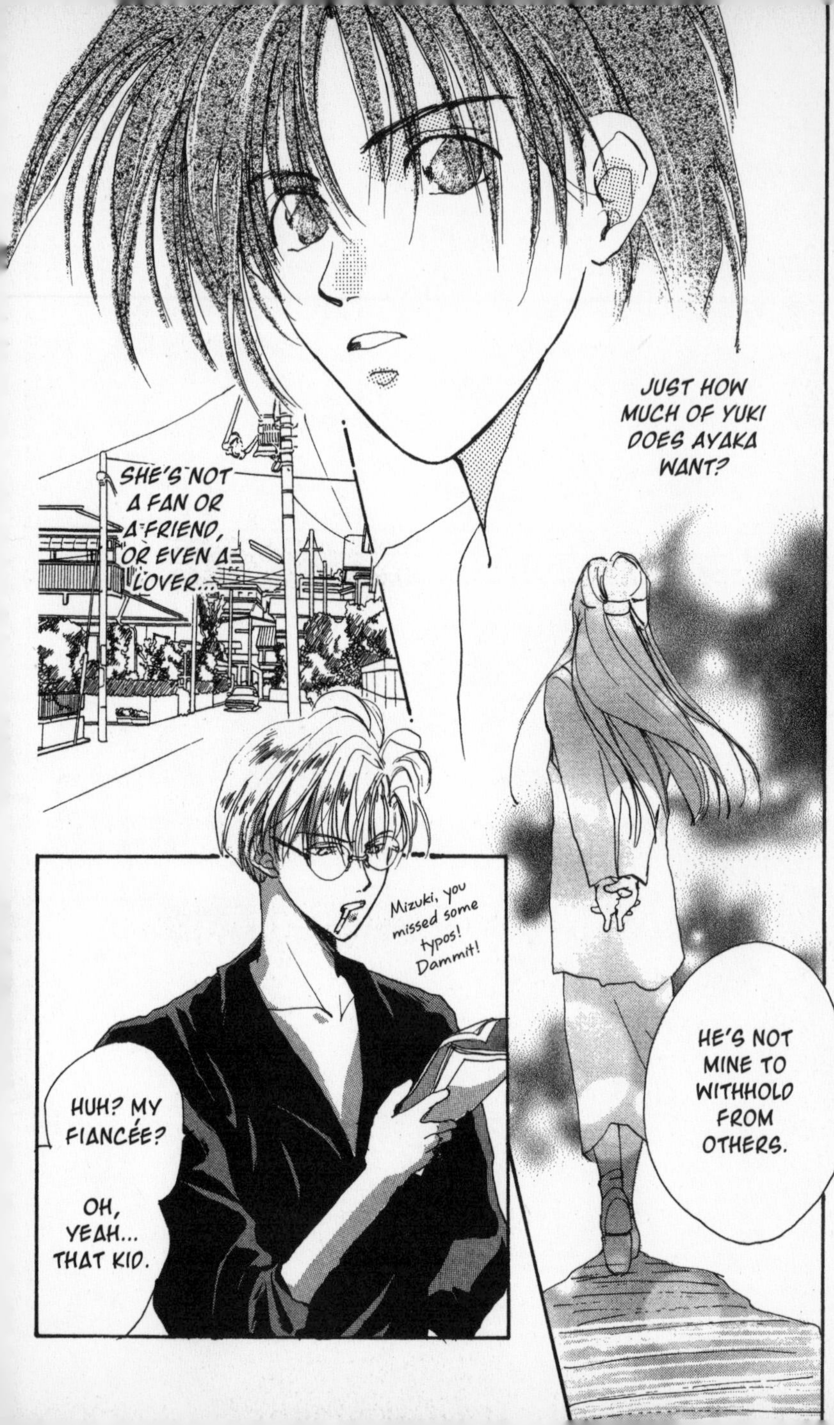
JUST HOW MUCH OF YUKI DOES AYAKA WANT?
SHE'S NOT A FAN OR A FRIEND, OR EVEN A LOVER...
HE'S NOT MINE TO WITHHOLD FROM OTHERS.
HUH? MY FIANCÉE?
OH, YEAH... THAT KID.
Mizuki, you missed some typos! Dammit!

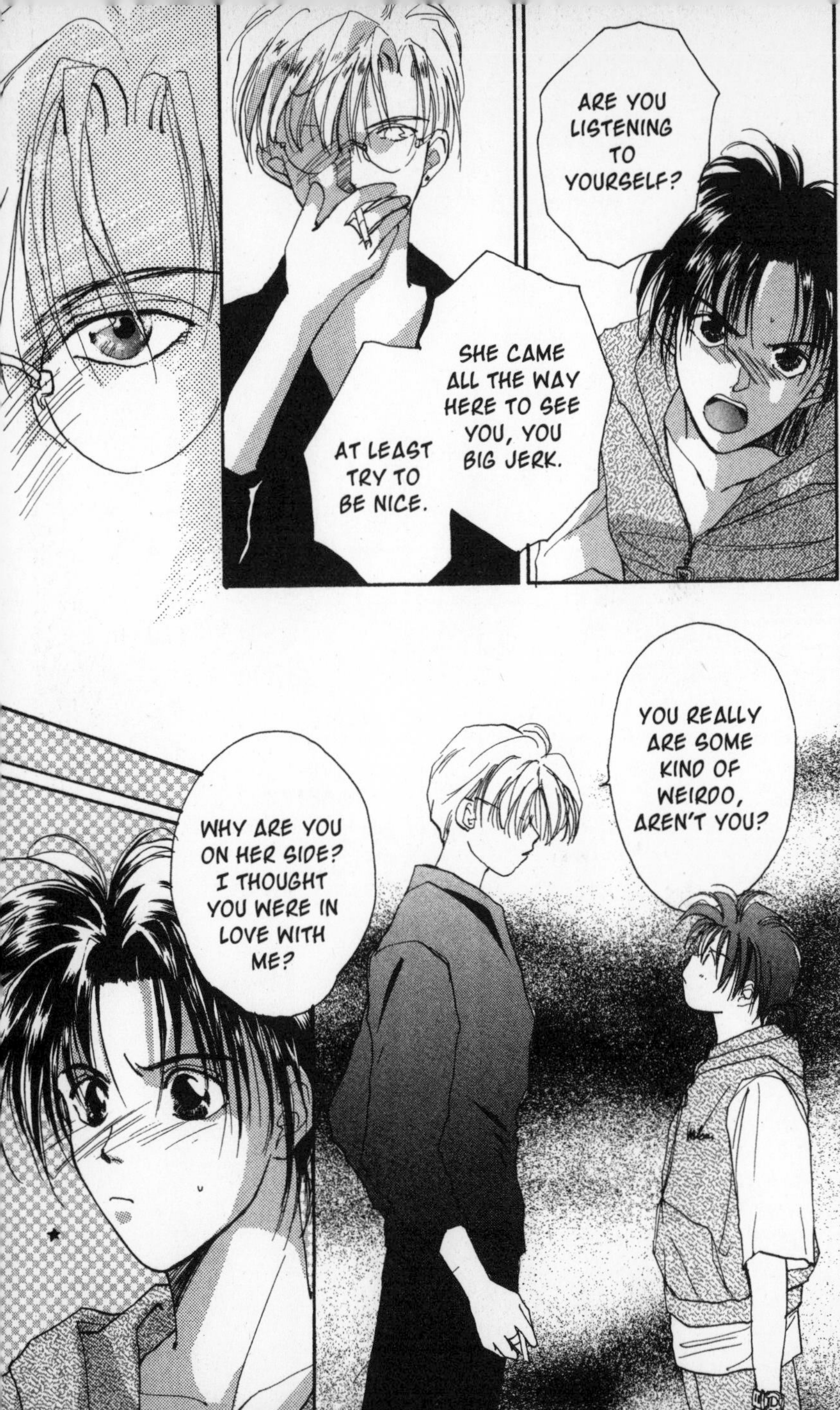
ARE YOU LISTENING TO YOURSELF?
SHE CAME ALL THE WAY HERE TO SEE YOU, YOU BIG JERK.
AT LEAST TRY TO BE NICE.
YOU REALLY ARE SOME KIND OF WEIRDO, AREN'T YOU?
WHY ARE YOU ON HER SIDE? I THOUGHT YOU WERE IN LOVE WITH ME?

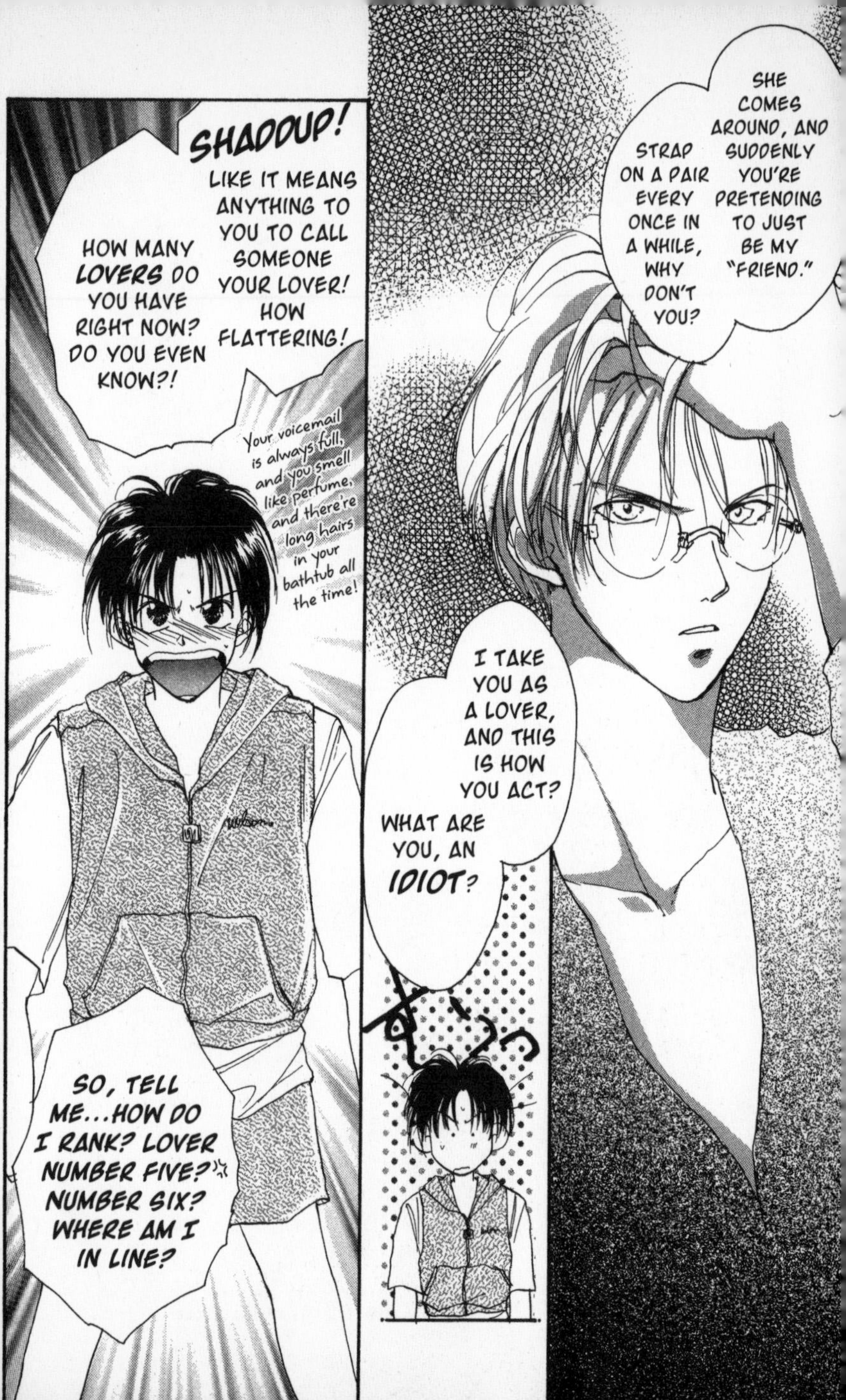
SHE COMES AROUND, AND SUDDENLY YOU'RE PRETENDING TO JUST BE MY "FRIEND."
STRAP ON A PAIR EVERY ONCE IN A WHILE, WHY DON'T YOU?
I TAKE YOU AS A LOVER, AND THIS IS HOW YOU ACT?
WHAT ARE YOU, AN IDIOT?
SHADDUP!
LIKE IT MEANS ANYTHING TO YOU TO CALL SOMEONE YOUR LOVER! HOW FLATTERING!
HOW MANY LOVERS DO YOU HAVE RIGHT NOW? DO YOU EVEN KNOW?!
Your voicemail is always full, and you smell like perfume, and there're long hairs in your bathtub all the time!
SO, TELL ME...HOW DO I RANK? LOVER NUMBER FIVE? NUMBER SIX? WHERE AM I IN LINE?

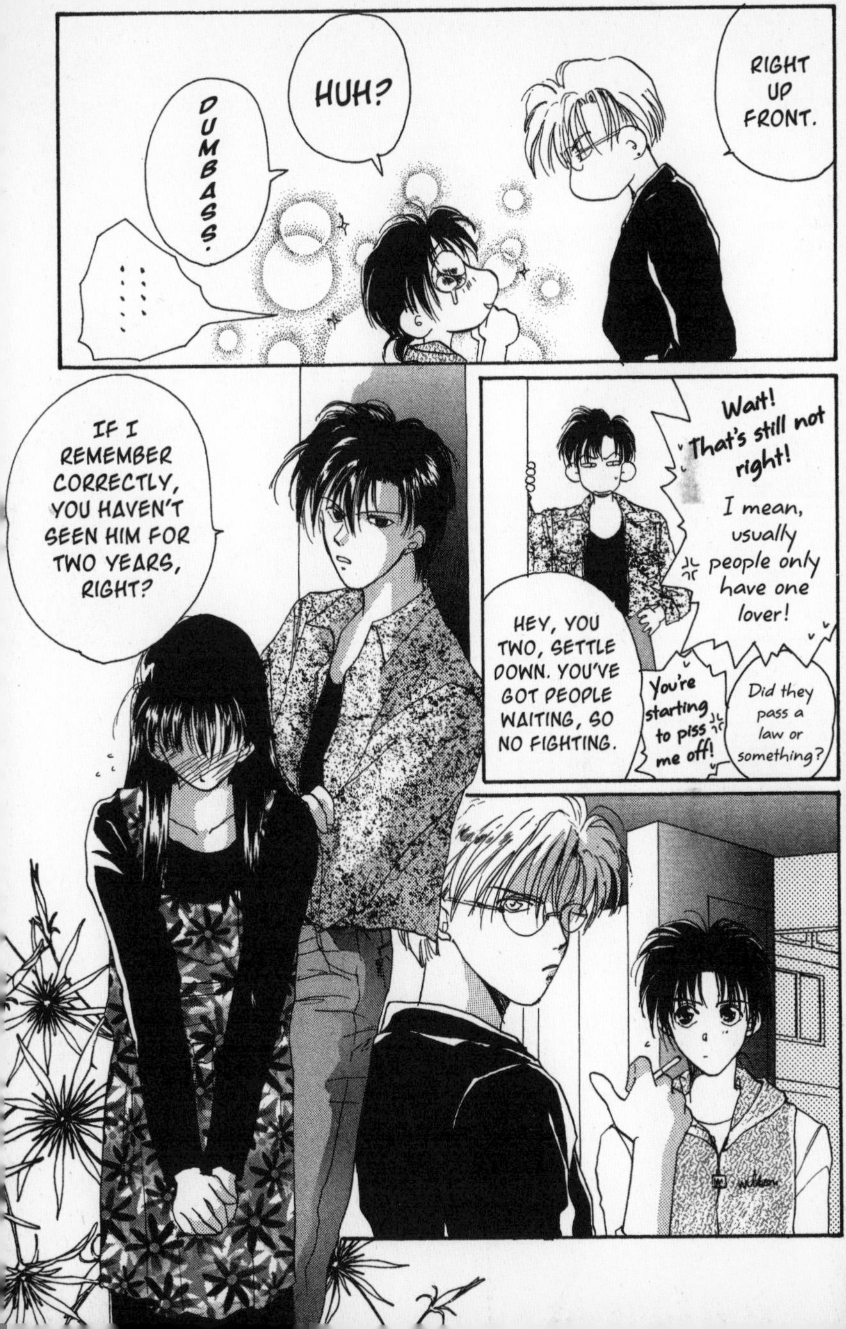
RIGHT UP FRONT.
HUH?
DUMBASS.
......
Wait! That's still not right! I mean, usually people only have one lover!
Did they pass a law or something?
You're starting to piss me off!
HEY, YOU TWO, SETTLE DOWN. YOU'VE GOT PEOPLE WAITING, SO NO FIGHTING.
IF I REMEMBER CORRECTLY, YOU HAVEN'T SEEN HIM FOR TWO YEARS, RIGHT?

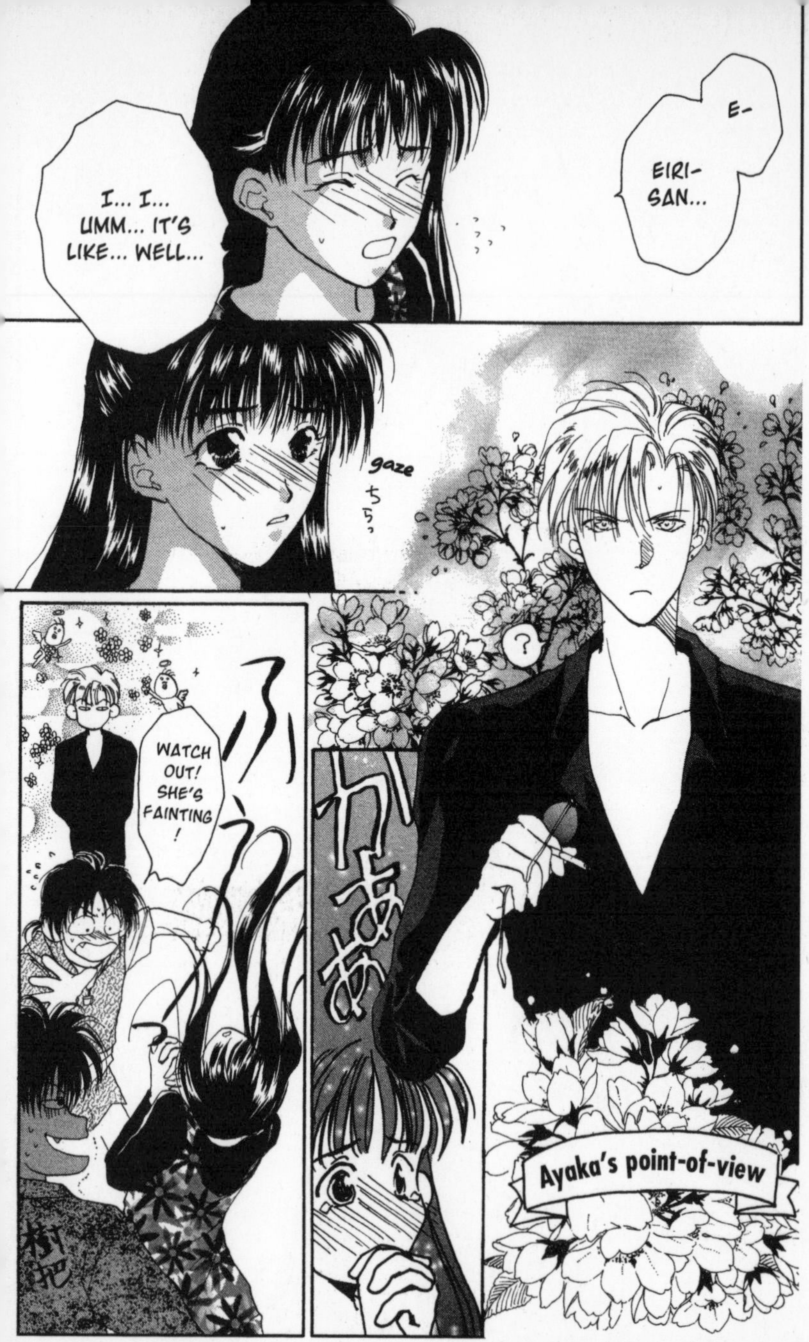
E- EIRI-SAN...
I... I... UMM... IT'S LIKE... WELL...
Ayaka's point-of-view
?
gaze
WATCH OUT! SHE'S FAINTING!

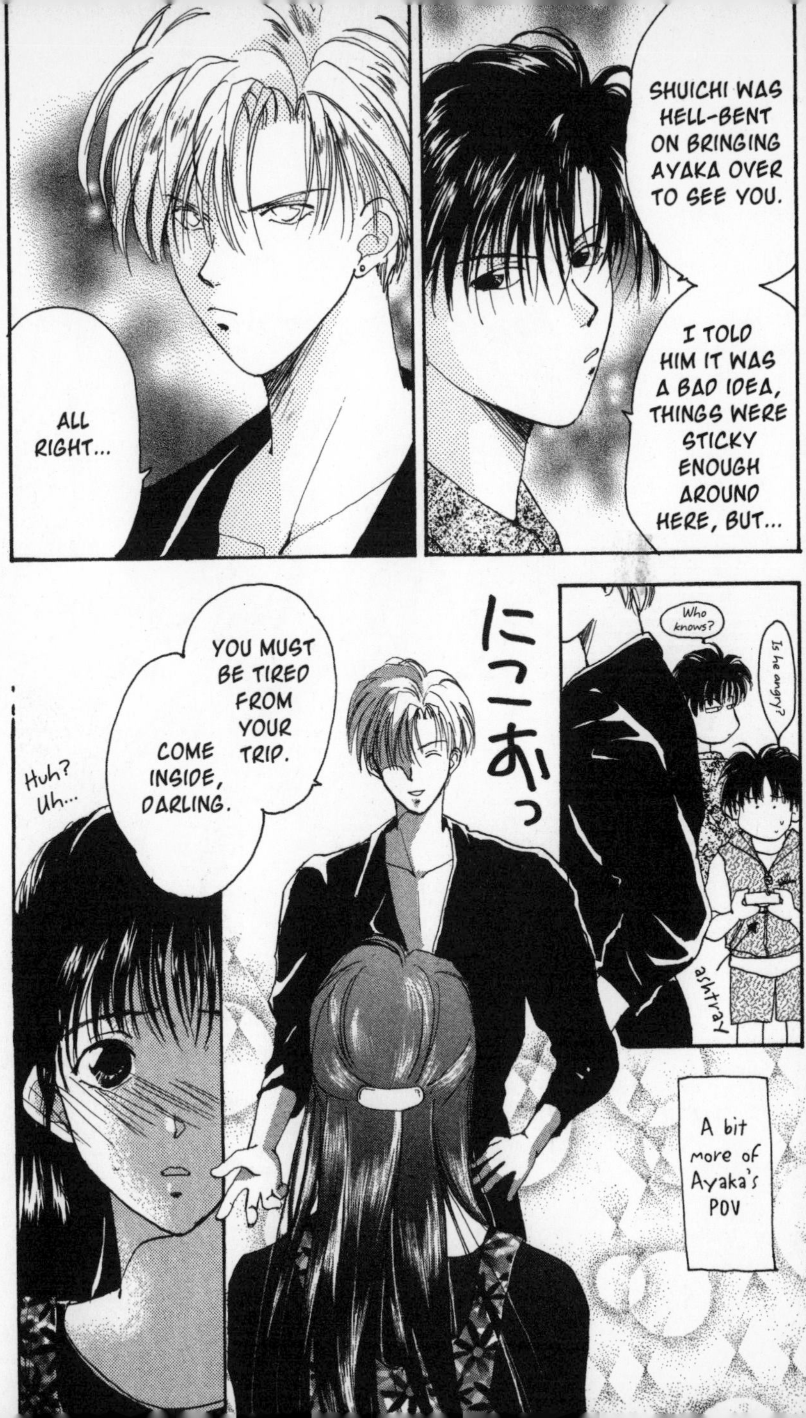
SHUICHI WAS HELL-BENT ON BRINGING AYAKA OVER TO SEE YOU.
I TOLD HIM IT WAS A BAD IDEA, THINGS WERE STICKY ENOUGH AROUND HERE, BUT...
ALL RIGHT...
Is he angry?
Who knows?
ashtray
にっこおっ
YOU MUST BE TIRED FROM YOUR TRIP. COME INSIDE, DARLING.
Huh? Uh...
A bit more of Ayaka's POV

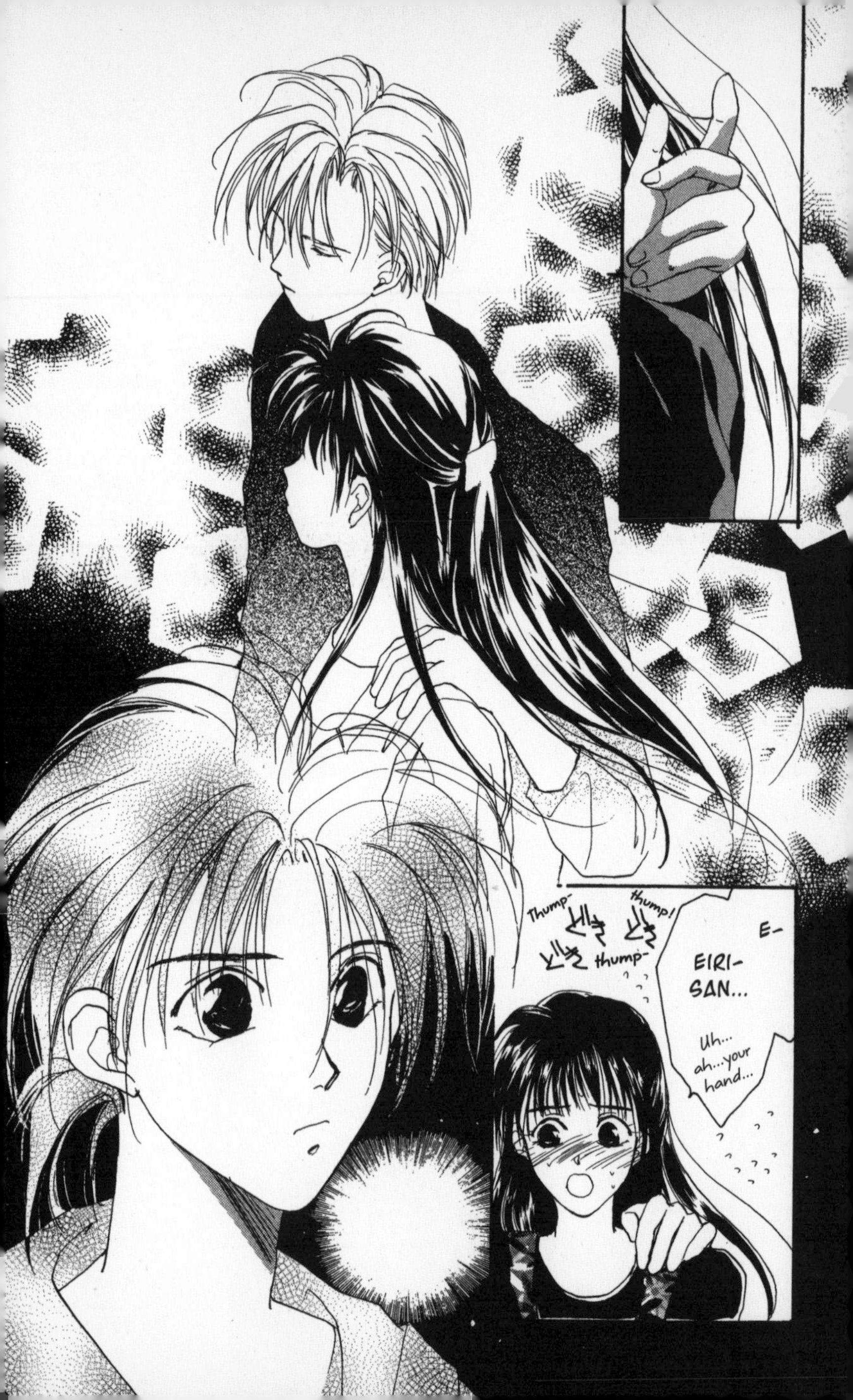

Thump- どきどき thump! どきどき thump-
E-
EIRI-SAN...
Uh... ah...your hand...

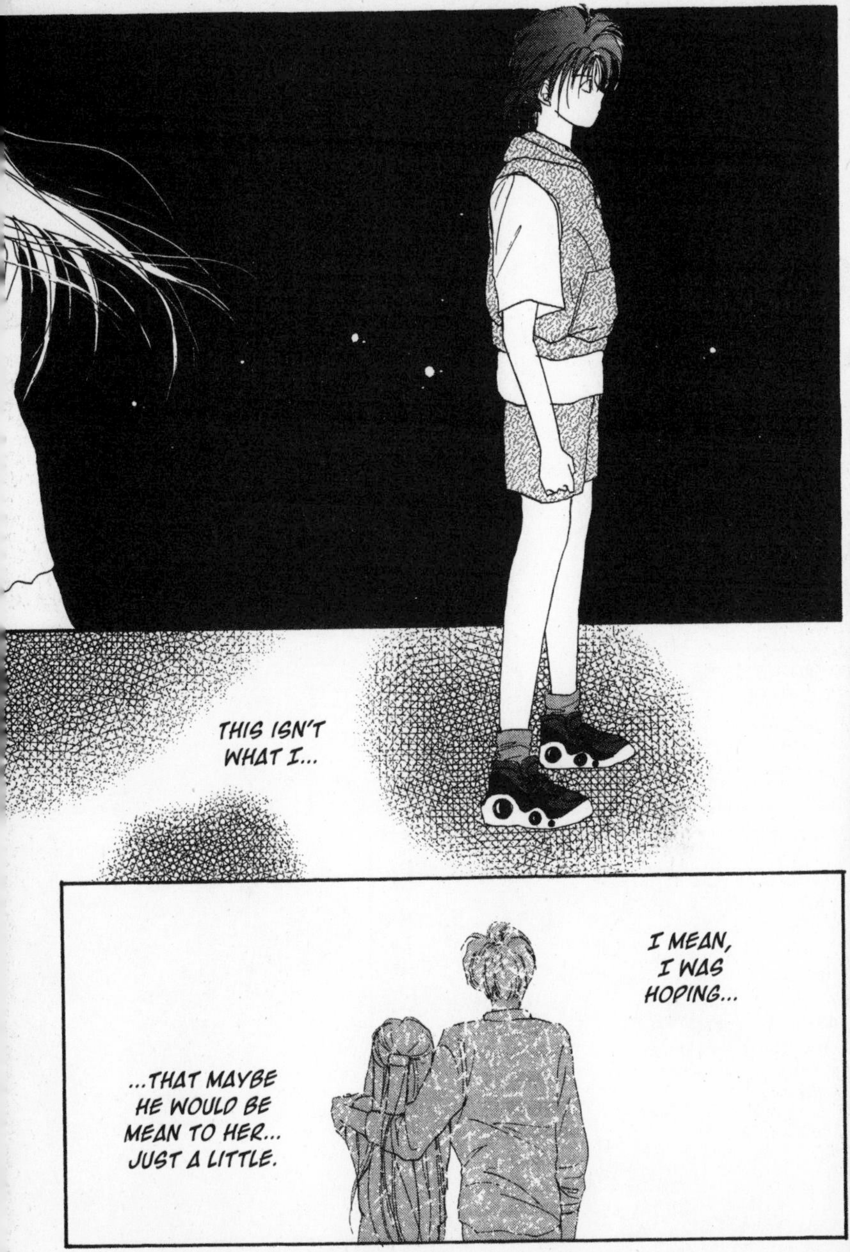
THIS ISN'T WHAT I...
I MEAN, I WAS HOPING...
...THAT MAYBE HE WOULD BE MEAN TO HER... JUST A LITTLE.

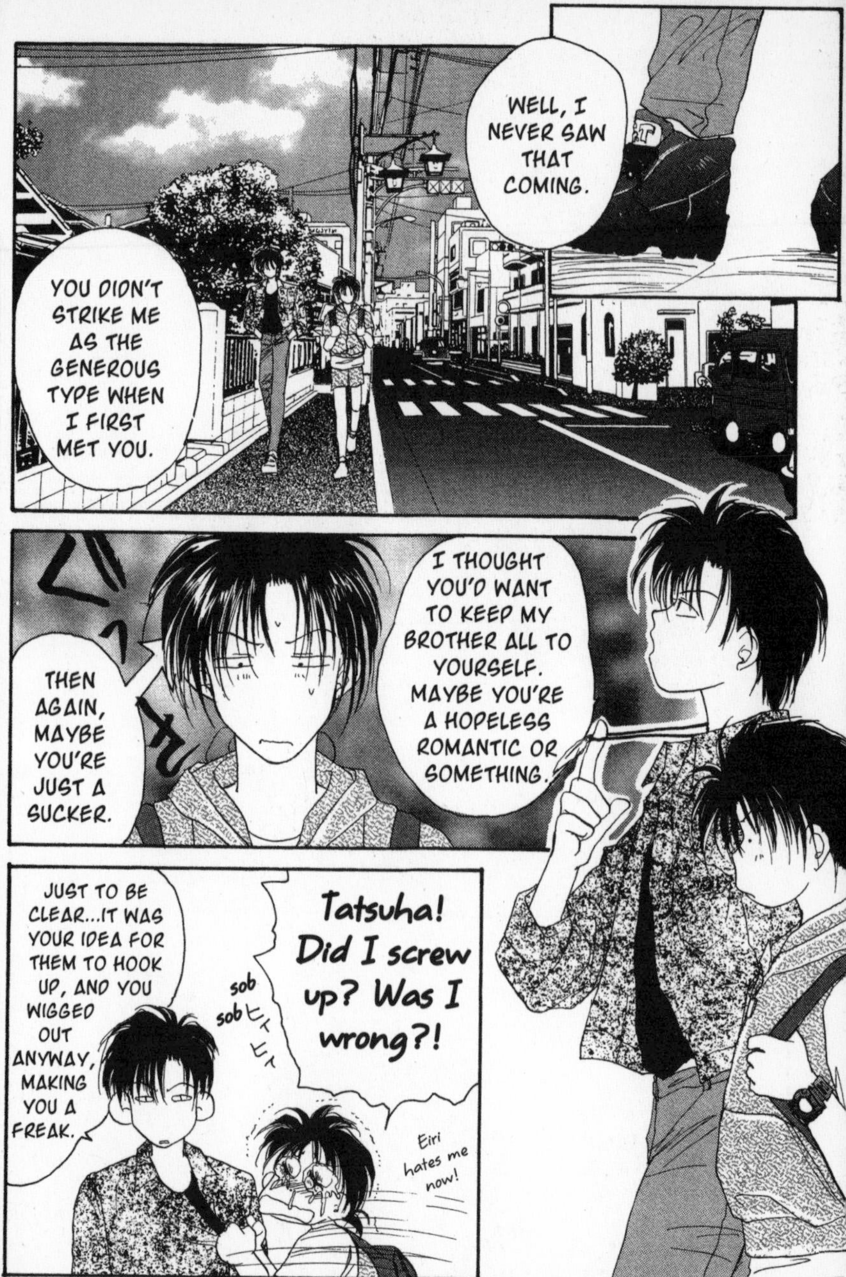
WELL, I NEVER SAW THAT COMING.
YOU DIDN'T STRIKE ME AS THE GENEROUS TYPE WHEN I FIRST MET YOU.
I THOUGHT YOU'D WANT TO KEEP MY BROTHER ALL TO YOURSELF. MAYBE YOU'RE A HOPELESS ROMANTIC OR SOMETHING.
THEN AGAIN, MAYBE YOU'RE JUST A SUCKER.
Tatsuha! Did I screw up? Was I wrong?!
sob sob
Eiri hates me now!
JUST TO BE CLEAR...IT WAS YOUR IDEA FOR THEM TO HOOK UP, AND YOU WIGGED OUT ANYWAY, MAKING YOU A FREAK.
16 years old
18 years old

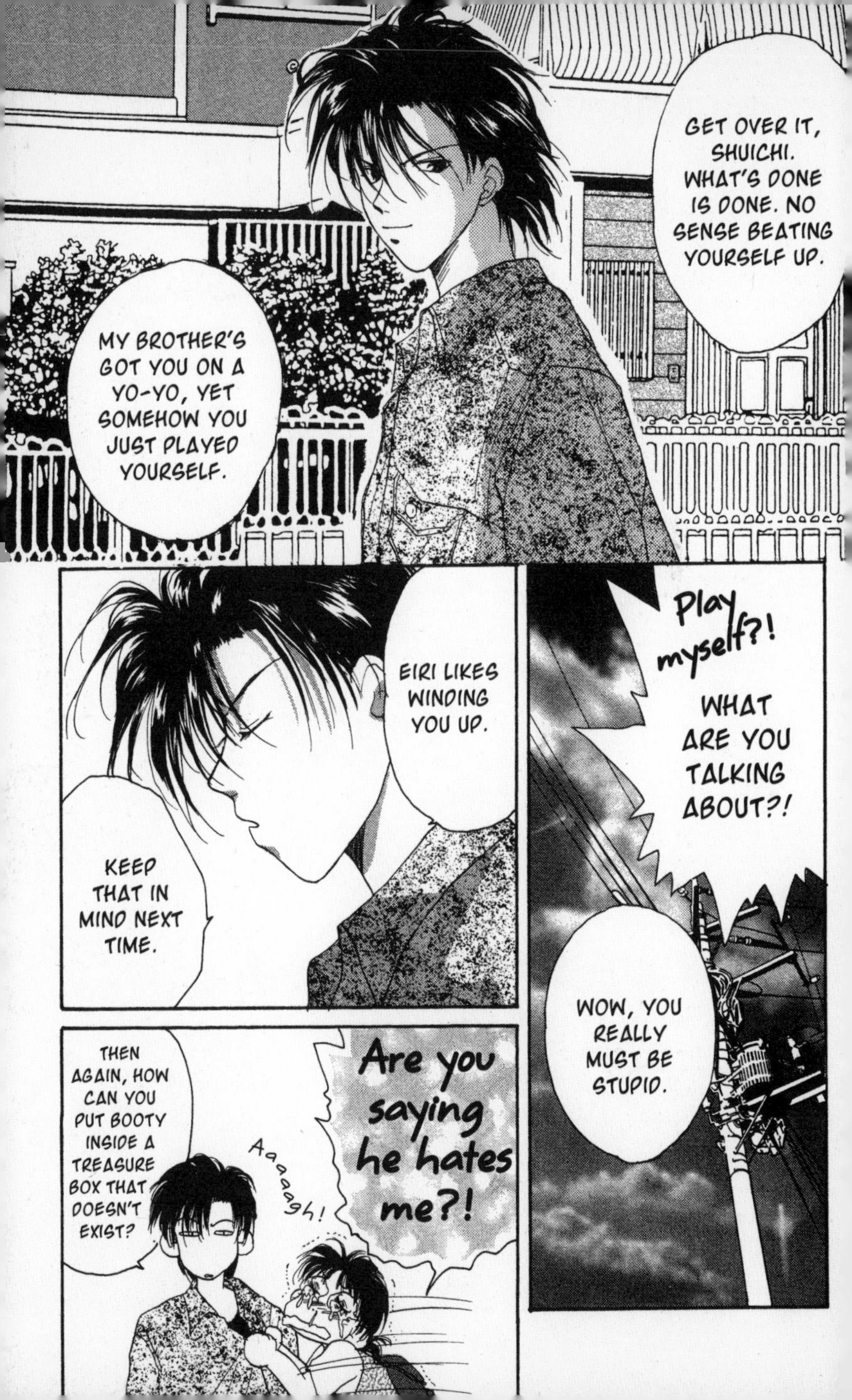
GET OVER IT, SHUICHI. WHAT'S DONE IS DONE. NO SENSE BEATING YOURSELF UP.
MY BROTHER'S GOT YOU ON A YO-YO, YET SOMEHOW YOU JUST PLAYED YOURSELF.
Play myself?!
WHAT ARE YOU TALKING ABOUT?!
WOW, YOU REALLY MUST BE STUPID.
EIRI LIKES WINDING YOU UP.
KEEP THAT IN MIND NEXT TIME.
Are you saying he hates me?!
Aaaaagh!
THEN AGAIN, HOW CAN YOU PUT BOOTY INSIDE A TREASURE BOX THAT DOESN'T EXIST?

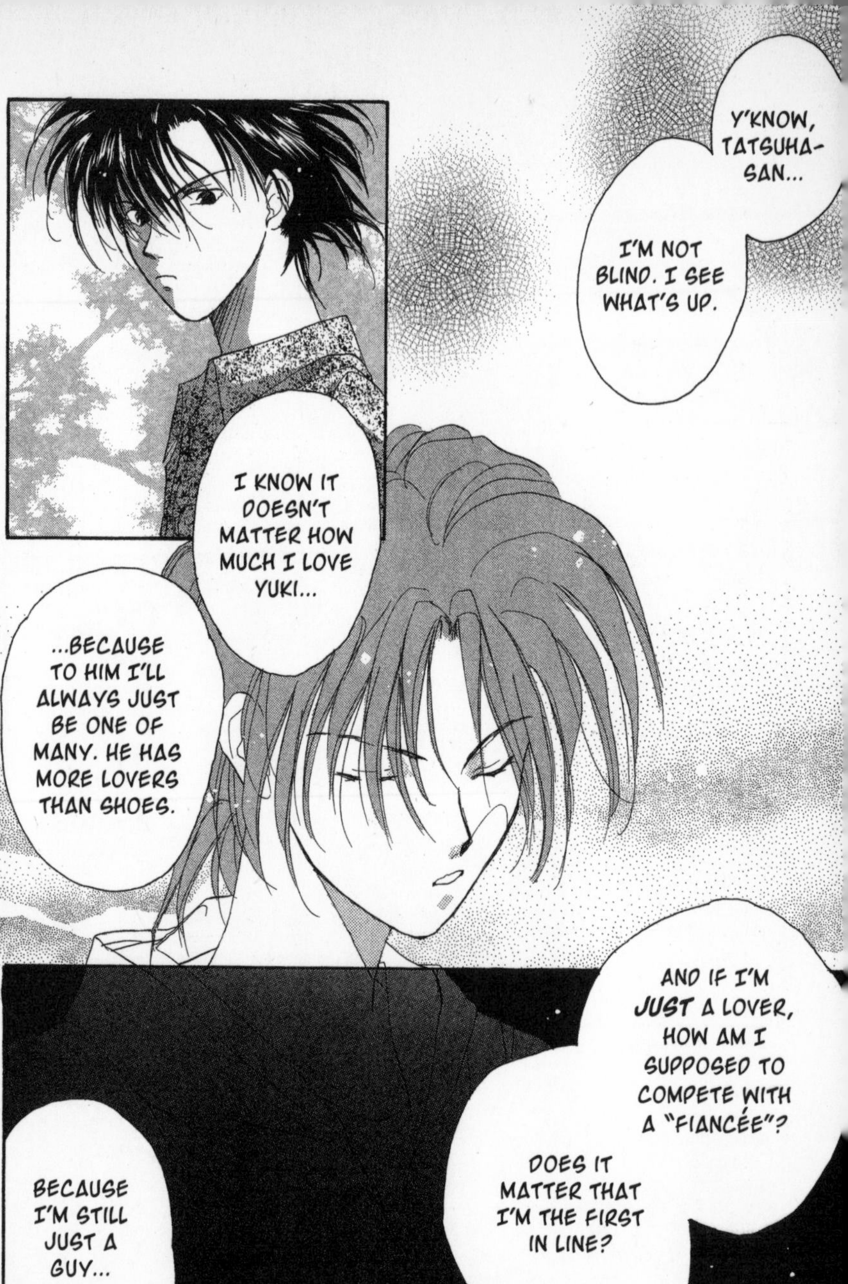
Y'KNOW, TATSUHA-SAN...
I'M NOT BLIND. I SEE WHAT'S UP.
I KNOW IT DOESN'T MATTER HOW MUCH I LOVE YUKI...
...BECAUSE TO HIM I'LL ALWAYS JUST BE ONE OF MANY. HE HAS MORE LOVERS THAN SHOES.
AND IF I'M *JUST* A LOVER, HOW AM I SUPPOSED TO COMPETE WITH A "FIANCÉE"?
DOES IT MATTER THAT I'M THE FIRST IN LINE?
BECAUSE I'M STILL JUST A GUY...

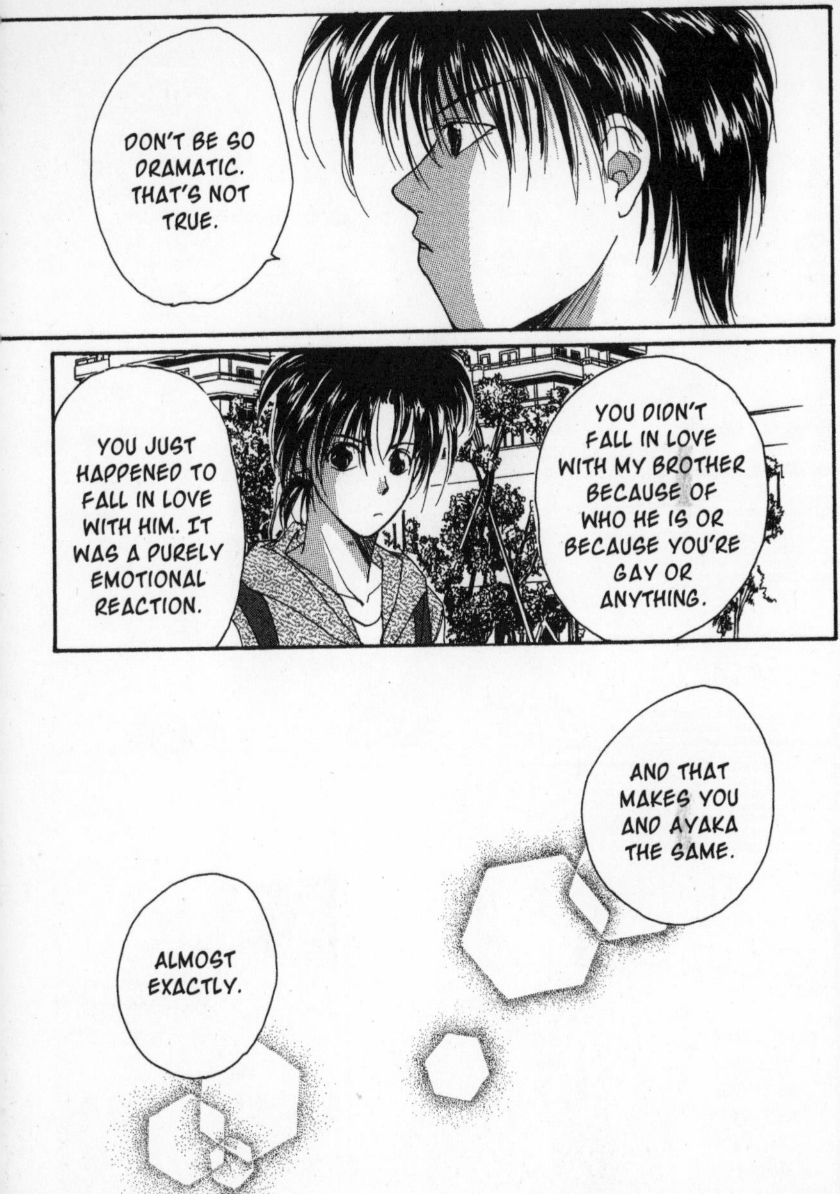
DON'T BE SO DRAMATIC. THAT'S NOT TRUE.
YOU DIDN'T FALL IN LOVE WITH MY BROTHER BECAUSE OF WHO HE IS OR BECAUSE YOU'RE GAY OR ANYTHING.
YOU JUST HAPPENED TO FALL IN LOVE WITH HIM. IT WAS A PURELY EMOTIONAL REACTION.
AND THAT MAKES YOU AND AYAKA THE SAME.
ALMOST EXACTLY.

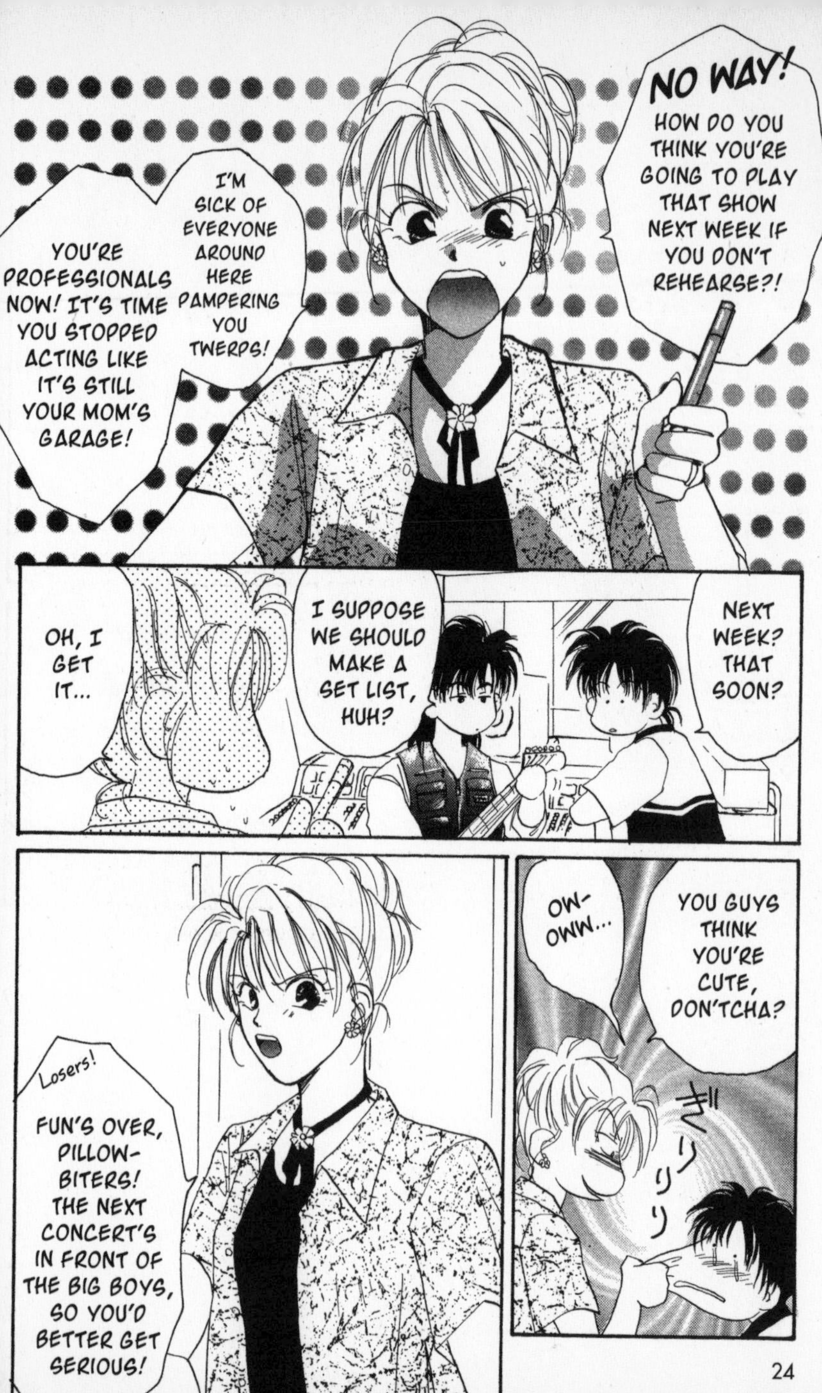
NO WAY! HOW DO YOU THINK YOU'RE GOING TO PLAY THAT SHOW NEXT WEEK IF YOU DON'T REHEARSE?!
I'M SICK OF EVERYONE AROUND HERE PAMPERING YOU TWERPS!
YOU'RE PROFESSIONALS NOW! IT'S TIME YOU STOPPED ACTING LIKE IT'S STILL YOUR MOM'S GARAGE!
NEXT WEEK? THAT SOON?
I SUPPOSE WE SHOULD MAKE A SET LIST, HUH?
OH, I GET IT...
YOU GUYS THINK YOU'RE CUTE, DON'TCHA?
OW-OWW...
ぎりりり
Losers!
FUN'S OVER, PILLOW-BITERS! THE NEXT CONCERT'S IN FRONT OF THE BIG BOYS, SO YOU'D BETTER GET SERIOUS!

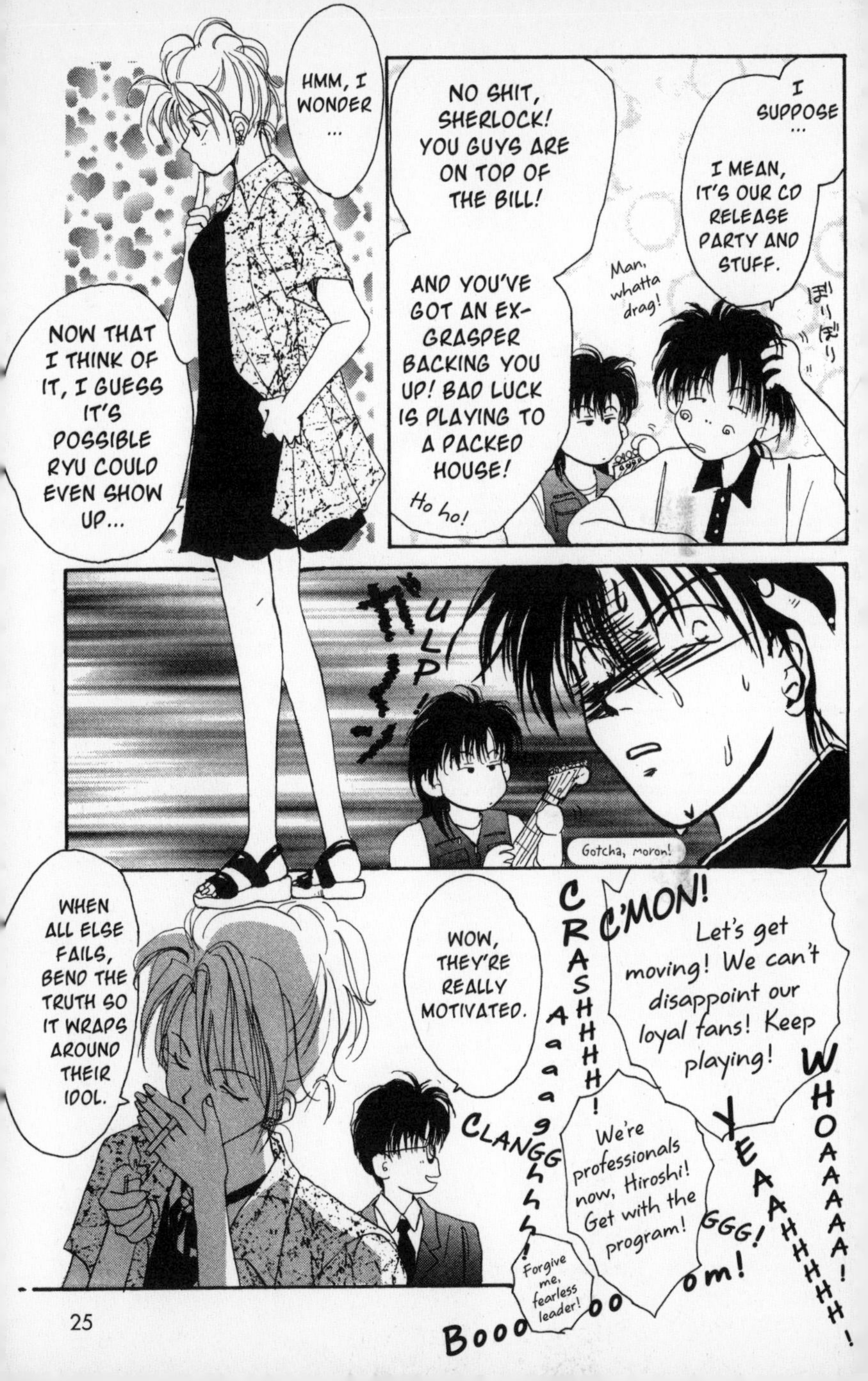

I SUPPOSE ... I MEAN, IT'S OUR CD RELEASE PARTY AND STUFF.
ぽりぽり
Man, whatta drag!
NO SHIT, SHERLOCK! YOU GUYS ARE ON TOP OF THE BILL!
AND YOU'VE GOT AN EX-GRASPER BACKING YOU UP! BAD LUCK IS PLAYING TO A PACKED HOUSE!
Ho ho!
HMM, I WONDER ...
NOW THAT I THINK OF IT, I GUESS IT'S POSSIBLE RYU COULD EVEN SHOW UP...
ULP!
Gotcha, moron!
C'MON! Let's get moving! We can't disappoint our loyal fans! Keep playing!
WHOAAAAAA!
YEAAAHHHHHH!
We're professionals now, Hiroshi! Get with the program!
GGG!
Forgive me, fearless leader!
CRASHHHH!
Aaaaagghhh!
CLANGGG!
Booooooom!
WOW, THEY'RE REALLY MOTIVATED.
WHEN ALL ELSE FAILS, BEND THE TRUTH SO IT WRAPS AROUND THEIR IDOL.

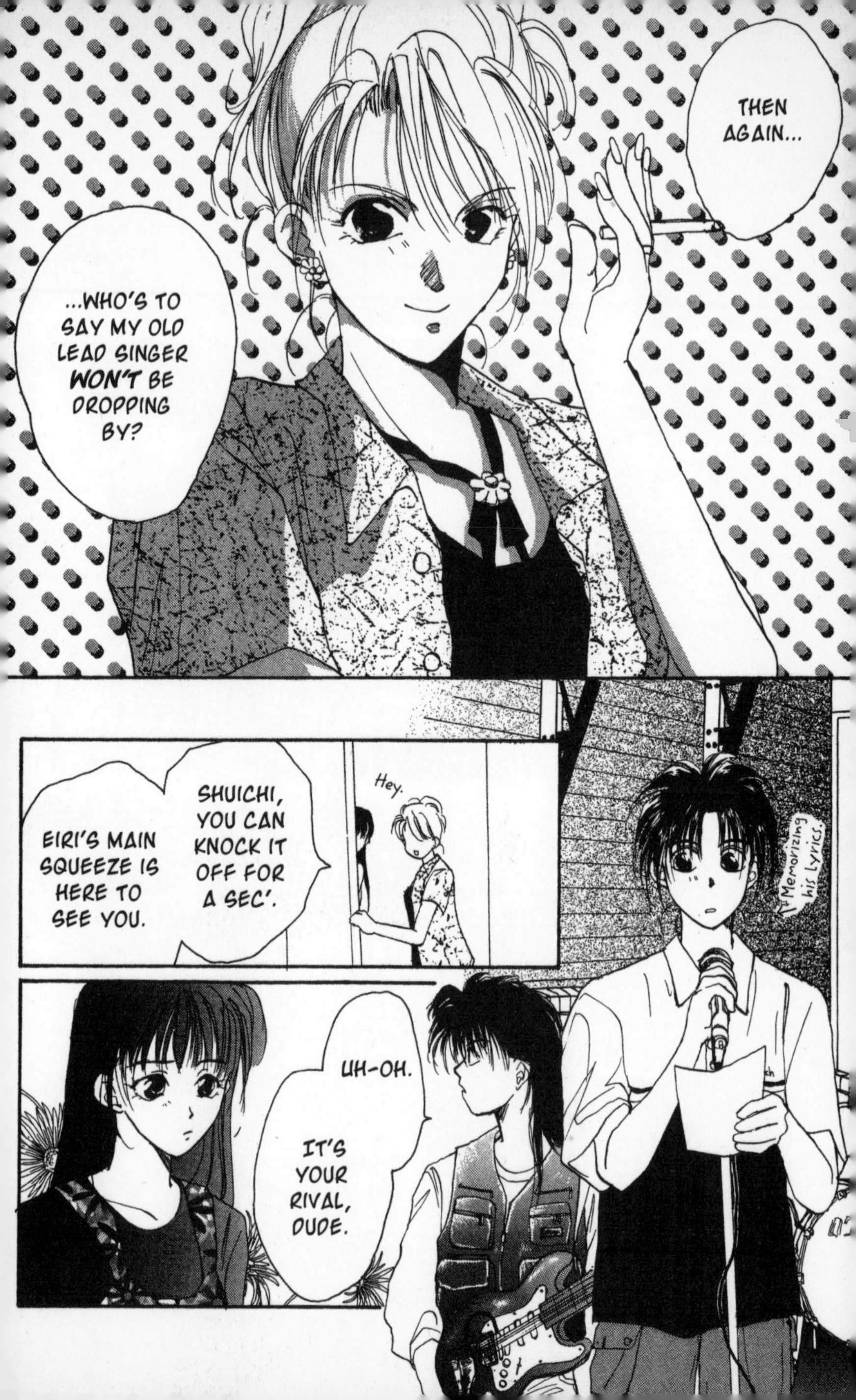
THEN AGAIN...
...WHO'S TO SAY MY OLD LEAD SINGER **WON'T** BE DROPPING BY?
Memorizing his Lyrics.
Hey.
SHUICHI, YOU CAN KNOCK IT OFF FOR A SEC'.
EIRI'S MAIN SQUEEZE IS HERE TO SEE YOU.
UH-OH.
IT'S YOUR RIVAL, DUDE.

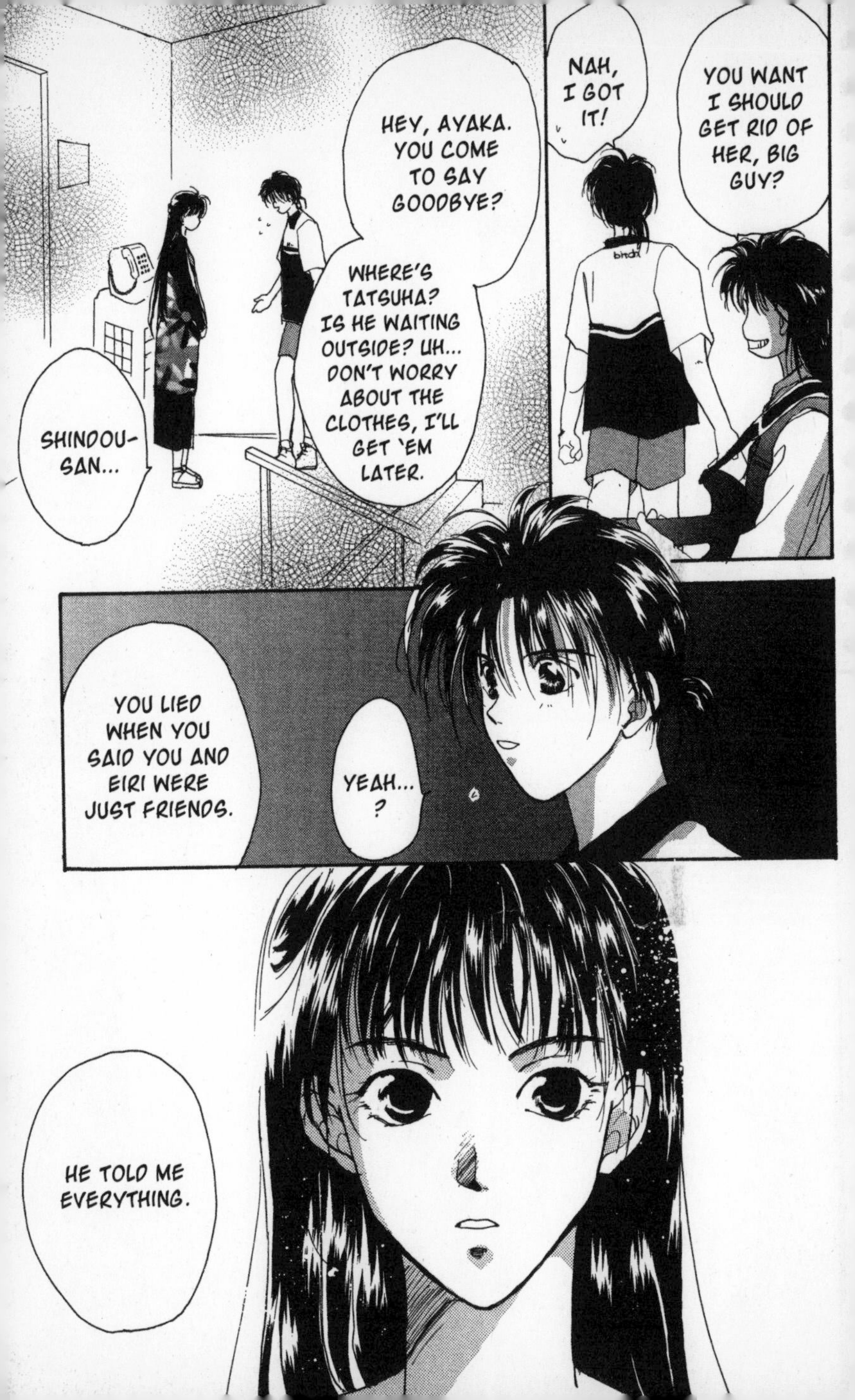
YOU WANT I SHOULD GET RID OF HER, BIG GUY?
NAH, I GOT IT!
HEY, AYAKA. YOU COME TO SAY GOODBYE?
WHERE'S TATSUHA? IS HE WAITING OUTSIDE? UH... DON'T WORRY ABOUT THE CLOTHES, I'LL GET 'EM LATER.
SHINDOU-SAN...
YEAH...?
YOU LIED WHEN YOU SAID YOU AND EIRI WERE JUST FRIENDS.
HE TOLD ME EVERYTHING.

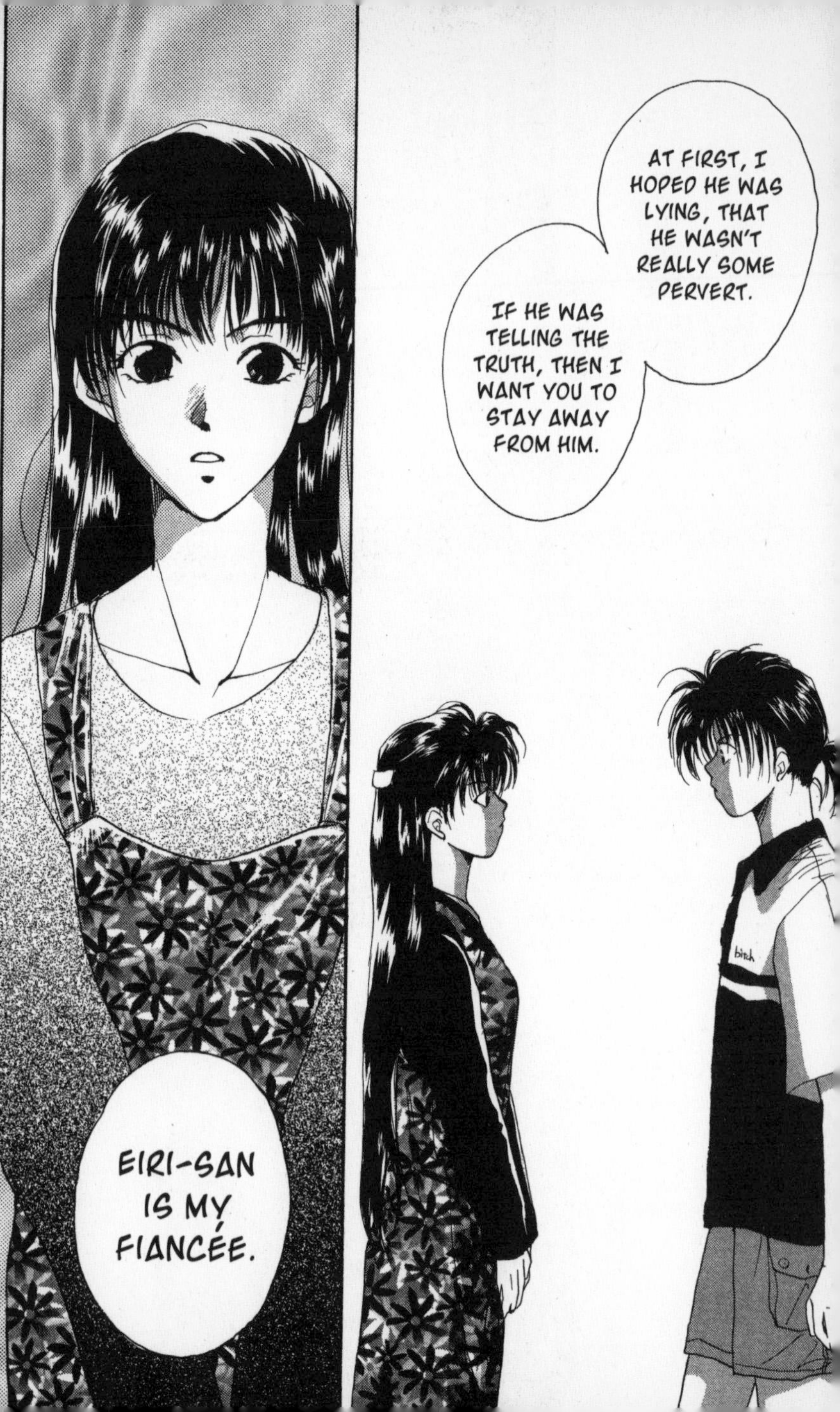
AT FIRST, I HOPED HE WAS LYING, THAT HE WASN'T REALLY SOME PERVERT.
IF HE WAS TELLING THE TRUTH, THEN I WANT YOU TO STAY AWAY FROM HIM.
EIRI-SAN IS MY FIANCÉE.

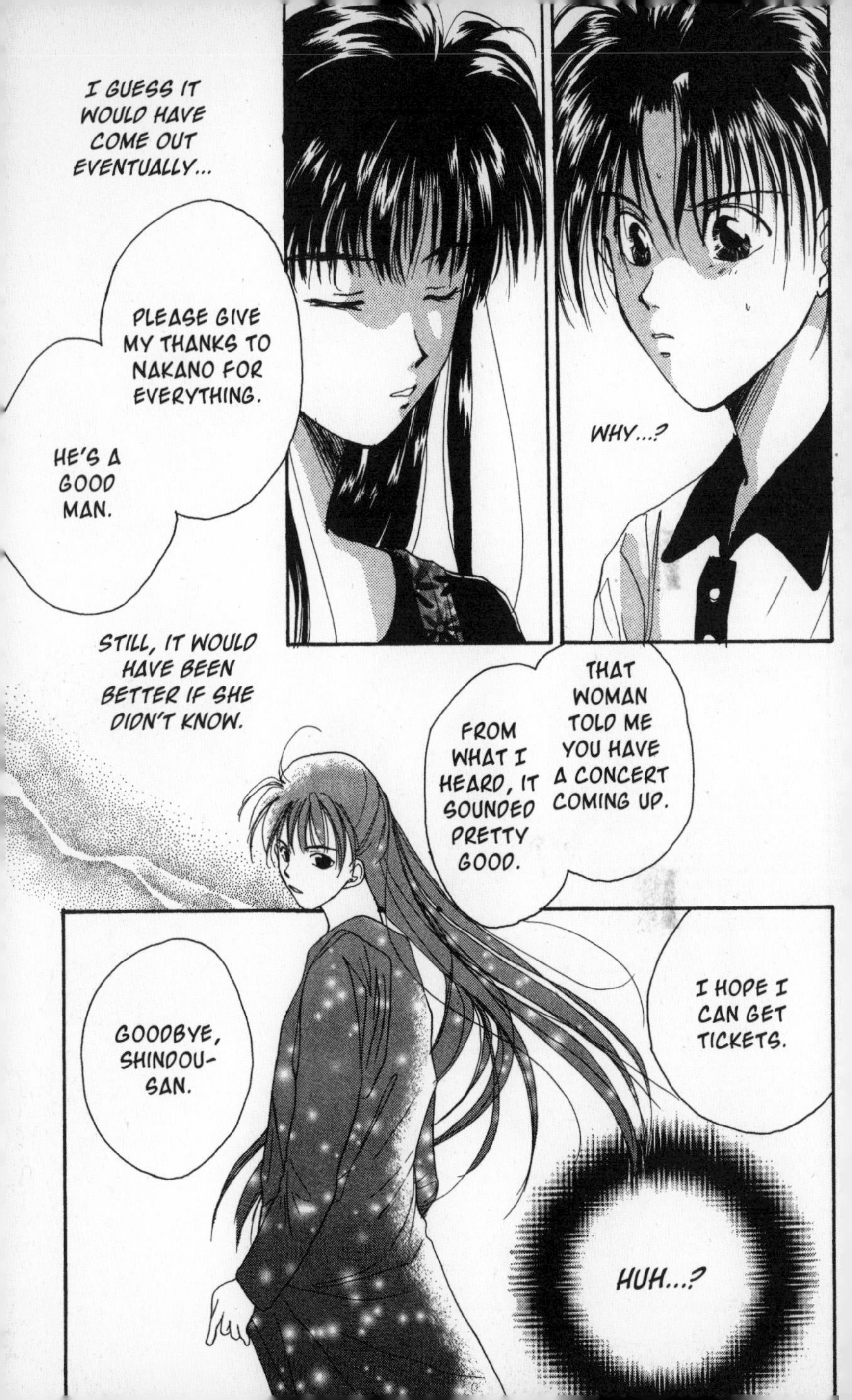
WHY...?
I GUESS IT WOULD HAVE COME OUT EVENTUALLY...
PLEASE GIVE MY THANKS TO NAKANO FOR EVERYTHING.
HE'S A GOOD MAN.
STILL, IT WOULD HAVE BEEN BETTER IF SHE DIDN'T KNOW.
THAT WOMAN TOLD ME YOU HAVE A CONCERT COMING UP.
FROM WHAT I HEARD, IT SOUNDED PRETTY GOOD.
I HOPE I CAN GET TICKETS.
GOODBYE, SHINDOU-SAN.
HUH...?

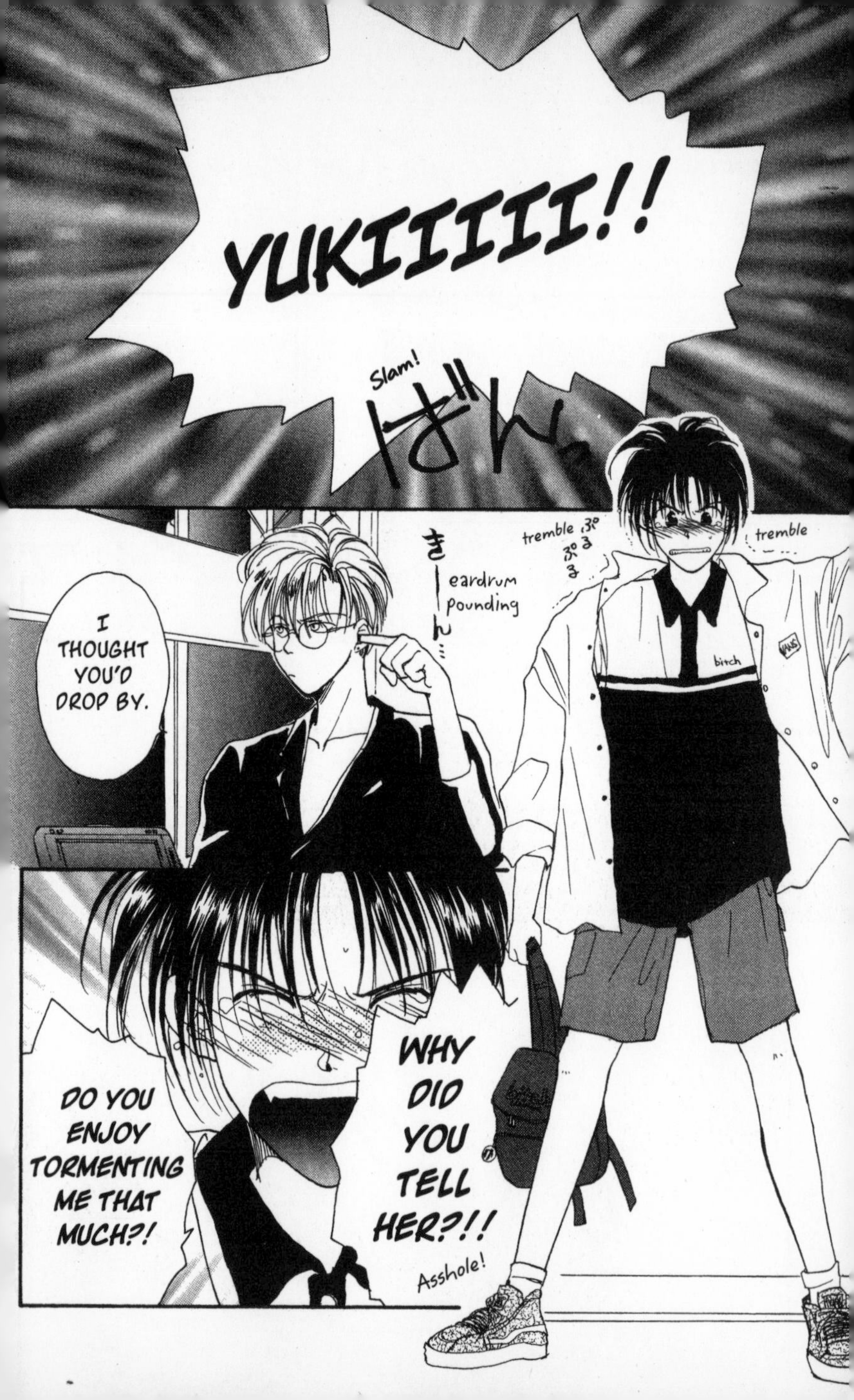

YUKIIIIII!!
Slam!
ばん
tremble
ぷるぷる
tremble
bitch
きーん
eardrum pounding
I THOUGHT YOU'D DROP BY.
WHY DID YOU TELL HER?!!
Asshole!
DO YOU ENJOY TORMENTING ME THAT MUCH?!

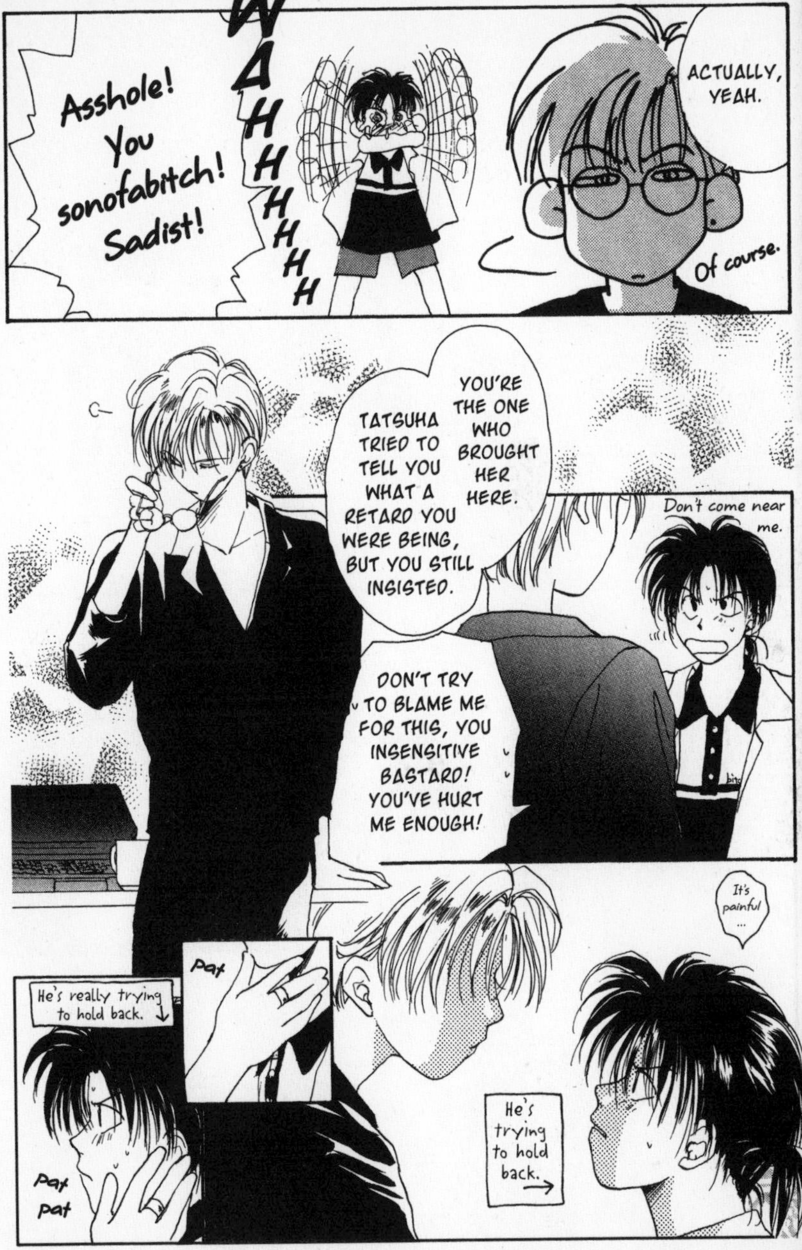
ACTUALLY, YEAH.
Of course.
WAHHHHHHH
Asshole! You sonofabitch! Sadist!
YOU'RE THE ONE WHO BROUGHT HER HERE. TATSUHA TRIED TO TELL YOU WHAT A RETARD YOU WERE BEING, BUT YOU STILL INSISTED.
Don't come near me.
DON'T TRY TO BLAME ME FOR THIS, YOU INSENSITIVE BASTARD! YOU'VE HURT ME ENOUGH!
It's painful...
He's trying to hold back.
pat
He's really trying to hold back.
pat pat

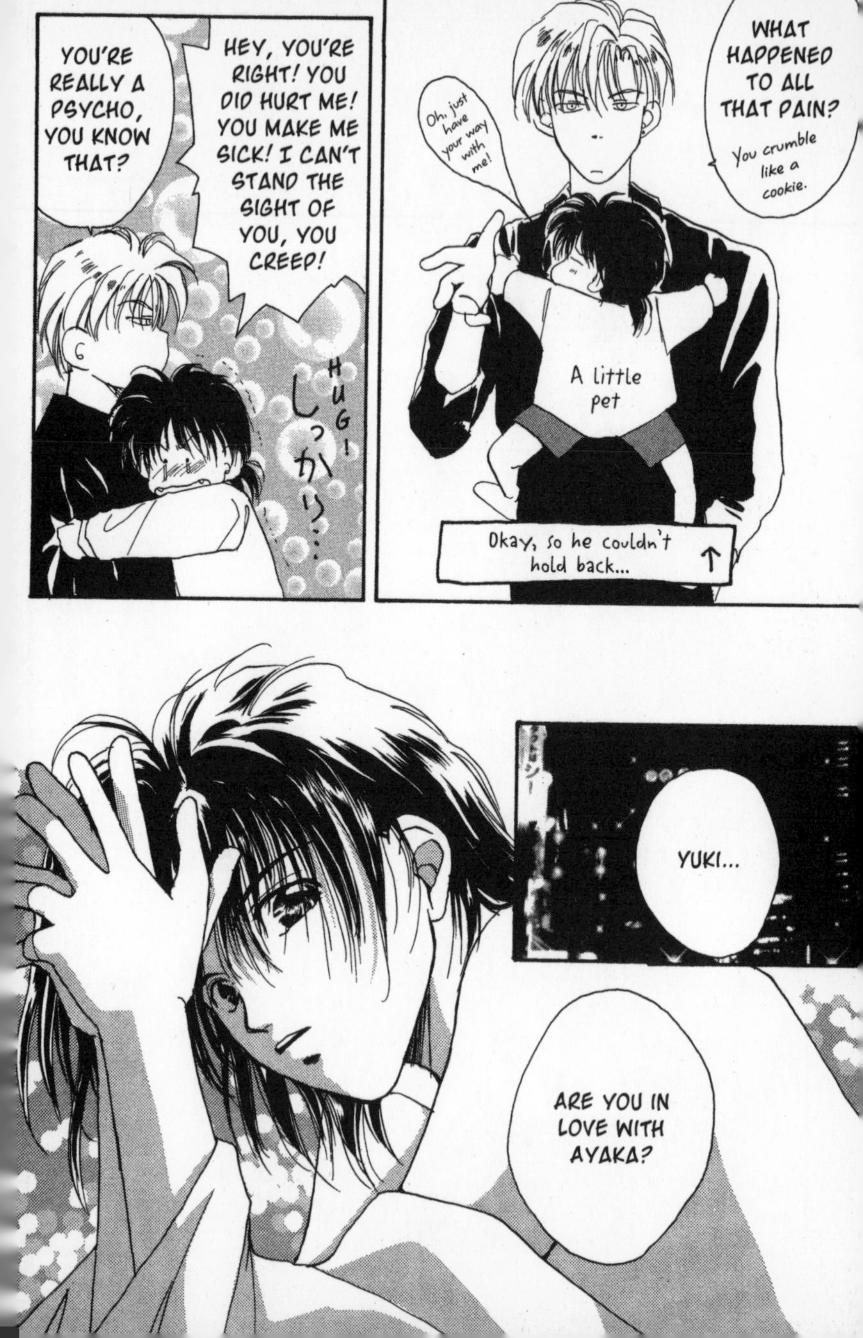
WHAT HAPPENED TO ALL THAT PAIN?
You crumble like a cookie.
Oh, just have your way with me!
A little pet
Okay, so he couldn't hold back... ↑
HEY, YOU'RE RIGHT! YOU DID HURT ME! YOU MAKE ME SICK! I CAN'T STAND THE SIGHT OF YOU, YOU CREEP!
YOU'RE REALLY A PSYCHO, YOU KNOW THAT?
HUG!
しっかり…
YUKI...
ARE YOU IN LOVE WITH AYAKA?

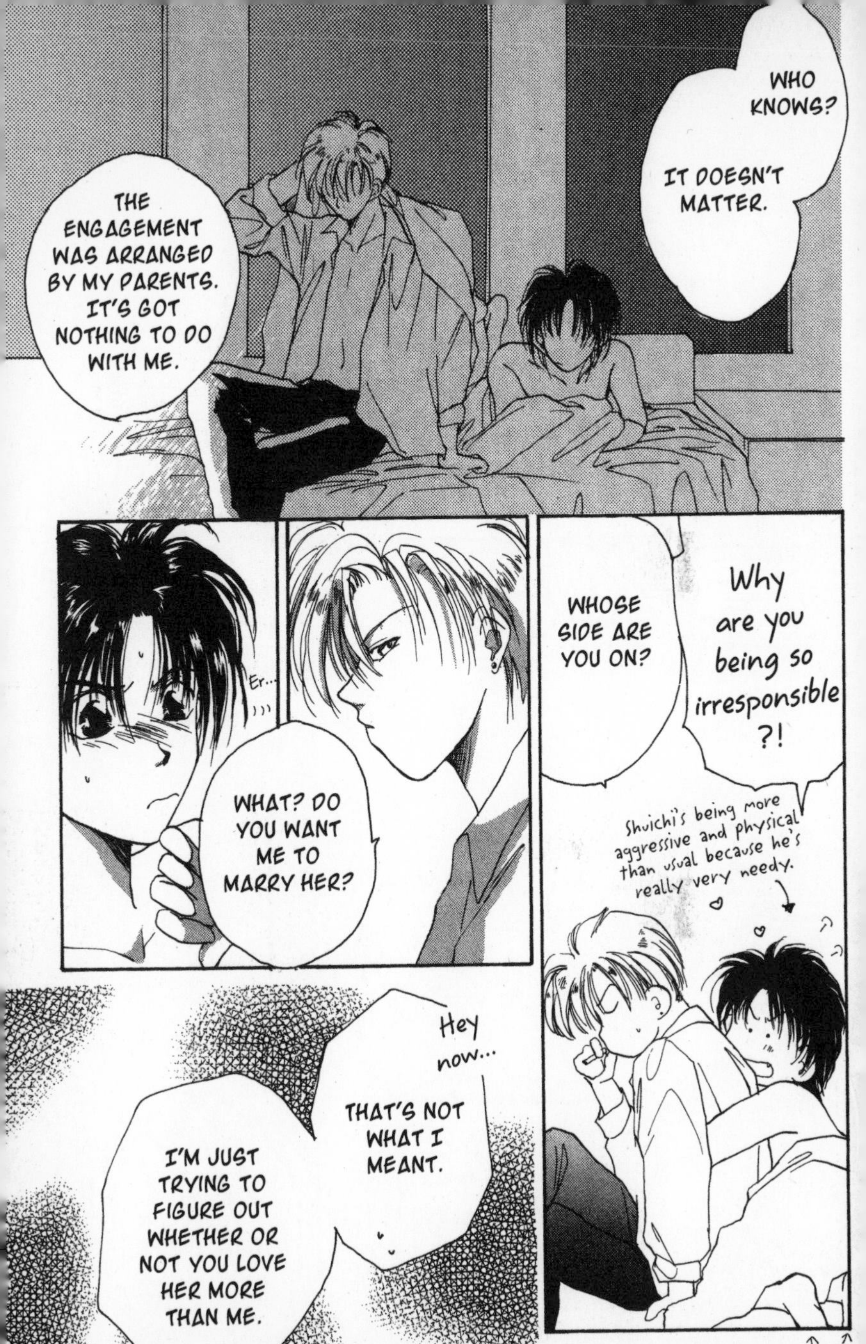
WHO KNOWS?
IT DOESN'T MATTER.
THE ENGAGEMENT WAS ARRANGED BY MY PARENTS. IT'S GOT NOTHING TO DO WITH ME.
Why are you being so irresponsible ?!
WHOSE SIDE ARE YOU ON?
Shuichi's being more aggressive and physical than usual because he's really very needy.
WHAT? DO YOU WANT ME TO MARRY HER?
Er...
Hey now...
THAT'S NOT WHAT I MEANT.
I'M JUST TRYING TO FIGURE OUT WHETHER OR NOT YOU LOVE HER MORE THAN ME.

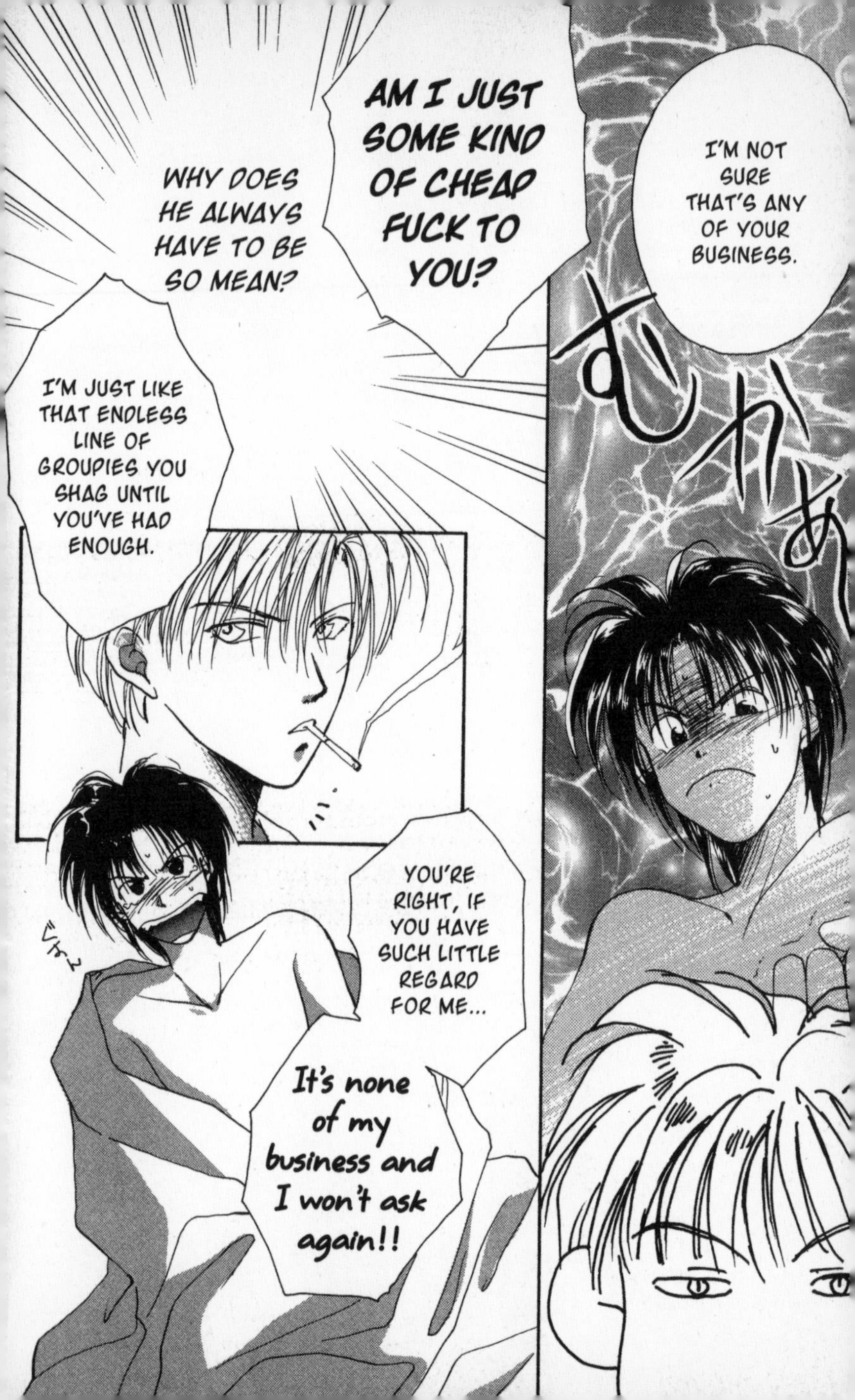
I'M NOT SURE THAT'S ANY OF YOUR BUSINESS.
むかあ
AM I JUST SOME KIND OF CHEAP FUCK TO YOU?
WHY DOES HE ALWAYS HAVE TO BE SO MEAN?
I'M JUST LIKE THAT ENDLESS LINE OF GROUPIES YOU SHAG UNTIL YOU'VE HAD ENOUGH.
YOU'RE RIGHT, IF YOU HAVE SUCH LITTLE REGARD FOR ME...
It's none of my business and I won't ask again!!

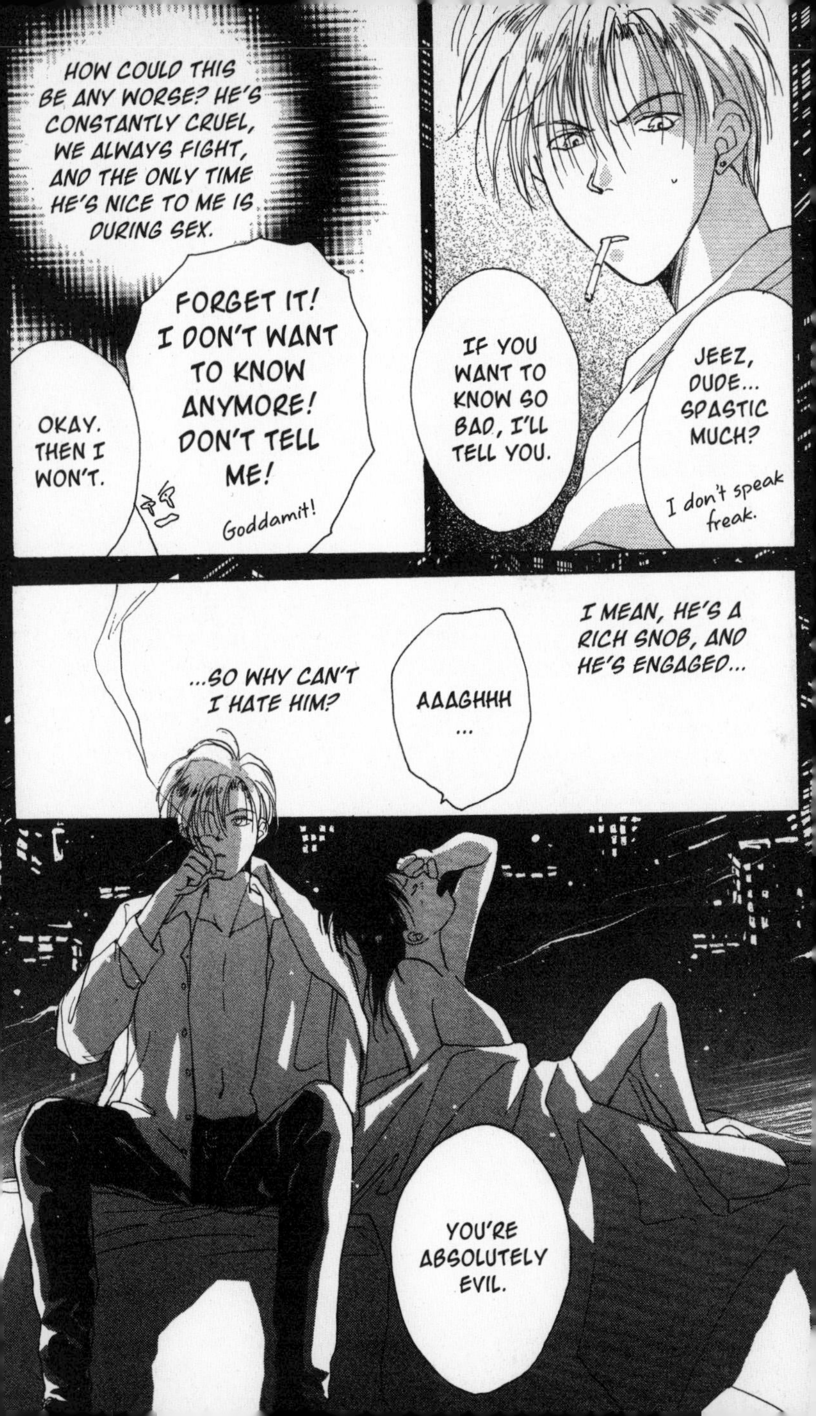
IF YOU WANT TO KNOW SO BAD, I'LL TELL YOU.
JEEZ, DUDE... SPASTIC MUCH?
I don't speak freak.
HOW COULD THIS BE ANY WORSE? HE'S CONSTANTLY CRUEL, WE ALWAYS FIGHT, AND THE ONLY TIME HE'S NICE TO ME IS DURING SEX.
FORGET IT! I DON'T WANT TO KNOW ANYMORE! DON'T TELL ME!
Goddamit!
OKAY. THEN I WON'T.
I MEAN, HE'S A RICH SNOB, AND HE'S ENGAGED...
AAAGHHH ...
...SO WHY CAN'T I HATE HIM?
YOU'RE ABSOLUTELY EVIL.

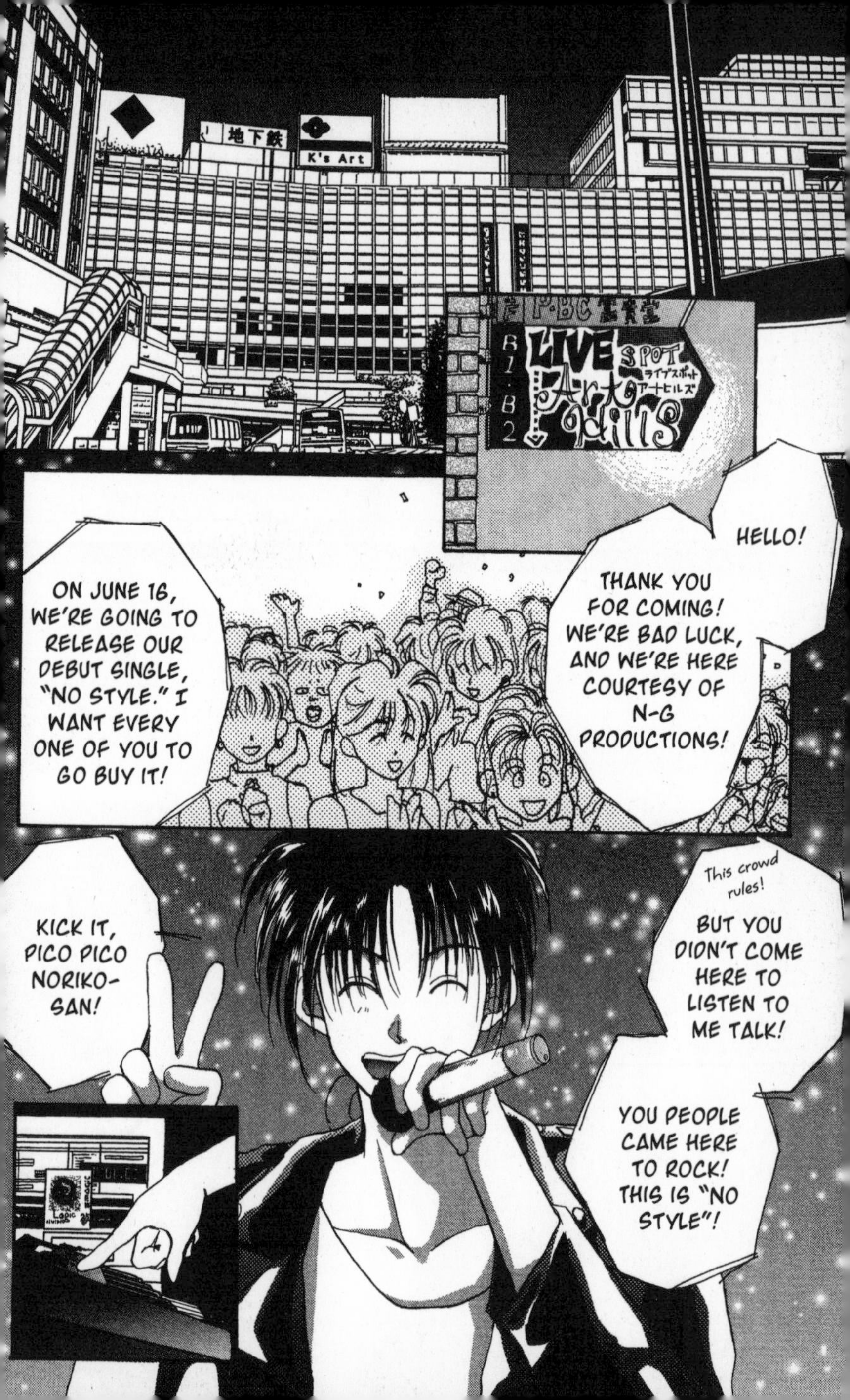
地下鉄
K's Art
LIVE SPOT
ライブスポット
アートヒルズ
Art Hills
B1・B2
HELLO!
THANK YOU FOR COMING! WE'RE BAD LUCK, AND WE'RE HERE COURTESY OF N-G PRODUCTIONS!
ON JUNE 16, WE'RE GOING TO RELEASE OUR DEBUT SINGLE, "NO STYLE." I WANT EVERY ONE OF YOU TO GO BUY IT!
This crowd rules!
BUT YOU DIDN'T COME HERE TO LISTEN TO ME TALK!
YOU PEOPLE CAME HERE TO ROCK! THIS IS "NO STYLE"!
KICK IT, PICO PICO NORIKO-SAN!

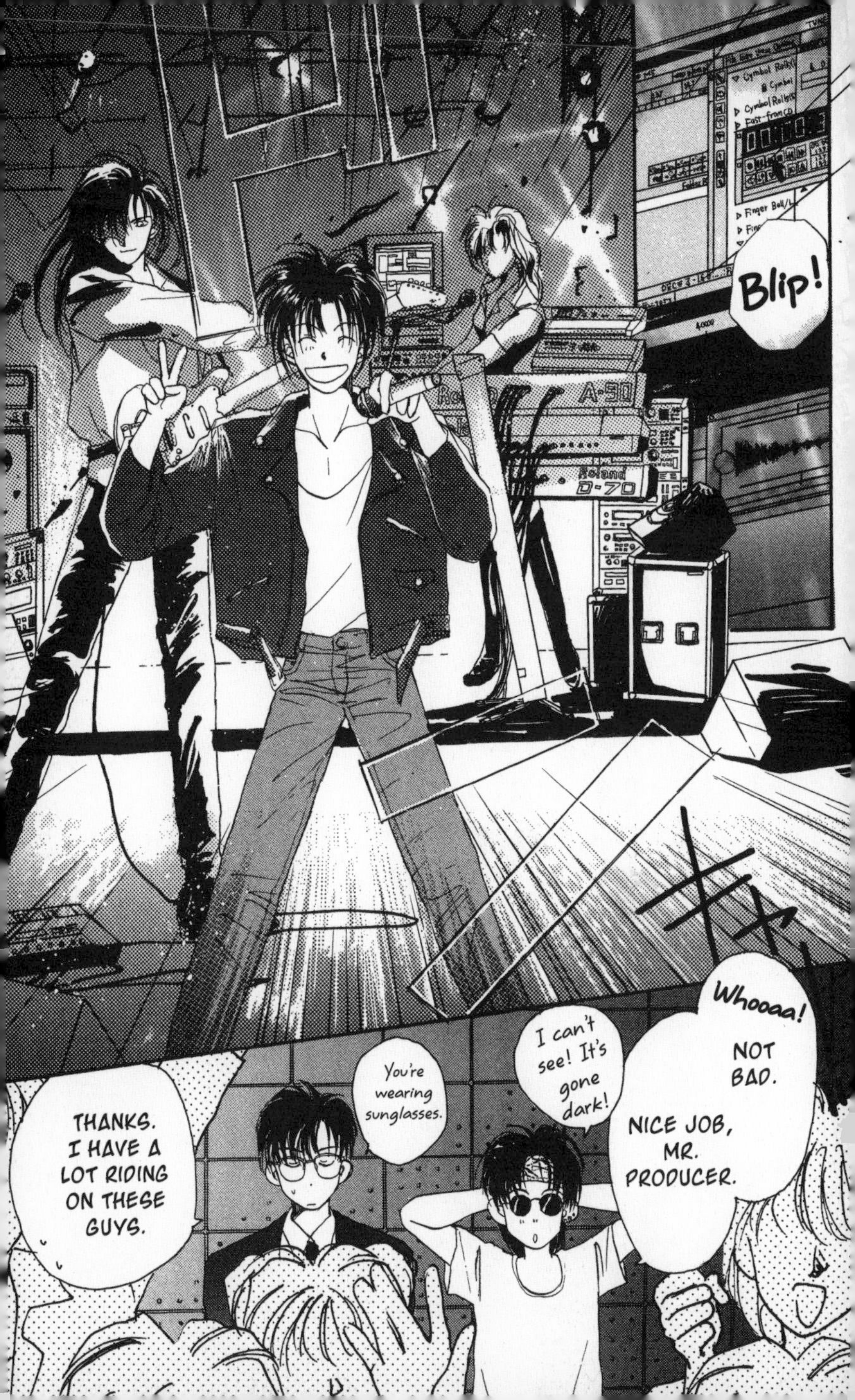

Blip!
Whoooa!
NOT BAD.
NICE JOB, MR. PRODUCER.
I can't see! It's gone dark!
You're wearing sunglasses.
THANKS. I HAVE A LOT RIDING ON THESE GUYS.

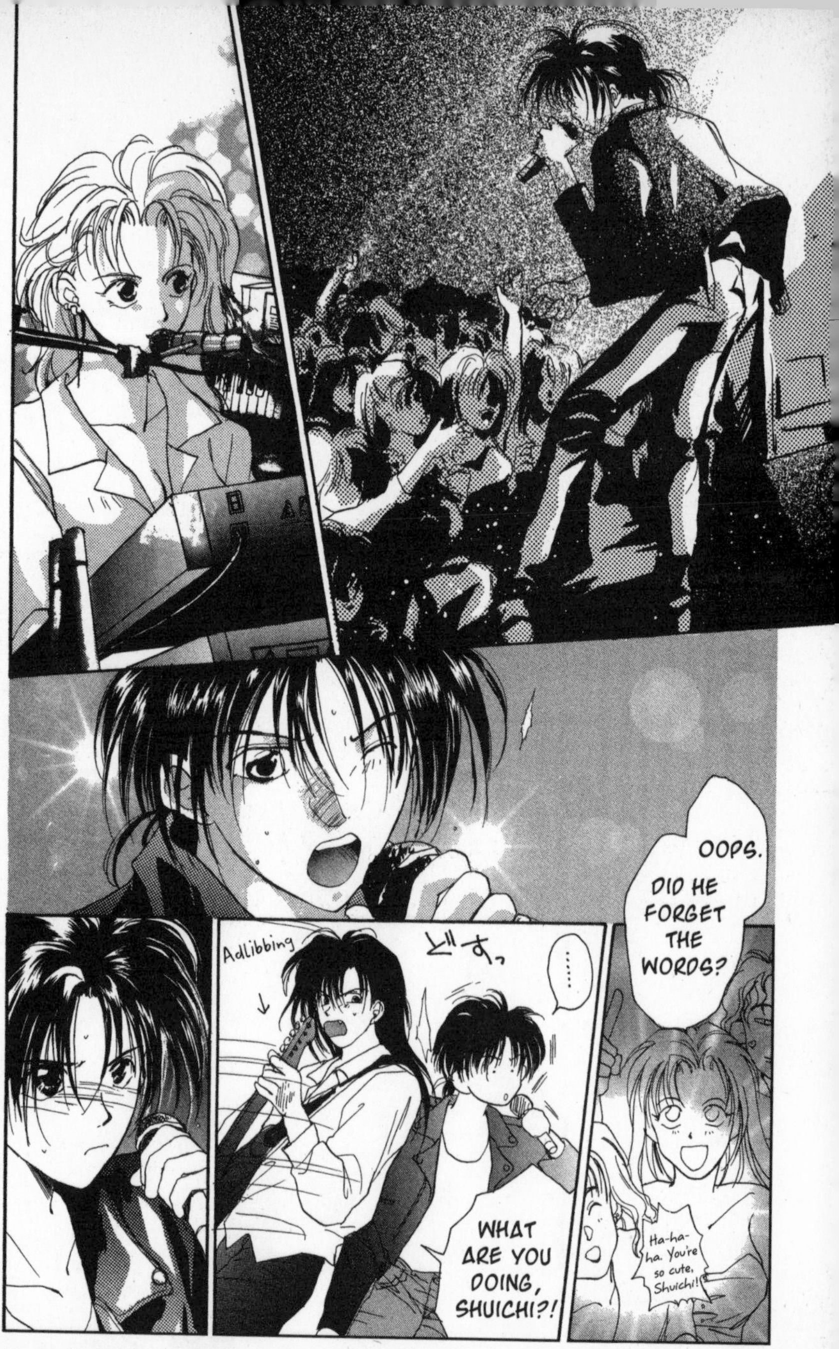
OOPS.
DID HE FORGET THE WORDS?
Ha-ha-ha. You're so cute, Shuichi!!
......
どすっ
Adlibbing
WHAT ARE YOU DOING, SHUICHI?!

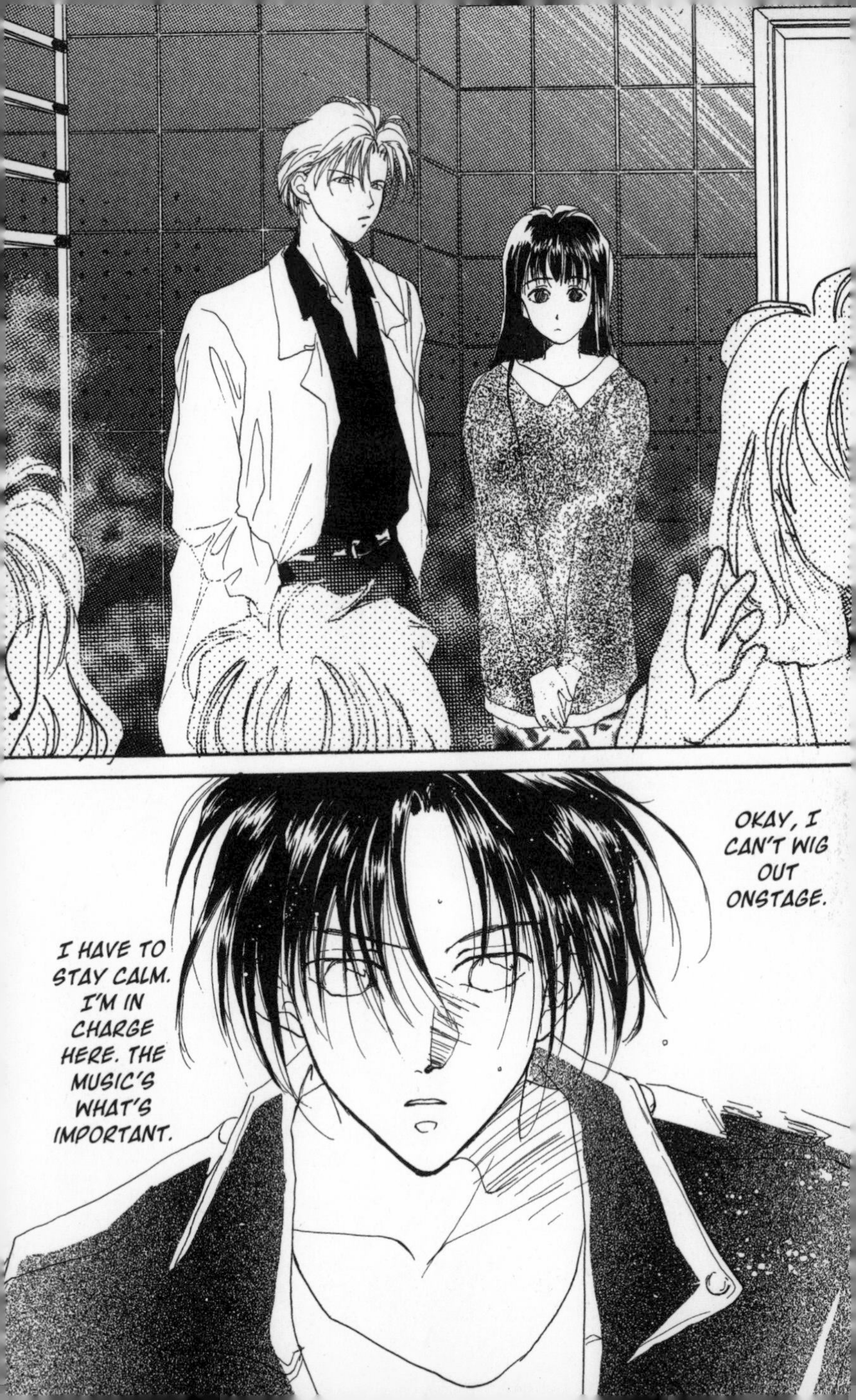
OKAY, I CAN'T WIG OUT ONSTAGE.
I HAVE TO STAY CALM. I'M IN CHARGE HERE. THE MUSIC'S WHAT'S IMPORTANT.

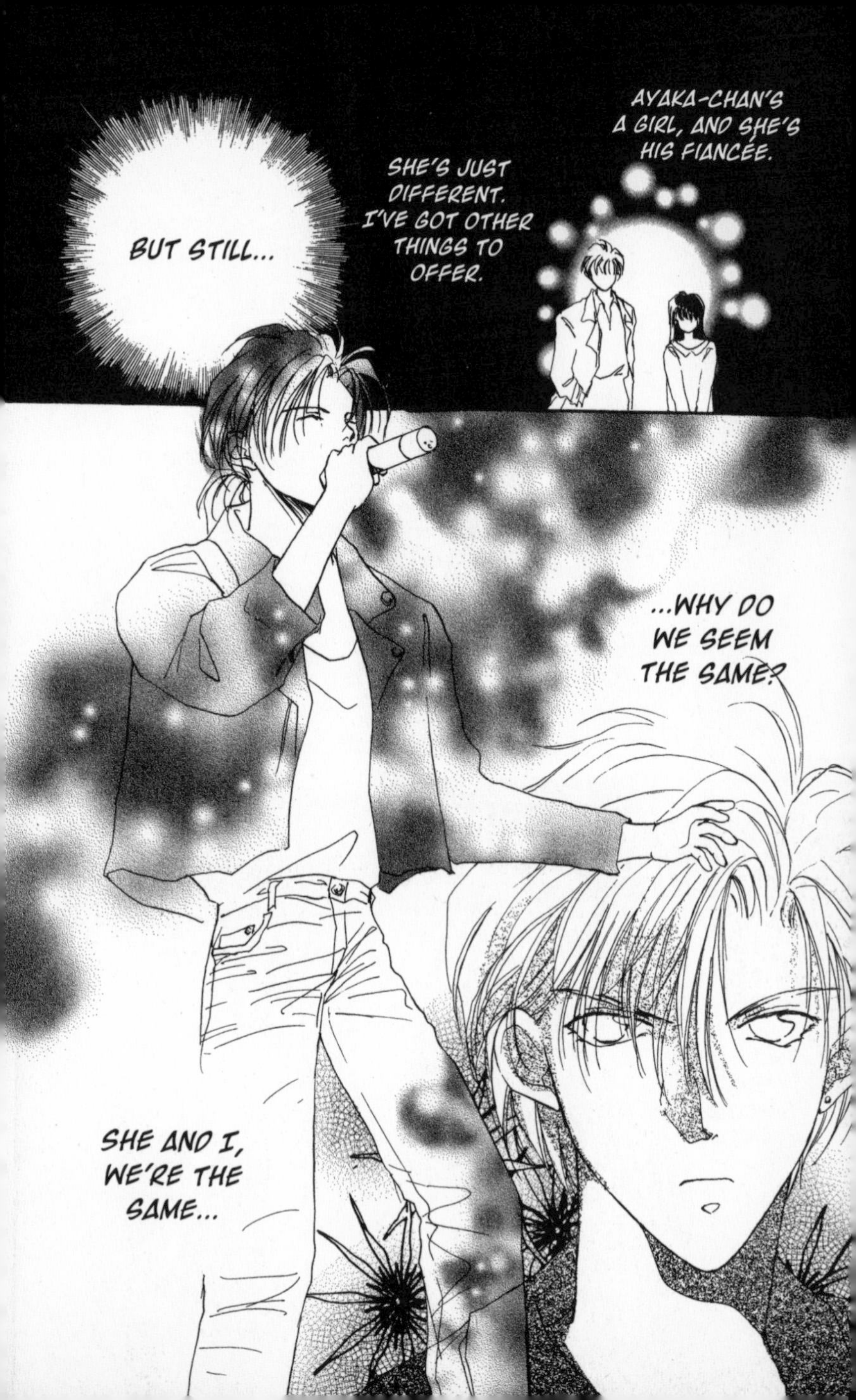
AYAKA-CHAN'S A GIRL, AND SHE'S HIS FIANCÉE.
SHE'S JUST DIFFERENT. I'VE GOT OTHER THINGS TO OFFER.
BUT STILL...
...WHY DO WE SEEM THE SAME?
SHE AND I, WE'RE THE SAME...

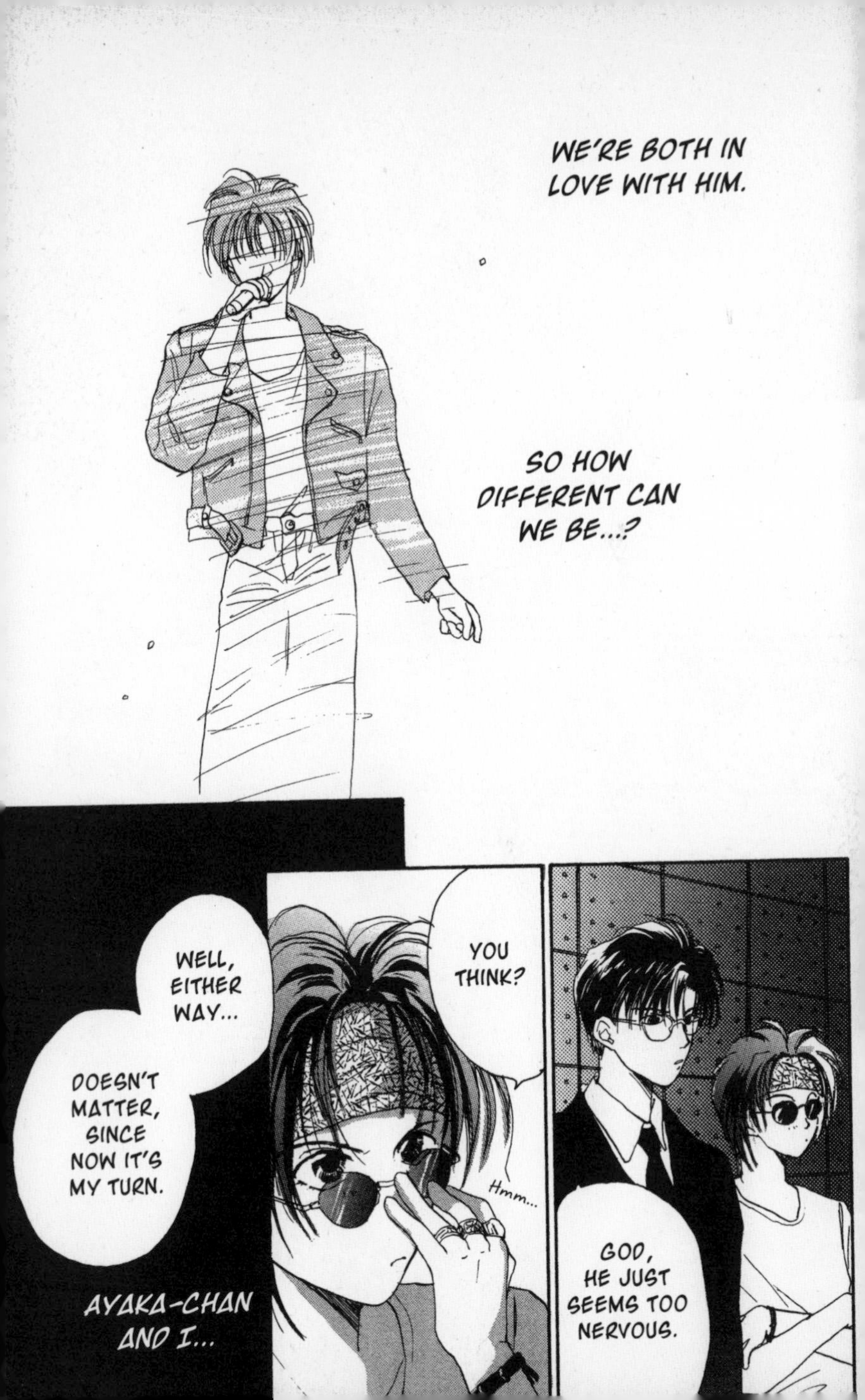
WE'RE BOTH IN LOVE WITH HIM.
SO HOW DIFFERENT CAN WE BE...?
GOD, HE JUST SEEMS TOO NERVOUS.
YOU THINK?
Hmm...
WELL, EITHER WAY...
DOESN'T MATTER, SINCE NOW IT'S MY TURN.
AYAKA-CHAN AND I...

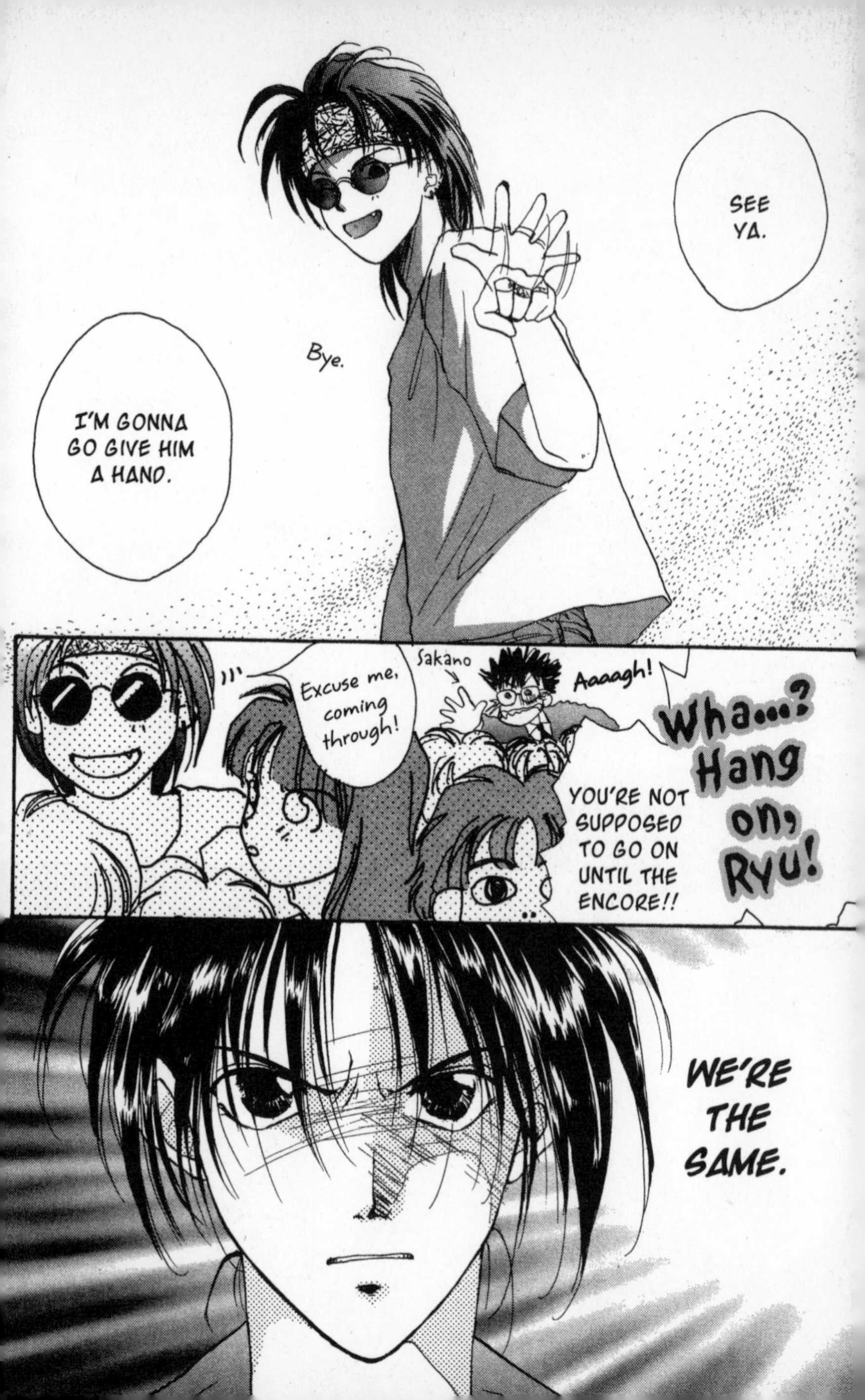
SEE YA.
Bye.
I'M GONNA GO GIVE HIM A HAND.
Wha...? Hang on, Ryu!
Aaaagh!
Sakano
YOU'RE NOT SUPPOSED TO GO ON UNTIL THE ENCORE!!
Excuse me, coming through!
WE'RE THE SAME.

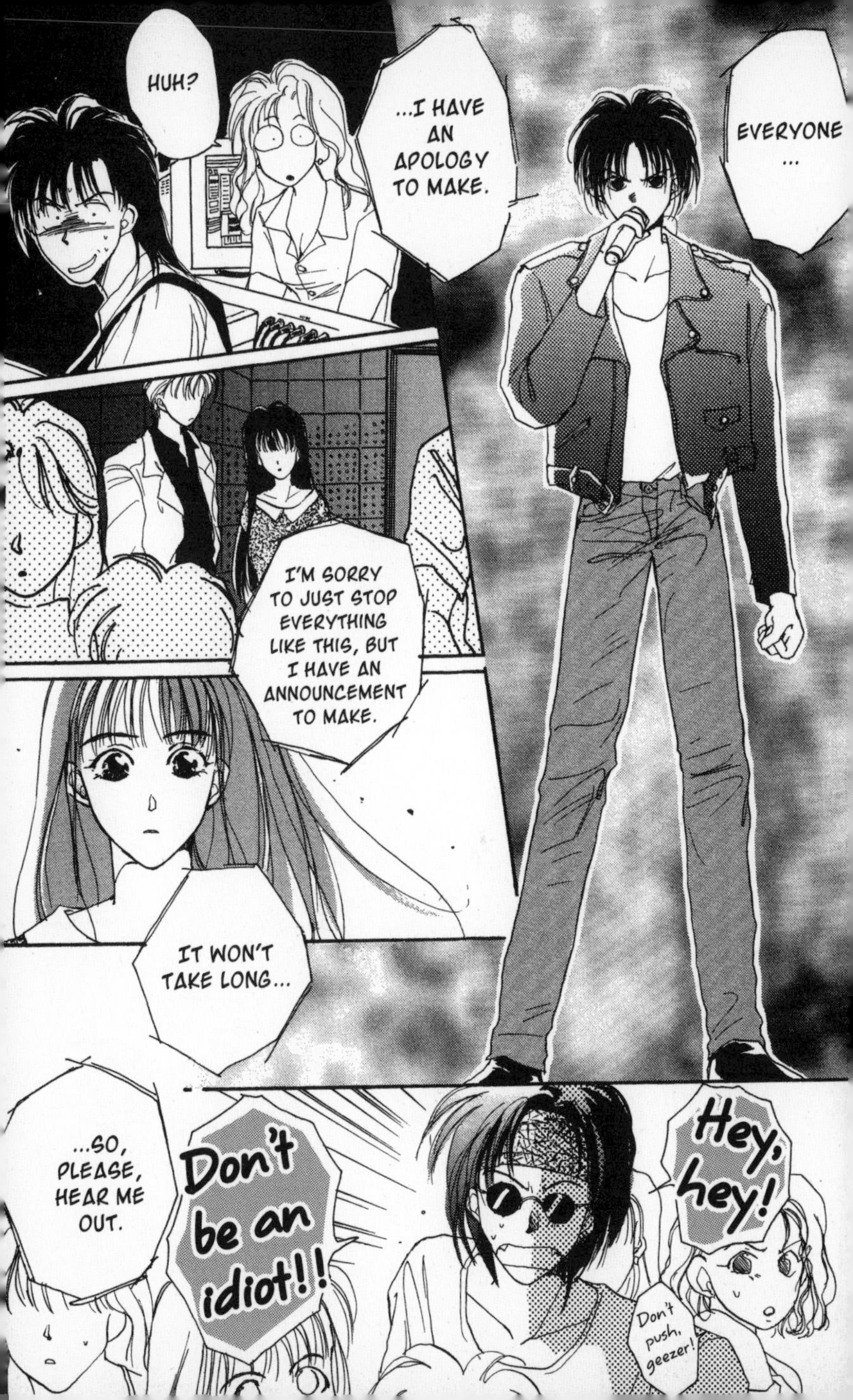
EVERYONE ...
...I HAVE AN APOLOGY TO MAKE.
HUH?
I'M SORRY TO JUST STOP EVERYTHING LIKE THIS, BUT I HAVE AN ANNOUNCEMENT TO MAKE.
IT WON'T TAKE LONG...
Hey, hey!
Don't push, geezer!
Don't be an idiot!!
...SO, PLEASE, HEAR ME OUT.

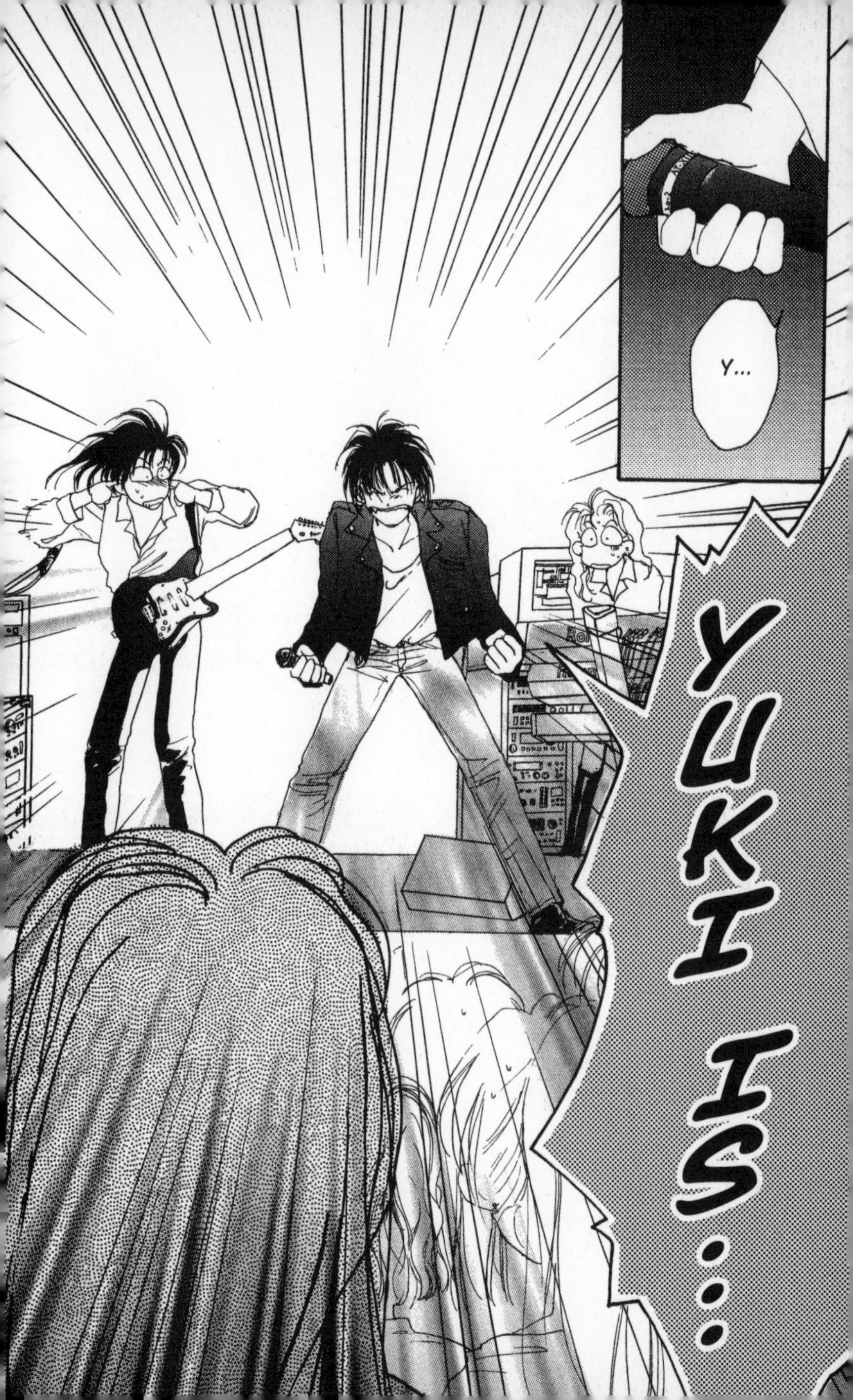
Y...
YUKI IS...

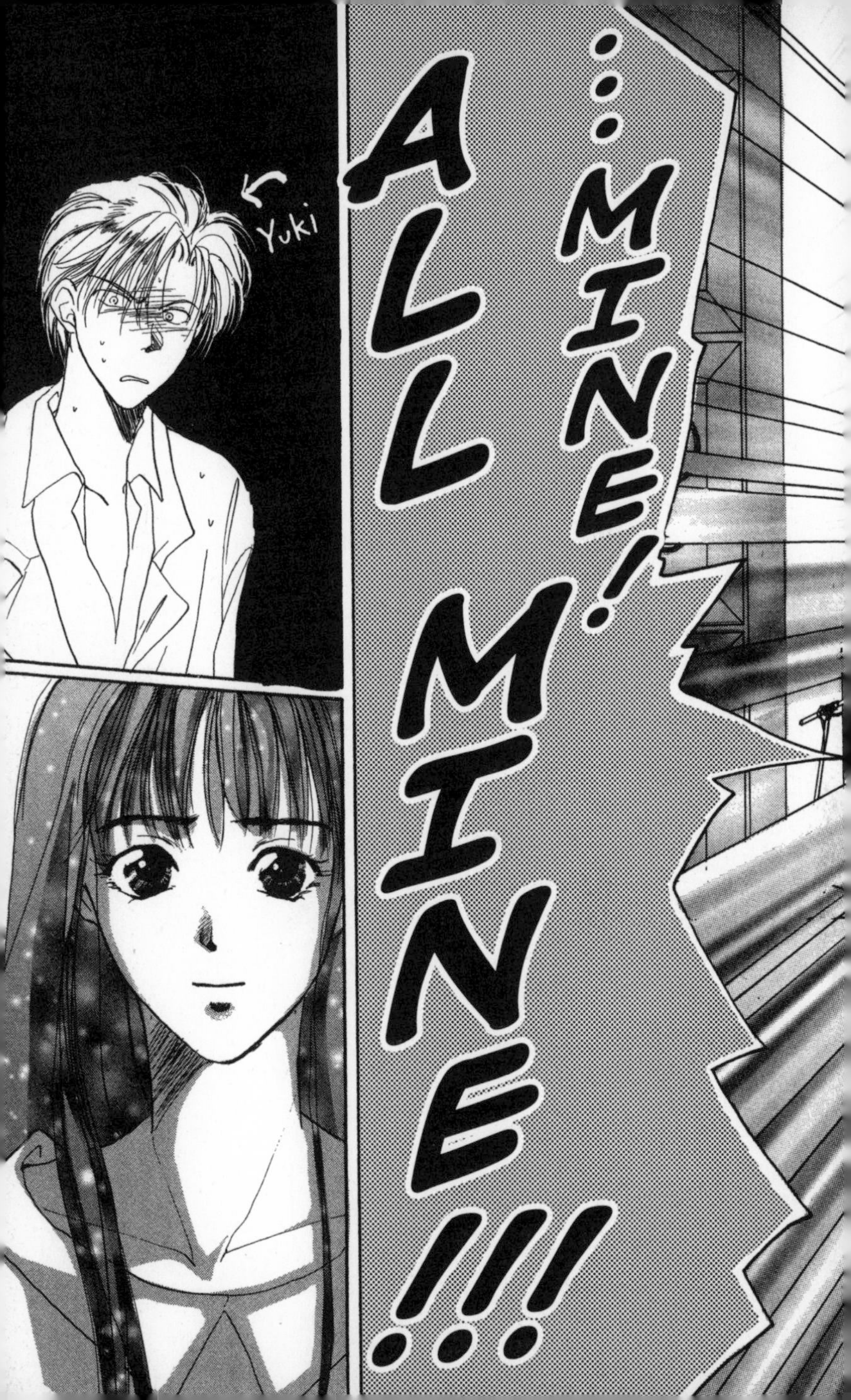
...MINE!
ALL MINE!!!
Yuki

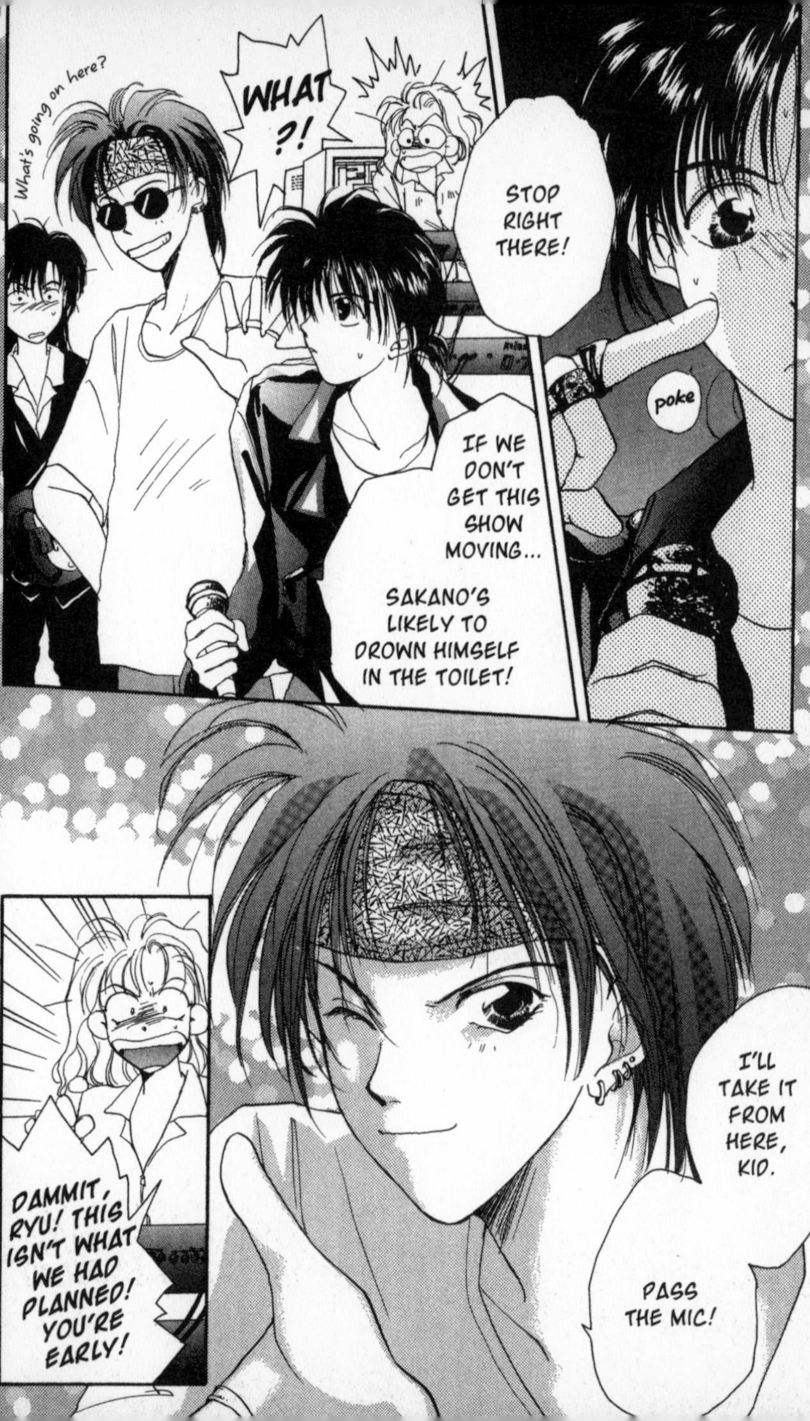
STOP RIGHT THERE!
poke
WHAT ?!
What's going on here?
IF WE DON'T GET THIS SHOW MOVING...
SAKANO'S LIKELY TO DROWN HIMSELF IN THE TOILET!
I'LL TAKE IT FROM HERE, KID.
PASS THE MIC!
DAMMIT, RYU! THIS ISN'T WHAT WE HAD PLANNED! YOU'RE EARLY!

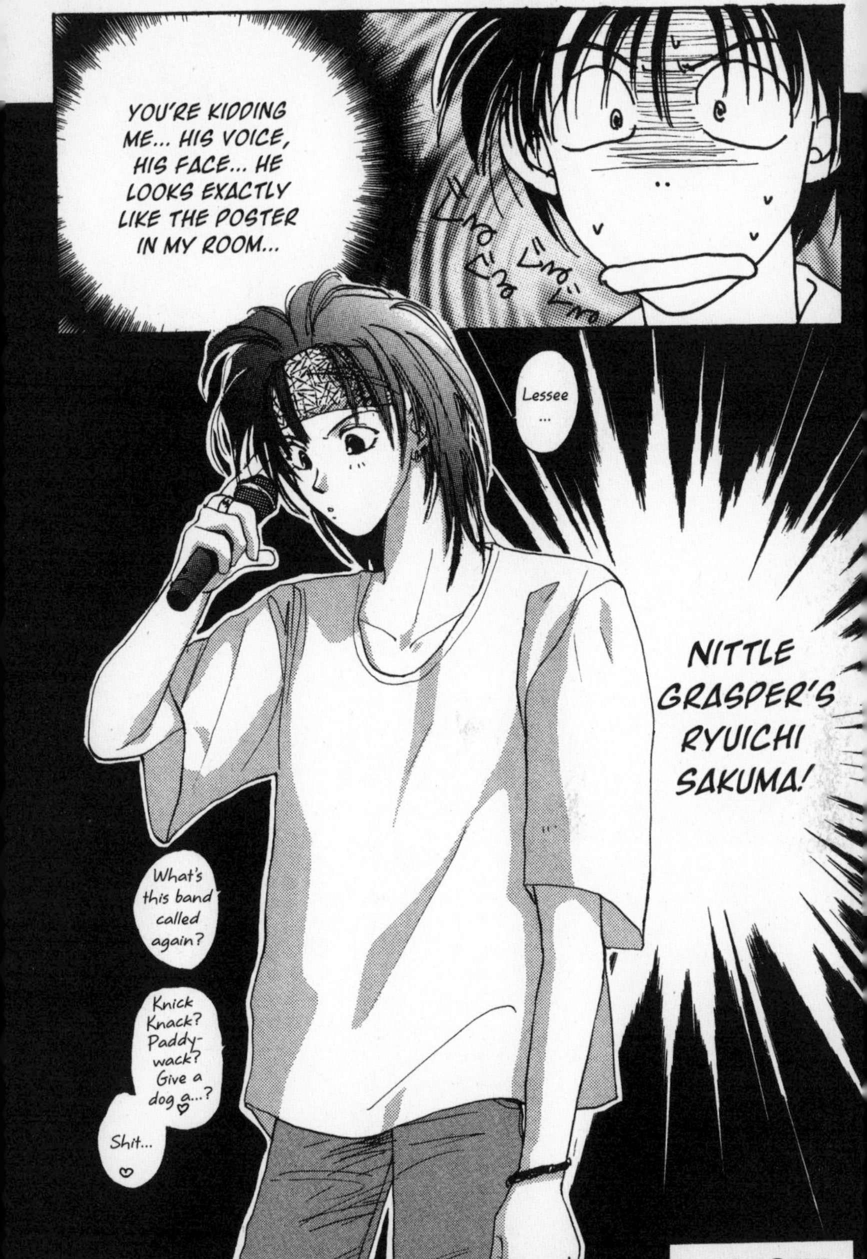
YOU'RE KIDDING ME... HIS VOICE, HIS FACE... HE LOOKS EXACTLY LIKE THE POSTER IN MY ROOM...
Lessee ...
NITTLE GRASPER'S RYUICHI SAKUMA!
...
What's this band called again?
Knick Knack? Paddy-wack? Give a dog a...?
Shit...
track9 END

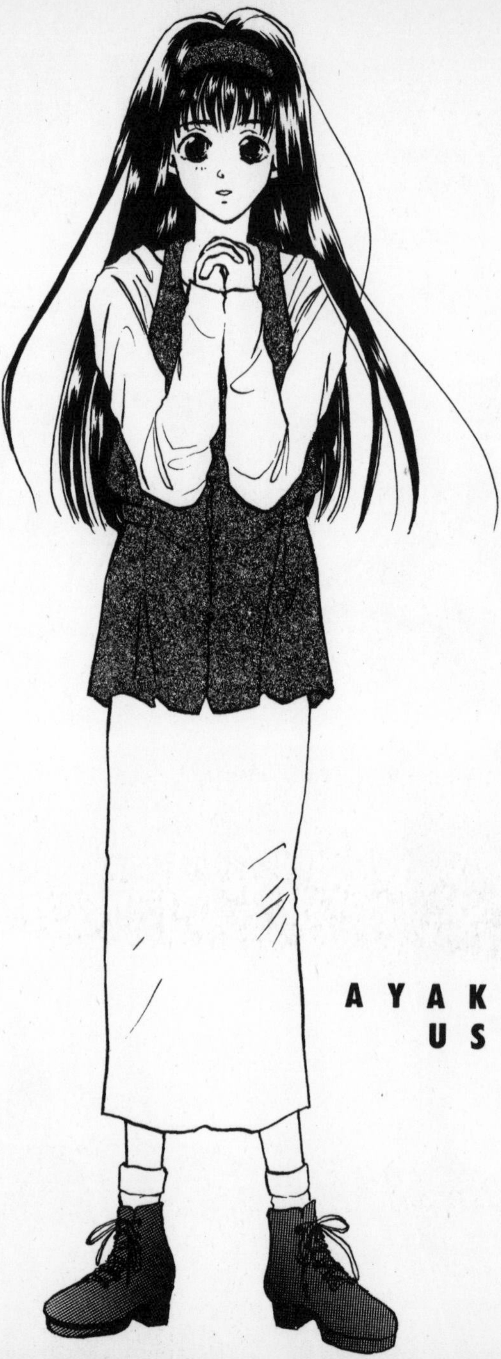

AYAKA
USAMI

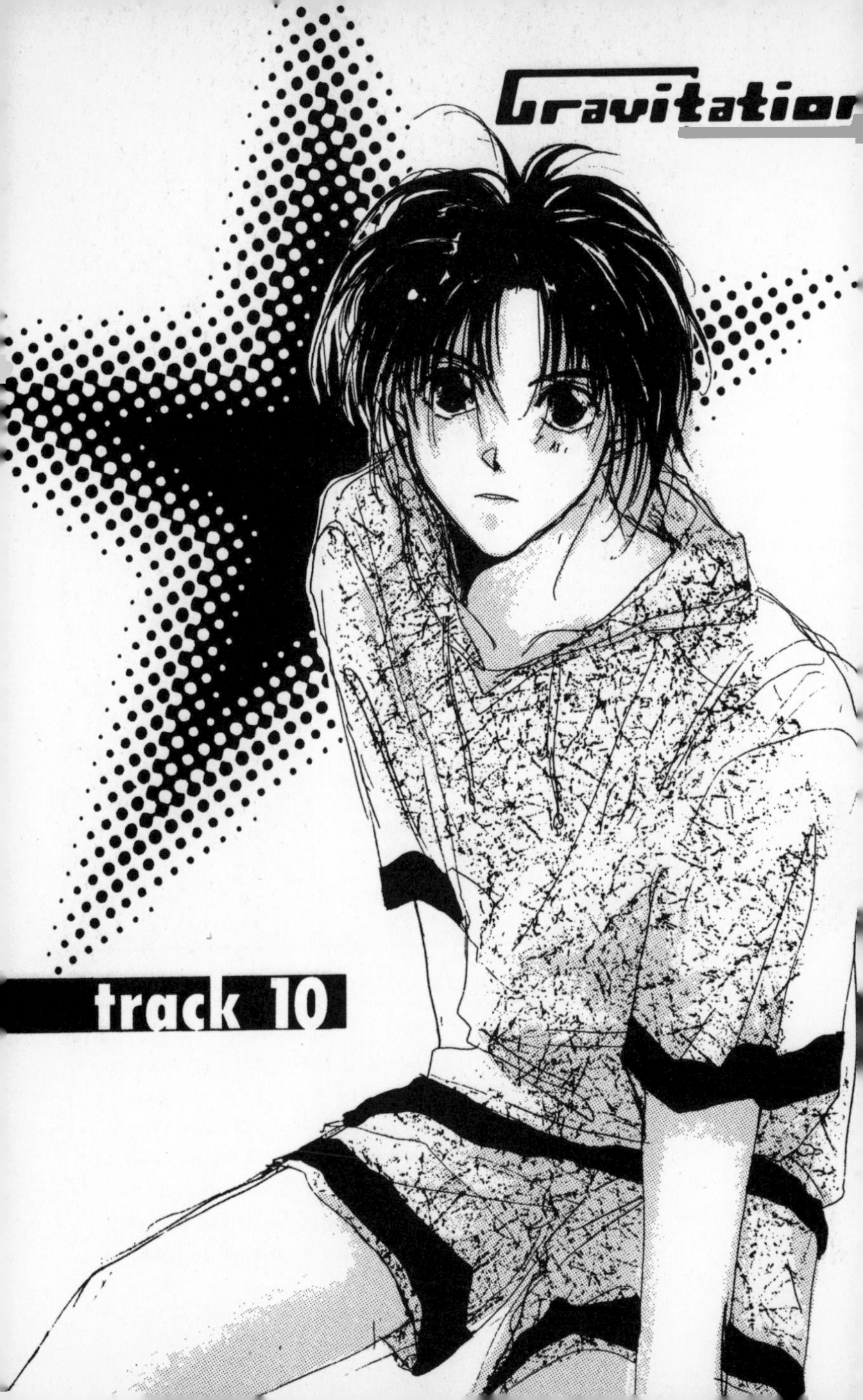
Gravitation
track 10

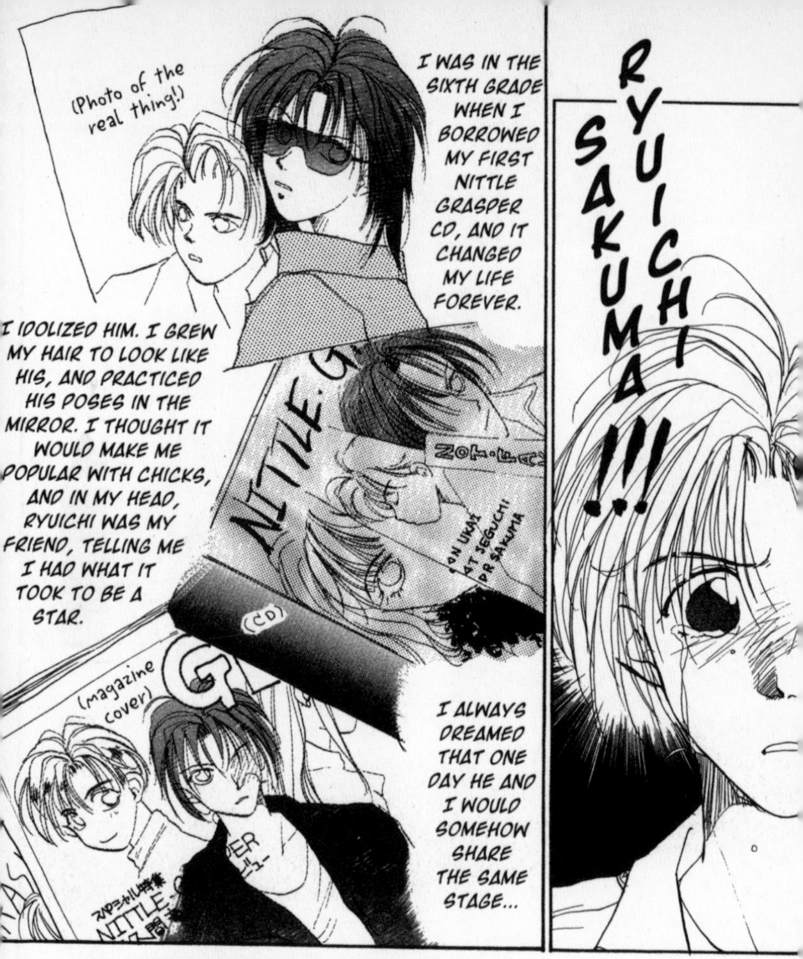
RYUICHI SAKUMA!!!
I WAS IN THE SIXTH GRADE WHEN I BORROWED MY FIRST NITTLE GRASPER CD, AND IT CHANGED MY LIFE FOREVER.
(Photo of the real thing!)
I IDOLIZED HIM. I GREW MY HAIR TO LOOK LIKE HIS, AND PRACTICED HIS POSES IN THE MIRROR. I THOUGHT IT WOULD MAKE ME POPULAR WITH CHICKS, AND IN MY HEAD, RYUICHI WAS MY FRIEND, TELLING ME I HAD WHAT IT TOOK TO BE A STAR.
(CD)
I ALWAYS DREAMED THAT ONE DAY HE AND I WOULD SOMEHOW SHARE THE SAME STAGE...
(magazine cover)

ABOUT GRAVITATION TRACK 10

The grand entrance of Ryuichi! This is what we've been waiting for! Yayyyy! Everything I've been doing has been leading up to this. Wait a second?! It's Track 10 already! Come on! You've gotta be kidding! Anyway, sometimes, since I designed them to look pretty much the same way, I have trouble telling him and Shuichi apart. Hey, is that Shu-chan? Or is it Ryu-chan? Jeez, even their names sound alike. But I gotta keep calm. If all else fails, I can always rely on their hair color to tell who's who! I just have to make sure to color them in right! Smile.

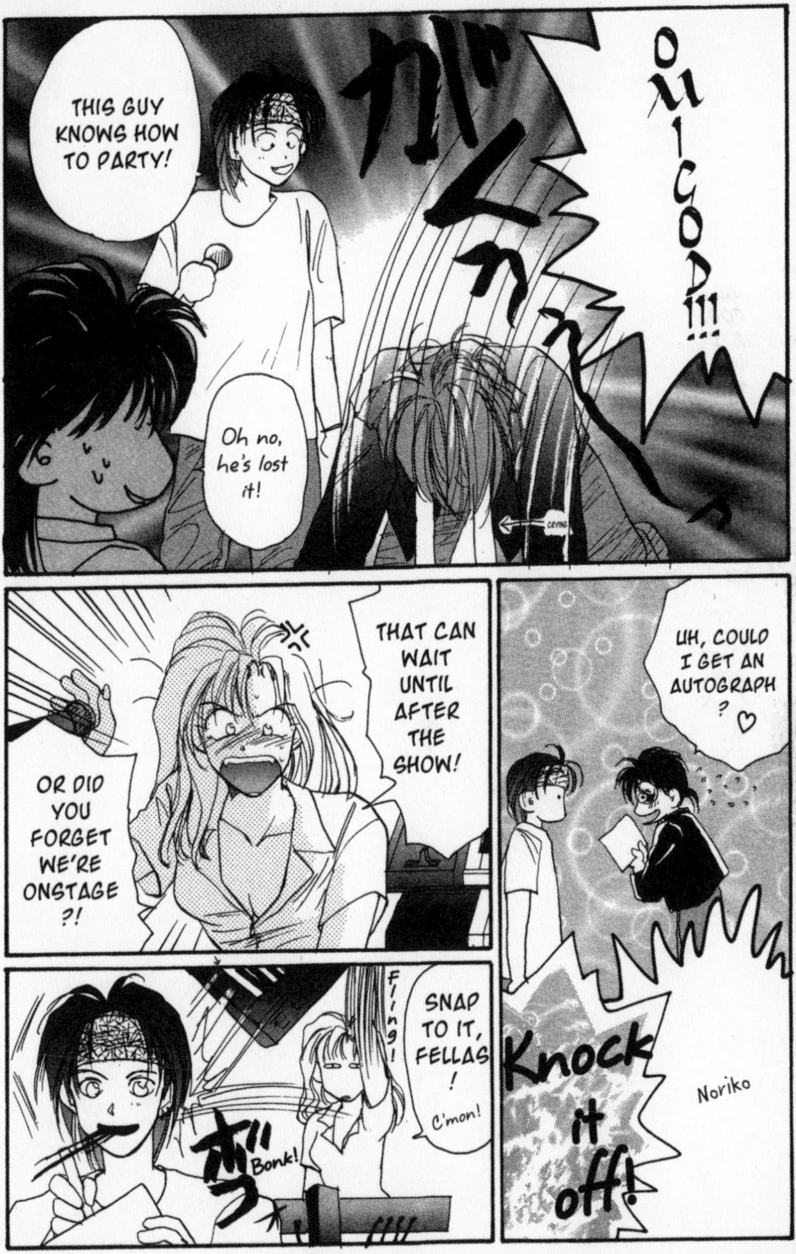
OH GOD!!!
CRYING
THIS GUY KNOWS HOW TO PARTY!
Oh no, he's lost it!
UH, COULD I GET AN AUTOGRAPH? ♡
Knock it off!
Noriko
THAT CAN WAIT UNTIL AFTER THE SHOW!
OR DID YOU FORGET WE'RE ONSTAGE?!
Fling!
SNAP TO IT, FELLAS!
C'mon!
Bonk!

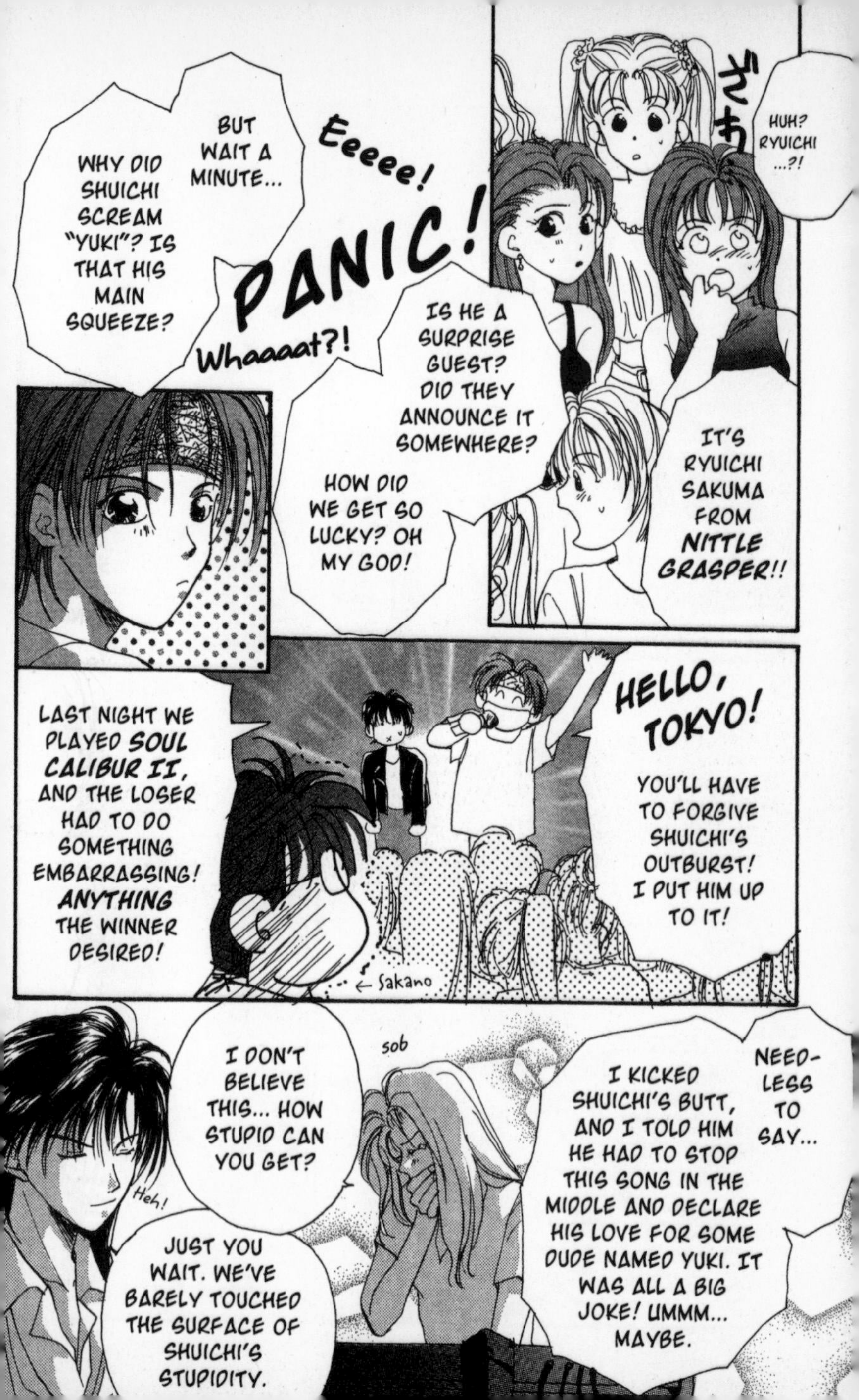
ざわ
HUH? RYUICHI ...?!
Eeeee!
PANIC!
Whaaaat?!
IS HE A SURPRISE GUEST? DID THEY ANNOUNCE IT SOMEWHERE?
IT'S RYUICHI SAKUMA FROM NITTLE GRASPER!!
HOW DID WE GET SO LUCKY? OH MY GOD!
BUT WAIT A MINUTE...
WHY DID SHUICHI SCREAM "YUKI"? IS THAT HIS MAIN SQUEEZE?
HELLO, TOKYO!
YOU'LL HAVE TO FORGIVE SHUICHI'S OUTBURST! I PUT HIM UP TO IT!
LAST NIGHT WE PLAYED SOUL CALIBUR II, AND THE LOSER HAD TO DO SOMETHING EMBARRASSING! ANYTHING THE WINNER DESIRED!
← Sakano
NEED-LESS TO SAY...
I KICKED SHUICHI'S BUTT, AND I TOLD HIM HE HAD TO STOP THIS SONG IN THE MIDDLE AND DECLARE HIS LOVE FOR SOME DUDE NAMED YUKI. IT WAS ALL A BIG JOKE! UMMM... MAYBE.
sob
I DON'T BELIEVE THIS... HOW STUPID CAN YOU GET?
Heh!
JUST YOU WAIT. WE'VE BARELY TOUCHED THE SURFACE OF SHUICHI'S STUPIDITY.

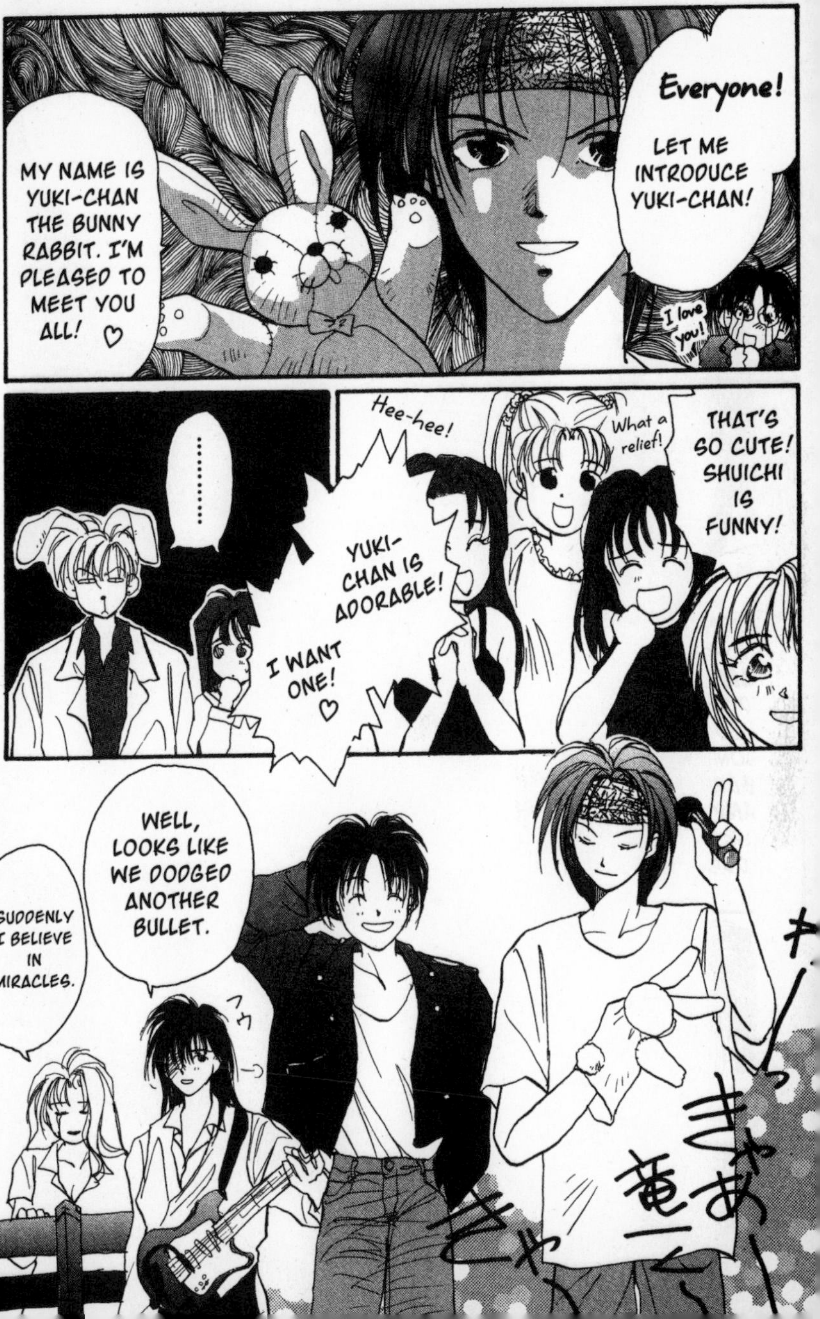
Everyone!
LET ME INTRODUCE YUKI-CHAN!
I love you!
MY NAME IS YUKI-CHAN THE BUNNY RABBIT. I'M PLEASED TO MEET YOU ALL! ♡
THAT'S SO CUTE! SHUICHI IS FUNNY!
What a relief!
Hee-hee!
YUKI-CHAN IS ADORABLE!
I WANT ONE! ♡
......
WELL, LOOKS LIKE WE DODGED ANOTHER BULLET.
SUDDENLY I BELIEVE IN MIRACLES.

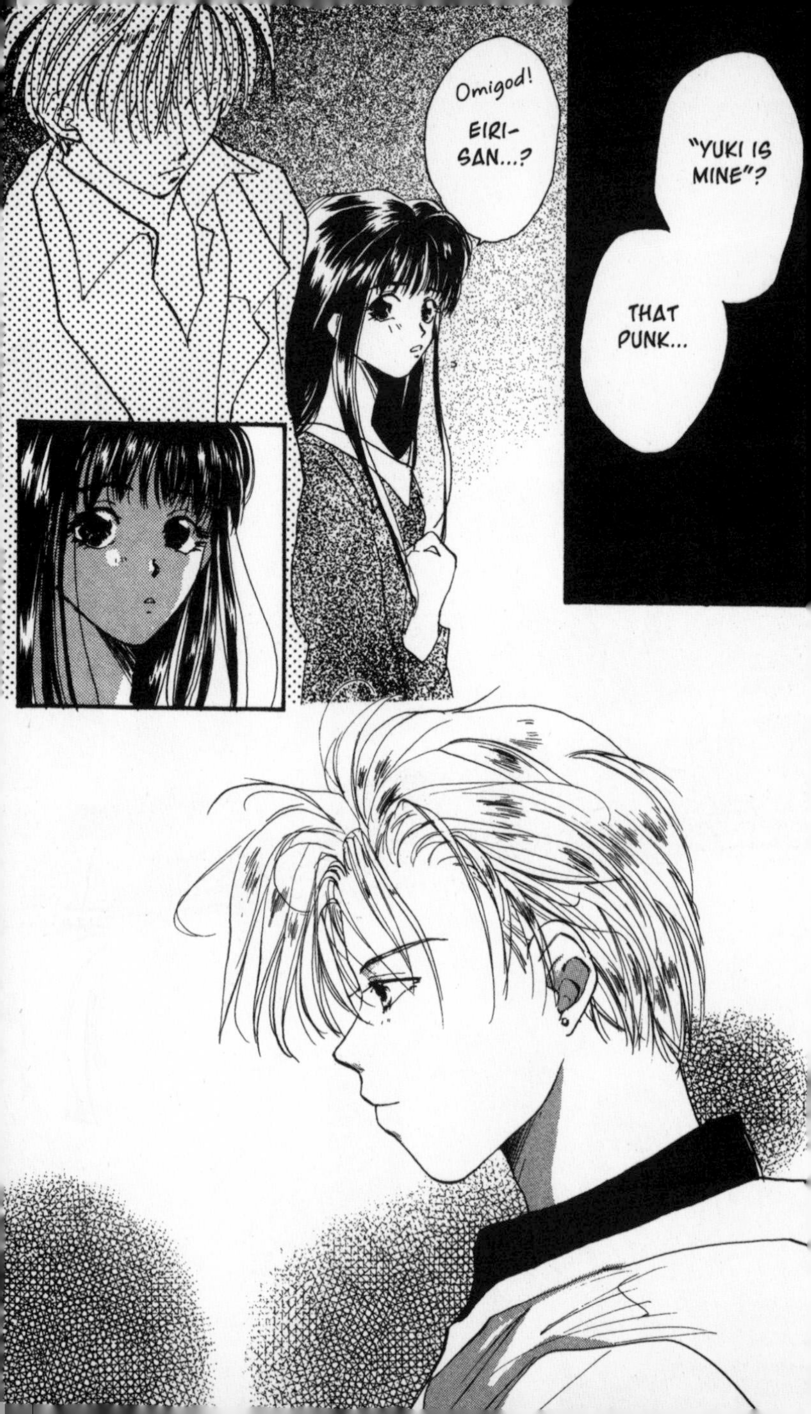
"YUKI IS MINE"?
THAT PUNK...
Omigod!
EIRI-SAN...?

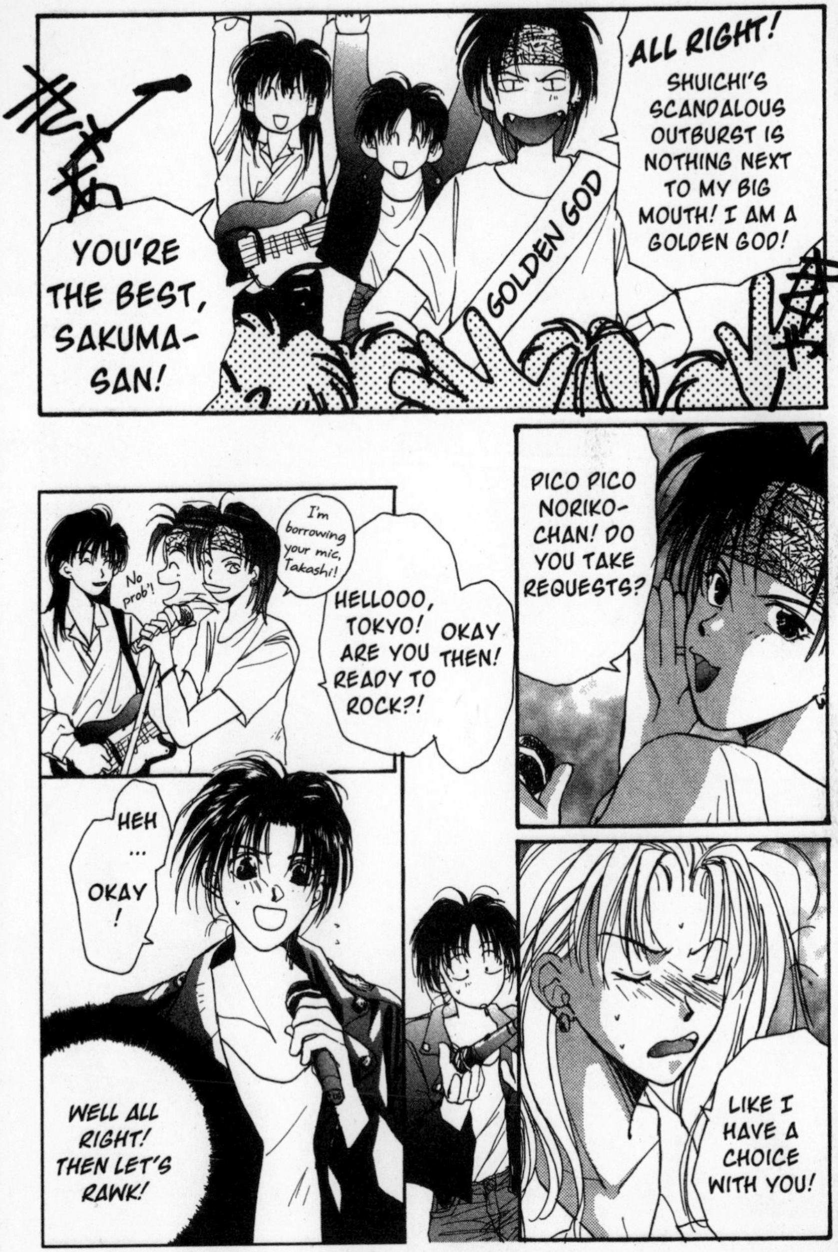
ALL RIGHT!
SHUICHI'S SCANDALOUS OUTBURST IS NOTHING NEXT TO MY BIG MOUTH! I AM A GOLDEN GOD!
GOLDEN GOD
YOU'RE THE BEST, SAKUMA-SAN!
PICO PICO NORIKO-CHAN! DO YOU TAKE REQUESTS?
I'm borrowing your mic, Takashi!
No prob'!
OKAY THEN!
HELLOOO, TOKYO! ARE YOU READY TO ROCK?!
LIKE I HAVE A CHOICE WITH YOU!
HEH ... OKAY!
WELL ALL RIGHT! THEN LET'S RAWK!

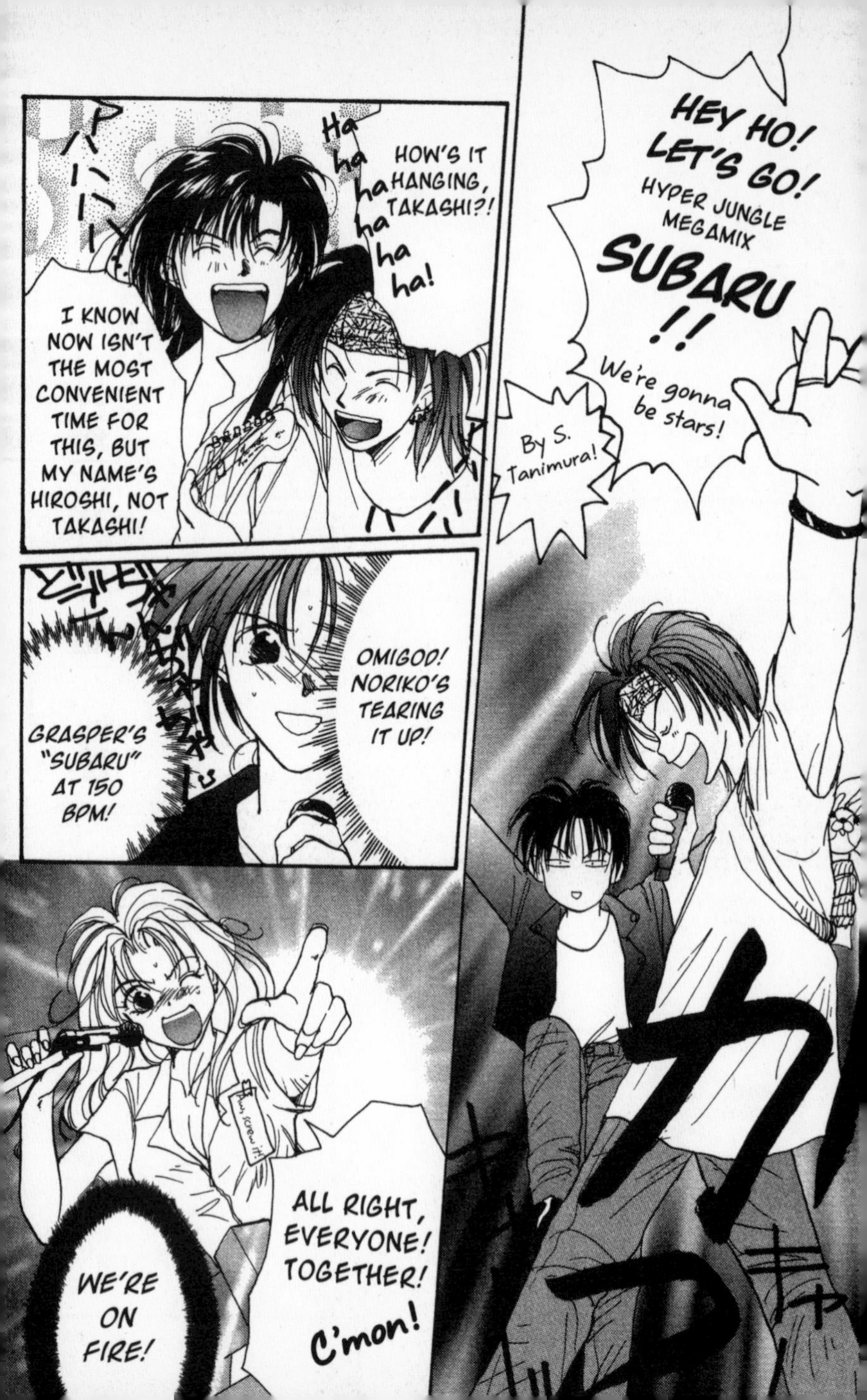
HEY HO! LET'S GO! HYPER JUNGLE MEGAMIX SUBARU!!
We're gonna be stars!
By S. Tanimura!
Ha ha ha ha ha ha!
HOW'S IT HANGING, TAKASHI?!
I KNOW NOW ISN'T THE MOST CONVENIENT TIME FOR THIS, BUT MY NAME'S HIROSHI, NOT TAKASHI!
OMIGOD! NORIKO'S TEARING IT UP!
GRASPER'S "SUBARU" AT 150 BPM!
Aw, screw it!
ALL RIGHT, EVERYONE! TOGETHER!
C'mon!
WE'RE ON FIRE!

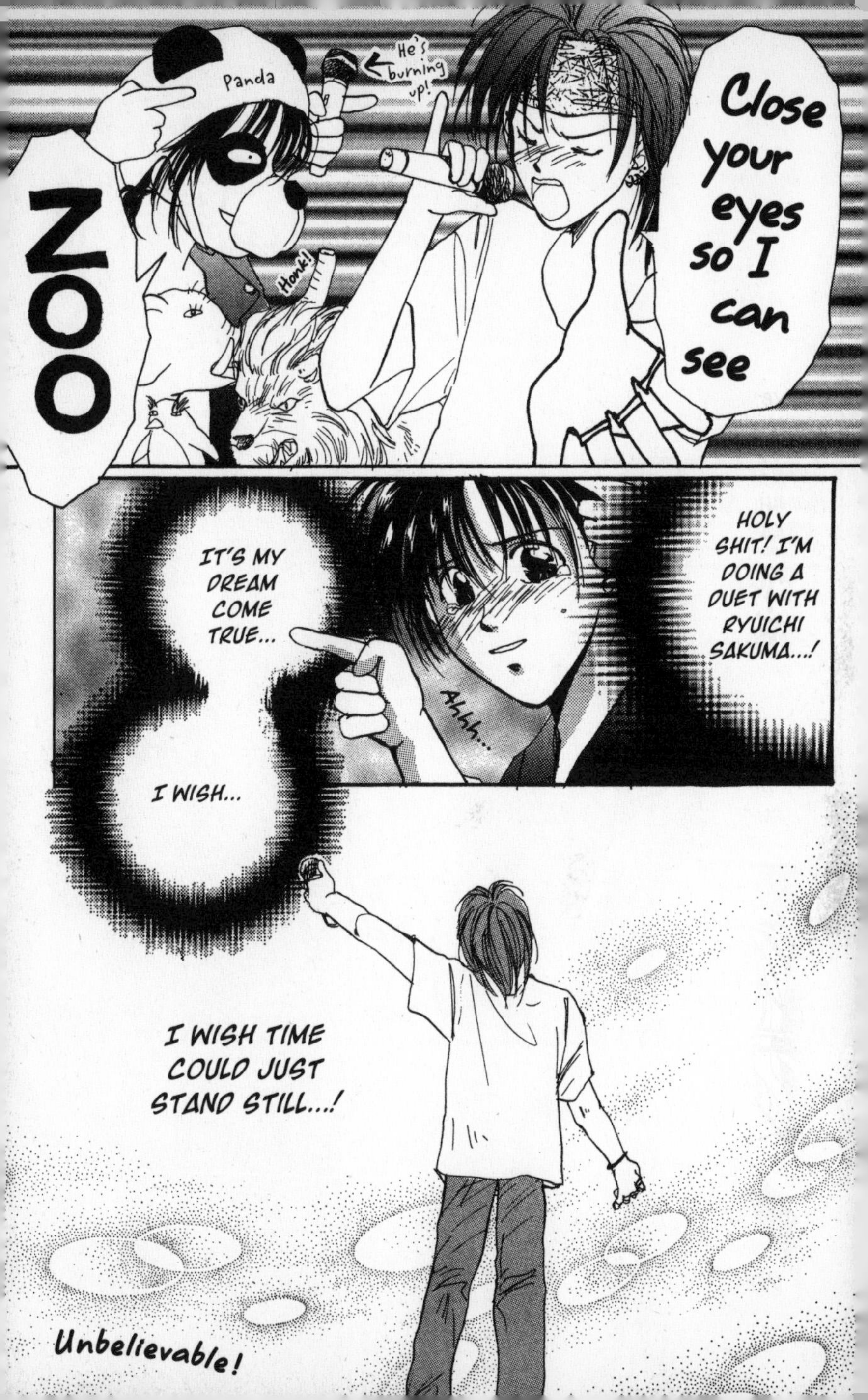
Close your eyes so I can see
He's burning up!
Panda
Honk!
ZOO
HOLY SHIT! I'M DOING A DUET WITH RYUICHI SAKUMA...!
Ahhh...
IT'S MY DREAM COME TRUE...
I WISH...
I WISH TIME COULD JUST STAND STILL...!
Unbelievable!

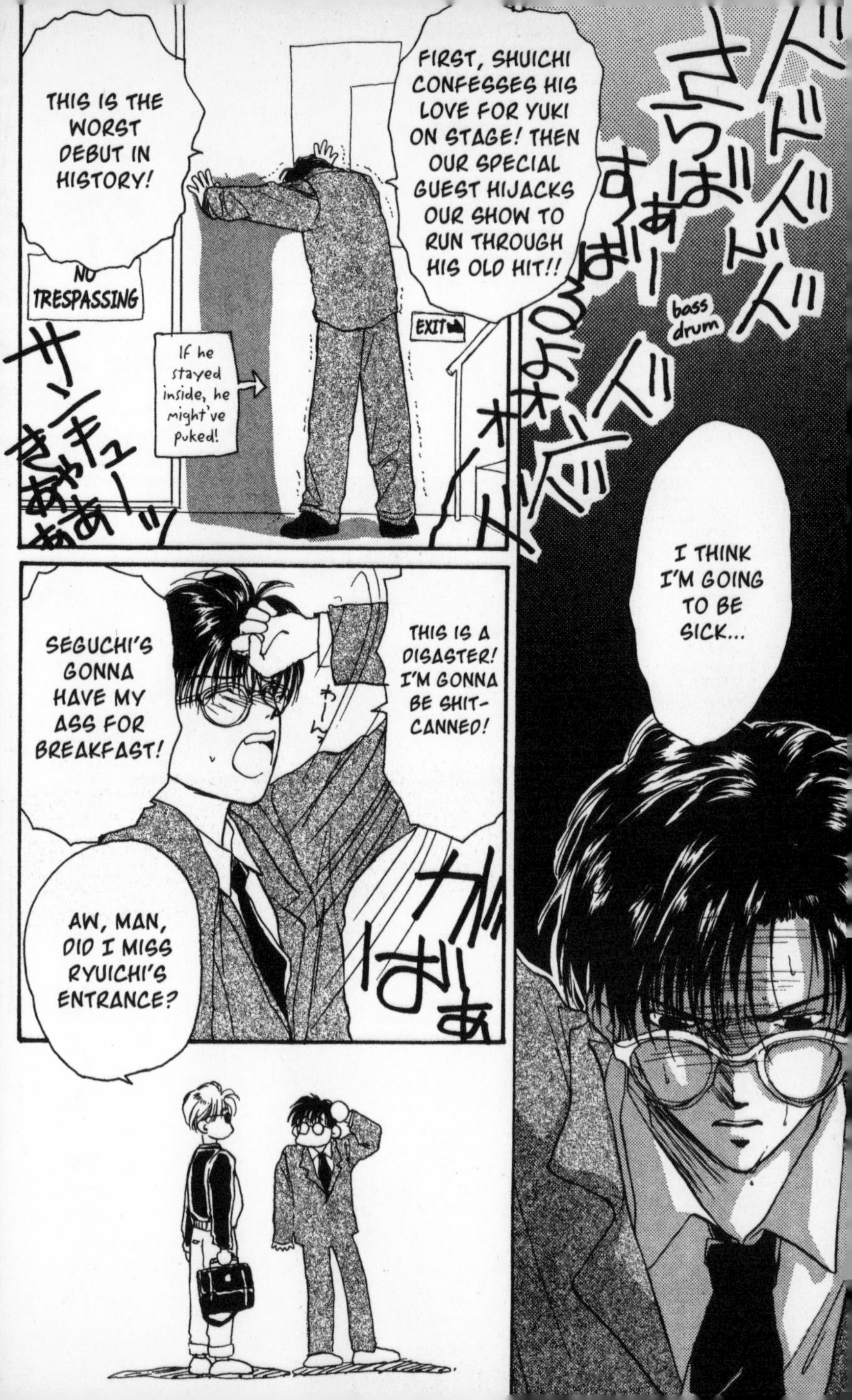
bass drum
I THINK I'M GOING TO BE SICK...
FIRST, SHUICHI CONFESSES HIS LOVE FOR YUKI ON STAGE! THEN OUR SPECIAL GUEST HIJACKS OUR SHOW TO RUN THROUGH HIS OLD HIT!!
THIS IS THE WORST DEBUT IN HISTORY!
EXIT
If he stayed inside, he might've puked!
NO TRESPASSING
THIS IS A DISASTER! I'M GONNA BE SHIT-CANNED!
SEGUCHI'S GONNA HAVE MY ASS FOR BREAKFAST!
AW, MAN, DID I MISS RYUICHI'S ENTRANCE?

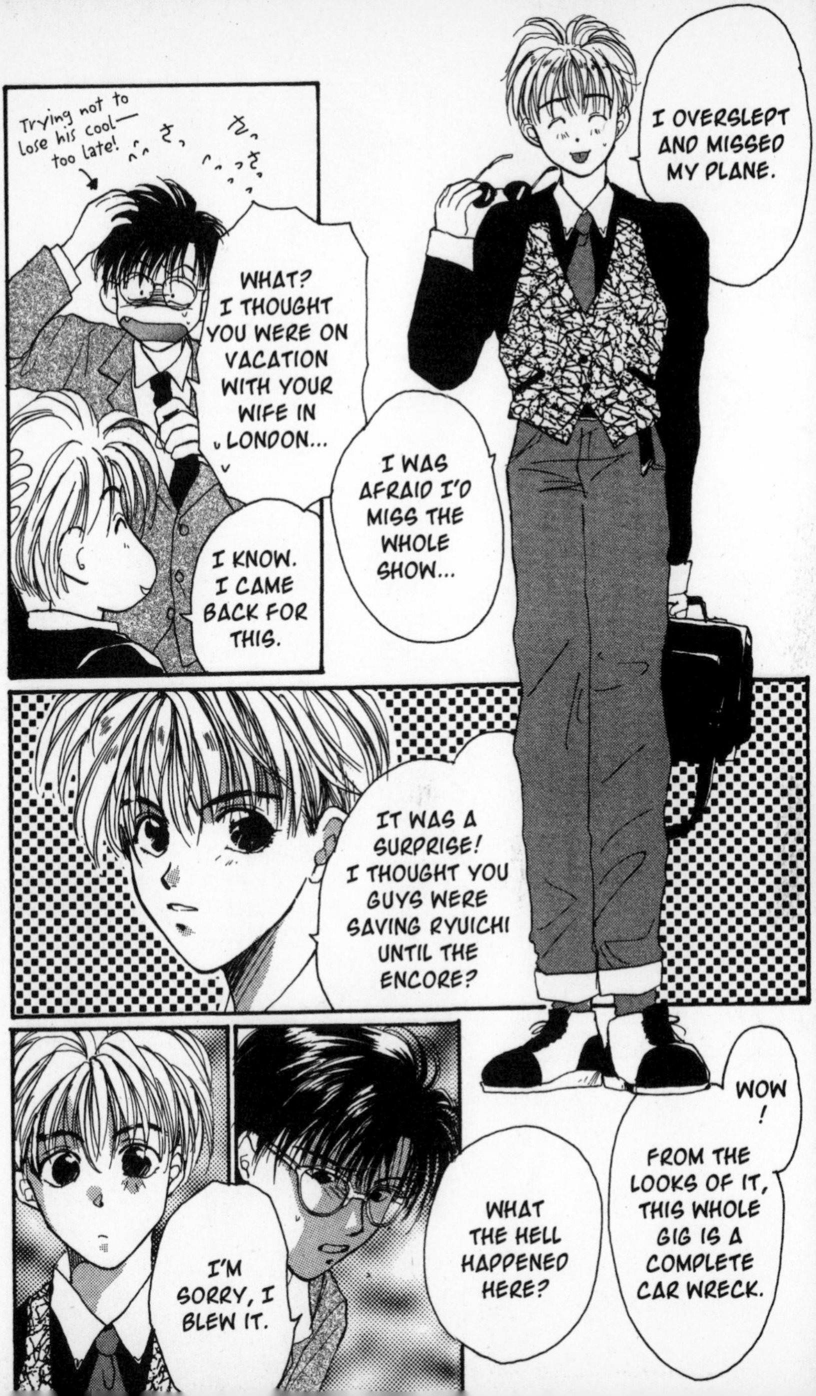
I OVERSLEPT AND MISSED MY PLANE.
Trying not to lose his cool— too late!
WHAT? I THOUGHT YOU WERE ON VACATION WITH YOUR WIFE IN LONDON...
I KNOW. I CAME BACK FOR THIS.
I WAS AFRAID I'D MISS THE WHOLE SHOW...
IT WAS A SURPRISE! I THOUGHT YOU GUYS WERE SAVING RYUICHI UNTIL THE ENCORE?
WOW!
FROM THE LOOKS OF IT, THIS WHOLE GIG IS A COMPLETE CAR WRECK.
WHAT THE HELL HAPPENED HERE?
I'M SORRY, I BLEW IT.

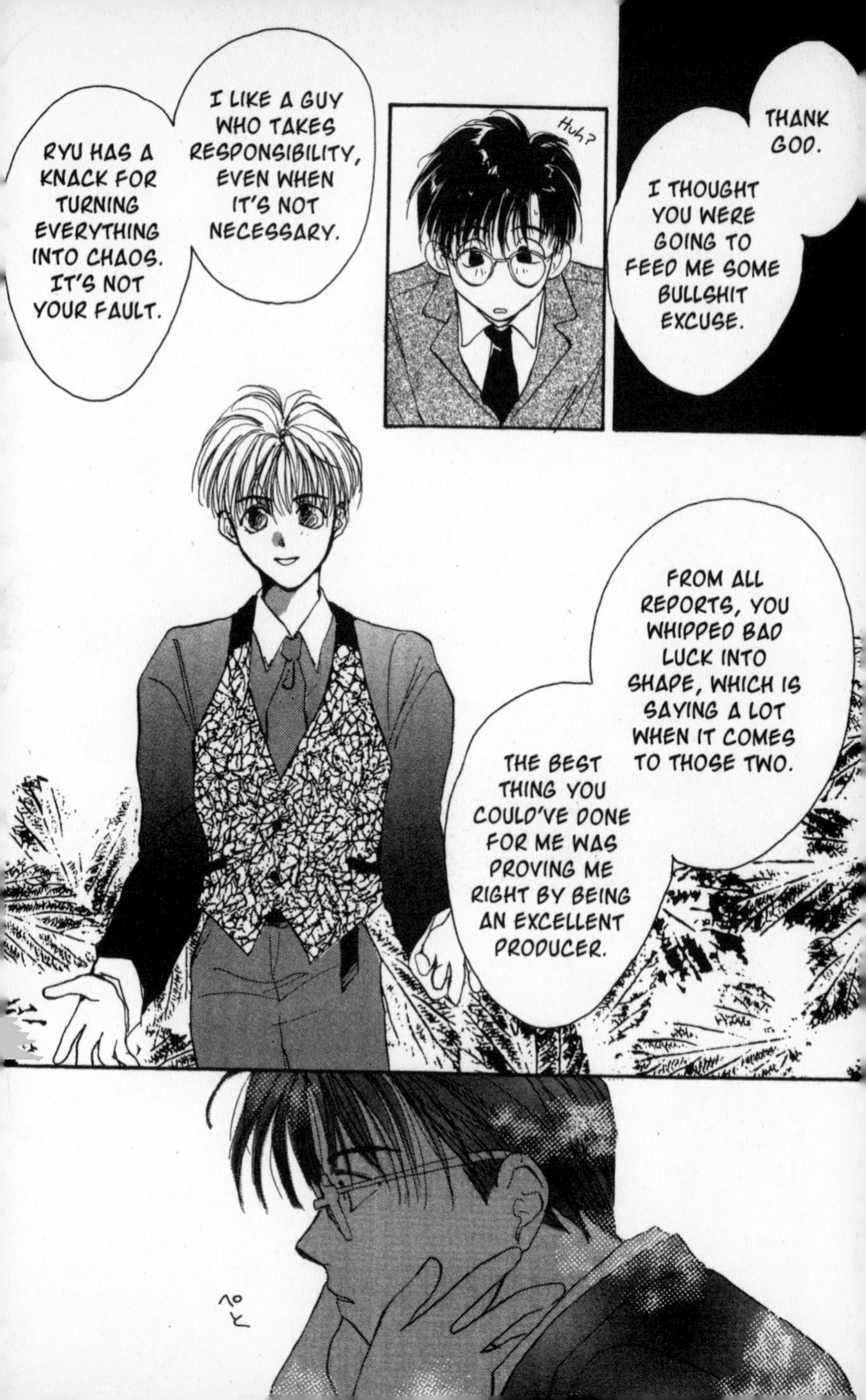
THANK GOD.
I THOUGHT YOU WERE GOING TO FEED ME SOME BULLSHIT EXCUSE.
Huh?
I LIKE A GUY WHO TAKES RESPONSIBILITY, EVEN WHEN IT'S NOT NECESSARY.
RYU HAS A KNACK FOR TURNING EVERYTHING INTO CHAOS. IT'S NOT YOUR FAULT.
FROM ALL REPORTS, YOU WHIPPED BAD LUCK INTO SHAPE, WHICH IS SAYING A LOT WHEN IT COMES TO THOSE TWO.
THE BEST THING YOU COULD'VE DONE FOR ME WAS PROVING ME RIGHT BY BEING AN EXCELLENT PRODUCER.
ぺと

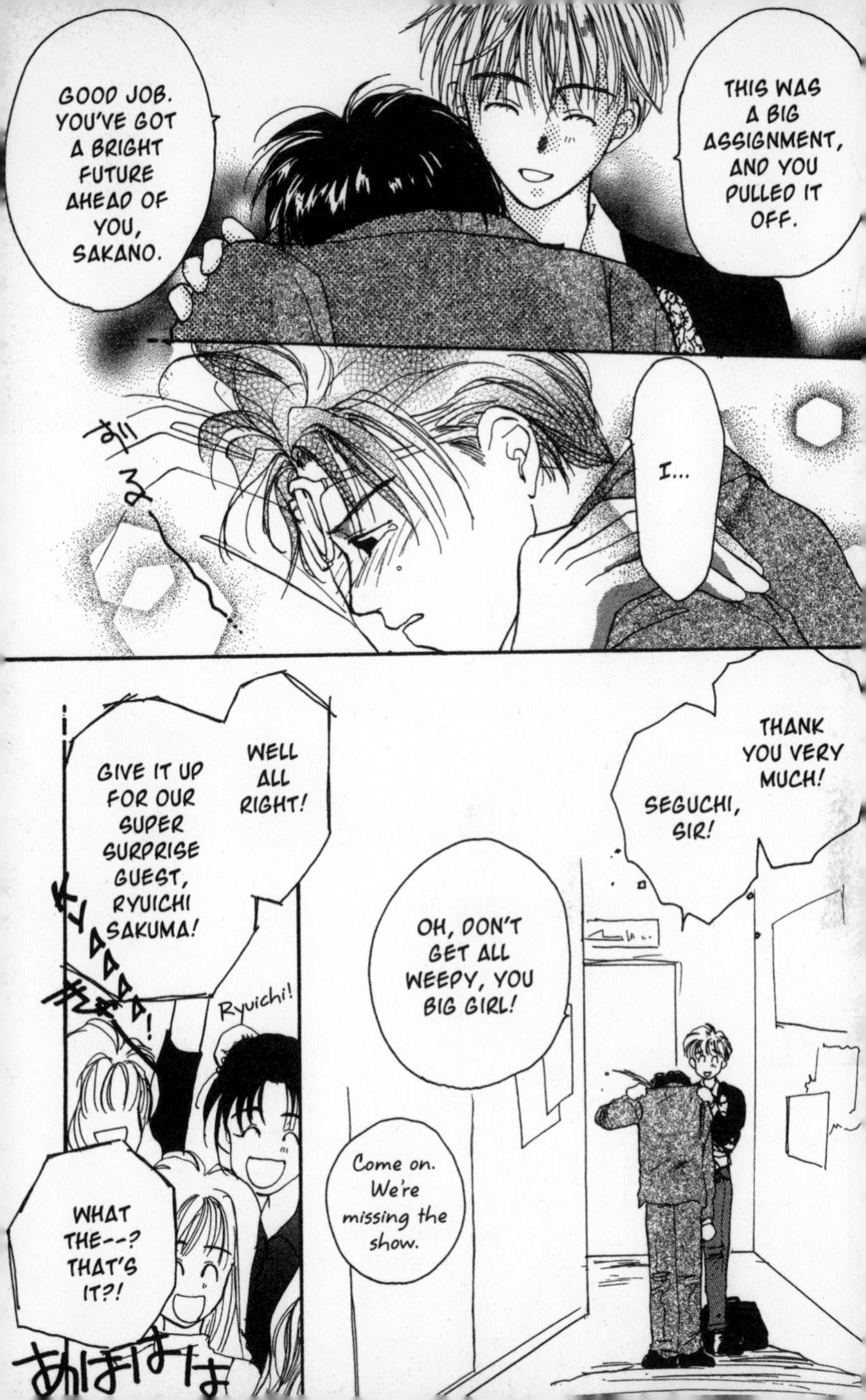
THIS WAS A BIG ASSIGNMENT, AND YOU PULLED IT OFF.
GOOD JOB. YOU'VE GOT A BRIGHT FUTURE AHEAD OF YOU, SAKANO.
I...
THANK YOU VERY MUCH!
SEGUCHI, SIR!
OH, DON'T GET ALL WEEPY, YOU BIG GIRL!
Come on. We're missing the show.
WELL ALL RIGHT!
GIVE IT UP FOR OUR SUPER SURPRISE GUEST, RYUICHI SAKUMA!
Ryuichi!
WHAT THE--? THAT'S IT?!

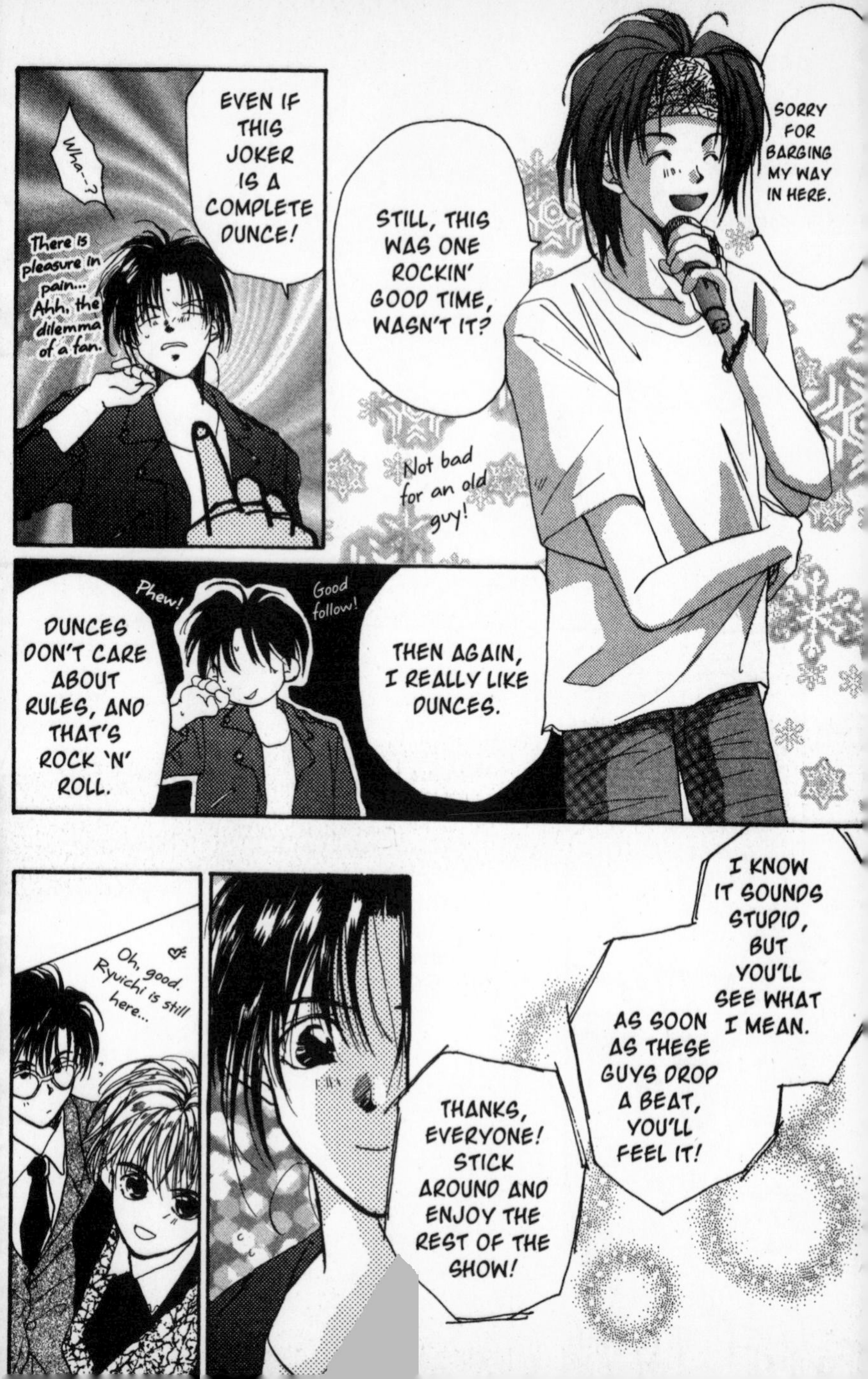
SORRY FOR BARGING MY WAY IN HERE.
STILL, THIS WAS ONE ROCKIN' GOOD TIME, WASN'T IT?
Not bad for an old guy!
EVEN IF THIS JOKER IS A COMPLETE DUNCE!
Wha--?
There is pleasure in pain... Ahh, the dilemma of a fan.
THEN AGAIN, I REALLY LIKE DUNCES.
Good follow!
Phew!
DUNCES DON'T CARE ABOUT RULES, AND THAT'S ROCK 'N' ROLL.
I KNOW IT SOUNDS STUPID, BUT YOU'LL SEE WHAT I MEAN.
AS SOON AS THESE GUYS DROP A BEAT, YOU'LL FEEL IT!
THANKS, EVERYONE! STICK AROUND AND ENJOY THE REST OF THE SHOW!
Oh, good. Ryuichi is still here...

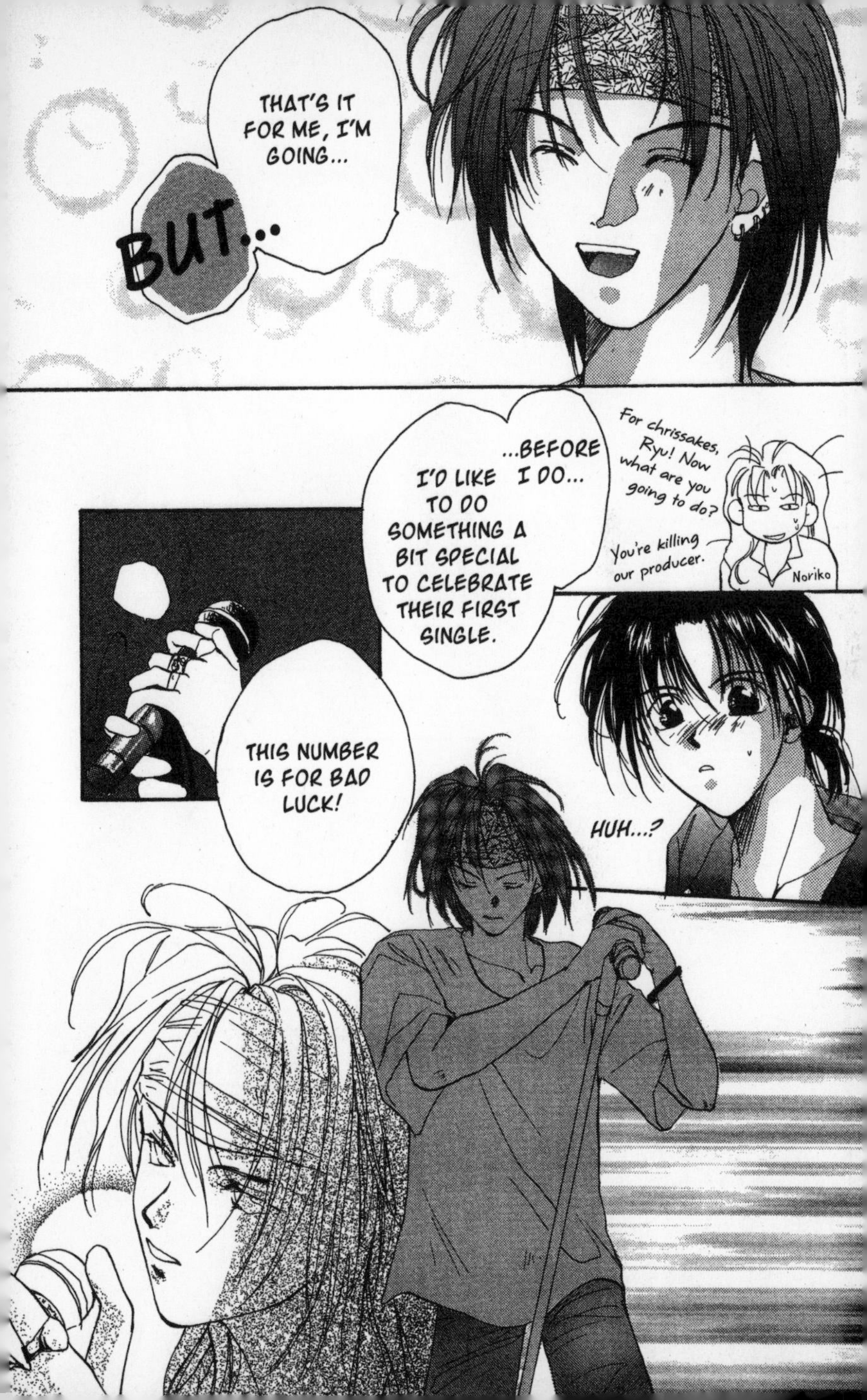
THAT'S IT FOR ME, I'M GOING...
BUT...
...BEFORE I DO... I'D LIKE TO DO SOMETHING A BIT SPECIAL TO CELEBRATE THEIR FIRST SINGLE.
For chrissakes, Ryu! Now what are you going to do?
You're killing our producer.
Noriko
THIS NUMBER IS FOR BAD LUCK!
HUH...?

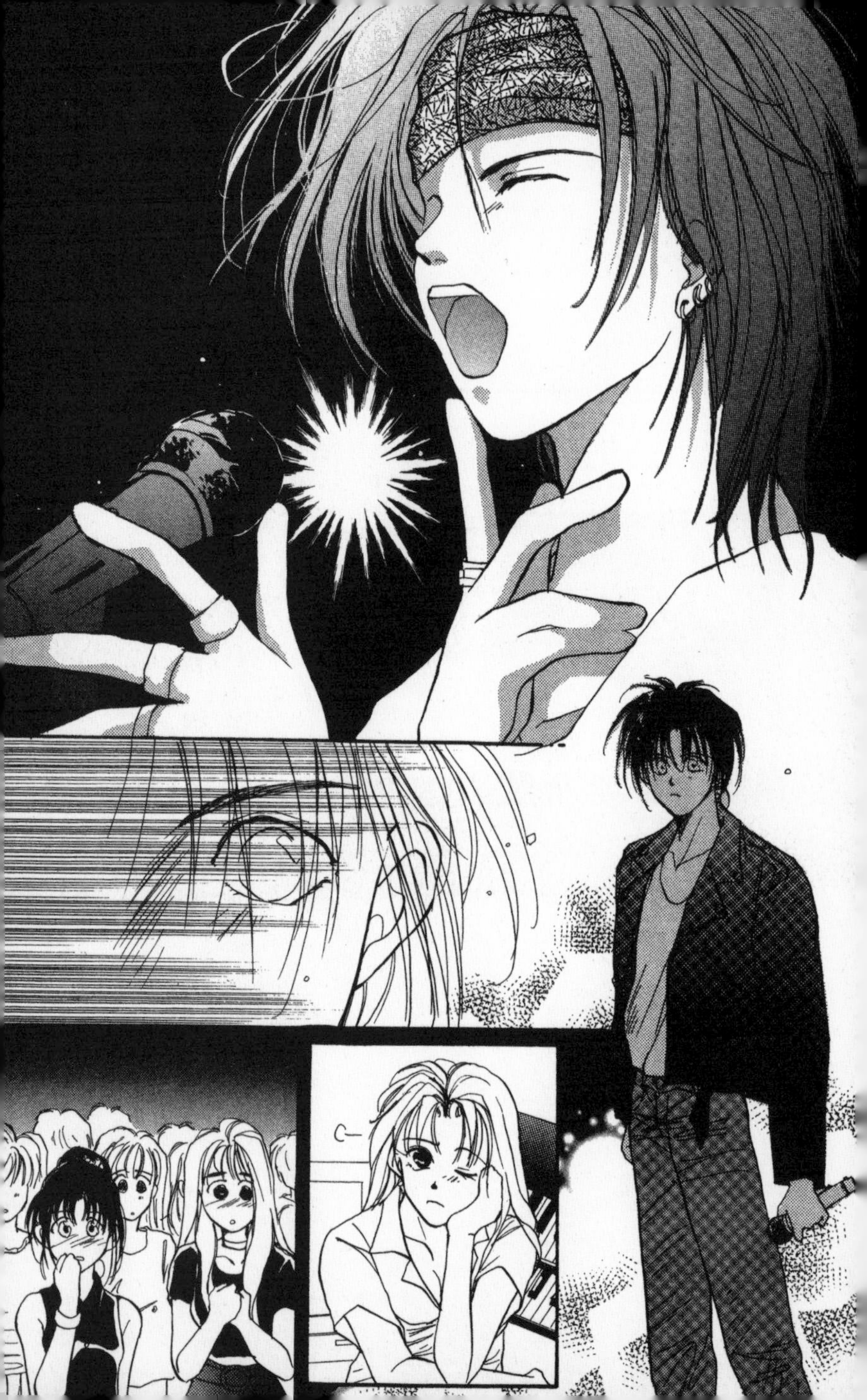
C—

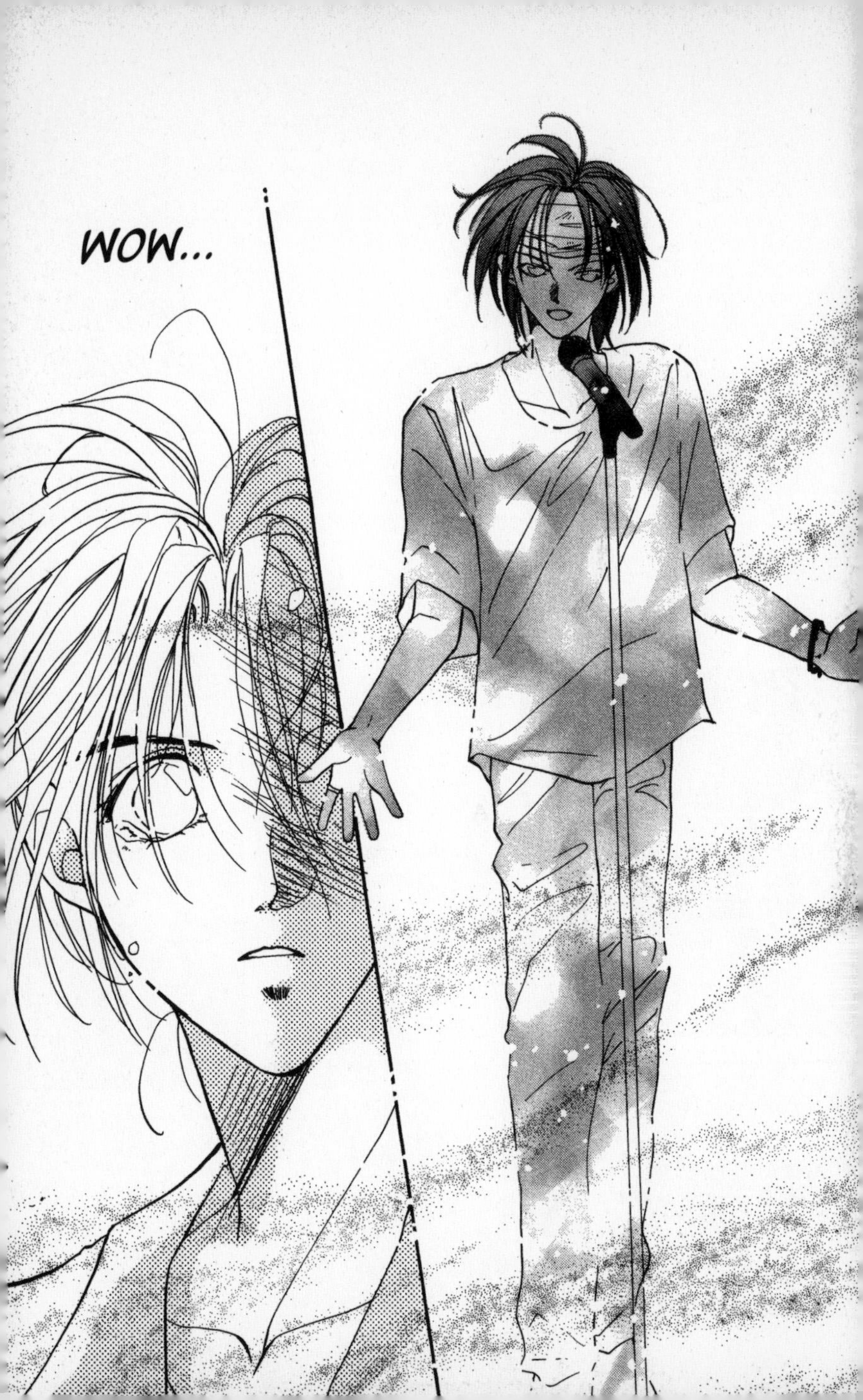
WOW...

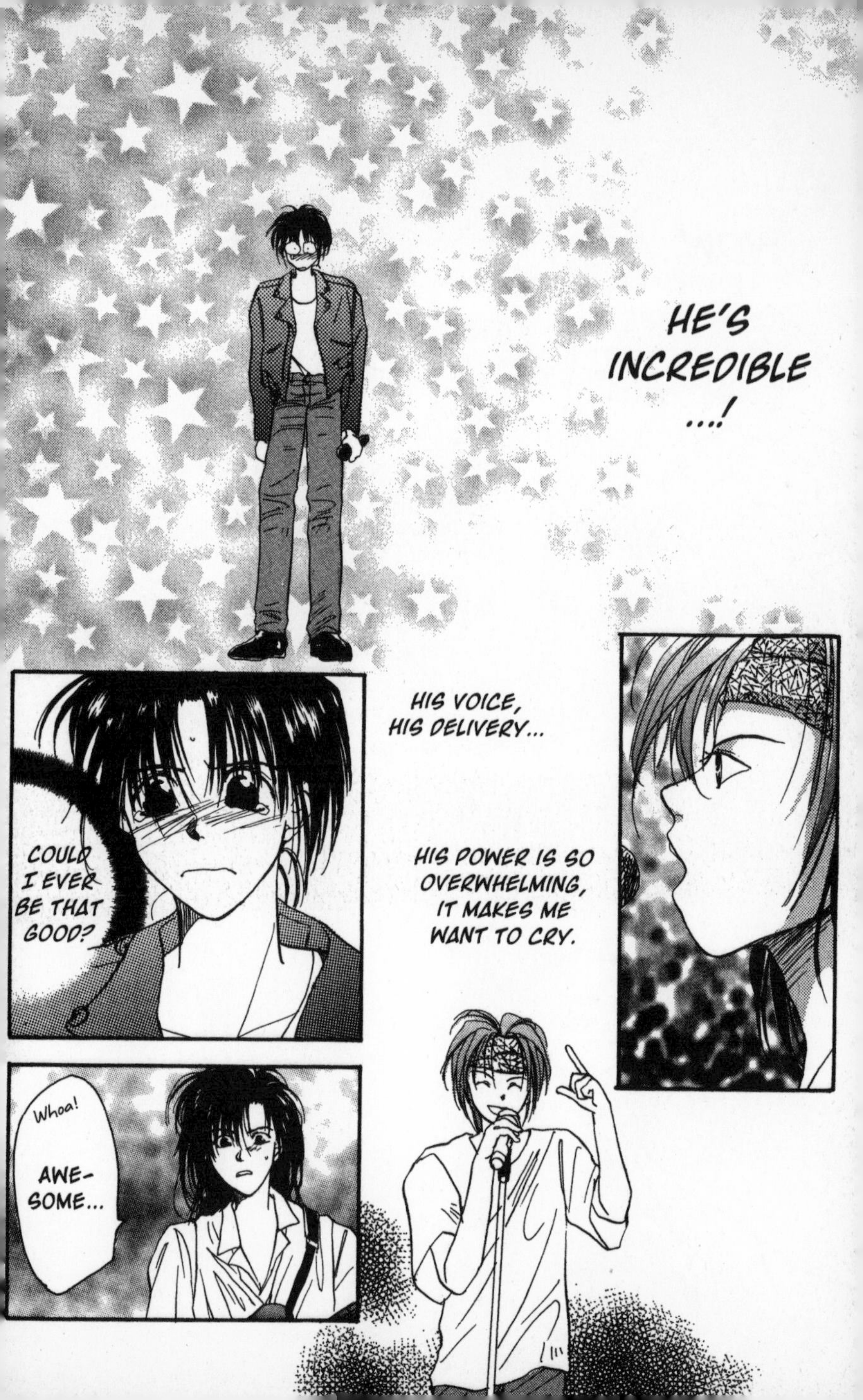
HE'S INCREDIBLE ...!
HIS VOICE, HIS DELIVERY...
HIS POWER IS SO OVERWHELMING, IT MAKES ME WANT TO CRY.
COULD I EVER BE THAT GOOD?
Whoa!
AWE-SOME...

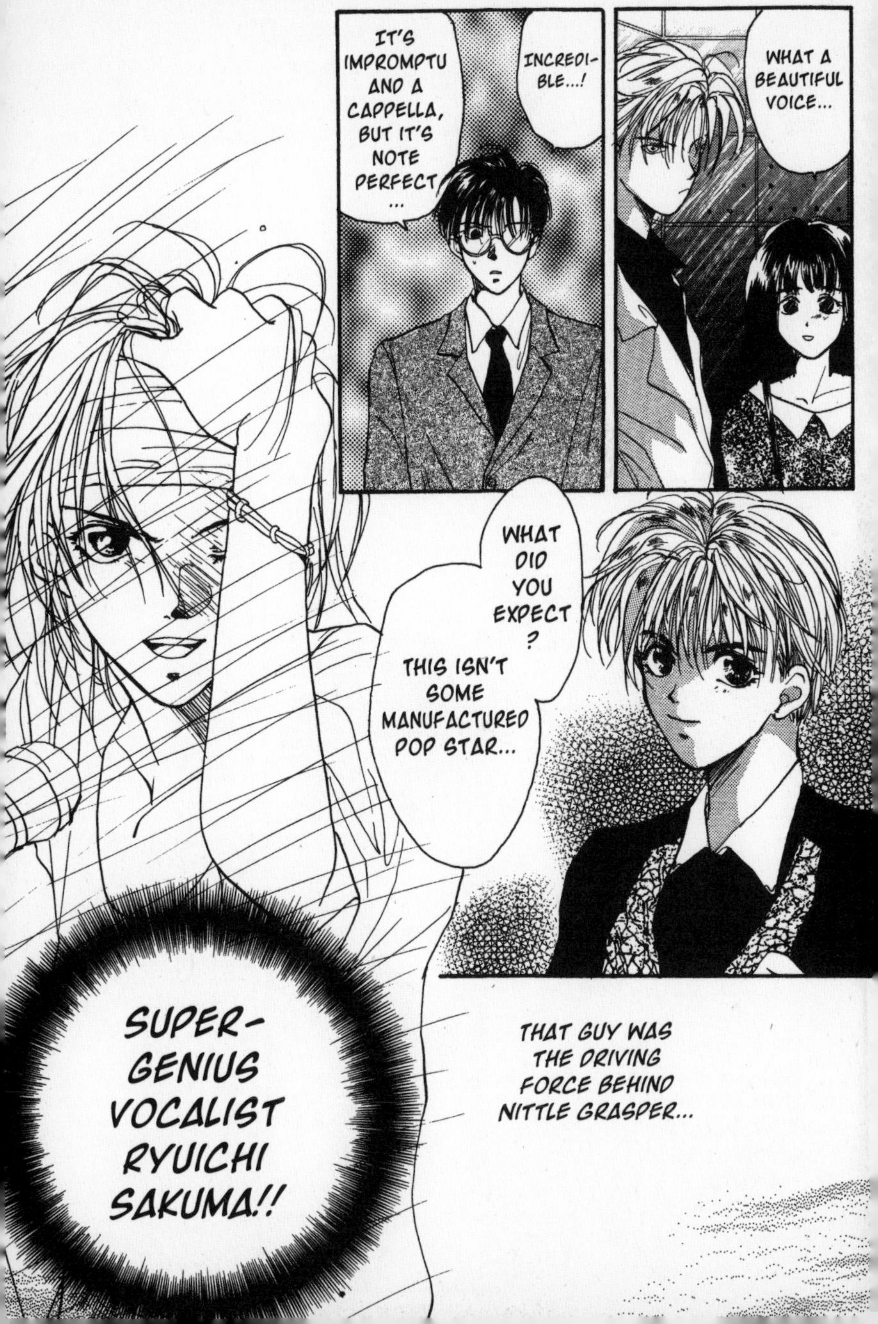

WHAT A BEAUTIFUL VOICE...
INCREDI-BLE...!
IT'S IMPROMPTU AND A CAPPELLA, BUT IT'S NOTE PERFECT...
WHAT DID YOU EXPECT?
THIS ISN'T SOME MANUFACTURED POP STAR...
THAT GUY WAS THE DRIVING FORCE BEHIND NITTLE GRASPER...
SUPER-GENIUS VOCALIST RYUICHI SAKUMA!!

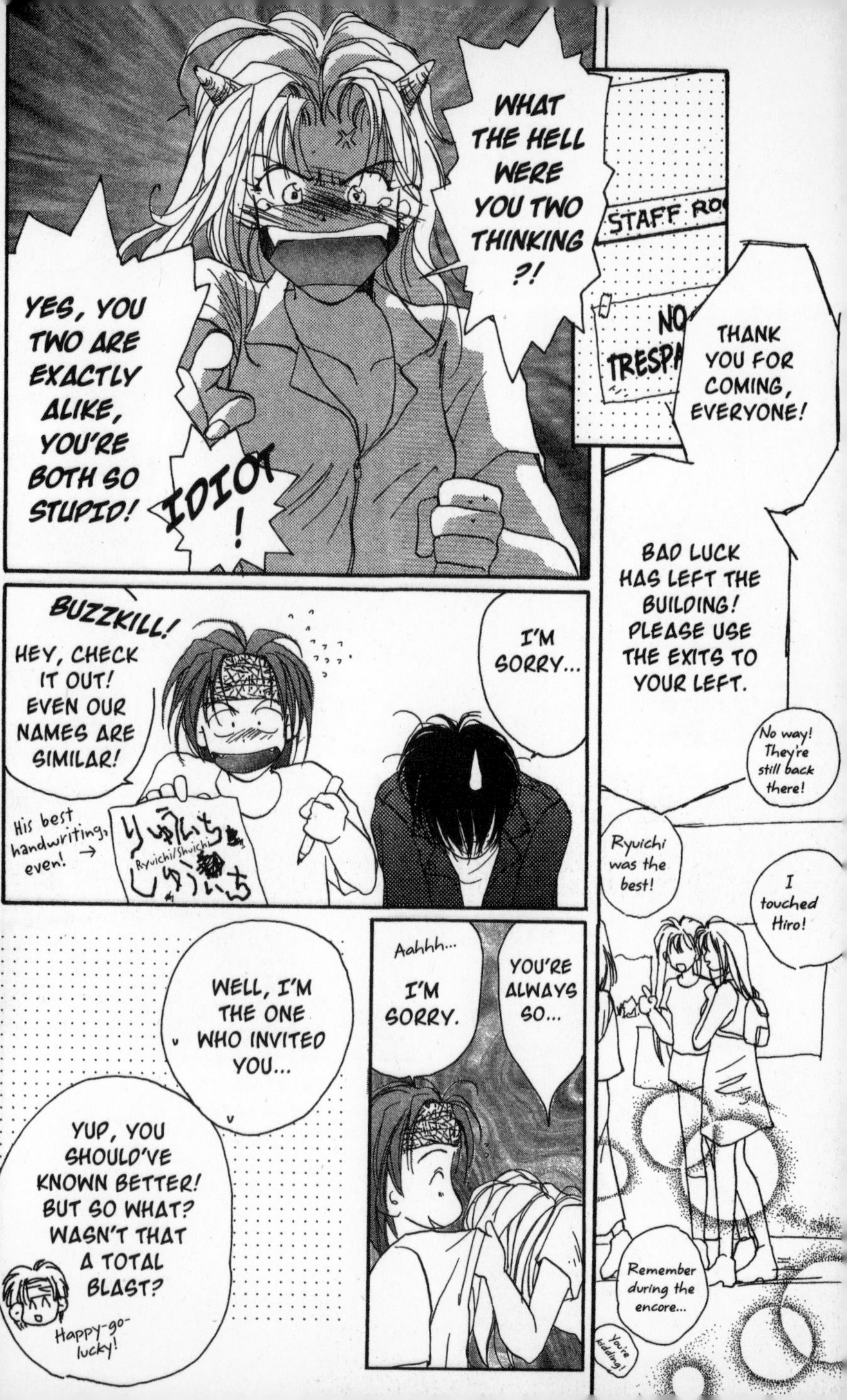
THANK YOU FOR COMING, EVERYONE!
BAD LUCK HAS LEFT THE BUILDING! PLEASE USE THE EXITS TO YOUR LEFT.
No way! They're still back there!
Ryuichi was the best!
I touched Hiro!
Remember during the encore...
You're kidding!
WHAT THE HELL WERE YOU TWO THINKING?!
YES, YOU TWO ARE EXACTLY ALIKE, YOU'RE BOTH SO STUPID!
IDIOT!
I'M SORRY...
BUZZKILL!
HEY, CHECK IT OUT! EVEN OUR NAMES ARE SIMILAR!
His best handwriting, even!
りゅういち
Ryuichi/Shuichi
しゅういち
YOU'RE ALWAYS SO...
Aahhh...
I'M SORRY.
WELL, I'M THE ONE WHO INVITED YOU...
YUP, YOU SHOULD'VE KNOWN BETTER! BUT SO WHAT? WASN'T THAT A TOTAL BLAST?
Happy-go-lucky!

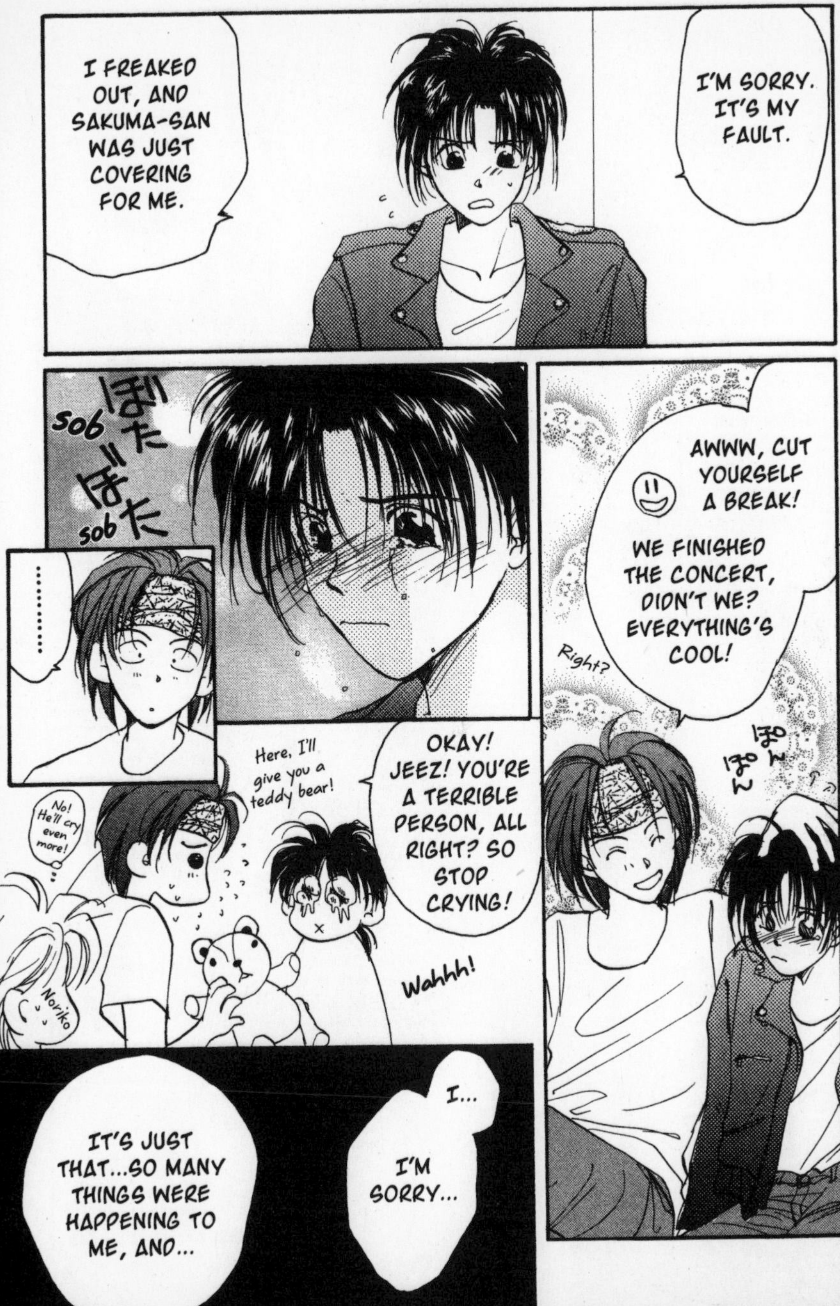
I'M SORRY. IT'S MY FAULT.
I FREAKED OUT, AND SAKUMA-SAN WAS JUST COVERING FOR ME.
AWWW, CUT YOURSELF A BREAK!
WE FINISHED THE CONCERT, DIDN'T WE? EVERYTHING'S COOL!
Right?
ぽんぽん
ぽたぽた sob sob
ぽたぽた sob
....
OKAY! JEEZ! YOU'RE A TERRIBLE PERSON, ALL RIGHT? SO STOP CRYING!
Here, I'll give you a teddy bear!
No! He'll cry even more!
Wahhh!
Noriko
I...
I'M SORRY...
IT'S JUST THAT...SO MANY THINGS WERE HAPPENING TO ME, AND...

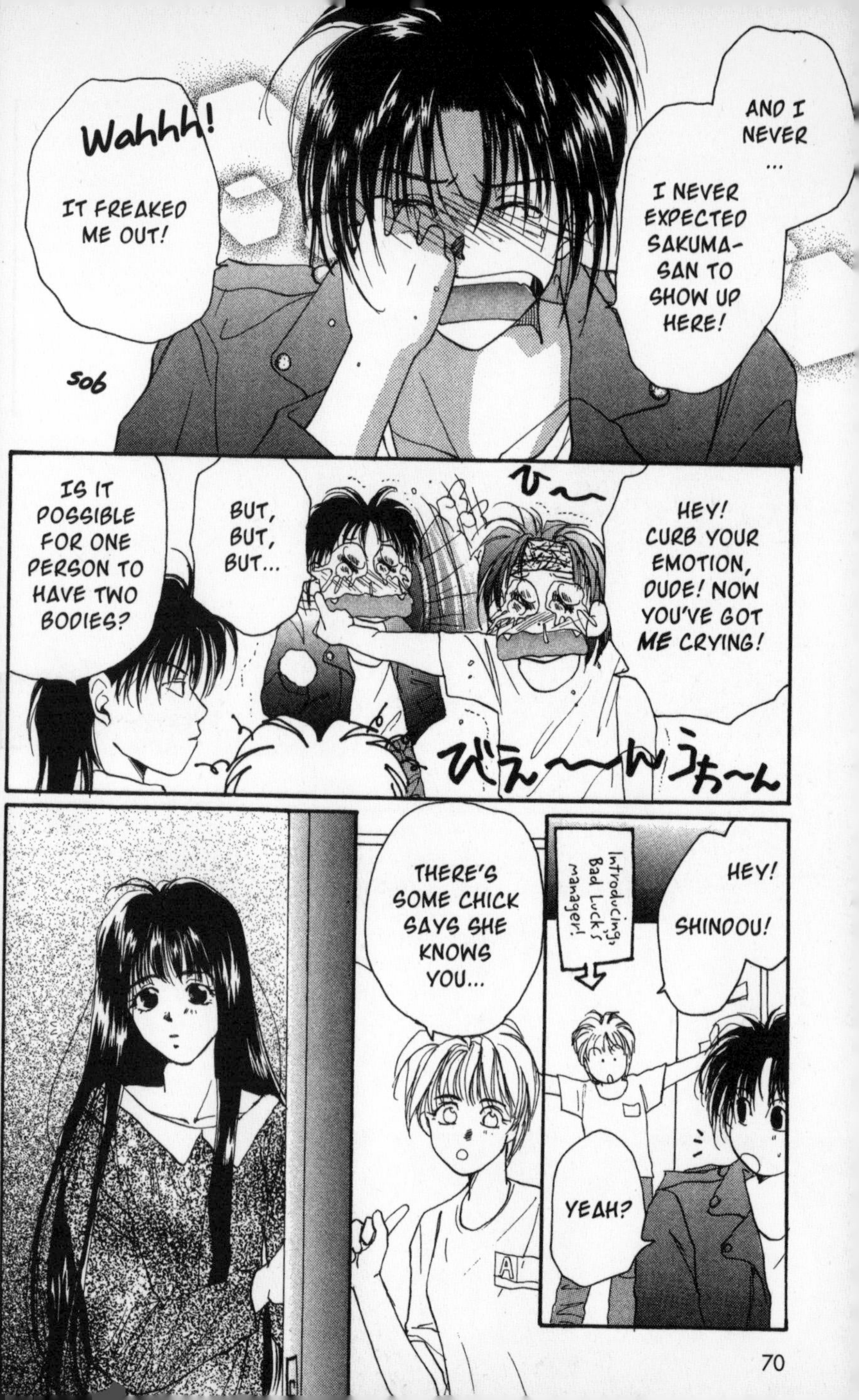
AND I NEVER ... I NEVER EXPECTED SAKUMA-SAN TO SHOW UP HERE!
Wahhh!
IT FREAKED ME OUT!
sob
ひ～
HEY! CURB YOUR EMOTION, DUDE! NOW YOU'VE GOT ME CRYING!
BUT, BUT, BUT...
IS IT POSSIBLE FOR ONE PERSON TO HAVE TWO BODIES?
びえ～～んうわ～ん
HEY! SHINDOU!
Introducing, Bad Luck's manager!
YEAH?
THERE'S SOME CHICK SAYS SHE KNOWS YOU...

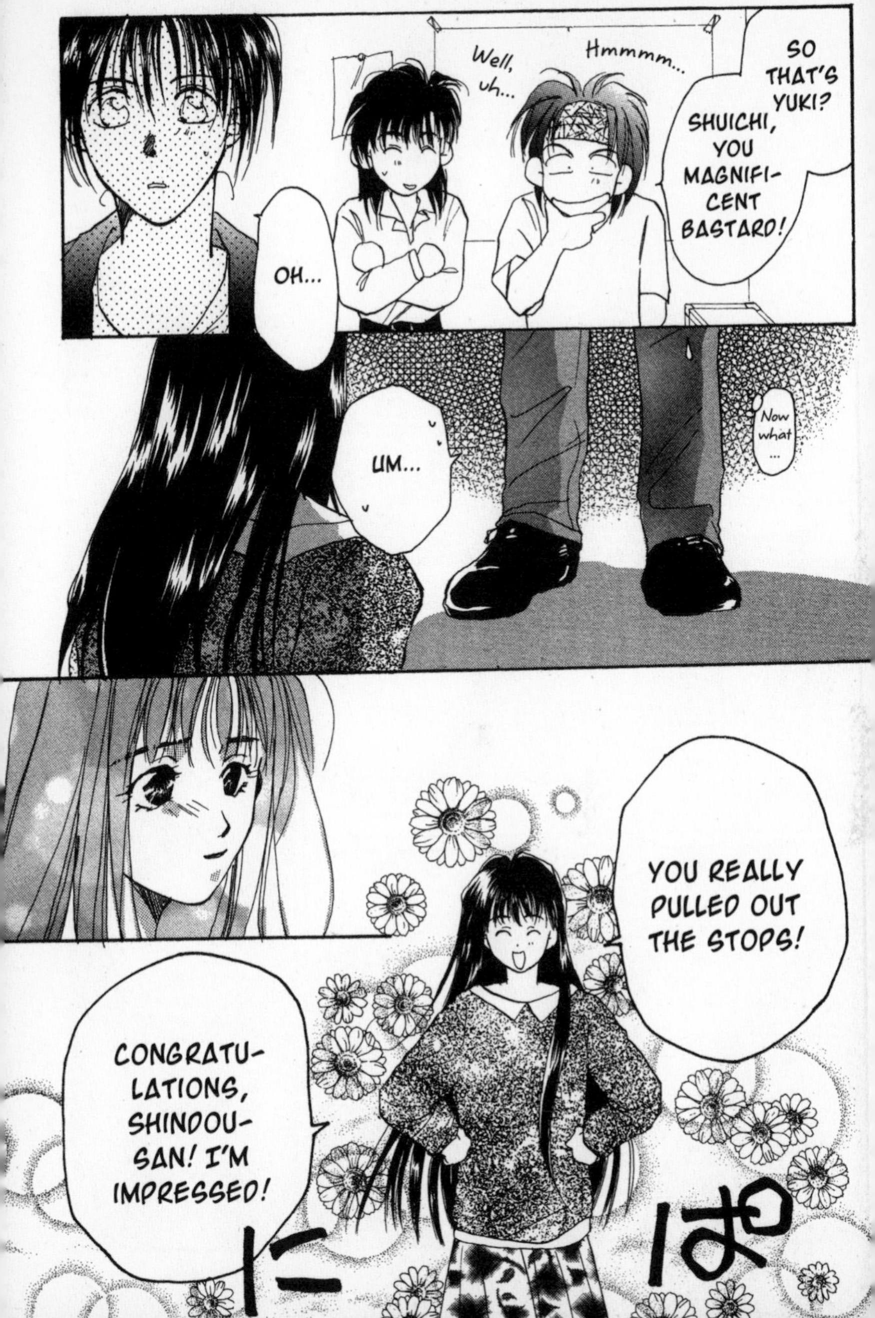
SO THAT'S YUKI? SHUICHI, YOU MAGNIFICENT BASTARD!
Hmmmm...
Well, uh...
OH...
Now what...
UM...
YOU REALLY PULLED OUT THE STOPS!
CONGRATULATIONS, SHINDOU-SAN! I'M IMPRESSED!
にーぱ

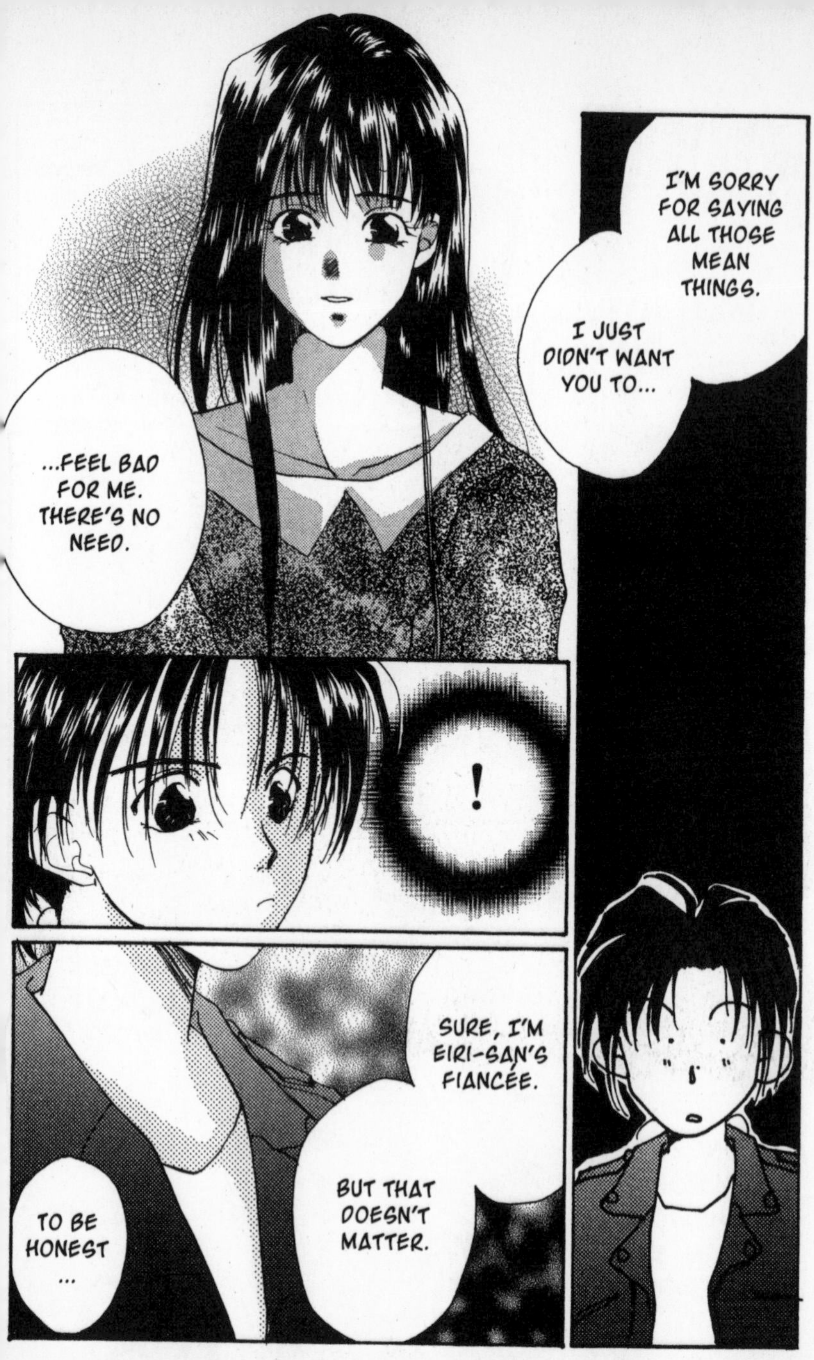
I'M SORRY FOR SAYING ALL THOSE MEAN THINGS.
I JUST DIDN'T WANT YOU TO...
...FEEL BAD FOR ME. THERE'S NO NEED.
!
SURE, I'M EIRI-SAN'S FIANCÉE.
BUT THAT DOESN'T MATTER.
TO BE HONEST ...

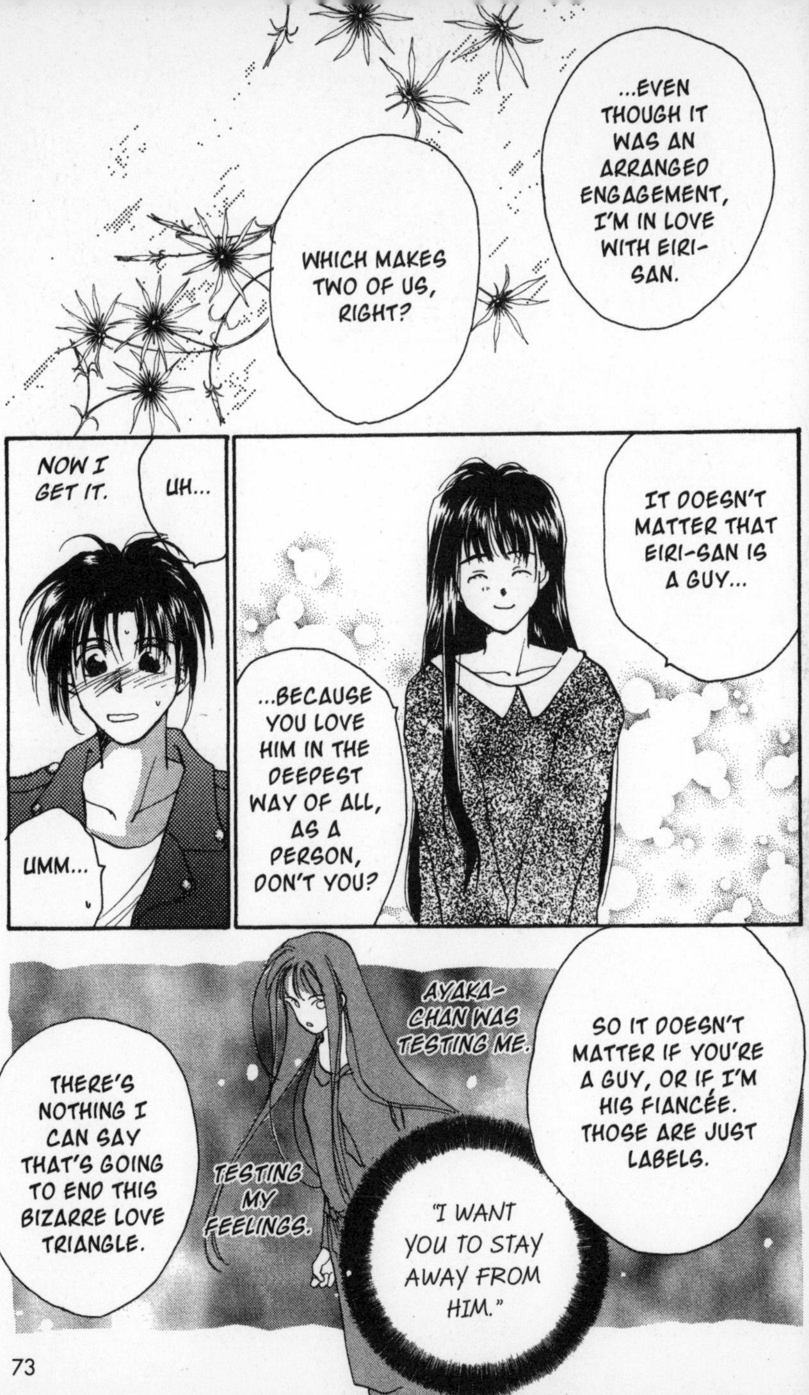

...EVEN THOUGH IT WAS AN ARRANGED ENGAGEMENT, I'M IN LOVE WITH EIRI-SAN.
WHICH MAKES TWO OF US, RIGHT?
IT DOESN'T MATTER THAT EIRI-SAN IS A GUY...
...BECAUSE YOU LOVE HIM IN THE DEEPEST WAY OF ALL, AS A PERSON, DON'T YOU?
UH...
NOW I GET IT.
UMM...
SO IT DOESN'T MATTER IF YOU'RE A GUY, OR IF I'M HIS FIANCÉE. THOSE ARE JUST LABELS.
AYAKA-CHAN WAS TESTING ME.
"I WANT YOU TO STAY AWAY FROM HIM."
TESTING MY FEELINGS.
THERE'S NOTHING I CAN SAY THAT'S GOING TO END THIS BIZARRE LOVE TRIANGLE.

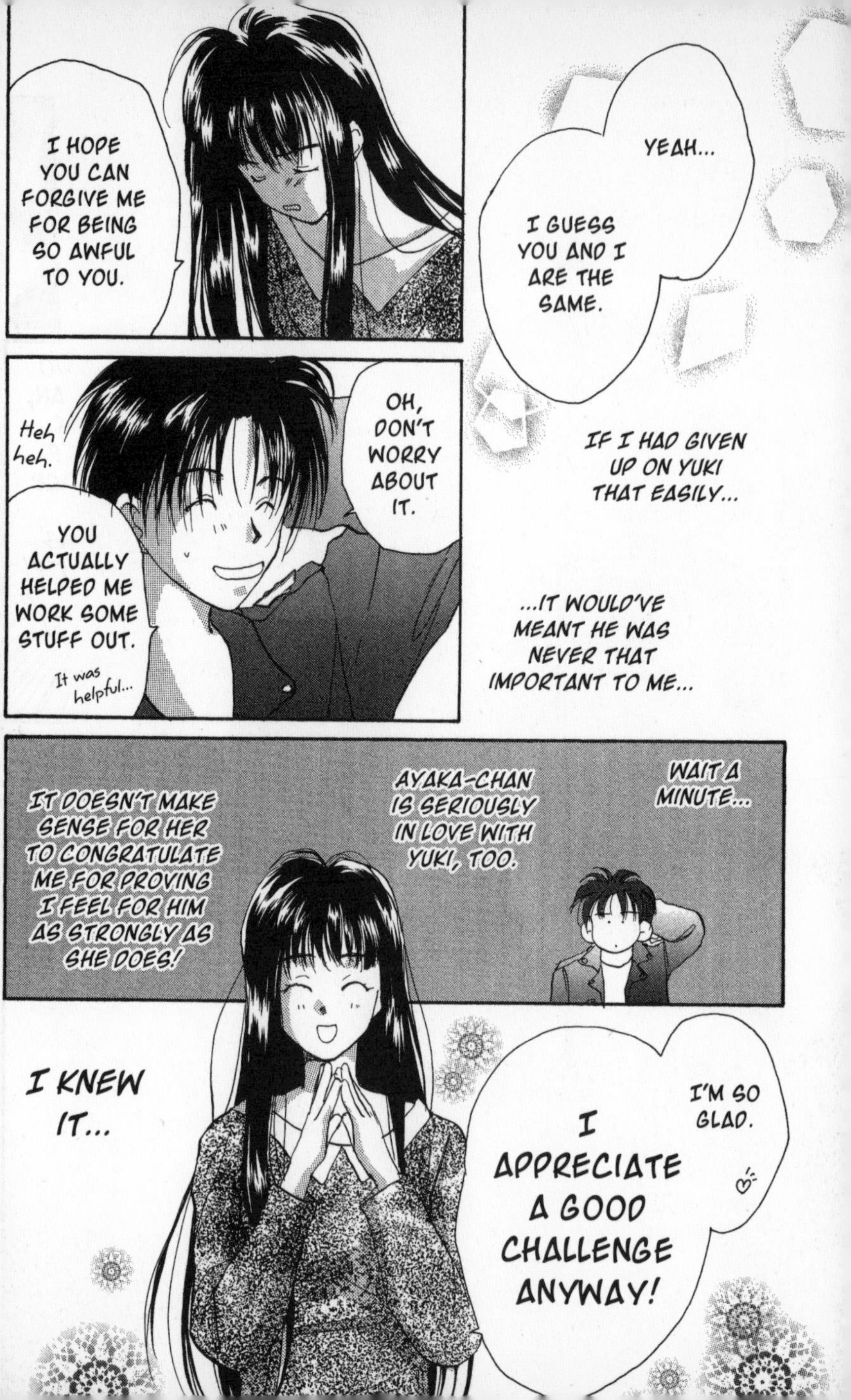

YEAH...
I GUESS YOU AND I ARE THE SAME.
IF I HAD GIVEN UP ON YUKI THAT EASILY...
...IT WOULD'VE MEANT HE WAS NEVER THAT IMPORTANT TO ME...
I HOPE YOU CAN FORGIVE ME FOR BEING SO AWFUL TO YOU.
OH, DON'T WORRY ABOUT IT.
Heh heh.
YOU ACTUALLY HELPED ME WORK SOME STUFF OUT.
It was helpful...
WAIT A MINUTE...
AYAKA-CHAN IS SERIOUSLY IN LOVE WITH YUKI, TOO.
IT DOESN'T MAKE SENSE FOR HER TO CONGRATULATE ME FOR PROVING I FEEL FOR HIM AS STRONGLY AS SHE DOES!
I'M SO GLAD.
I APPRECIATE A GOOD CHALLENGE ANYWAY!
I KNEW IT...

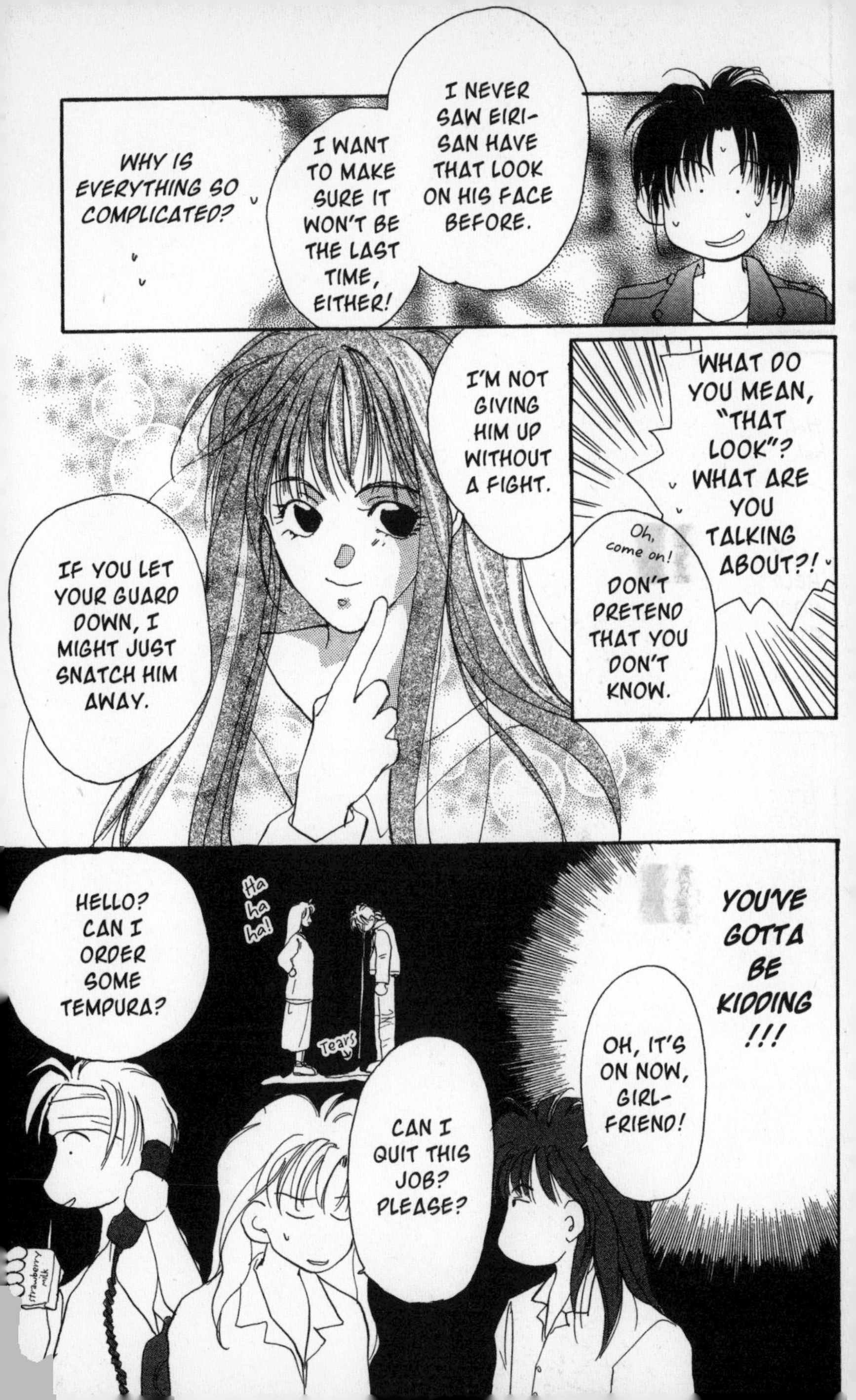
I NEVER SAW EIRI-SAN HAVE THAT LOOK ON HIS FACE BEFORE.
I WANT TO MAKE SURE IT WON'T BE THE LAST TIME, EITHER!
WHY IS EVERYTHING SO COMPLICATED?
WHAT DO YOU MEAN, "THAT LOOK"? WHAT ARE YOU TALKING ABOUT?!
Oh, come on! DON'T PRETEND THAT YOU DON'T KNOW.
I'M NOT GIVING HIM UP WITHOUT A FIGHT.
IF YOU LET YOUR GUARD DOWN, I MIGHT JUST SNATCH HIM AWAY.
YOU'VE GOTTA BE KIDDING!!!
OH, IT'S ON NOW, GIRL-FRIEND!
CAN I QUIT THIS JOB? PLEASE?
Ha ha ha!
Tears
HELLO? CAN I ORDER SOME TEMPURA?
strawberry milk

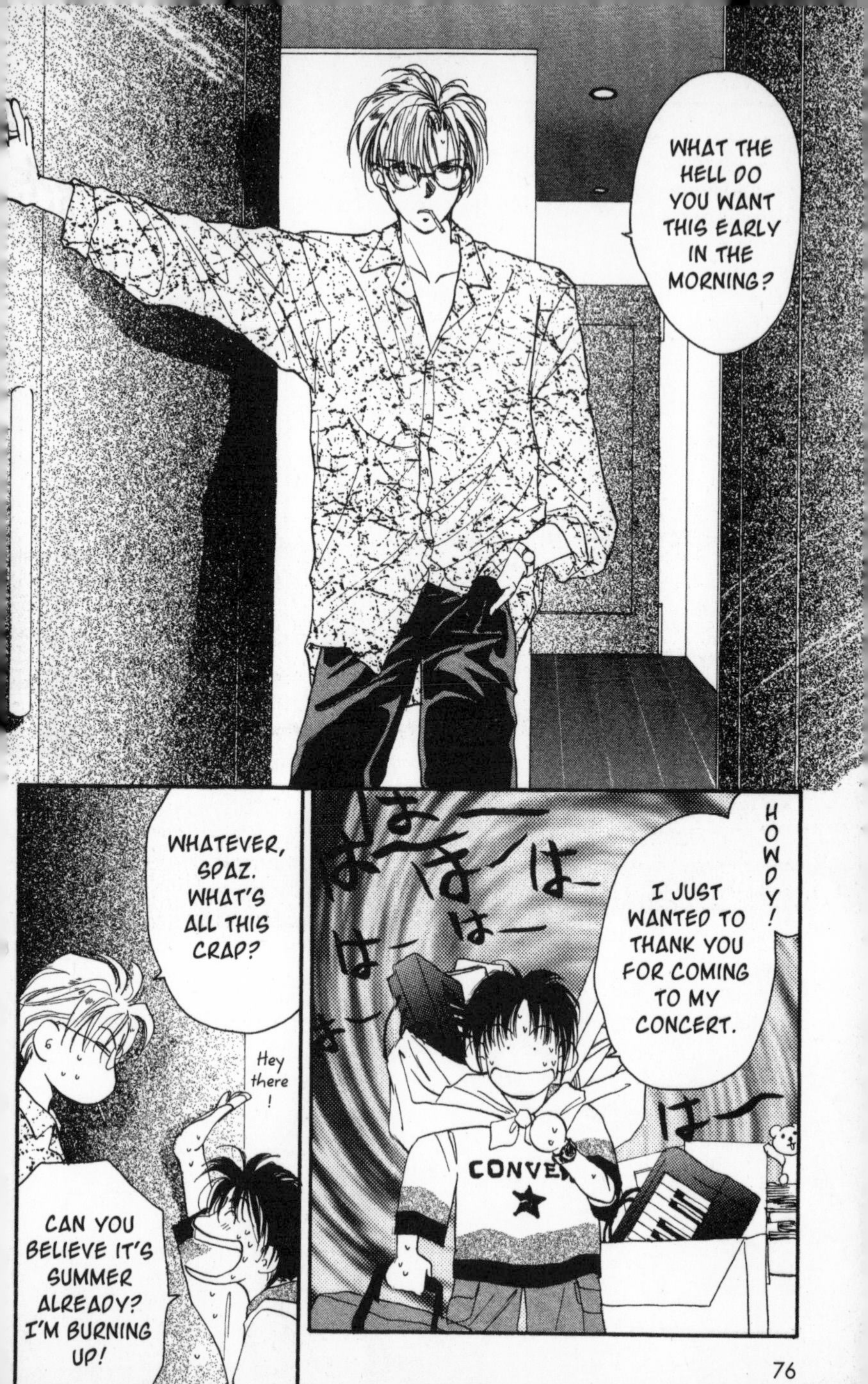
WHAT THE HELL DO YOU WANT THIS EARLY IN THE MORNING?
HOWDY!
I JUST WANTED TO THANK YOU FOR COMING TO MY CONCERT.
CONVE
WHATEVER, SPAZ. WHAT'S ALL THIS CRAP?
Hey there!
CAN YOU BELIEVE IT'S SUMMER ALREADY? I'M BURNING UP!

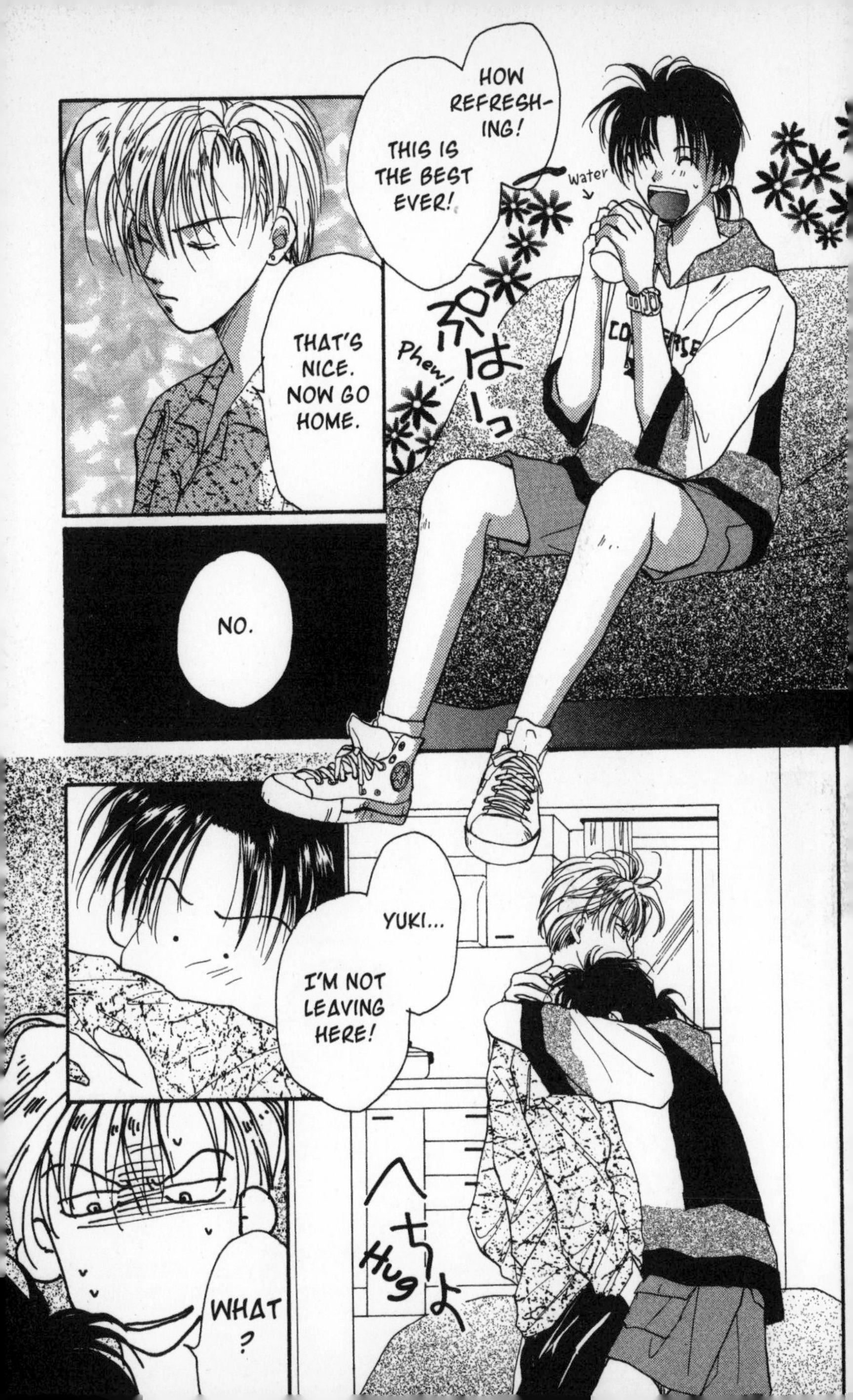
HOW REFRESHING!
THIS IS THE BEST EVER!
Water
ぷはーっ
Phew!
THAT'S NICE. NOW GO HOME.
NO.
YUKI...
I'M NOT LEAVING HERE!
へちょ
Hug
WHAT?

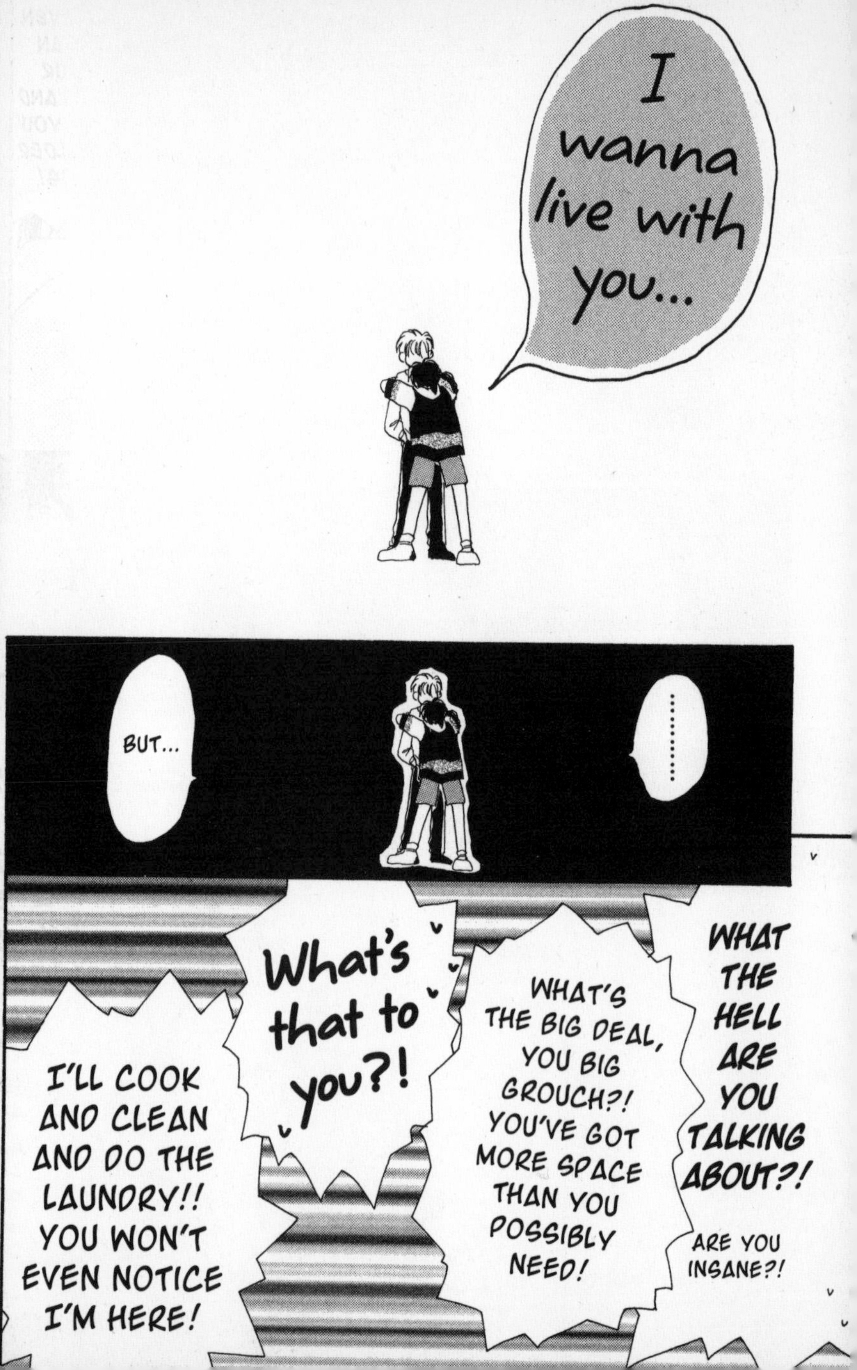
I wanna live with you...
....
BUT...
WHAT THE HELL ARE YOU TALKING ABOUT?!
ARE YOU INSANE?!
WHAT'S THE BIG DEAL, YOU BIG GROUCH?! YOU'VE GOT MORE SPACE THAN YOU POSSIBLY NEED!
What's that to you?!
I'LL COOK AND CLEAN AND DO THE LAUNDRY!! YOU WON'T EVEN NOTICE I'M HERE!

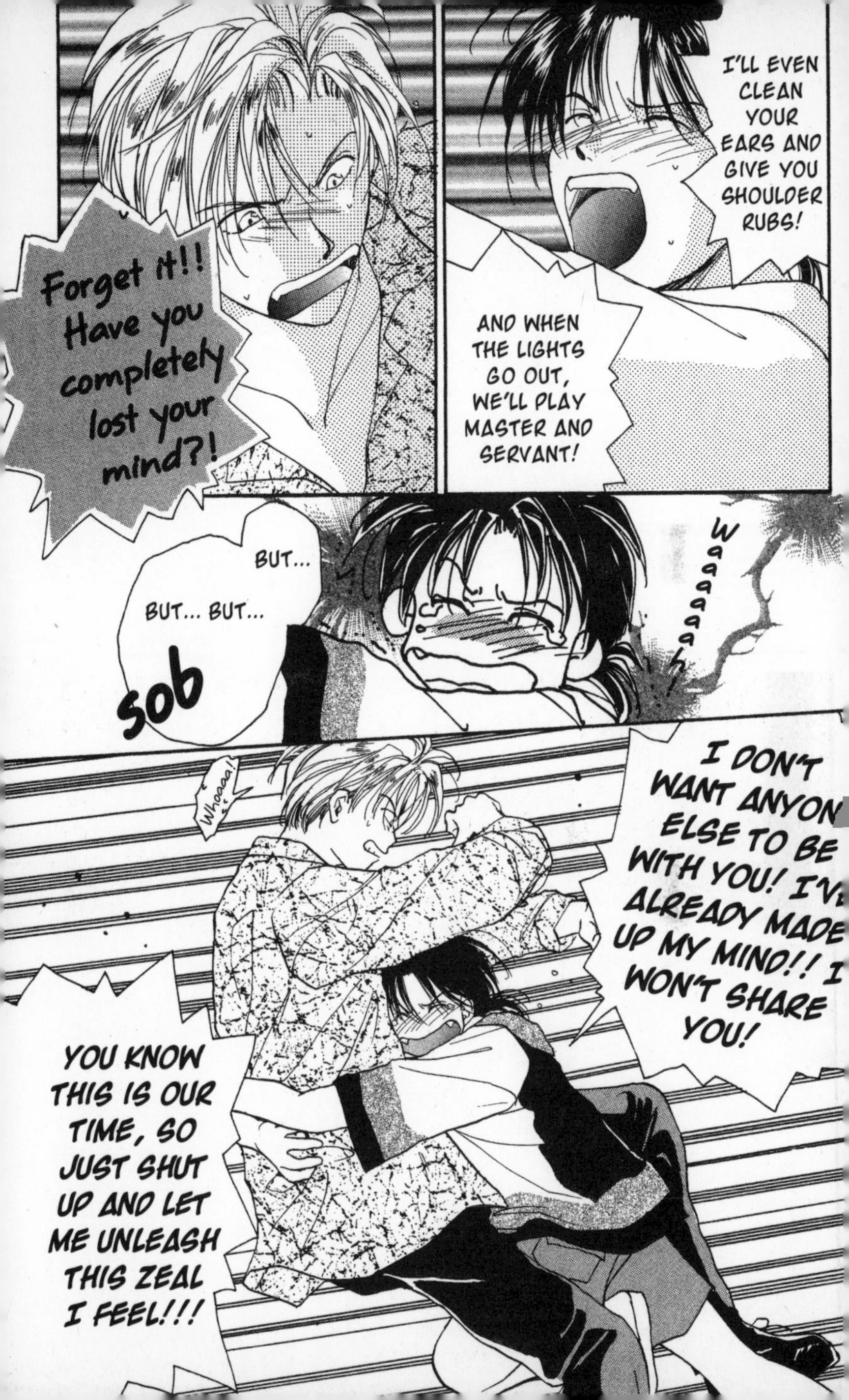

I'LL EVEN CLEAN YOUR EARS AND GIVE YOU SHOULDER RUBS!
AND WHEN THE LIGHTS GO OUT, WE'LL PLAY MASTER AND SERVANT!
Forget it!! Have you completely lost your mind?!
Waaaaaaah!
BUT...
BUT... BUT...
sob
Whoaaa!
I DON'T WANT ANYON ELSE TO BE WITH YOU! I'V ALREADY MADE UP MY MIND!! I WON'T SHARE YOU!
YOU KNOW THIS IS OUR TIME, SO JUST SHUT UP AND LET ME UNLEASH THIS ZEAL I FEEL!!!

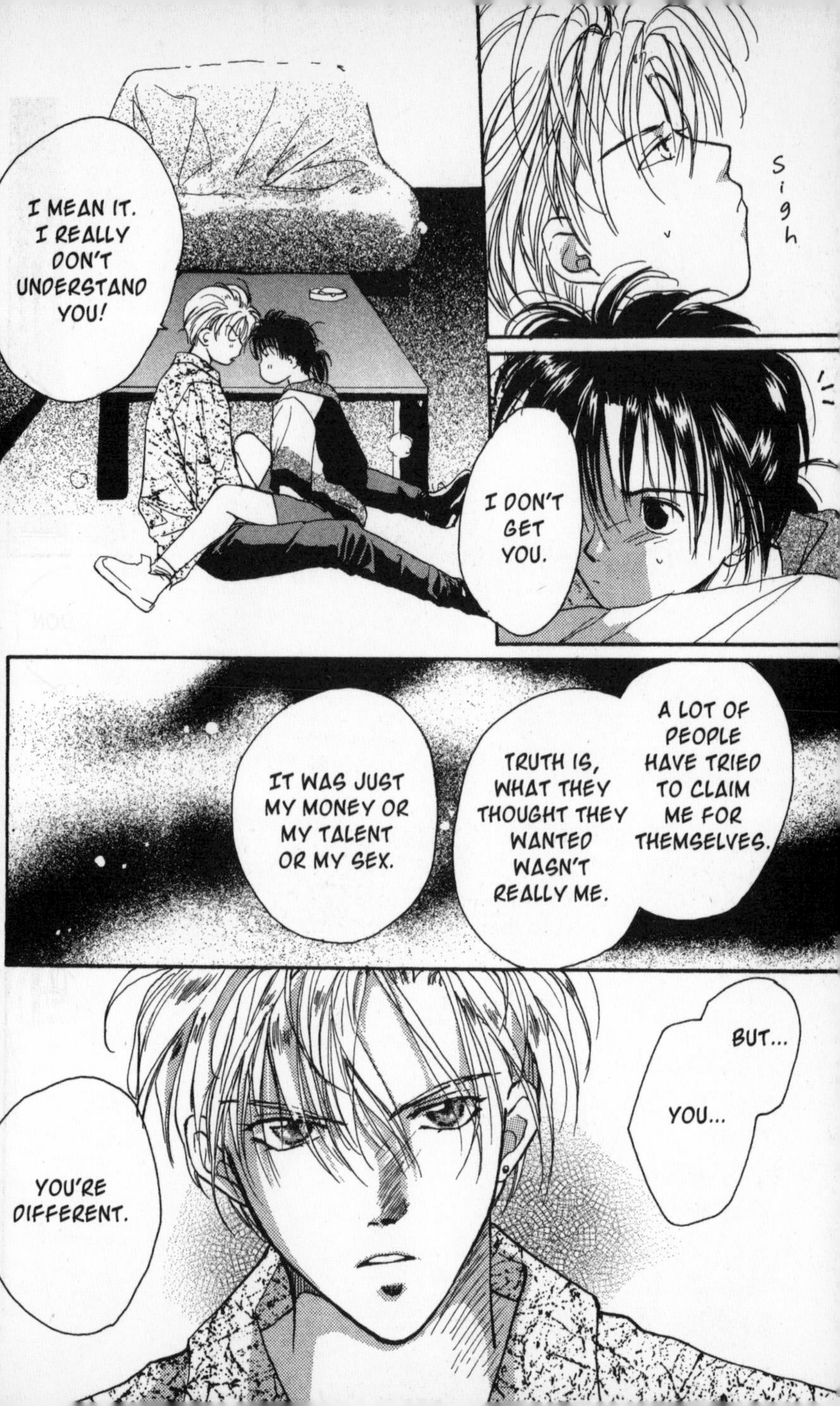
Sigh
I DON'T GET YOU.
I MEAN IT. I REALLY DON'T UNDERSTAND YOU!
A LOT OF PEOPLE HAVE TRIED TO CLAIM ME FOR THEMSELVES.
TRUTH IS, WHAT THEY THOUGHT THEY WANTED WASN'T REALLY ME.
IT WAS JUST MY MONEY OR MY TALENT OR MY SEX.
BUT...
YOU...
YOU'RE DIFFERENT.

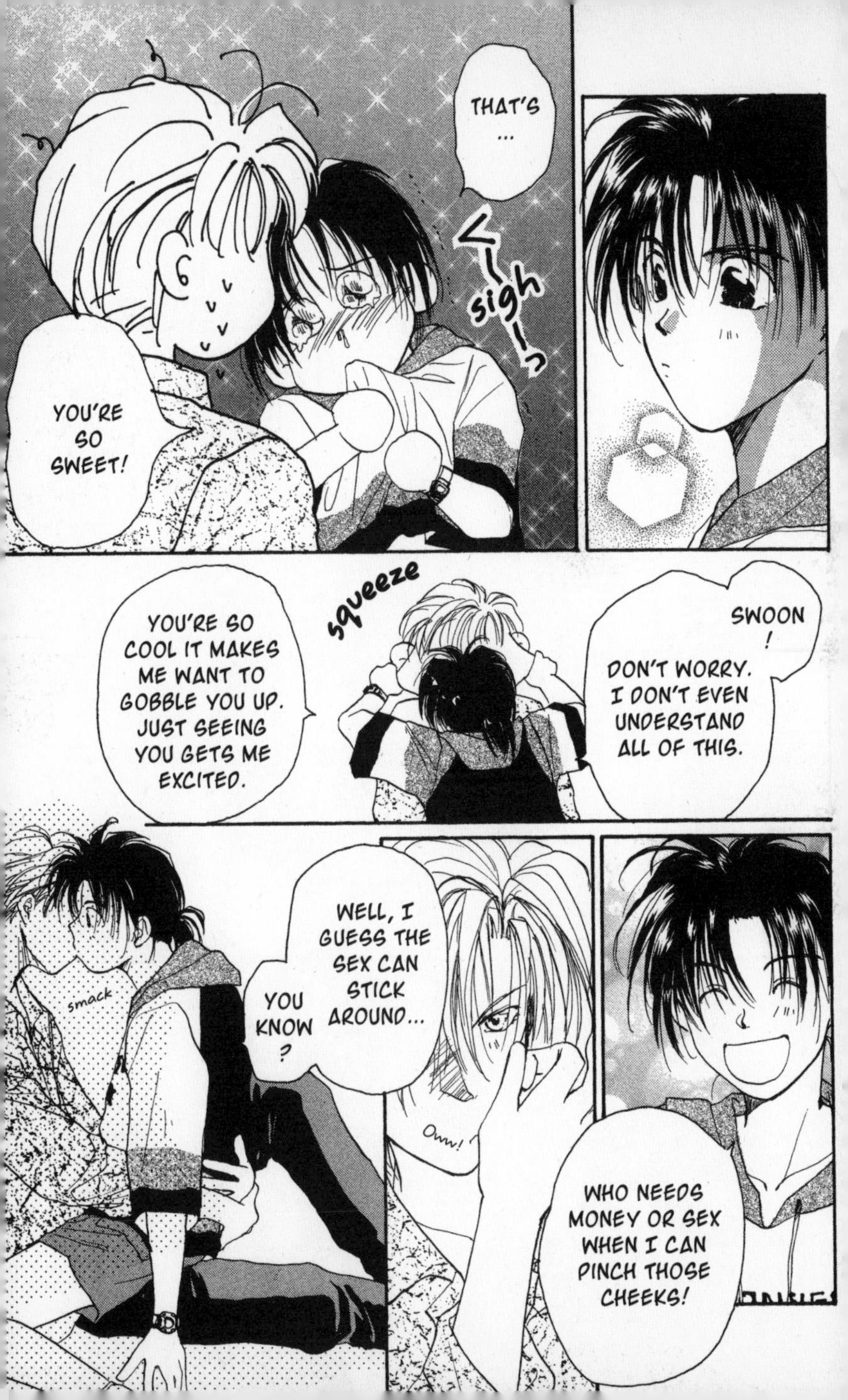
THAT'S ...
sigh
YOU'RE SO SWEET!
SWOON!
DON'T WORRY. I DON'T EVEN UNDERSTAND ALL OF THIS.
squeeze
YOU'RE SO COOL IT MAKES ME WANT TO GOBBLE YOU UP. JUST SEEING YOU GETS ME EXCITED.
WHO NEEDS MONEY OR SEX WHEN I CAN PINCH THOSE CHEEKS!
WELL, I GUESS THE SEX CAN STICK AROUND...
YOU KNOW?
Oww!
smack

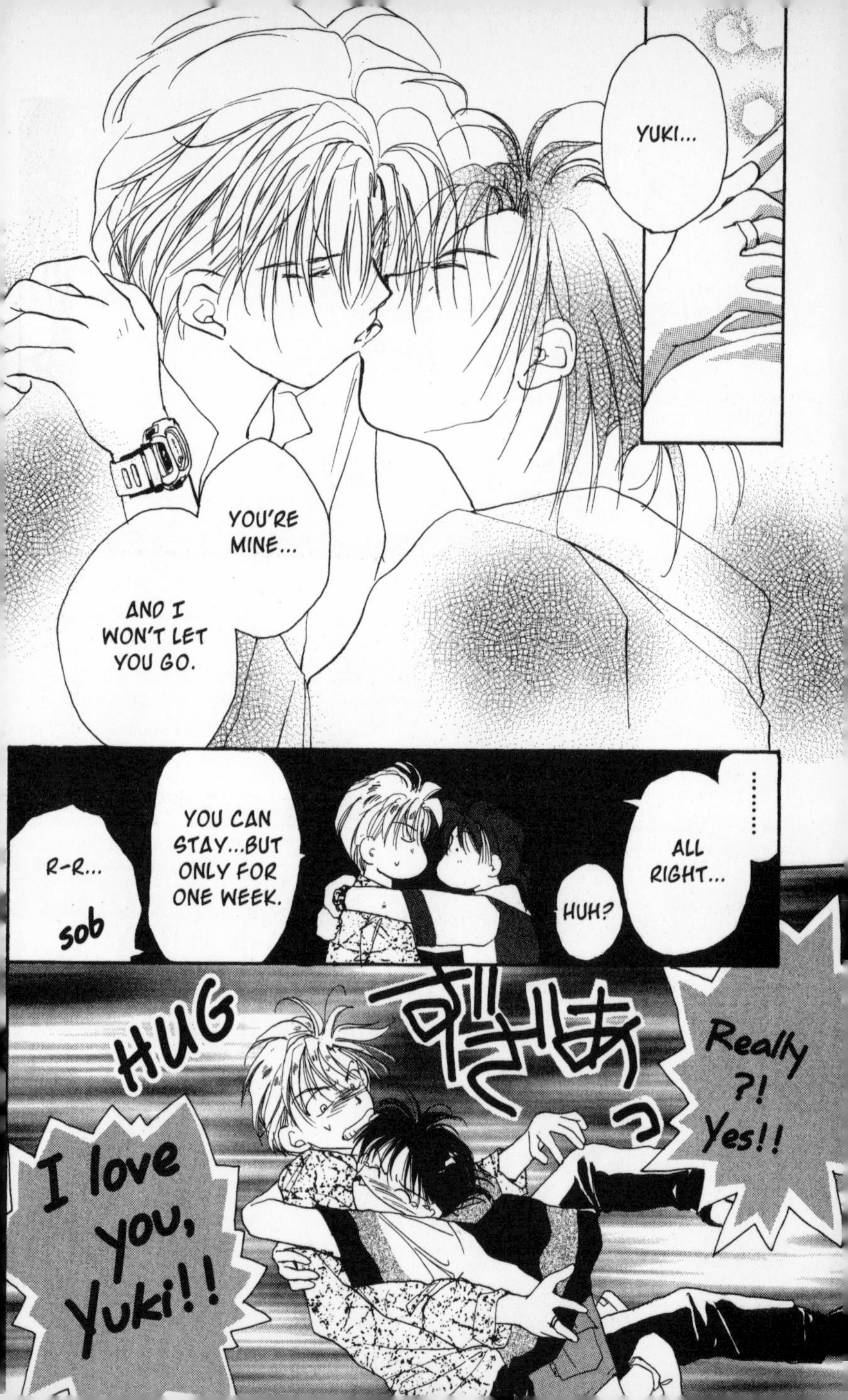
YUKI...
YOU'RE MINE...
AND I WON'T LET YOU GO.
......
ALL RIGHT...
HUH?
YOU CAN STAY...BUT ONLY FOR ONE WEEK.
R-R...
sob
Really?! Yes!!
ずぎあっ
HUG
I love you, Yuki!!

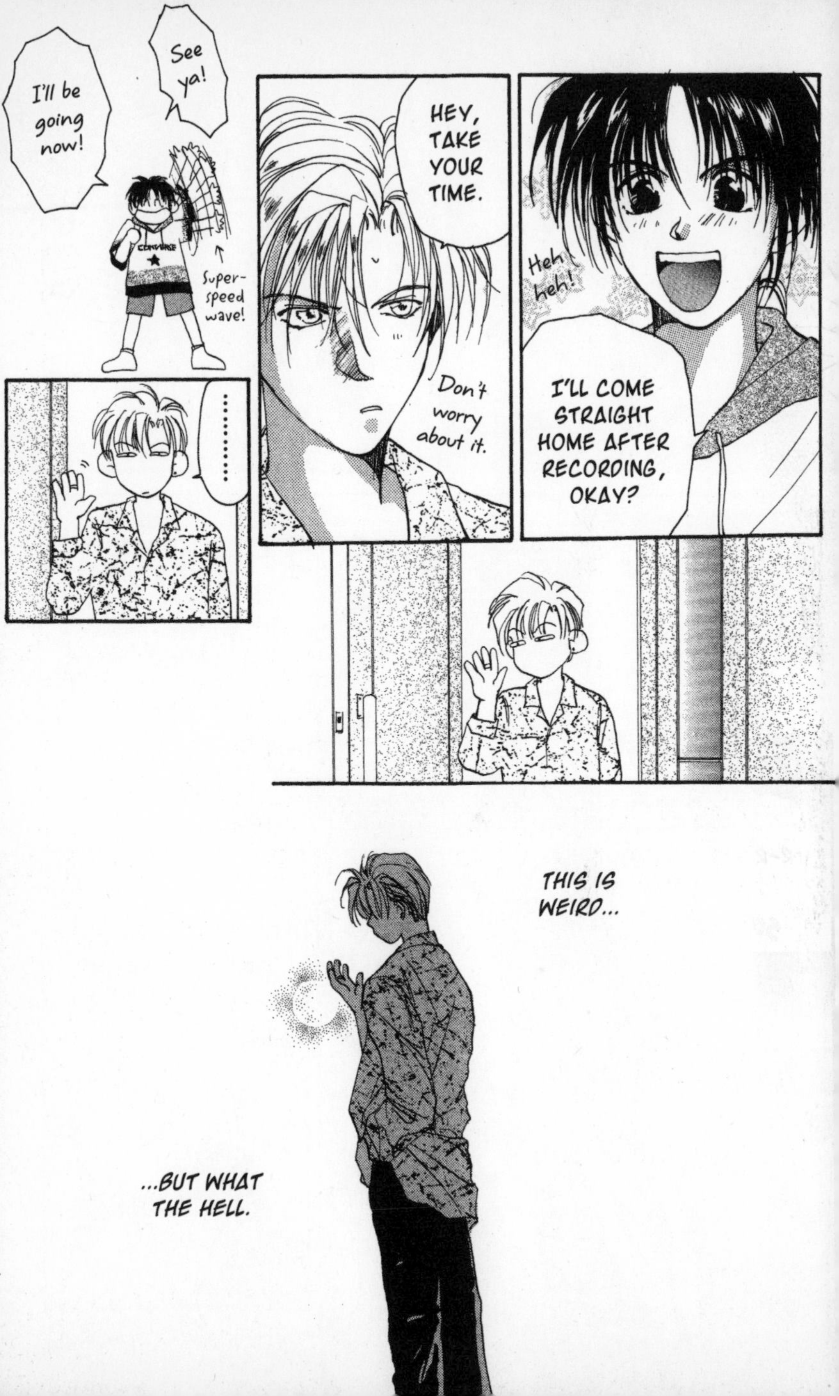
Heh heh!
I'LL COME STRAIGHT HOME AFTER RECORDING, OKAY?
HEY, TAKE YOUR TIME.
Don't worry about it.
See ya!
I'll be going now!
Super-speed wave!
……
THIS IS WEIRD...
...BUT WHAT THE HELL.

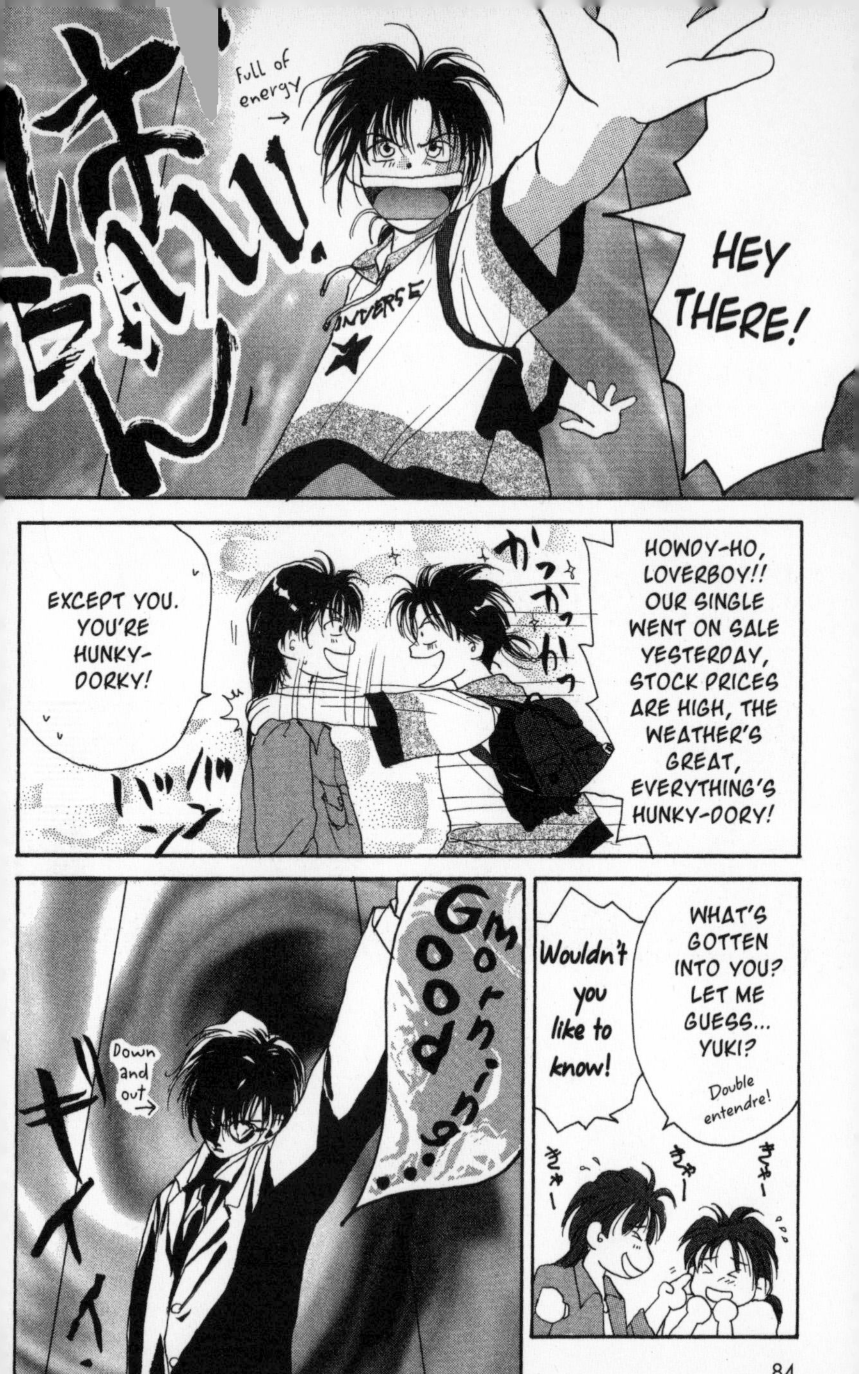

Full of energy →
HEY THERE!
HOWDY-HO, LOVERBOY!! OUR SINGLE WENT ON SALE YESTERDAY, STOCK PRICES ARE HIGH, THE WEATHER'S GREAT, EVERYTHING'S HUNKY-DORY!
EXCEPT YOU. YOU'RE HUNKY-DORKY!
WHAT'S GOTTEN INTO YOU? LET ME GUESS... YUKI?
Double entendre!
Wouldn't you like to know!
Good mor-ning...
Down and out →

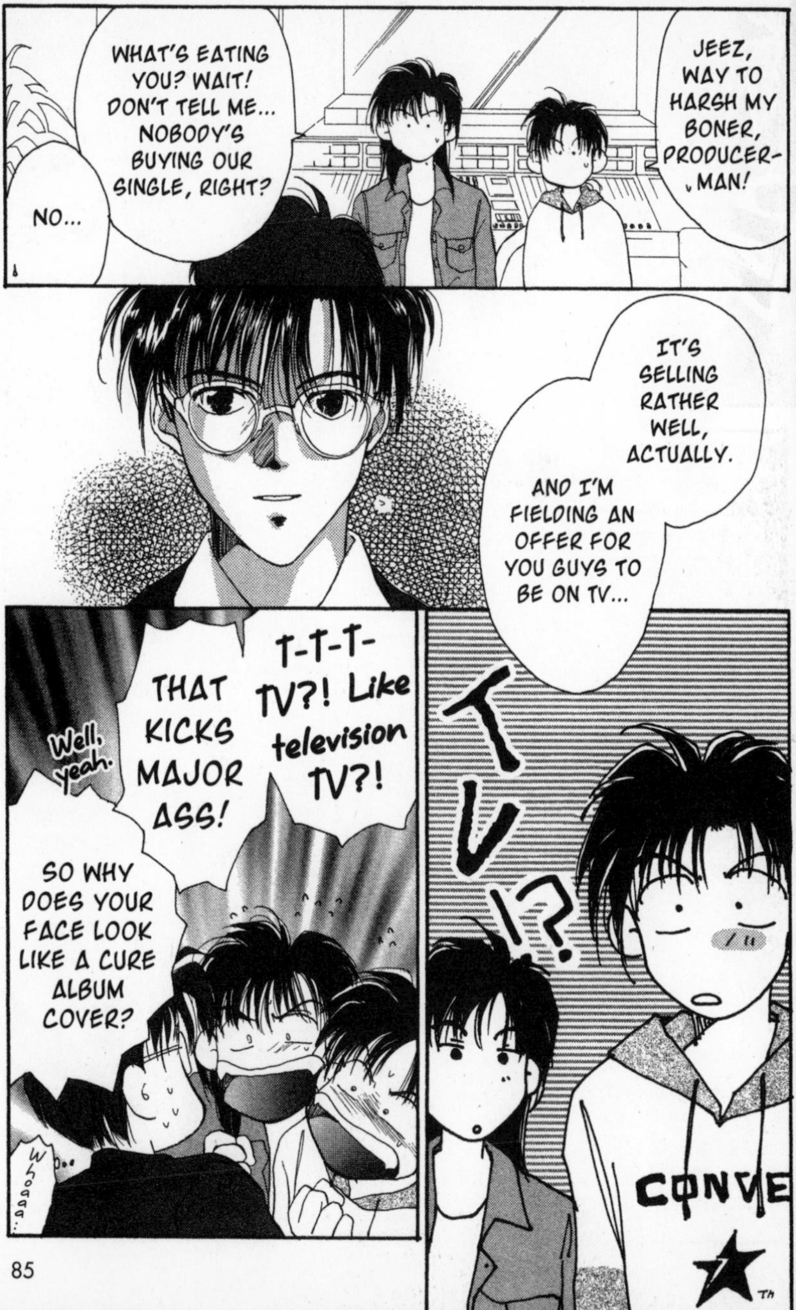
JEEZ, WAY TO HARSH MY BONER, PRODUCER-MAN!
WHAT'S EATING YOU? WAIT! DON'T TELL ME... NOBODY'S BUYING OUR SINGLE, RIGHT?
NO...
IT'S SELLING RATHER WELL, ACTUALLY.
AND I'M FIELDING AN OFFER FOR YOU GUYS TO BE ON TV...
TV!?
CONVE
T-T-T-TV?! Like television TV?!
THAT KICKS MAJOR ASS!
Well, yeah.
SO WHY DOES YOUR FACE LOOK LIKE A CURE ALBUM COVER?
Whoaaa...

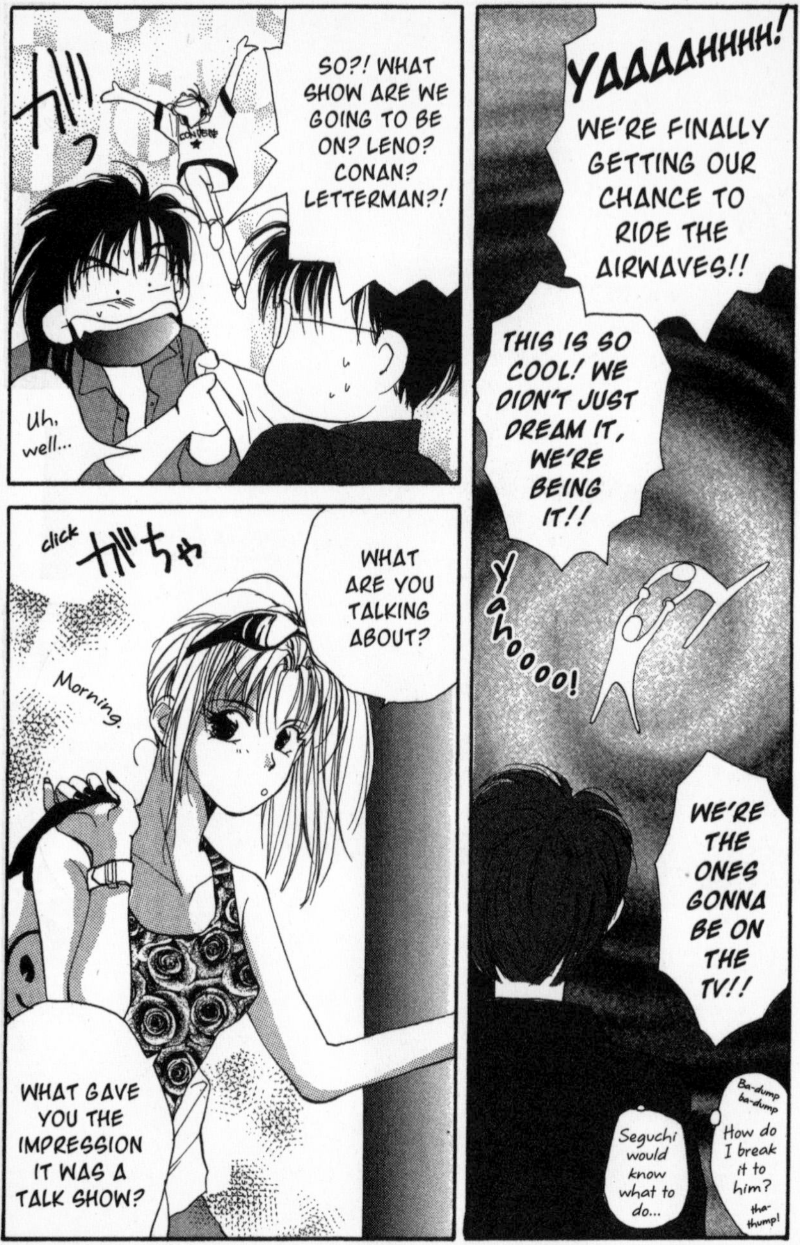

YAAAAHHHH!
WE'RE FINALLY GETTING OUR CHANCE TO RIDE THE AIRWAVES!!
THIS IS SO COOL! WE DIDN'T JUST DREAM IT, WE'RE BEING IT!!
Yahooooo!
WE'RE THE ONES GONNA BE ON THE TV!!
Ba-dump ba-dump
How do I break it to him?
tha-thump!
Seguchi would know what to do...
SO?! WHAT SHOW ARE WE GOING TO BE ON? LENO? CONAN? LETTERMAN?!
Uh, well...
click
がちゃ
WHAT ARE YOU TALKING ABOUT?
Morning.
WHAT GAVE YOU THE IMPRESSION IT WAS A TALK SHOW?

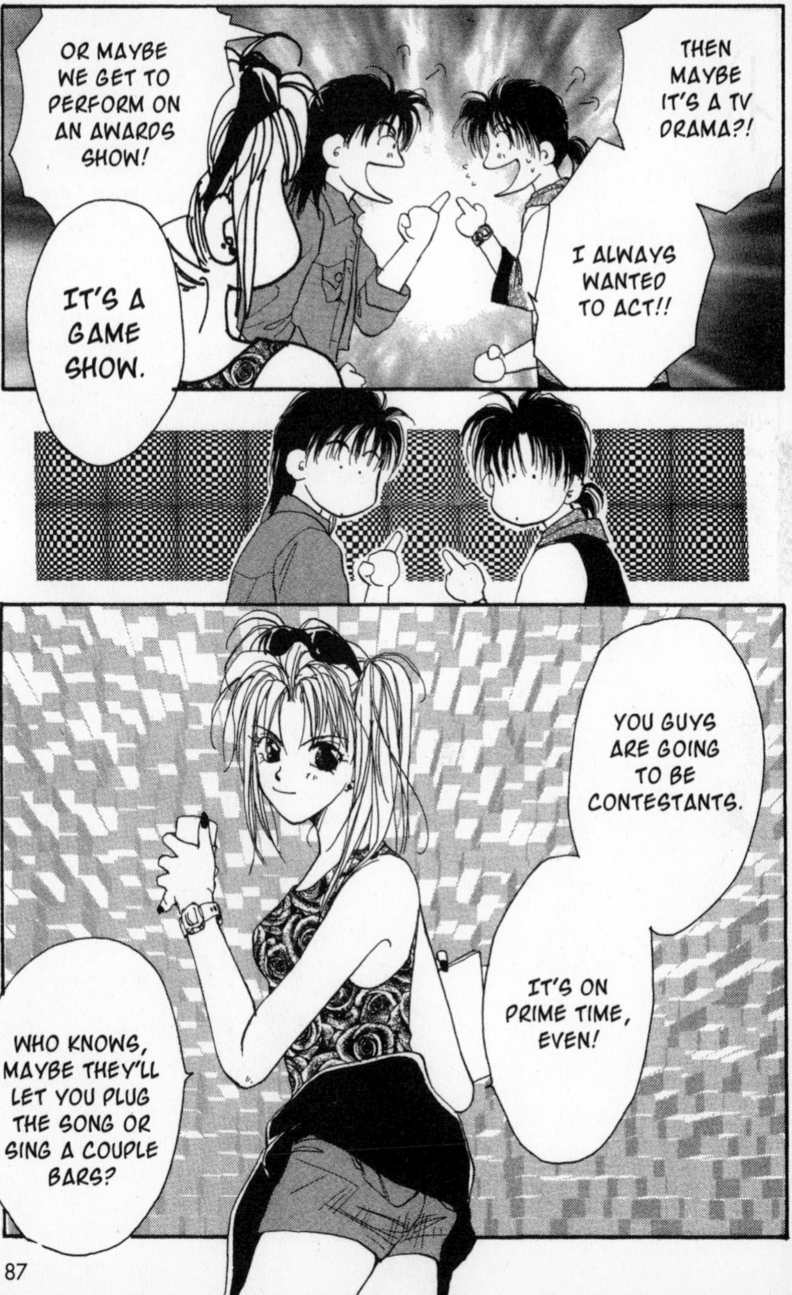
THEN MAYBE IT'S A TV DRAMA?!
I ALWAYS WANTED TO ACT!!
OR MAYBE WE GET TO PERFORM ON AN AWARDS SHOW!
IT'S A GAME SHOW.
YOU GUYS ARE GOING TO BE CONTESTANTS.
IT'S ON PRIME TIME, EVEN!
WHO KNOWS, MAYBE THEY'LL LET YOU PLUG THE SONG OR SING A COUPLE BARS?

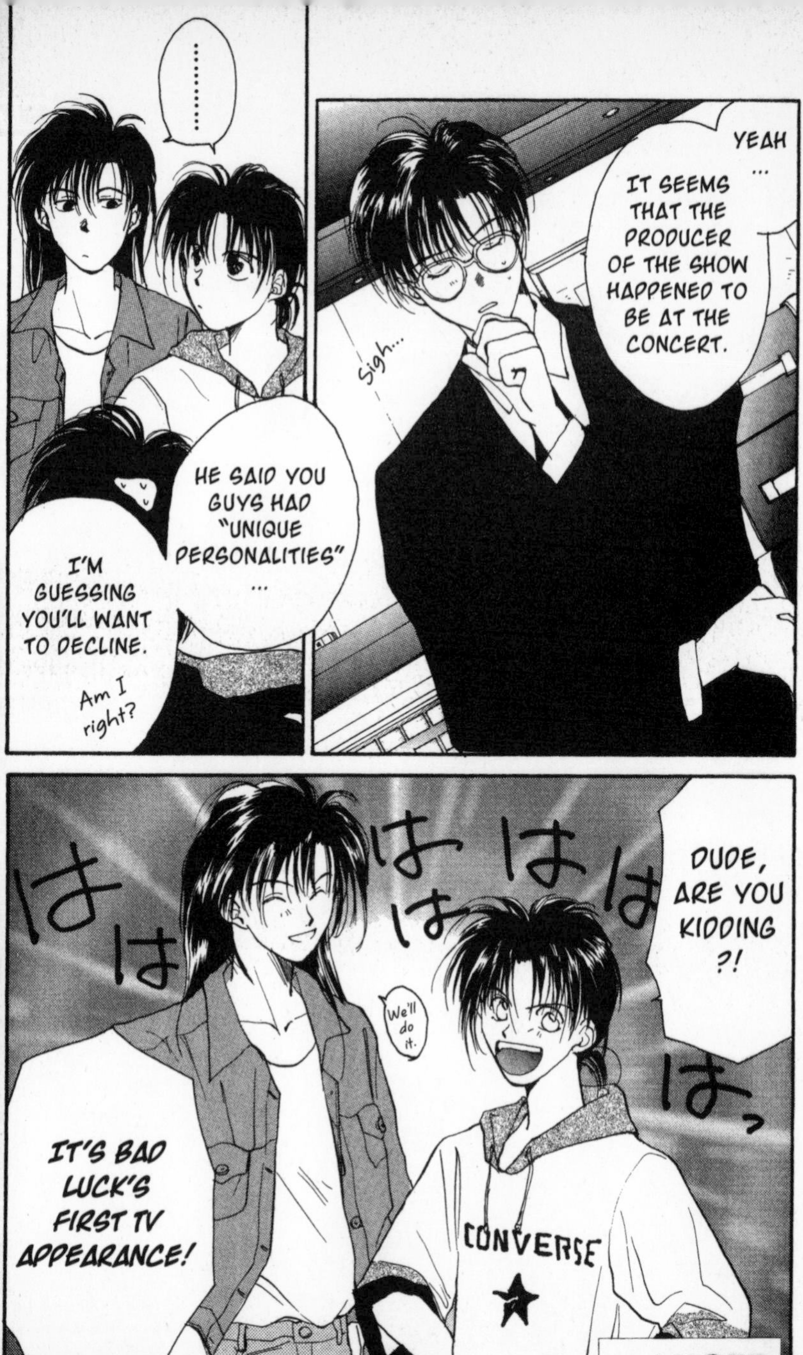
YEAH ... IT SEEMS THAT THE PRODUCER OF THE SHOW HAPPENED TO BE AT THE CONCERT.
Sigh...
......
HE SAID YOU GUYS HAD "UNIQUE PERSONALITIES" ...
I'M GUESSING YOU'LL WANT TO DECLINE.
Am I right?
DUDE, ARE YOU KIDDING ?!
ははははははは、
We'll do it.
IT'S BAD LUCK'S FIRST TV APPEARANCE!
track10▶END

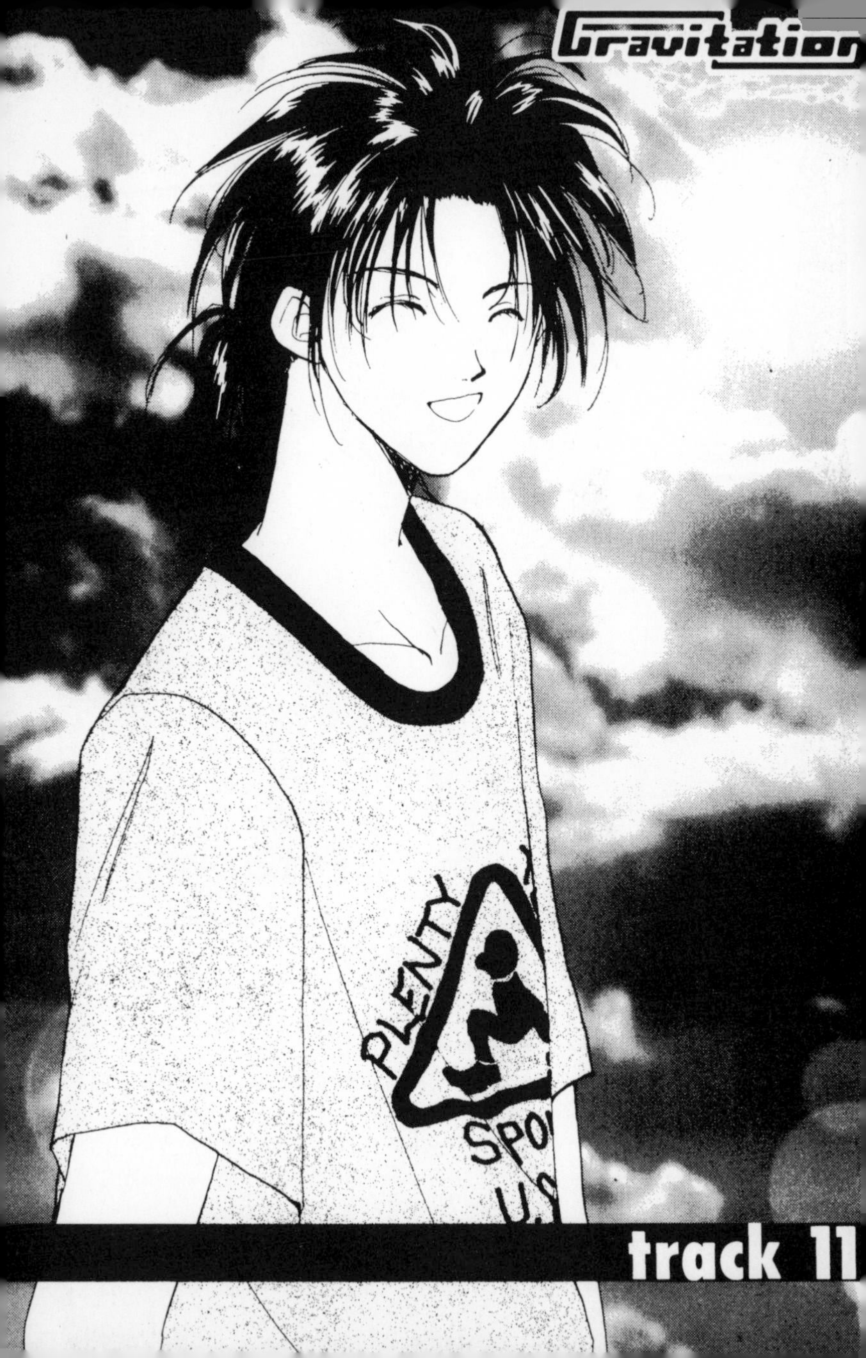
Gravitation
track 11
PLENTY

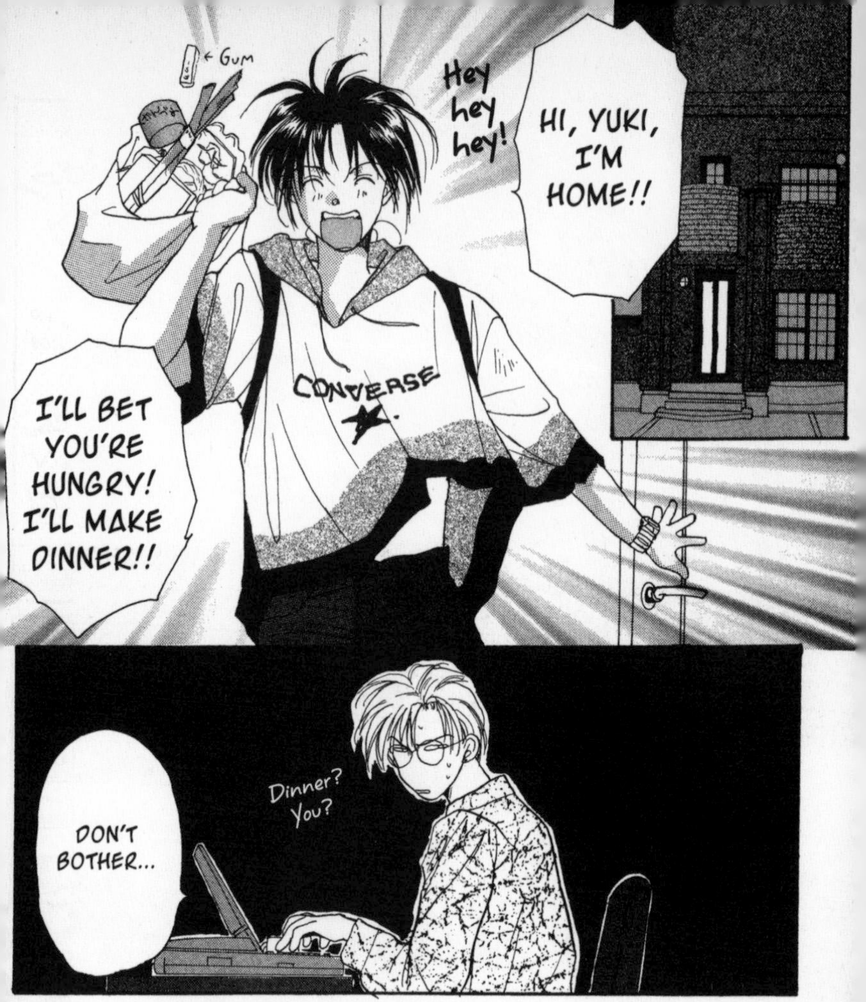
HI, YUKI, I'M HOME!!
Hey hey hey!
← Gum
I'LL BET YOU'RE HUNGRY! I'LL MAKE DINNER!!
Dinner? You?
DON'T BOTHER...

ABOUT GRAVITATION TRACK 11

So we finally made it this far. When these two first met, they didn't even know each other's names. Just look where they are now! It's almost like they're newlyweds the way they're so lovey dovey. Congrats! I hope you two will continue to be happy. I'll bet they take baths together and wash each other's backs. How nice. Shindou, aren't you having fun? Shindou, are you happy now? Shindou? Okay. Good. Glad to hear that. Enjoy the moment. I bid you adieu.

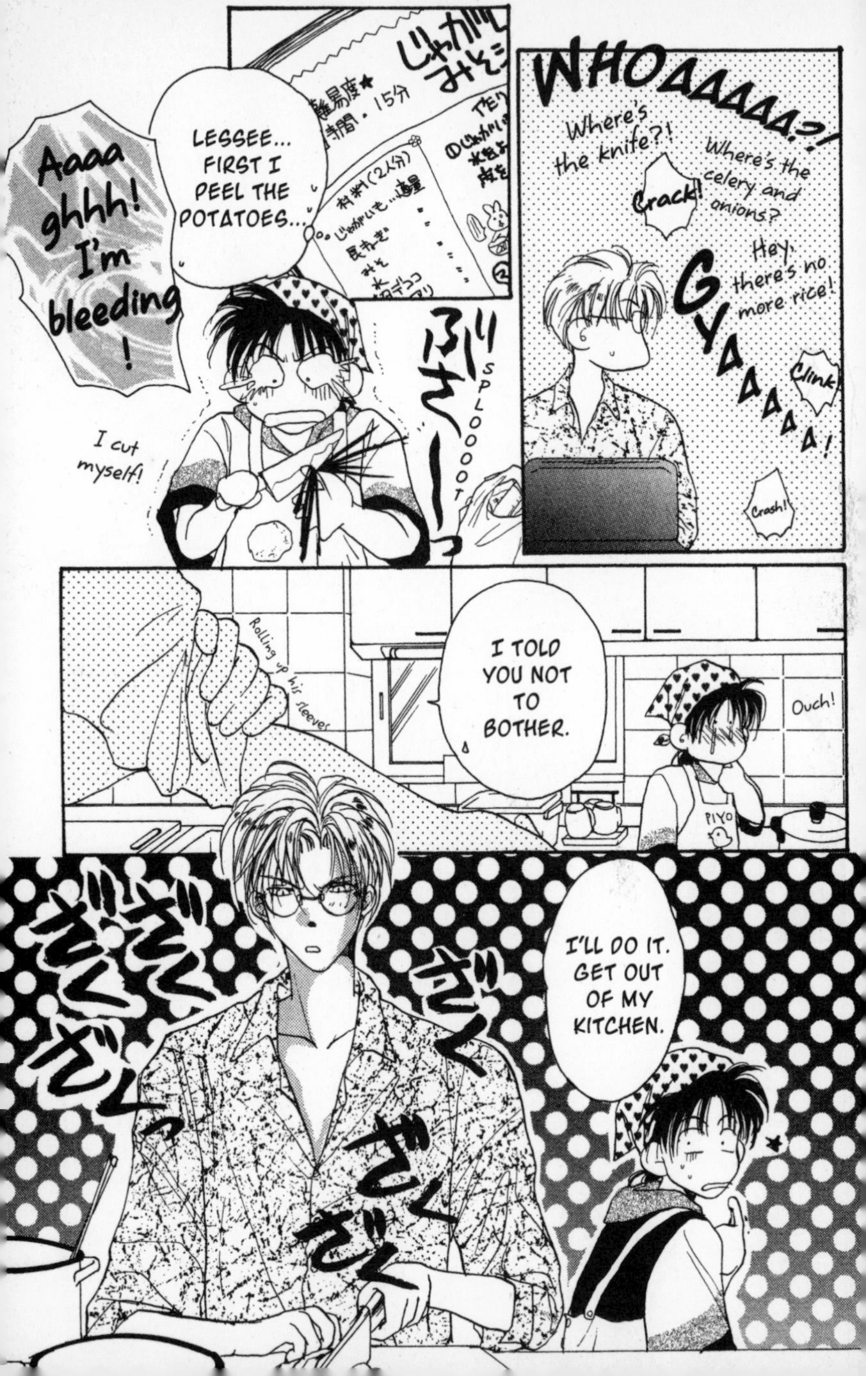
WHOAAAAAA?!
Where's the knife?!
Where's the celery and onions?
Crack!
Hey, there's no more rice!
GYAAAAAAA!
Clink
Crash!
LESSEE... FIRST I PEEL THE POTATOES...
Aaaa ghhh! I'm bleeding!
SPLOOOOOOT
I cut myself!
Ouch!
I TOLD YOU NOT TO BOTHER.
Rolling up his sleeves
I'LL DO IT. GET OUT OF MY KITCHEN.

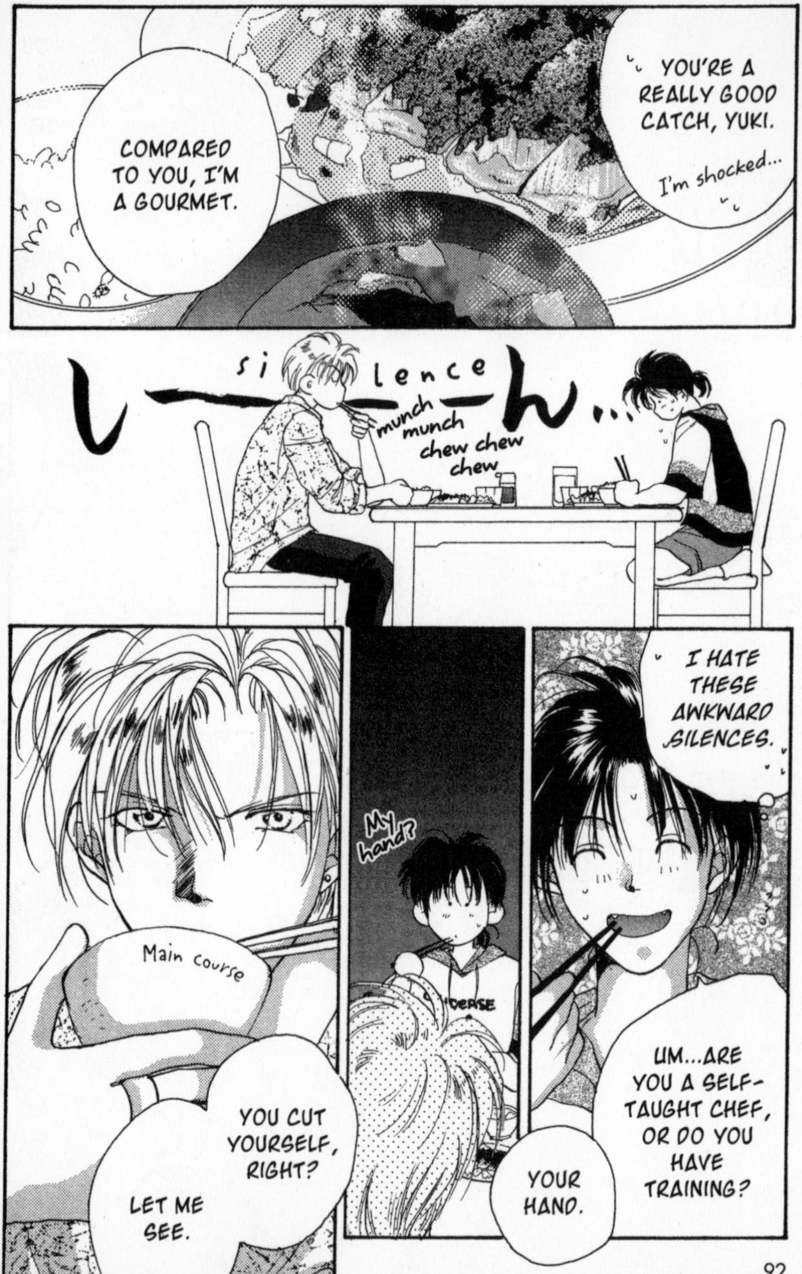
YOU'RE A REALLY GOOD CATCH, YUKI.
I'm shocked...
COMPARED TO YOU, I'M A GOURMET.
silence
しーーーん…
munch munch
chew chew chew
I HATE THESE AWKWARD SILENCES.
UM...ARE YOU A SELF-TAUGHT CHEF, OR DO YOU HAVE TRAINING?
YOUR HAND.
My hand?
Main course
YOU CUT YOURSELF, RIGHT?
LET ME SEE.

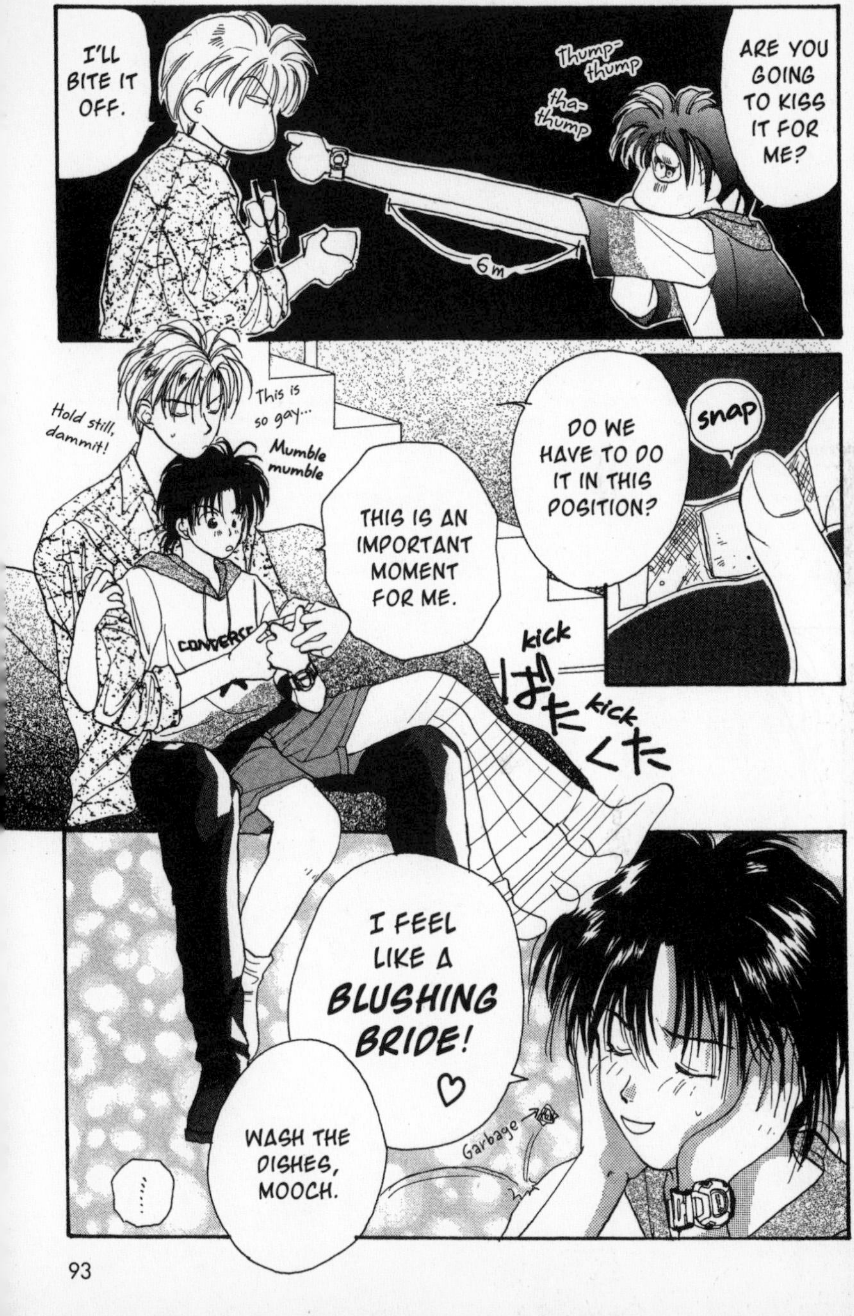
ARE YOU GOING TO KISS IT FOR ME?
Thump-thump
tha-thump
6m
I'LL BITE IT OFF.
snap
DO WE HAVE TO DO IT IN THIS POSITION?
THIS IS AN IMPORTANT MOMENT FOR ME.
Mumble mumble
This is so gay...
Hold still, dammit!
kick
ぱたくた
kick
I FEEL LIKE A **BLUSHING BRIDE!** ♡
Garbage
WASH THE DISHES, MOOCH.
......

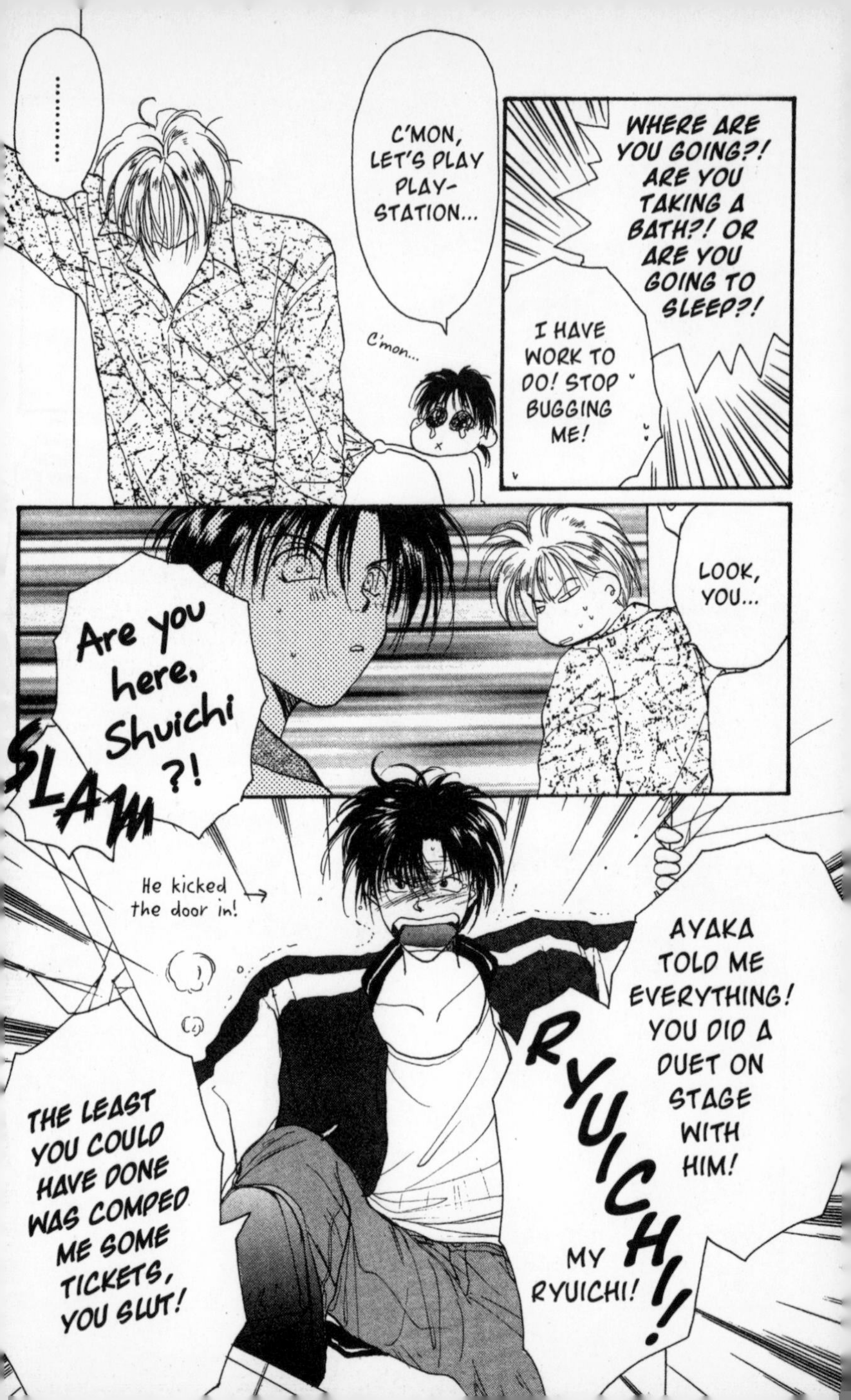

WHERE ARE YOU GOING?! ARE YOU TAKING A BATH?! OR ARE YOU GOING TO SLEEP?!
I HAVE WORK TO DO! STOP BUGGING ME!
C'MON, LET'S PLAY PLAY-STATION...
C'mon...
......
LOOK, YOU...
Are you here, Shuichi?!
SLAM
He kicked the door in!
AYAKA TOLD ME EVERYTHING! YOU DID A DUET ON STAGE WITH HIM!
RYUICHI!!
MY RYUICHI!
THE LEAST YOU COULD HAVE DONE WAS COMPED ME SOME TICKETS, YOU SLUT!

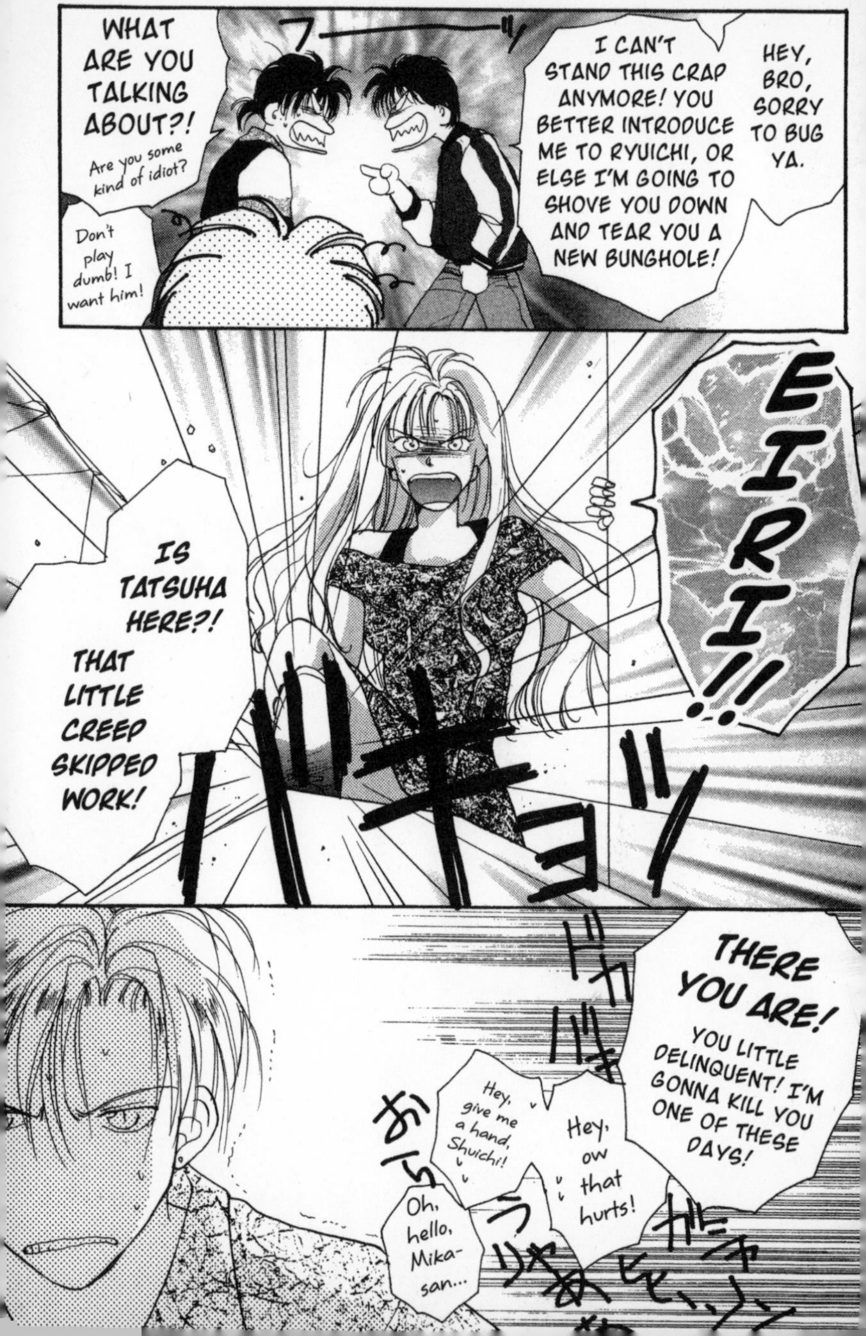
HEY, BRO, SORRY TO BUG YA.
I CAN'T STAND THIS CRAP ANYMORE! YOU BETTER INTRODUCE ME TO RYUICHI, OR ELSE I'M GOING TO SHOVE YOU DOWN AND TEAR YOU A NEW BUNGHOLE!
WHAT ARE YOU TALKING ABOUT?!
Are you some kind of idiot?
Don't play dumb! I want him!
EIRI!!
IS TATSUHA HERE?! THAT LITTLE CREEP SKIPPED WORK!
バキョッ
THERE YOU ARE!
YOU LITTLE DELINQUENT! I'M GONNA KILL YOU ONE OF THESE DAYS!
Hey, ow that hurts!
Hey, give me a hand, Shuichi!
Oh, hello, Mika-san...

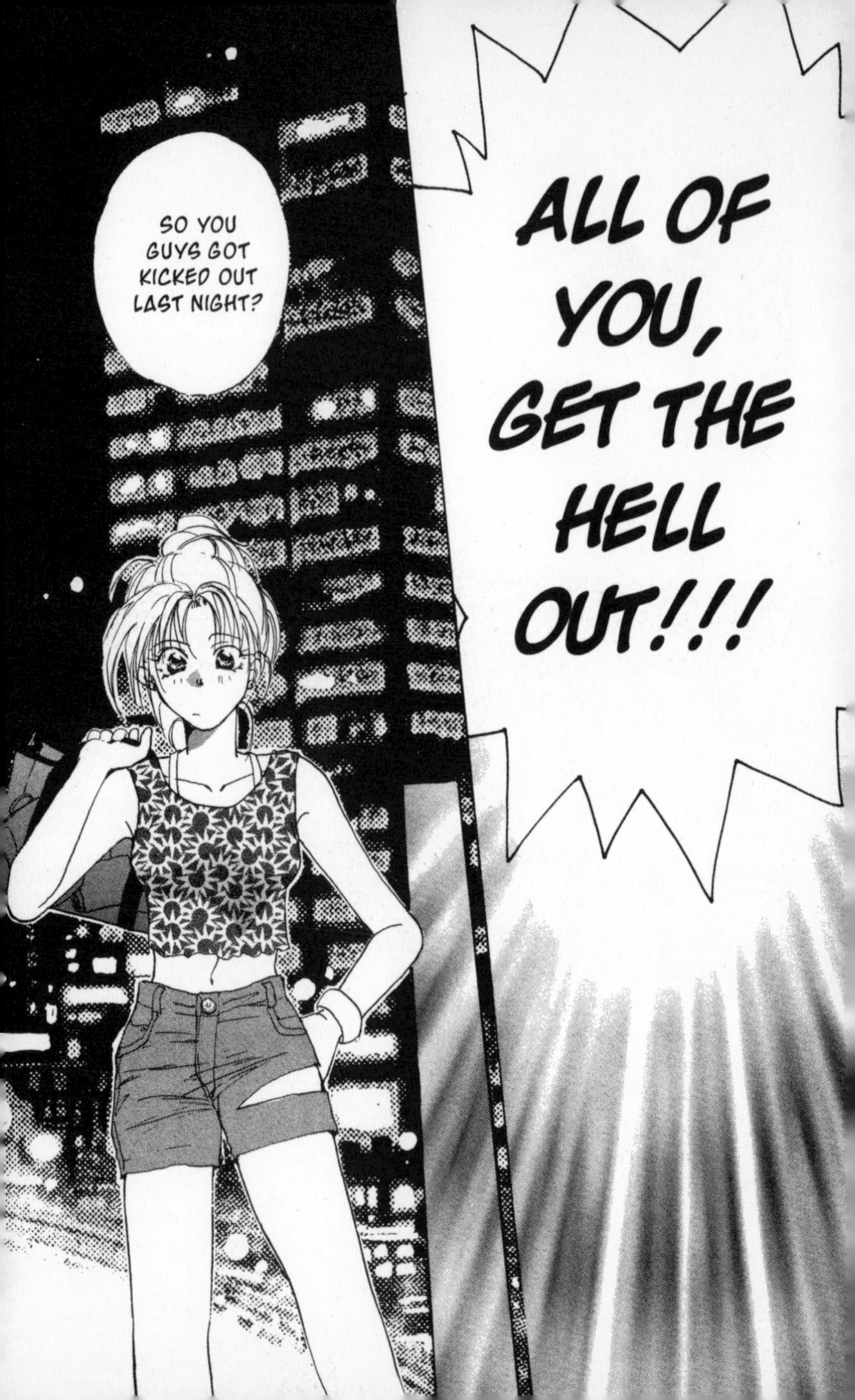
ALL OF YOU, GET THE HELL OUT!!!
SO YOU GUYS GOT KICKED OUT LAST NIGHT?

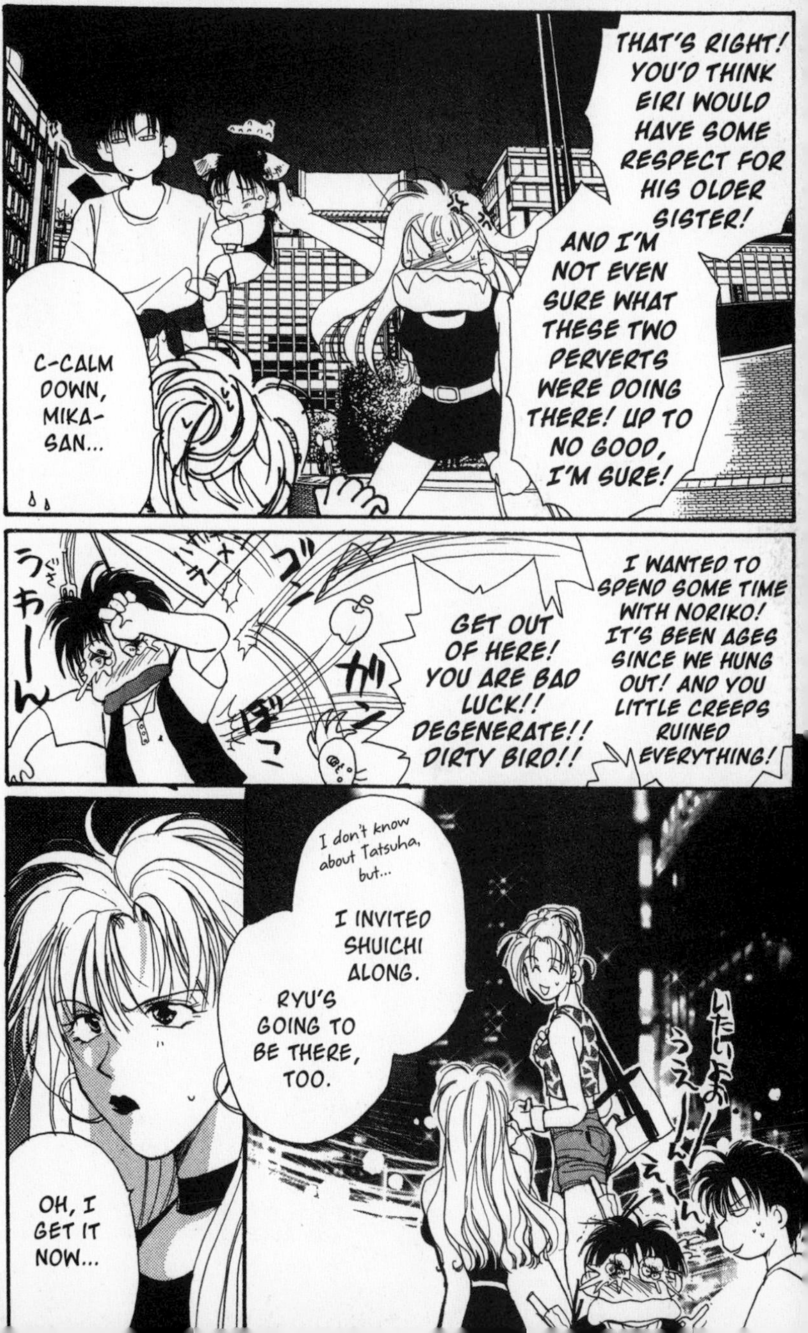
THAT'S RIGHT! YOU'D THINK EIRI WOULD HAVE SOME RESPECT FOR HIS OLDER SISTER!
AND I'M NOT EVEN SURE WHAT THESE TWO PERVERTS WERE DOING THERE! UP TO NO GOOD, I'M SURE!
C-CALM DOWN, MIKA-SAN...
I WANTED TO SPEND SOME TIME WITH NORIKO! IT'S BEEN AGES SINCE WE HUNG OUT! AND YOU LITTLE CREEPS RUINED EVERYTHING!
GET OUT OF HERE! YOU ARE BAD LUCK!! DEGENERATE!! DIRTY BIRD!!
うわーん
I don't know about Tatsuha, but...
I INVITED SHUICHI ALONG.
RYU'S GOING TO BE THERE, TOO.
いたいよぉ うえーん えーん
OH, I GET IT NOW...

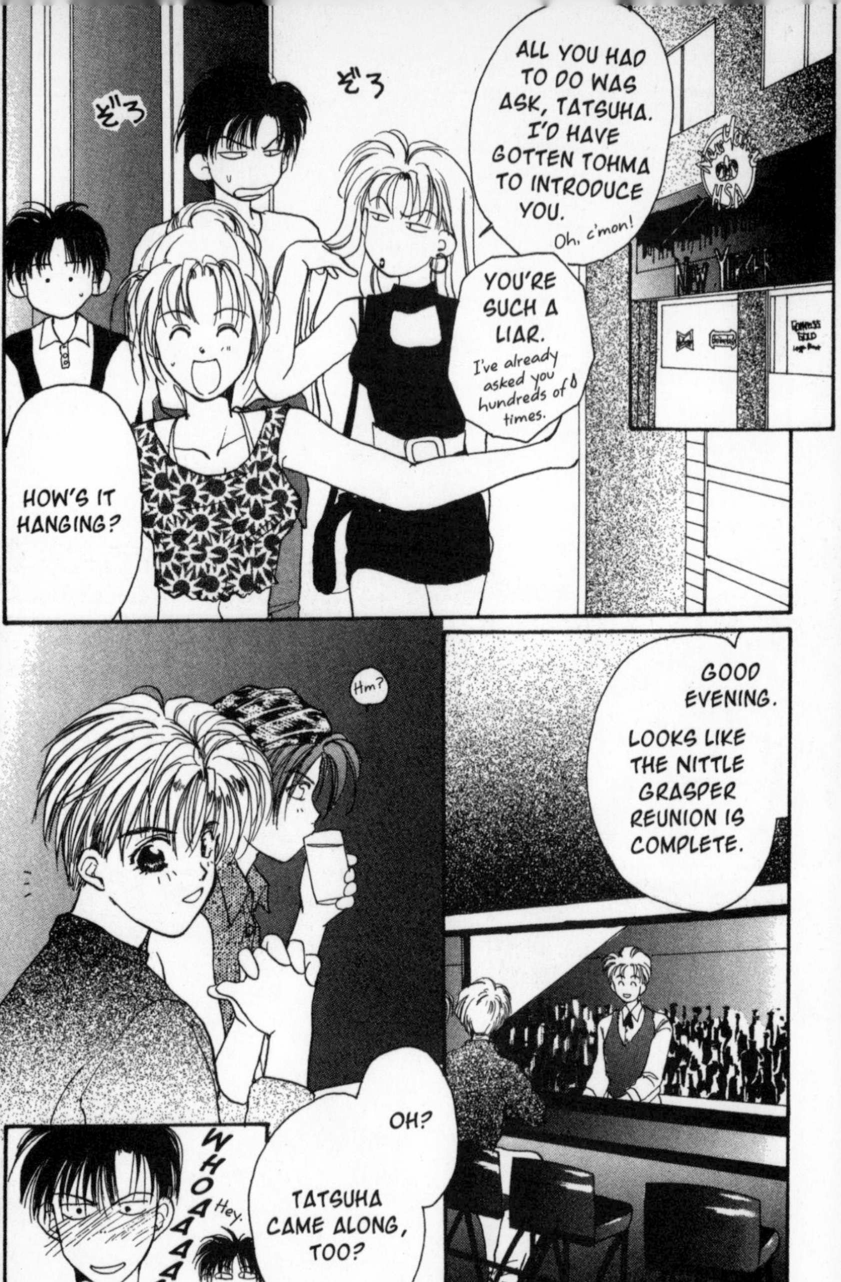
ぞろ
ぞろ
ALL YOU HAD TO DO WAS ASK, TATSUHA. I'D HAVE GOTTEN TOHMA TO INTRODUCE YOU.
Oh, c'mon!
YOU'RE SUCH A LIAR.
I've already asked you hundreds of times.
HOW'S IT HANGING?
GOOD EVENING.
LOOKS LIKE THE NITTLE GRASPER REUNION IS COMPLETE.
Hm?
OH?
TATSUHA CAME ALONG, TOO?
WHOAAAAAAA!
Hey.

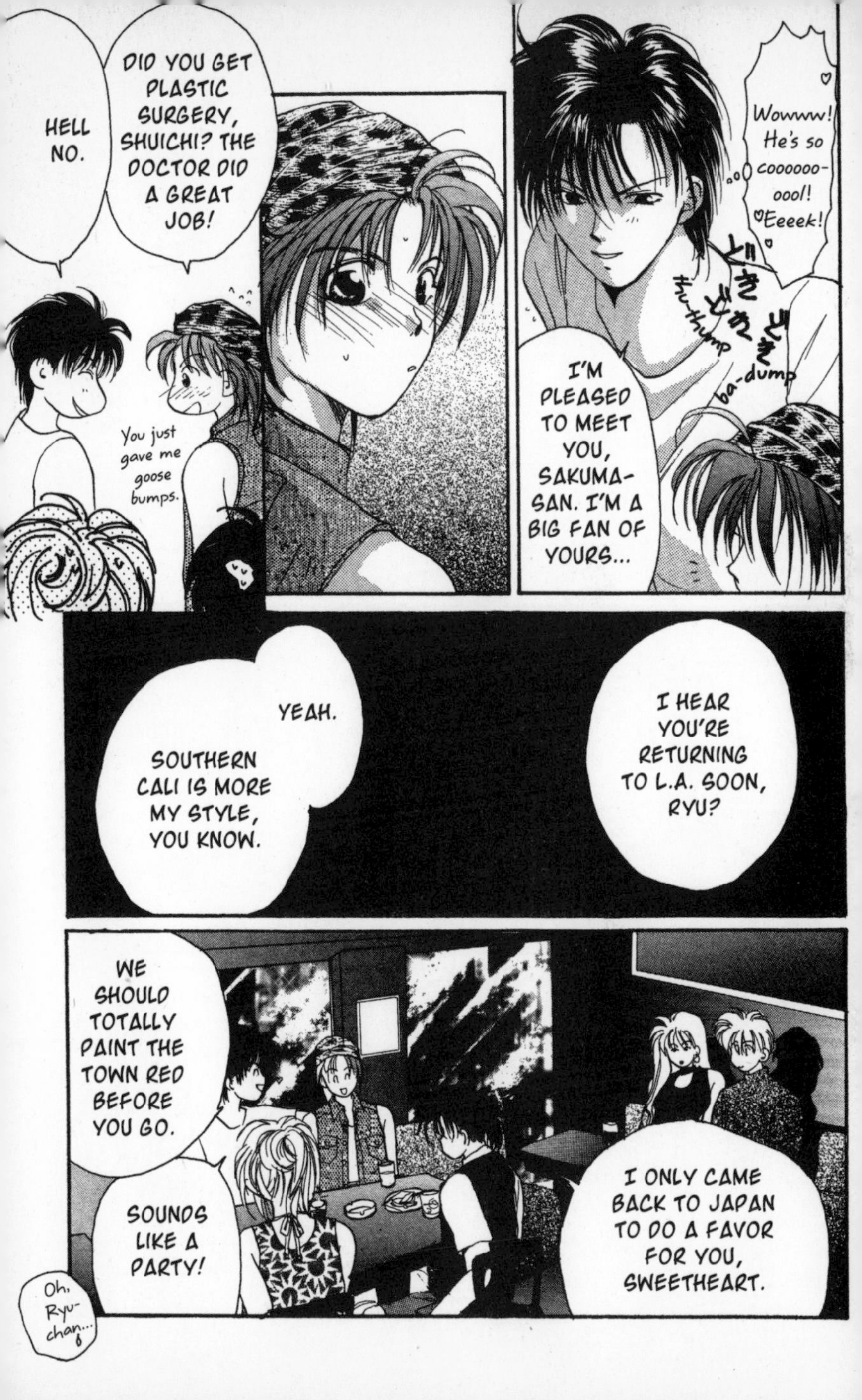
Wowww! He's so cooooooo-oool! Eeeek!
thu-thump
ba-dump
I'M PLEASED TO MEET YOU, SAKUMA-SAN. I'M A BIG FAN OF YOURS...
DID YOU GET PLASTIC SURGERY, SHUICHI? THE DOCTOR DID A GREAT JOB!
HELL NO.
You just gave me goose bumps.
I HEAR YOU'RE RETURNING TO L.A. SOON, RYU?
YEAH.
SOUTHERN CALI IS MORE MY STYLE, YOU KNOW.
I ONLY CAME BACK TO JAPAN TO DO A FAVOR FOR YOU, SWEETHEART.
WE SHOULD TOTALLY PAINT THE TOWN RED BEFORE YOU GO.
SOUNDS LIKE A PARTY!
Oh, Ryu-chan...

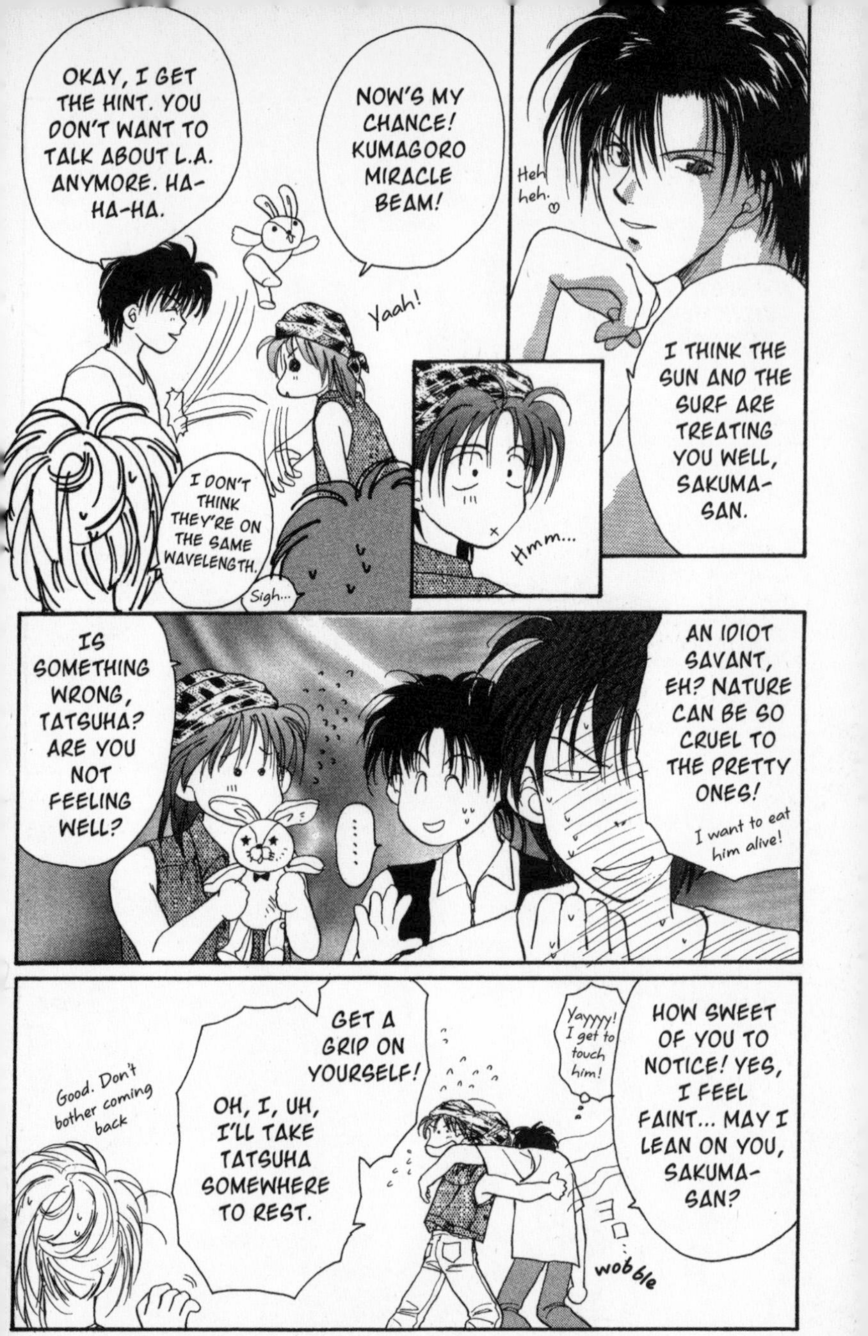
Heh heh.
I THINK THE SUN AND THE SURF ARE TREATING YOU WELL, SAKUMA-SAN.
Hmm...
NOW'S MY CHANCE! KUMAGORO MIRACLE BEAM!
Yaah!
OKAY, I GET THE HINT. YOU DON'T WANT TO TALK ABOUT L.A. ANYMORE. HA-HA-HA.
I DON'T THINK THEY'RE ON THE SAME WAVELENGTH.
Sigh...
AN IDIOT SAVANT, EH? NATURE CAN BE SO CRUEL TO THE PRETTY ONES!
I want to eat him alive!
......
IS SOMETHING WRONG, TATSUHA? ARE YOU NOT FEELING WELL?
HOW SWEET OF YOU TO NOTICE! YES, I FEEL FAINT... MAY I LEAN ON YOU, SAKUMA-SAN?
Yayyyy! I get to touch him!
wobble
GET A GRIP ON YOURSELF!
OH, I, UH, I'LL TAKE TATSUHA SOMEWHERE TO REST.
Good. Don't bother coming back

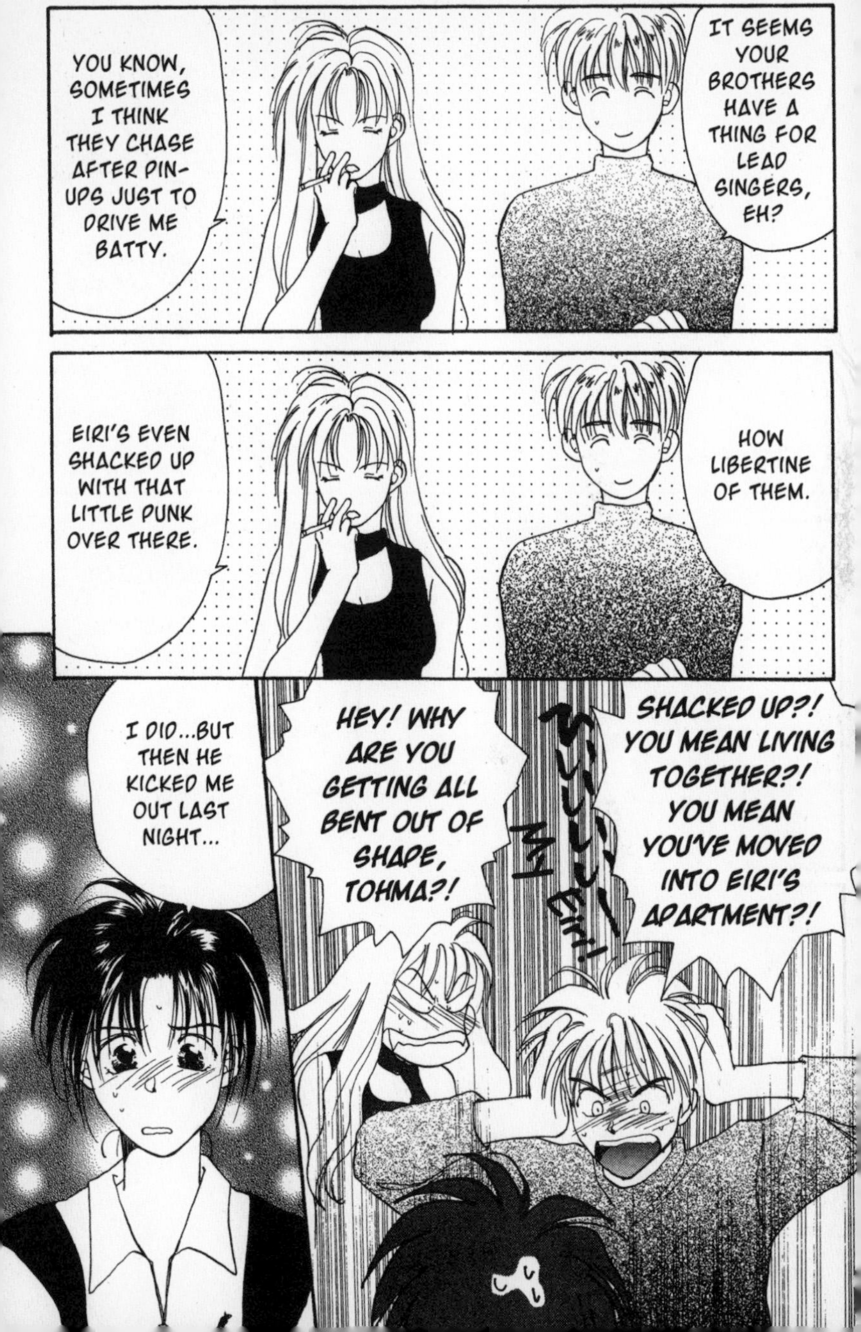
IT SEEMS YOUR BROTHERS HAVE A THING FOR LEAD SINGERS, EH?
YOU KNOW, SOMETIMES I THINK THEY CHASE AFTER PIN-UPS JUST TO DRIVE ME BATTY.
HOW LIBERTINE OF THEM.
EIRI'S EVEN SHACKED UP WITH THAT LITTLE PUNK OVER THERE.
SHACKED UP?! YOU MEAN LIVING TOGETHER?! YOU MEAN YOU'VE MOVED INTO EIRI'S APARTMENT?!
MY Eiri!!
HEY! WHY ARE YOU GETTING ALL BENT OUT OF SHAPE, TOHMA?!
I DID...BUT THEN HE KICKED ME OUT LAST NIGHT...

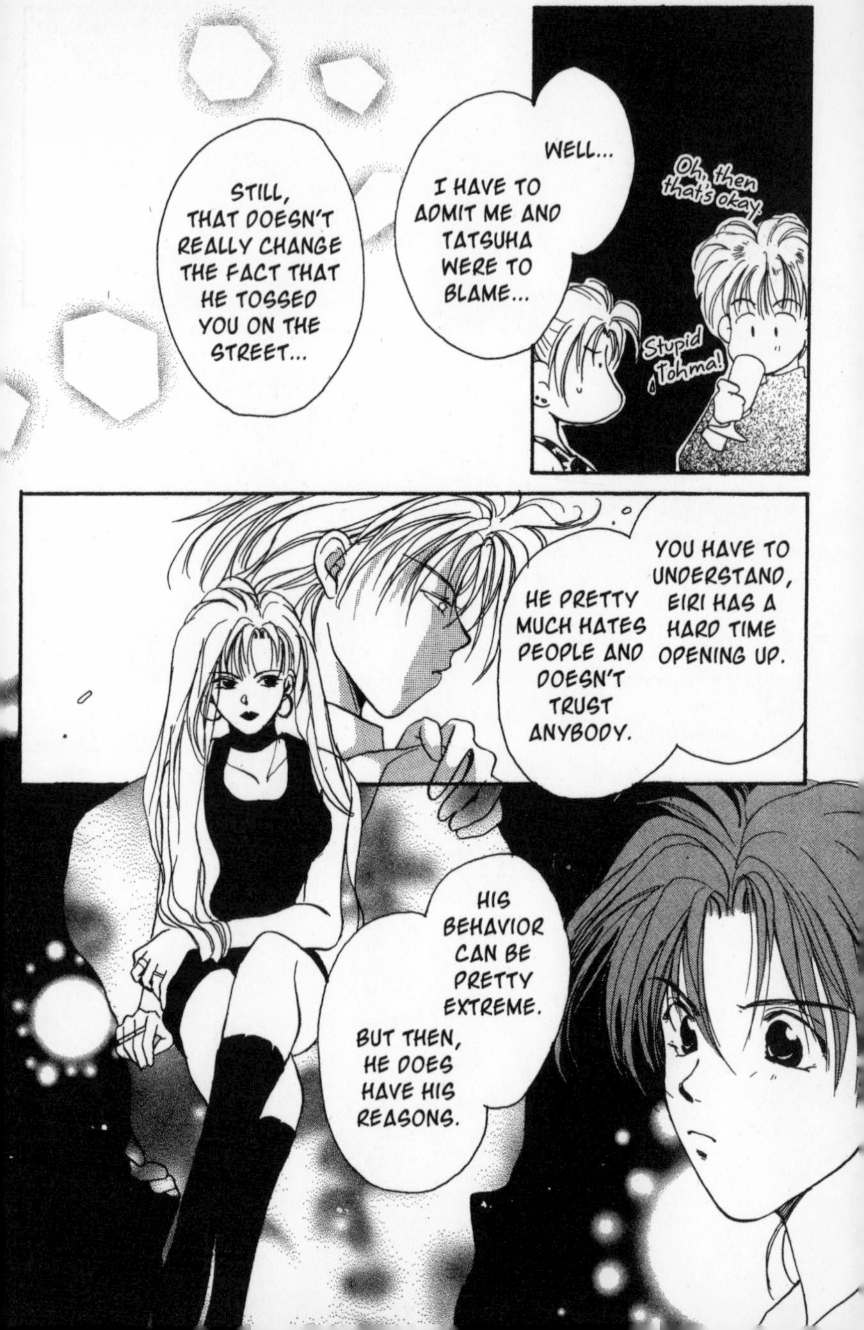
WELL...
I HAVE TO ADMIT ME AND TATSUHA WERE TO BLAME...
Oh, then that's okay.
Stupid Tohma!
STILL, THAT DOESN'T REALLY CHANGE THE FACT THAT HE TOSSED YOU ON THE STREET...
YOU HAVE TO UNDERSTAND, EIRI HAS A HARD TIME OPENING UP.
HE PRETTY MUCH HATES PEOPLE AND DOESN'T TRUST ANYBODY.
HIS BEHAVIOR CAN BE PRETTY EXTREME.
BUT THEN, HE DOES HAVE HIS REASONS.

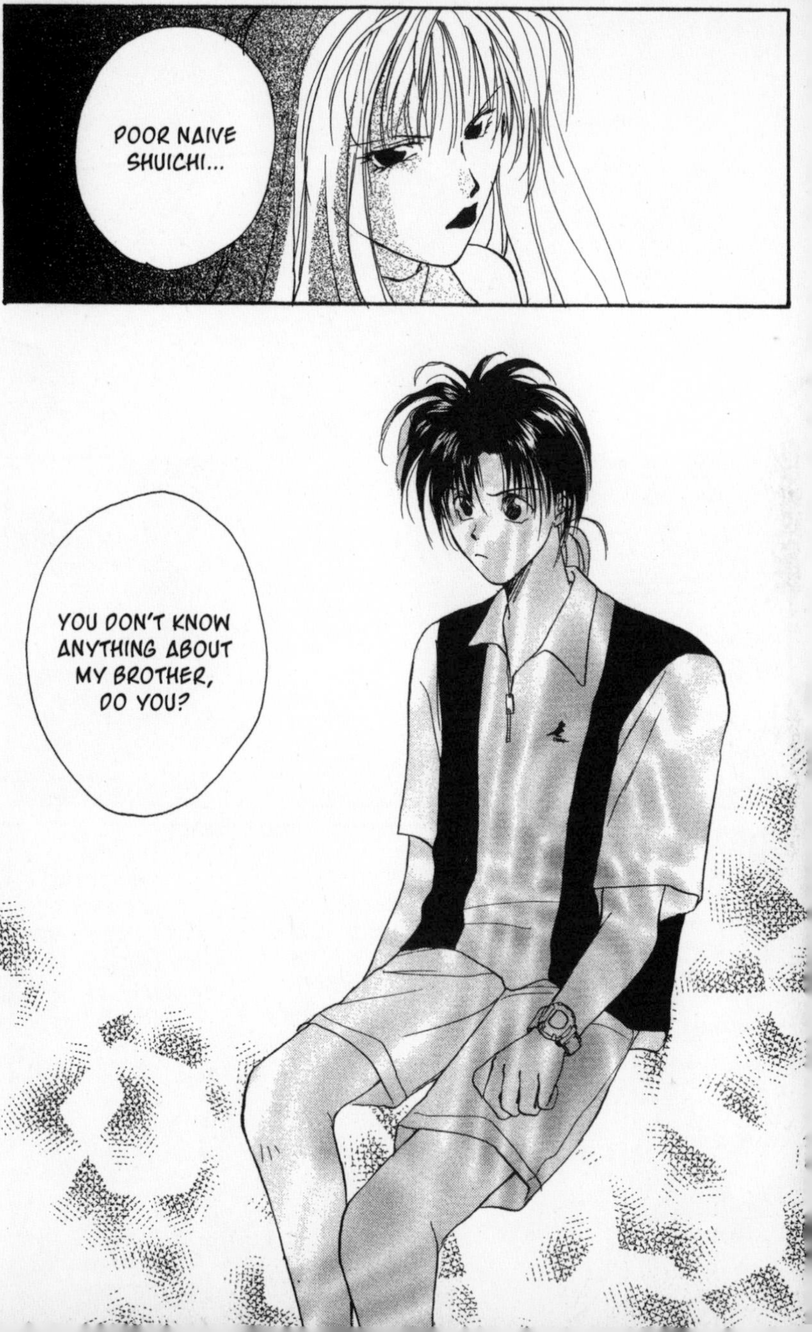
POOR NAIVE SHUICHI...
YOU DON'T KNOW ANYTHING ABOUT MY BROTHER, DO YOU?

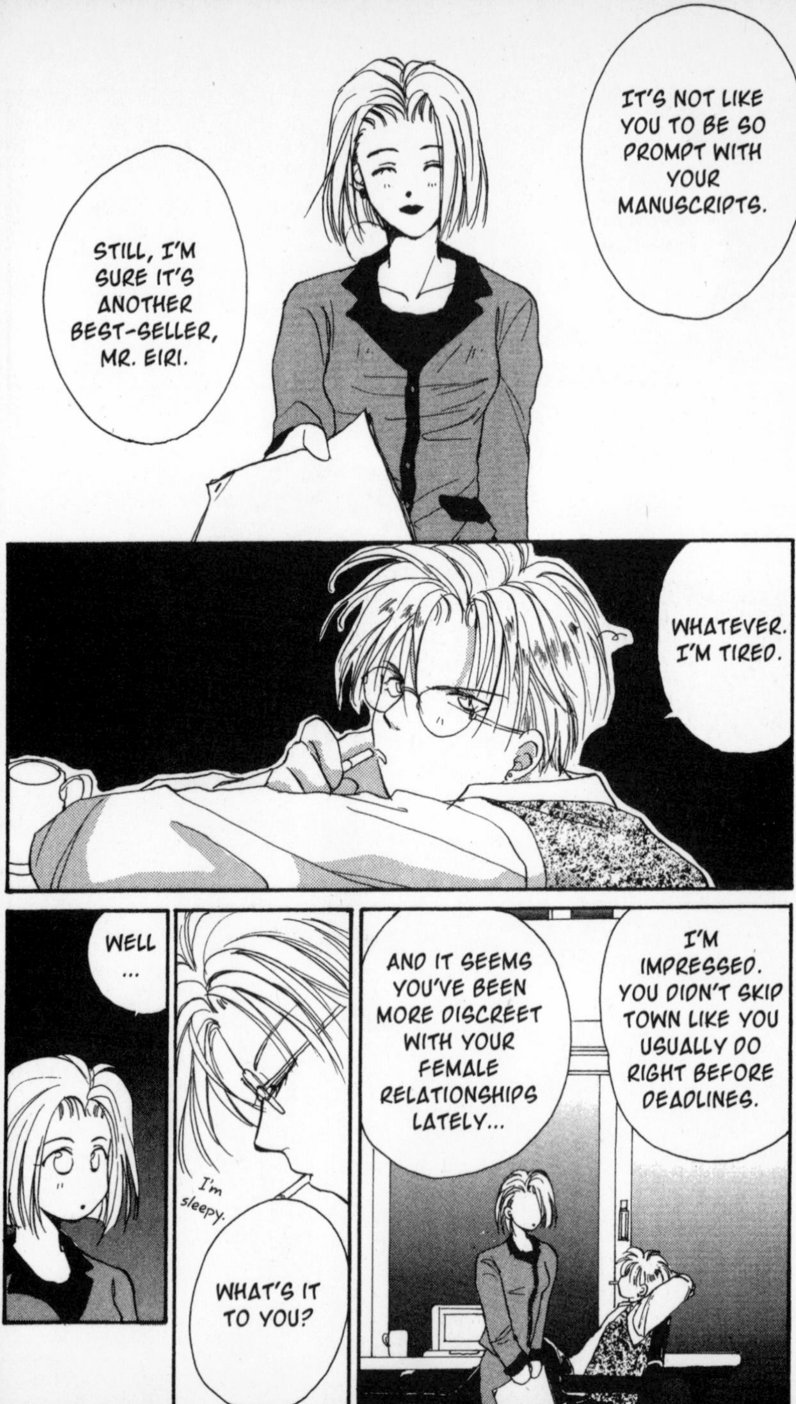
IT'S NOT LIKE YOU TO BE SO PROMPT WITH YOUR MANUSCRIPTS.
STILL, I'M SURE IT'S ANOTHER BEST-SELLER, MR. EIRI.
WHATEVER. I'M TIRED.
I'M IMPRESSED. YOU DIDN'T SKIP TOWN LIKE YOU USUALLY DO RIGHT BEFORE DEADLINES.
AND IT SEEMS YOU'VE BEEN MORE DISCREET WITH YOUR FEMALE RELATIONSHIPS LATELY...
I'm sleepy.
WHAT'S IT TO YOU?
WELL ...

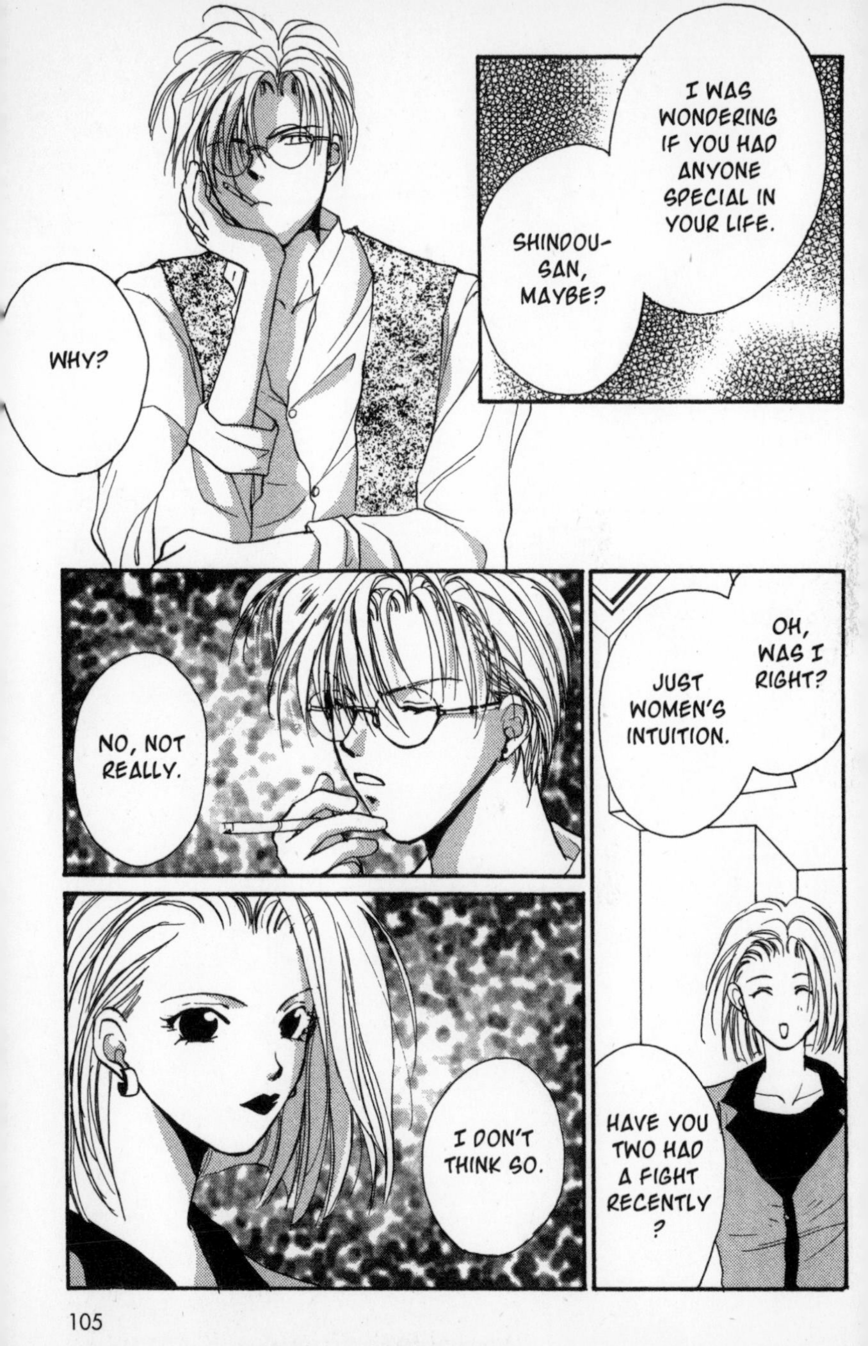
I WAS WONDERING IF YOU HAD ANYONE SPECIAL IN YOUR LIFE.
SHINDOU-SAN, MAYBE?
WHY?
OH, WAS I RIGHT?
JUST WOMEN'S INTUITION.
HAVE YOU TWO HAD A FIGHT RECENTLY?
NO, NOT REALLY.
I DON'T THINK SO.

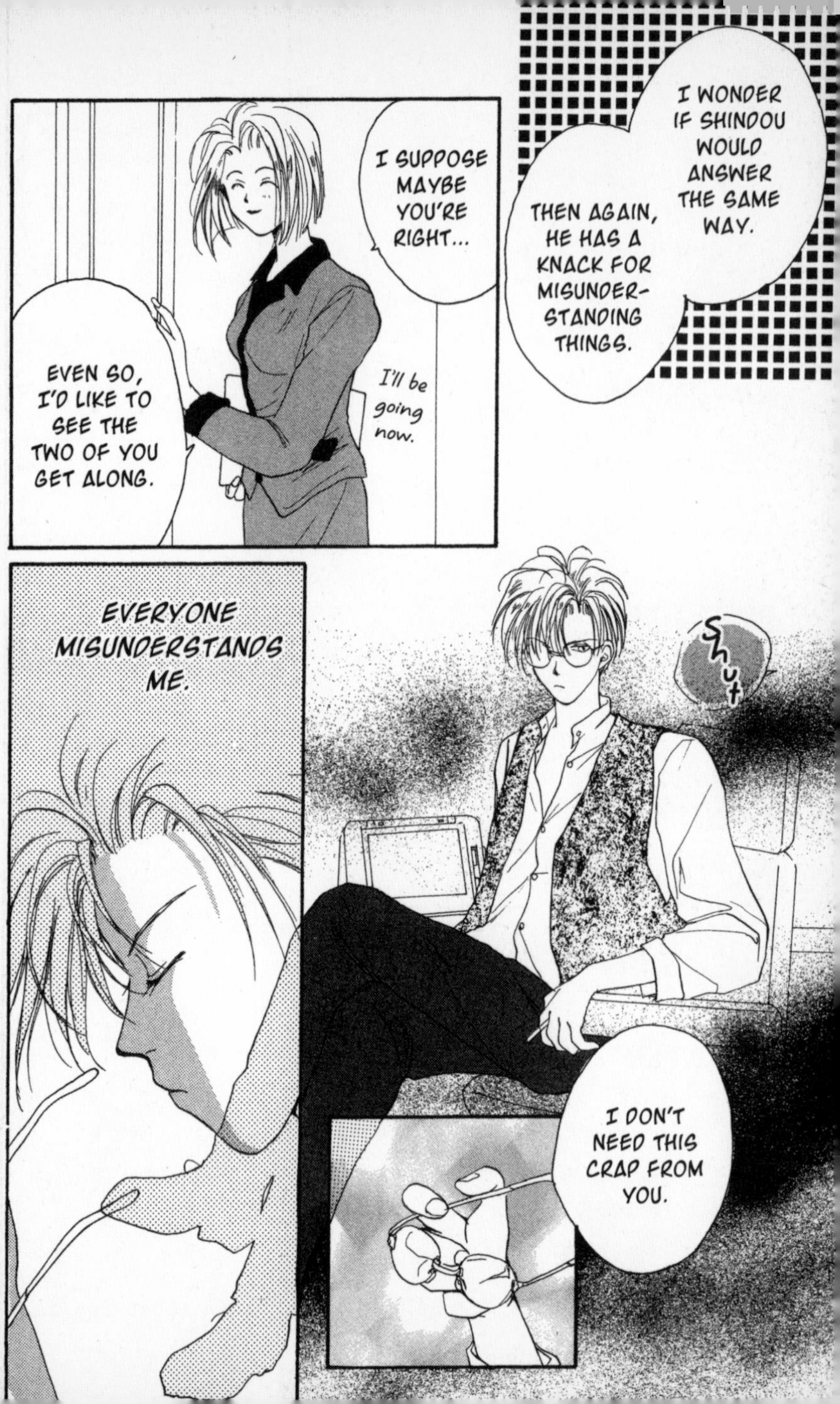
I WONDER IF SHINDOU WOULD ANSWER THE SAME WAY.
THEN AGAIN, HE HAS A KNACK FOR MISUNDER-STANDING THINGS.
I SUPPOSE MAYBE YOU'RE RIGHT...
I'll be going now.
EVEN SO, I'D LIKE TO SEE THE TWO OF YOU GET ALONG.
Shut
I DON'T NEED THIS CRAP FROM YOU.
EVERYONE MISUNDERSTANDS ME.

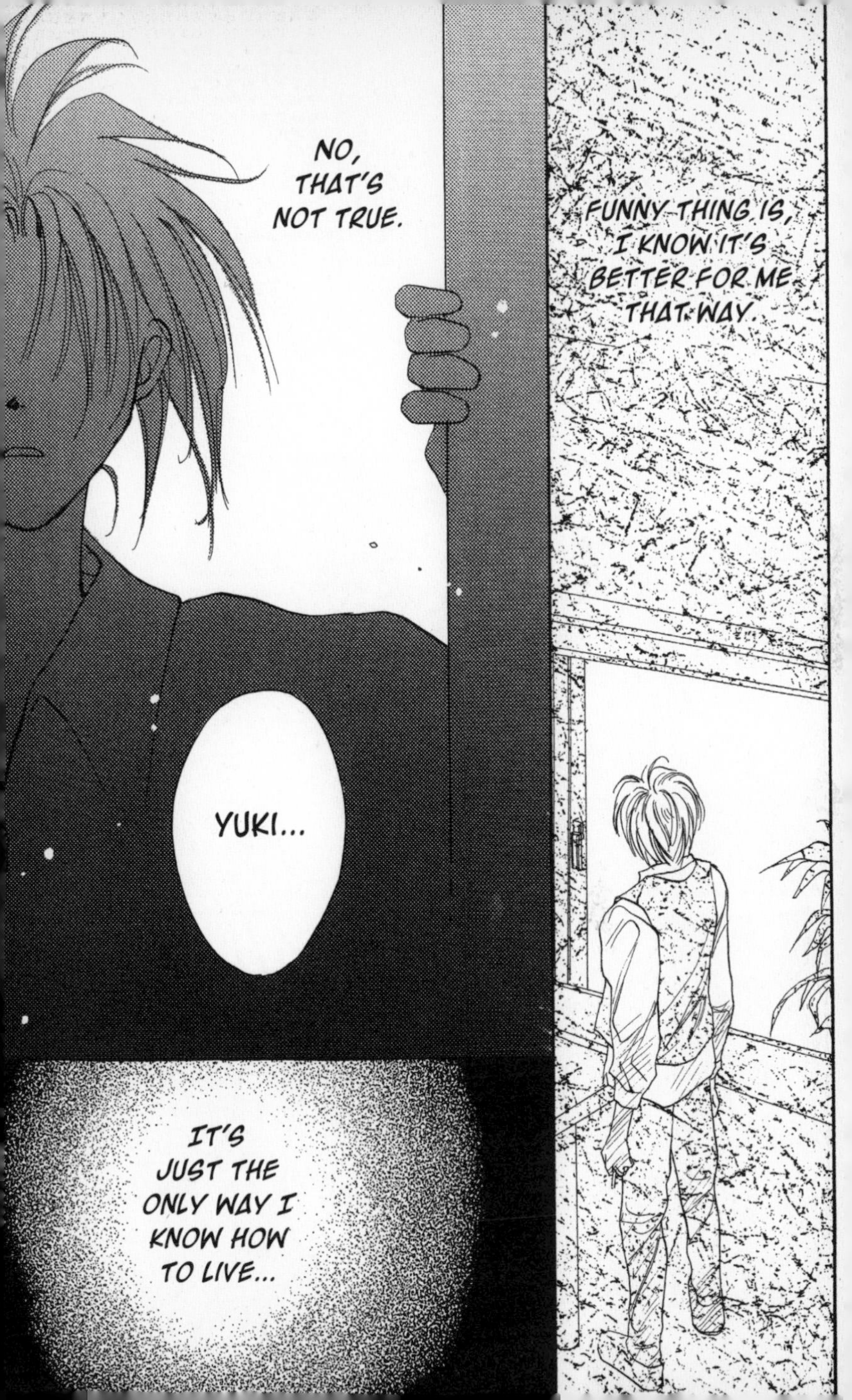
FUNNY THING IS, I KNOW IT'S BETTER FOR ME THAT WAY.
NO, THAT'S NOT TRUE.
YUKI...
IT'S JUST THE ONLY WAY I KNOW HOW TO LIVE...

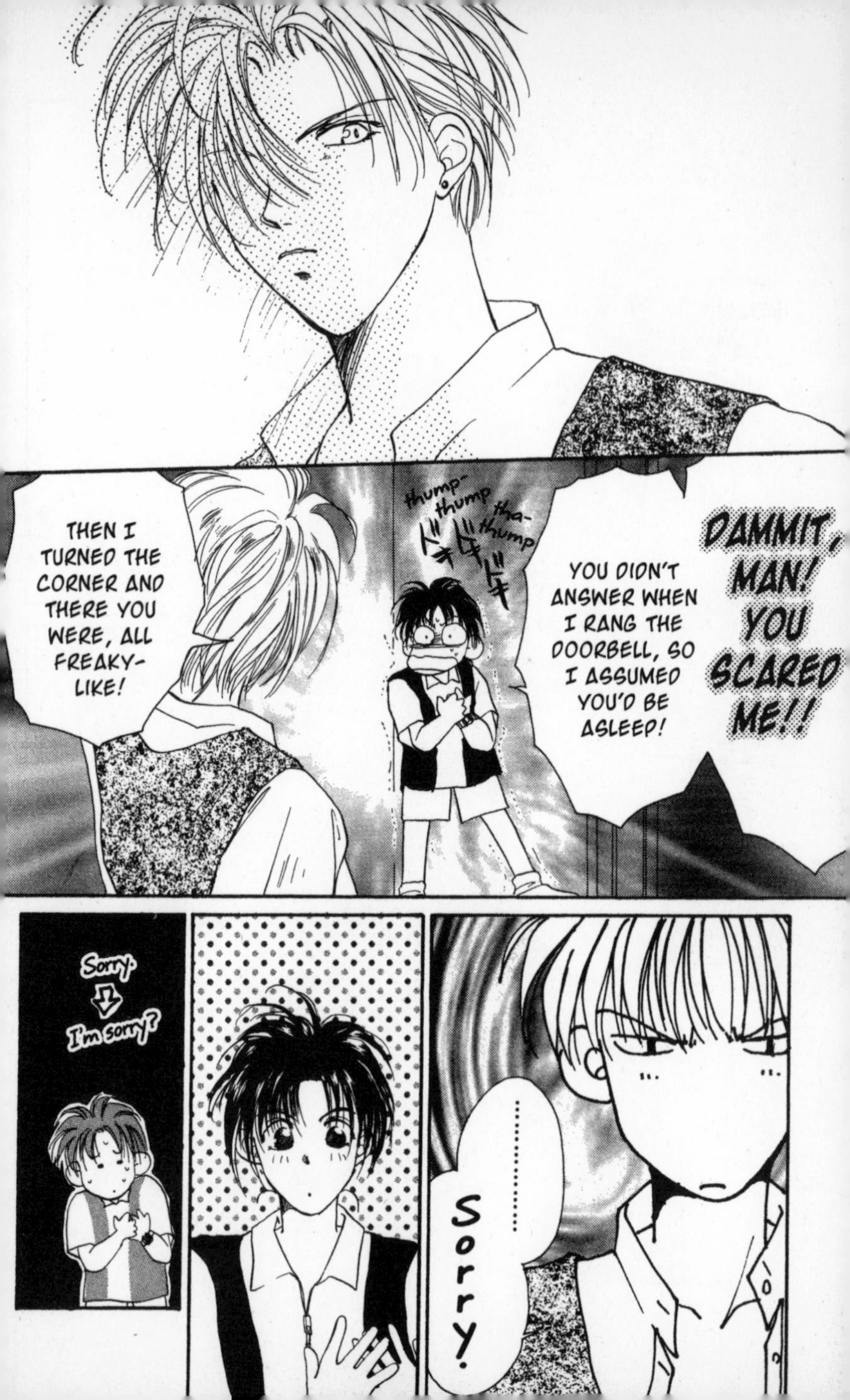
DAMMIT, MAN! YOU SCARED ME!!
YOU DIDN'T ANSWER WHEN I RANG THE DOORBELL, SO I ASSUMED YOU'D BE ASLEEP!
thump-thump tha-thump
THEN I TURNED THE CORNER AND THERE YOU WERE, ALL FREAKY-LIKE!
...... Sorry.
Sorry. ⇩ I'm sorry?

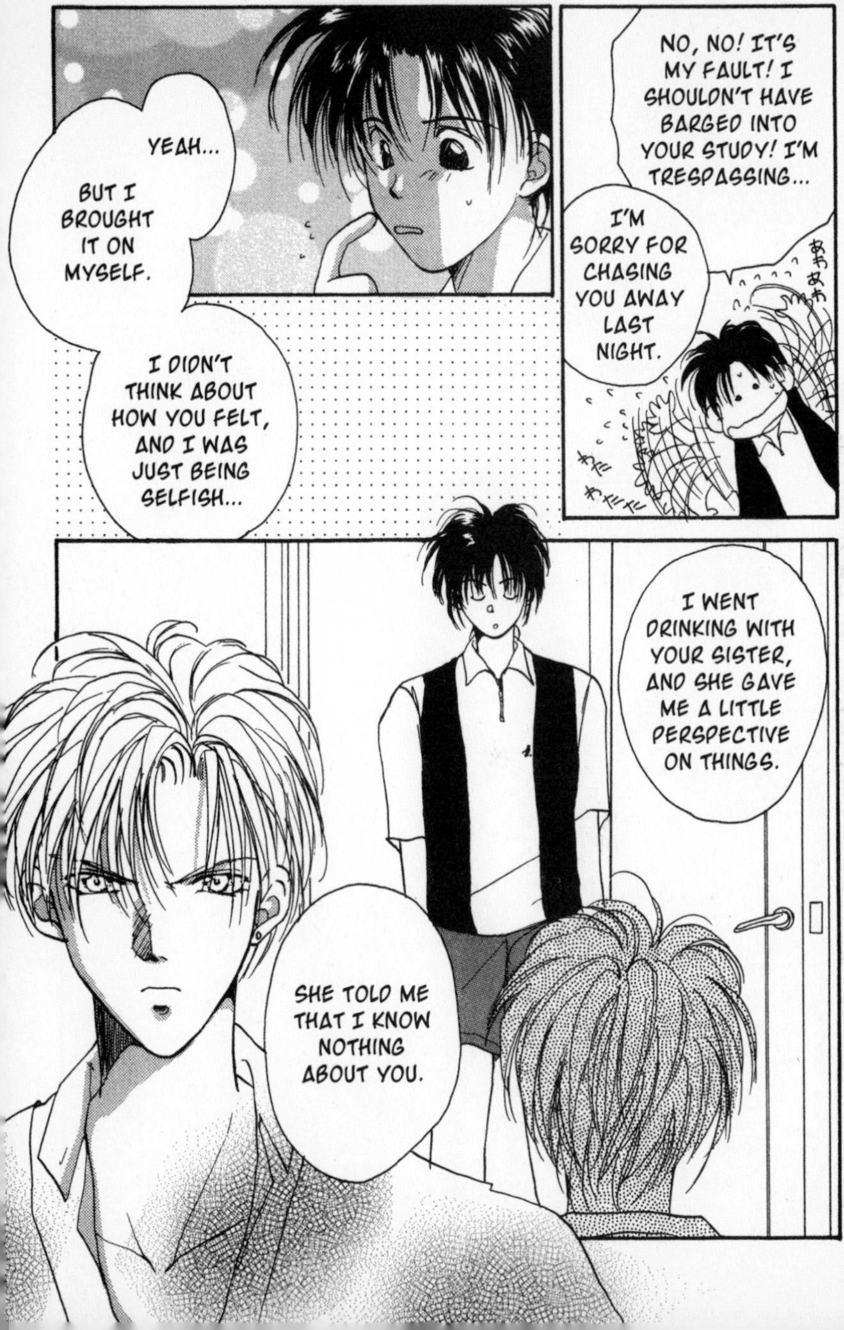
NO, NO! IT'S MY FAULT! I SHOULDN'T HAVE BARGED INTO YOUR STUDY! I'M TRESPASSING...
I'M SORRY FOR CHASING YOU AWAY LAST NIGHT.
YEAH...
BUT I BROUGHT IT ON MYSELF.
I DIDN'T THINK ABOUT HOW YOU FELT, AND I WAS JUST BEING SELFISH...
I WENT DRINKING WITH YOUR SISTER, AND SHE GAVE ME A LITTLE PERSPECTIVE ON THINGS.
SHE TOLD ME THAT I KNOW NOTHING ABOUT YOU.

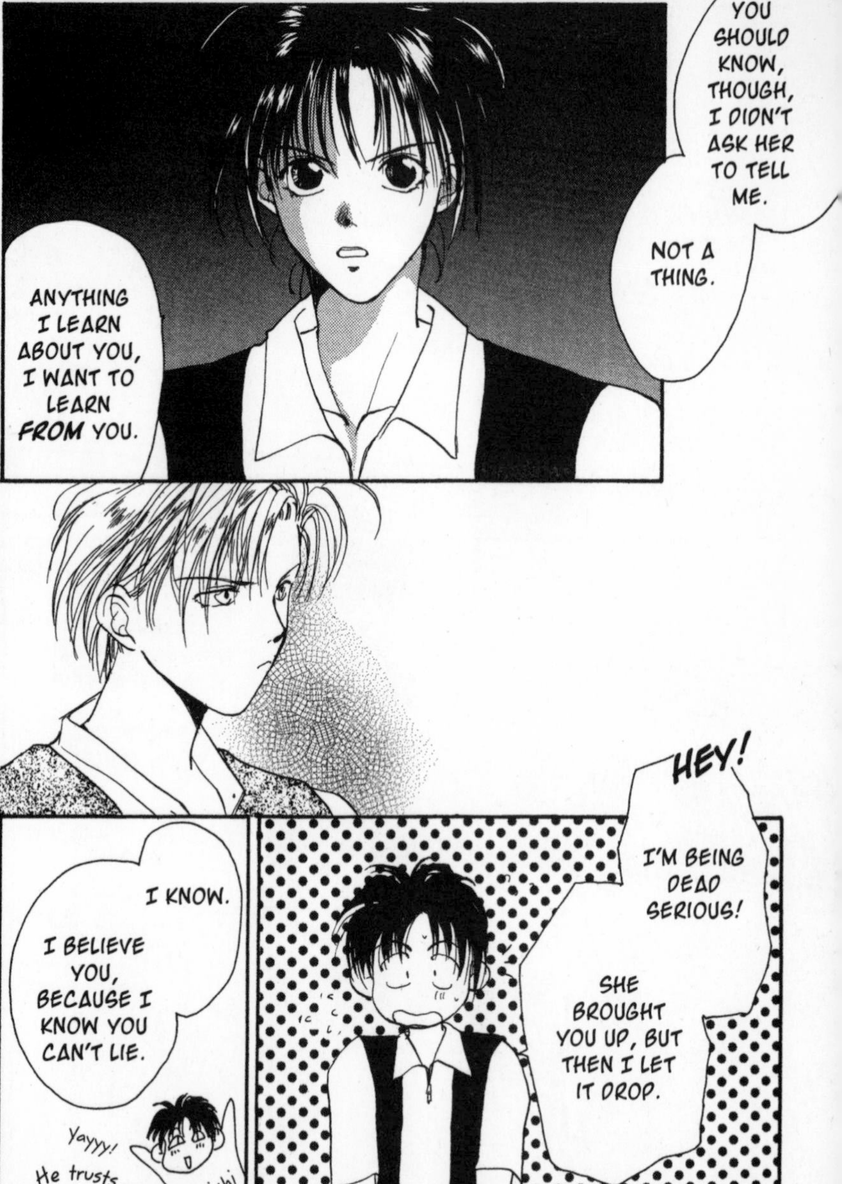

YOU SHOULD KNOW, THOUGH, I DIDN'T ASK HER TO TELL ME.
NOT A THING.
ANYTHING I LEARN ABOUT YOU, I WANT TO LEARN FROM YOU.
HEY!
I'M BEING DEAD SERIOUS!
SHE BROUGHT YOU UP, BUT THEN I LET IT DROP.
I KNOW.
I BELIEVE YOU, BECAUSE I KNOW YOU CAN'T LIE.
Yayyy! He trusts me!
Shuichi

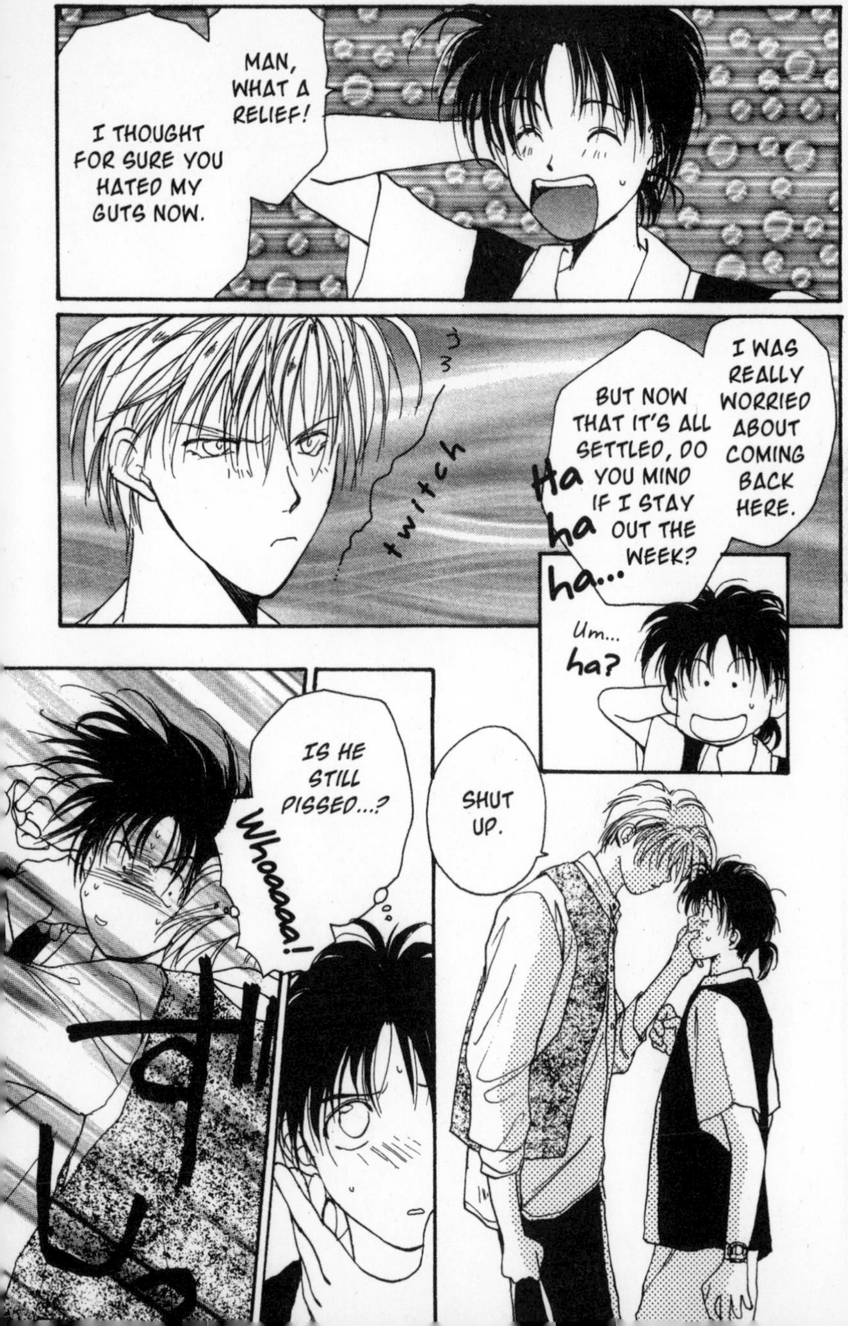
MAN, WHAT A RELIEF!
I THOUGHT FOR SURE YOU HATED MY GUTS NOW.
I WAS REALLY WORRIED ABOUT COMING BACK HERE.
BUT NOW THAT IT'S ALL SETTLED, DO YOU MIND IF I STAY OUT THE WEEK?
Ha ha ha...
twitch
Um... ha?
SHUT UP.
IS HE STILL PISSED...?
Whoaaaa!

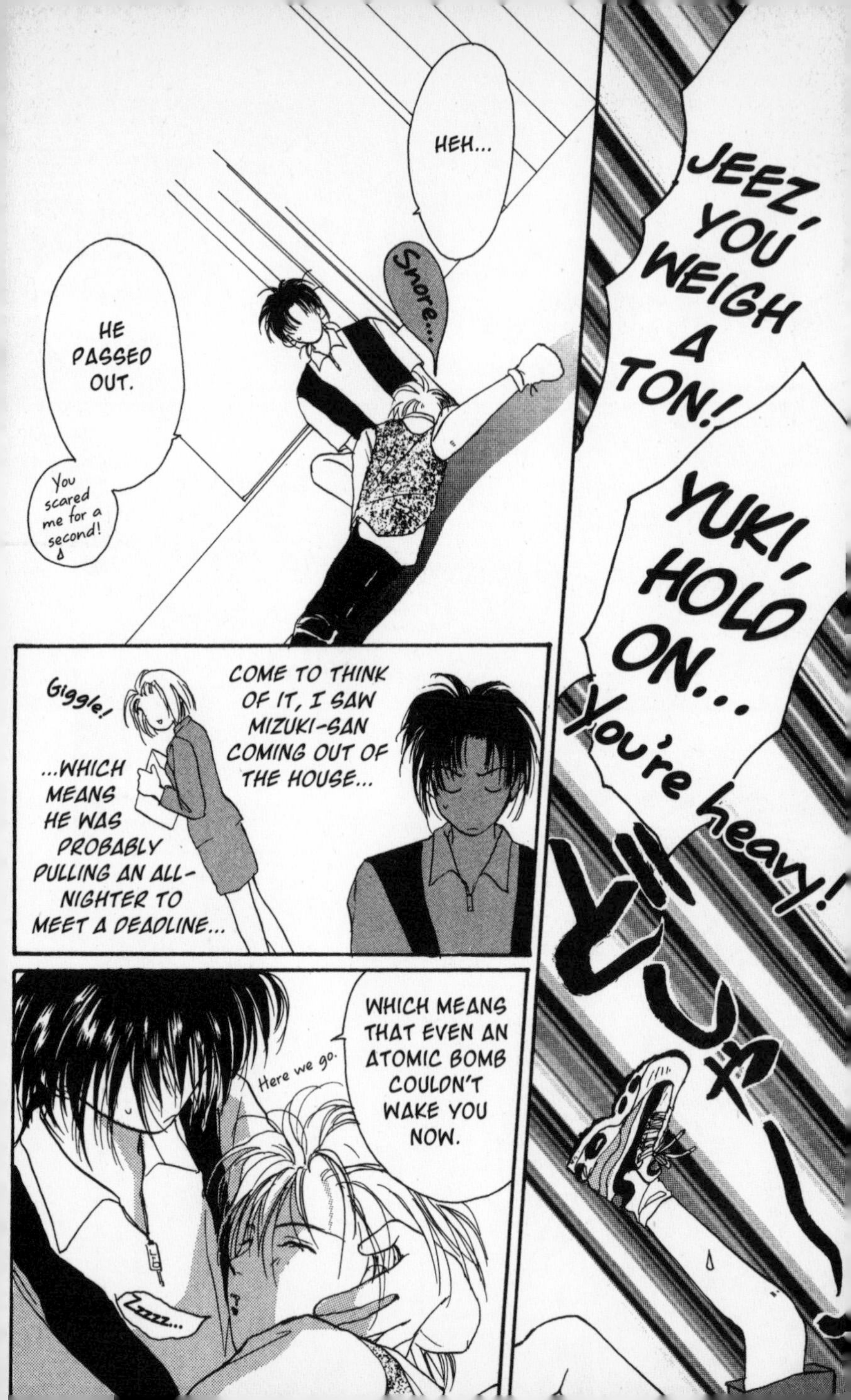
JEEZ, YOU WEIGH A TON!
YUKI, HOLD ON...
You're heavy!
HEH...
Snore...
HE PASSED OUT.
You scared me for a second!
COME TO THINK OF IT, I SAW MIZUKI-SAN COMING OUT OF THE HOUSE...
Giggle!
...WHICH MEANS HE WAS PROBABLY PULLING AN ALL-NIGHTER TO MEET A DEADLINE...
WHICH MEANS THAT EVEN AN ATOMIC BOMB COULDN'T WAKE YOU NOW.
Here we go.
Zzzz...

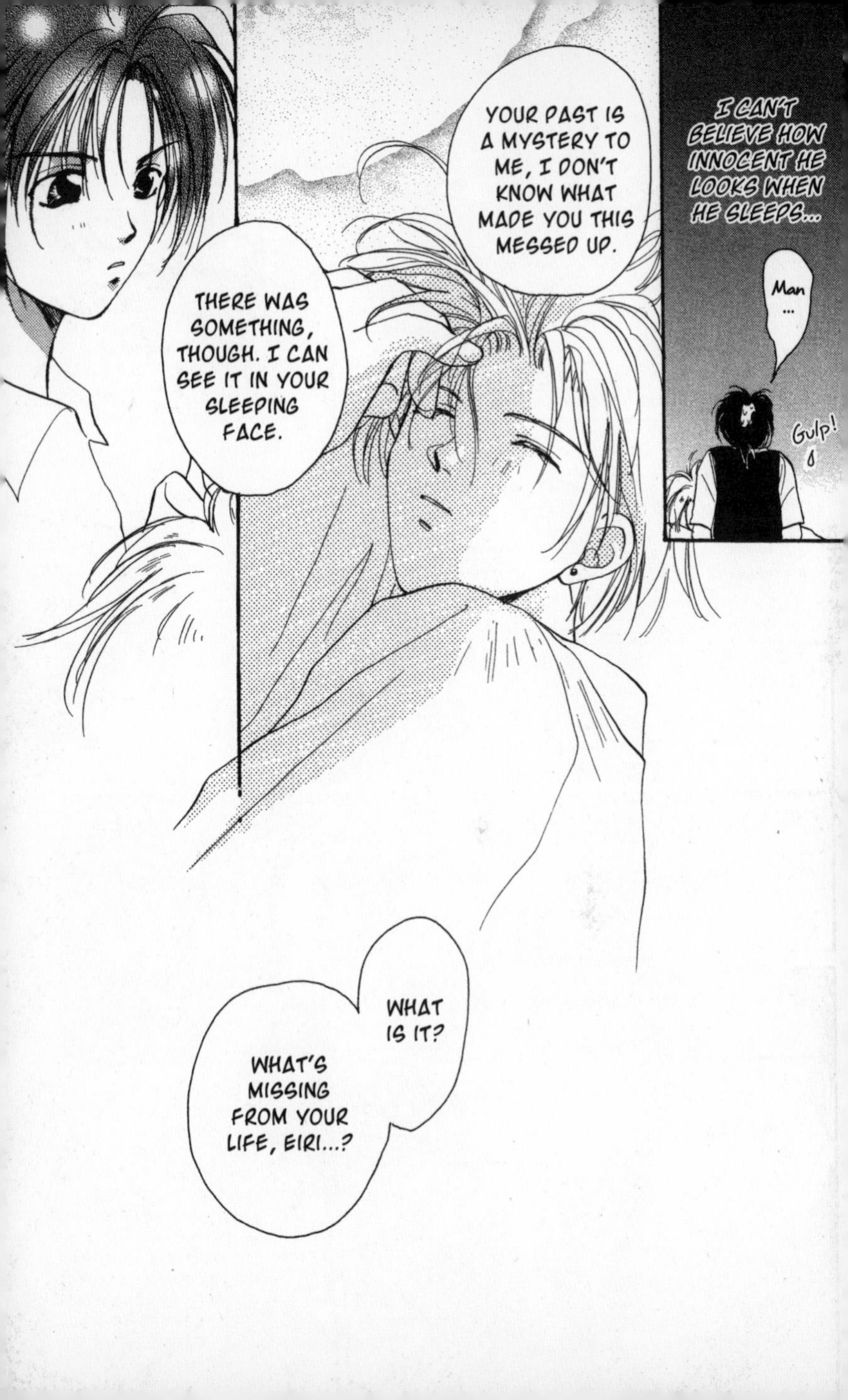
I CAN'T BELIEVE HOW INNOCENT HE LOOKS WHEN HE SLEEPS...
Man ...
Gulp!
YOUR PAST IS A MYSTERY TO ME, I DON'T KNOW WHAT MADE YOU THIS MESSED UP.
THERE WAS SOMETHING, THOUGH. I CAN SEE IT IN YOUR SLEEPING FACE.
WHAT IS IT?
WHAT'S MISSING FROM YOUR LIFE, EIRI...?

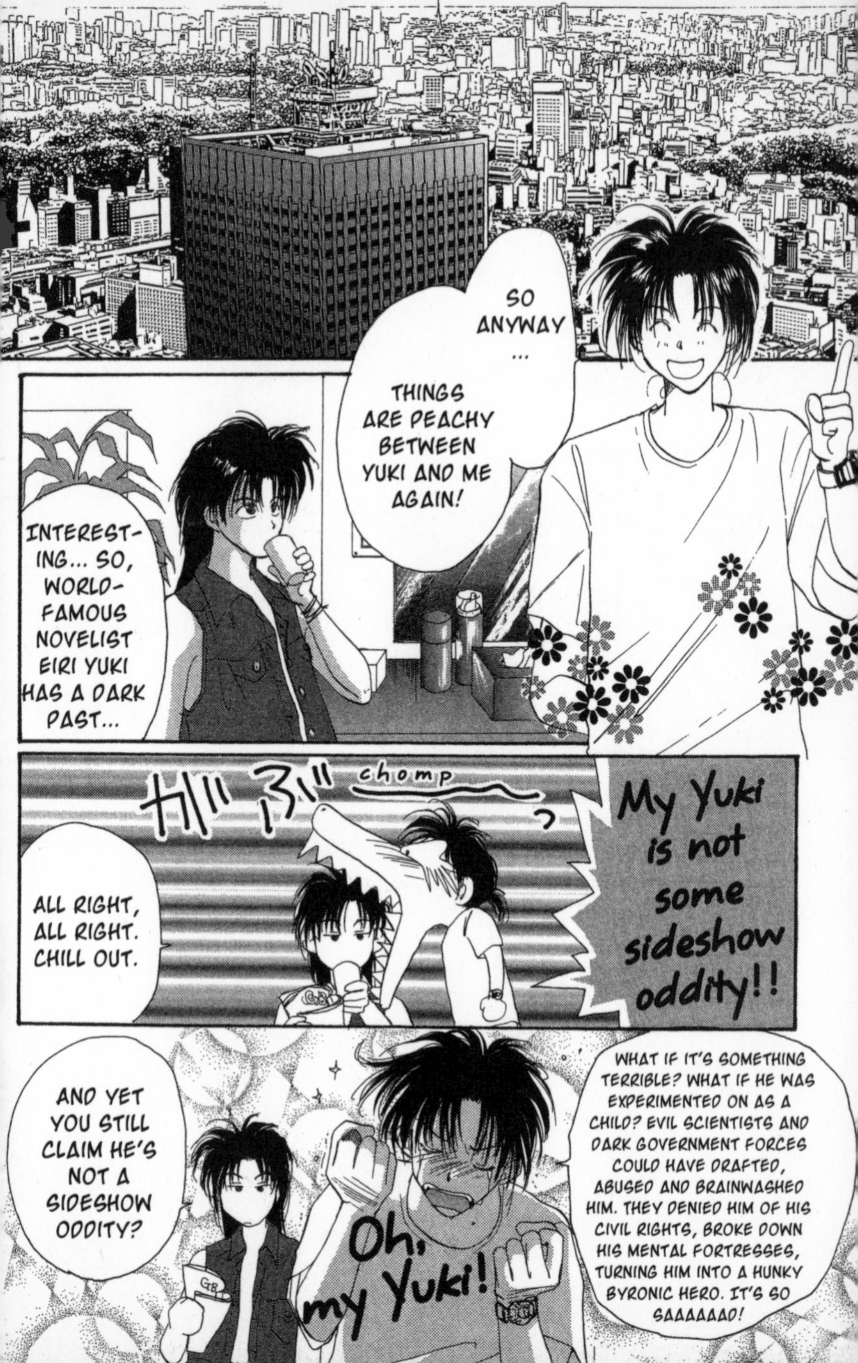
SO ANYWAY ... THINGS ARE PEACHY BETWEEN YUKI AND ME AGAIN!
INTEREST-ING... SO, WORLD-FAMOUS NOVELIST EIRI YUKI HAS A DARK PAST...
My Yuki is not some sideshow oddity!!
ガぶ chomp
ALL RIGHT, ALL RIGHT. CHILL OUT.
WHAT IF IT'S SOMETHING TERRIBLE? WHAT IF HE WAS EXPERIMENTED ON AS A CHILD? EVIL SCIENTISTS AND DARK GOVERNMENT FORCES COULD HAVE DRAFTED, ABUSED AND BRAINWASHED HIM. THEY DENIED HIM OF HIS CIVIL RIGHTS, BROKE DOWN HIS MENTAL FORTRESSES, TURNING HIM INTO A HUNKY BYRONIC HERO. IT'S SO SAAAAAAD!
Oh, my Yuki!
AND YET YOU STILL CLAIM HE'S NOT A SIDESHOW ODDITY?

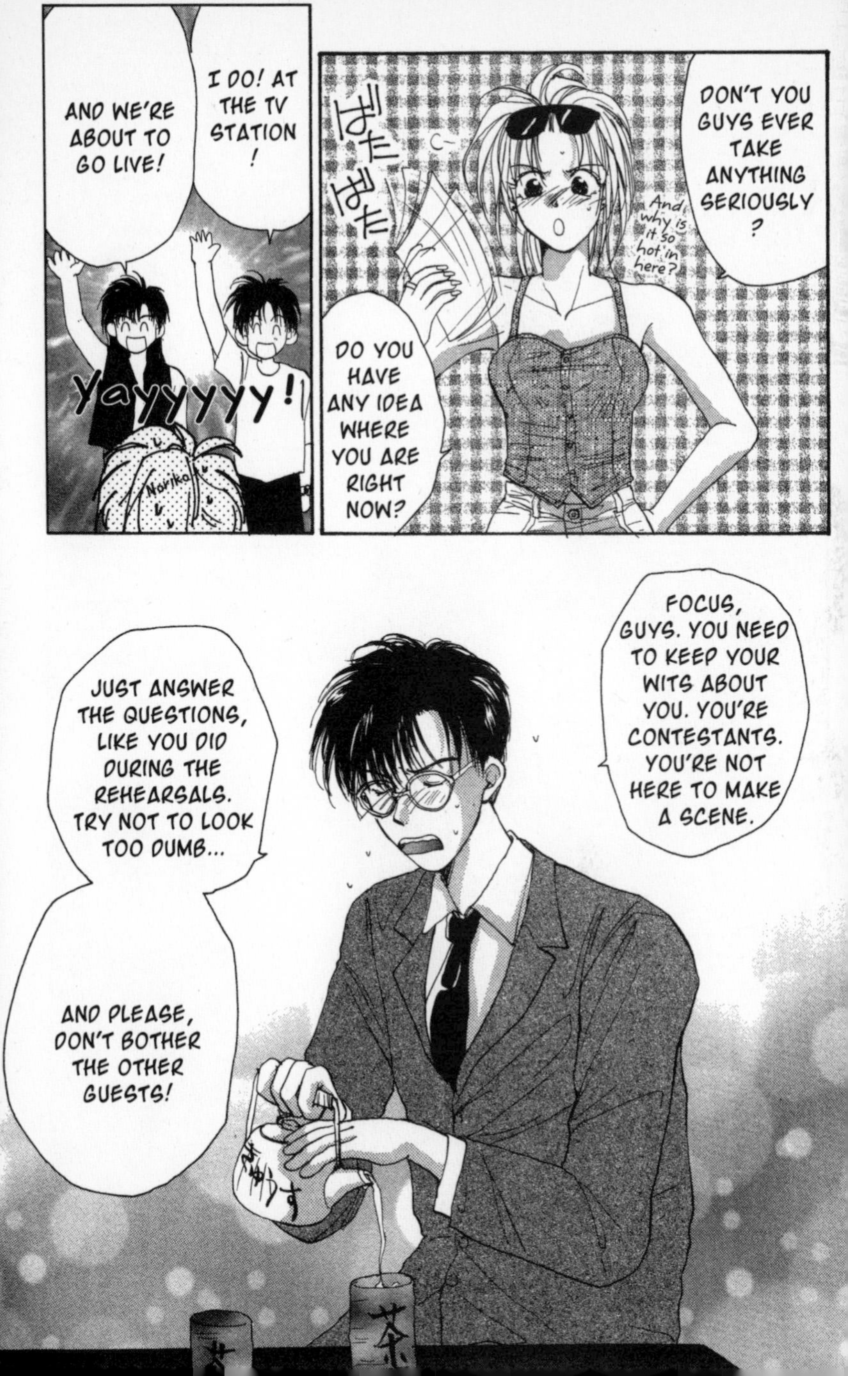
DON'T YOU GUYS EVER TAKE ANYTHING SERIOUSLY?
And why is it so hot in here?
ぱたぱた
DO YOU HAVE ANY IDEA WHERE YOU ARE RIGHT NOW?
I DO! AT THE TV STATION!
AND WE'RE ABOUT TO GO LIVE!
Yayyyyy!
Noriko
FOCUS, GUYS. YOU NEED TO KEEP YOUR WITS ABOUT YOU. YOU'RE CONTESTANTS. YOU'RE NOT HERE TO MAKE A SCENE.
JUST ANSWER THE QUESTIONS, LIKE YOU DID DURING THE REHEARSALS. TRY NOT TO LOOK TOO DUMB...
AND PLEASE, DON'T BOTHER THE OTHER GUESTS!
茶

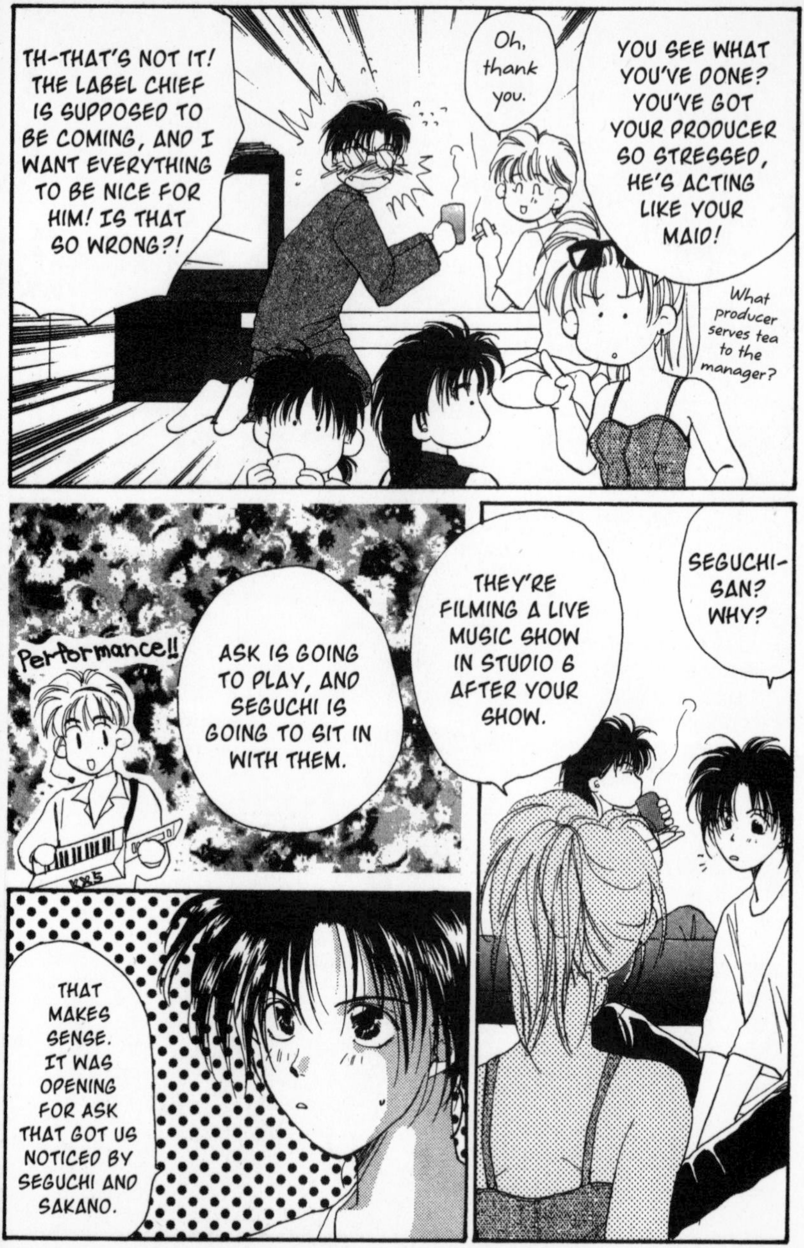
YOU SEE WHAT YOU'VE DONE? YOU'VE GOT YOUR PRODUCER SO STRESSED, HE'S ACTING LIKE YOUR MAID!
Oh, thank you.
TH-THAT'S NOT IT! THE LABEL CHIEF IS SUPPOSED TO BE COMING, AND I WANT EVERYTHING TO BE NICE FOR HIM! IS THAT SO WRONG?!
What producer serves tea to the manager?
SEGUCHI-SAN? WHY?
THEY'RE FILMING A LIVE MUSIC SHOW IN STUDIO 6 AFTER YOUR SHOW.
ASK IS GOING TO PLAY, AND SEGUCHI IS GOING TO SIT IN WITH THEM.
Performance!!
THAT MAKES SENSE. IT WAS OPENING FOR ASK THAT GOT US NOTICED BY SEGUCHI AND SAKANO.

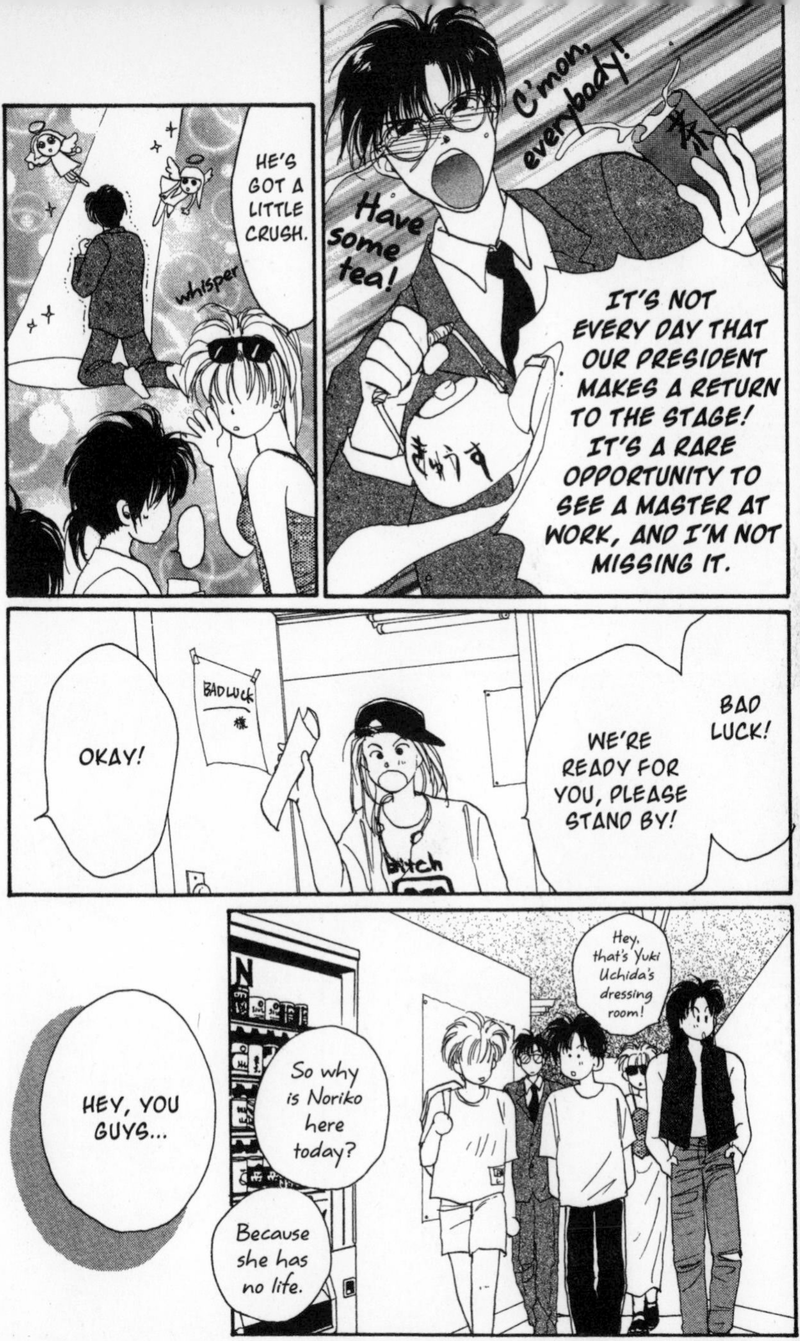
C'mon, everybody!
Have some tea!
IT'S NOT EVERY DAY THAT OUR PRESIDENT MAKES A RETURN TO THE STAGE! IT'S A RARE OPPORTUNITY TO SEE A MASTER AT WORK, AND I'M NOT MISSING IT.
HE'S GOT A LITTLE CRUSH.
whisper
BAD LUCK!
WE'RE READY FOR YOU, PLEASE STAND BY!
BAD LUCK
OKAY!
Hey, that's Yuki Uchida's dressing room!
So why is Noriko here today?
Because she has no life.
HEY, YOU GUYS...

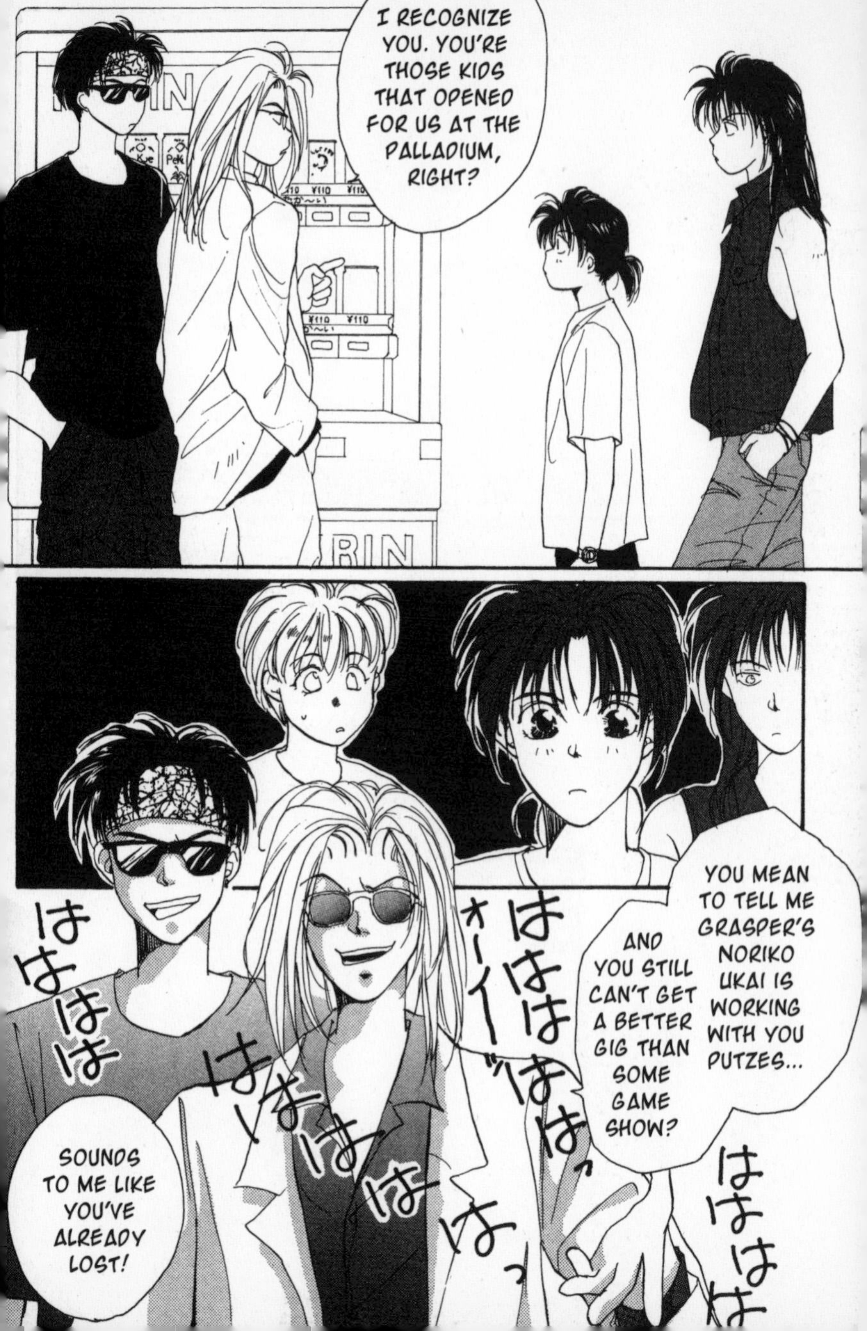
I RECOGNIZE YOU. YOU'RE THOSE KIDS THAT OPENED FOR US AT THE PALLADIUM, RIGHT?
YOU MEAN TO TELL ME GRASPER'S NORIKO UKAI IS WORKING WITH YOU PUTZES...
AND YOU STILL CAN'T GET A BETTER GIG THAN SOME GAME SHOW?
SOUNDS TO ME LIKE YOU'VE ALREADY LOST!
ははは

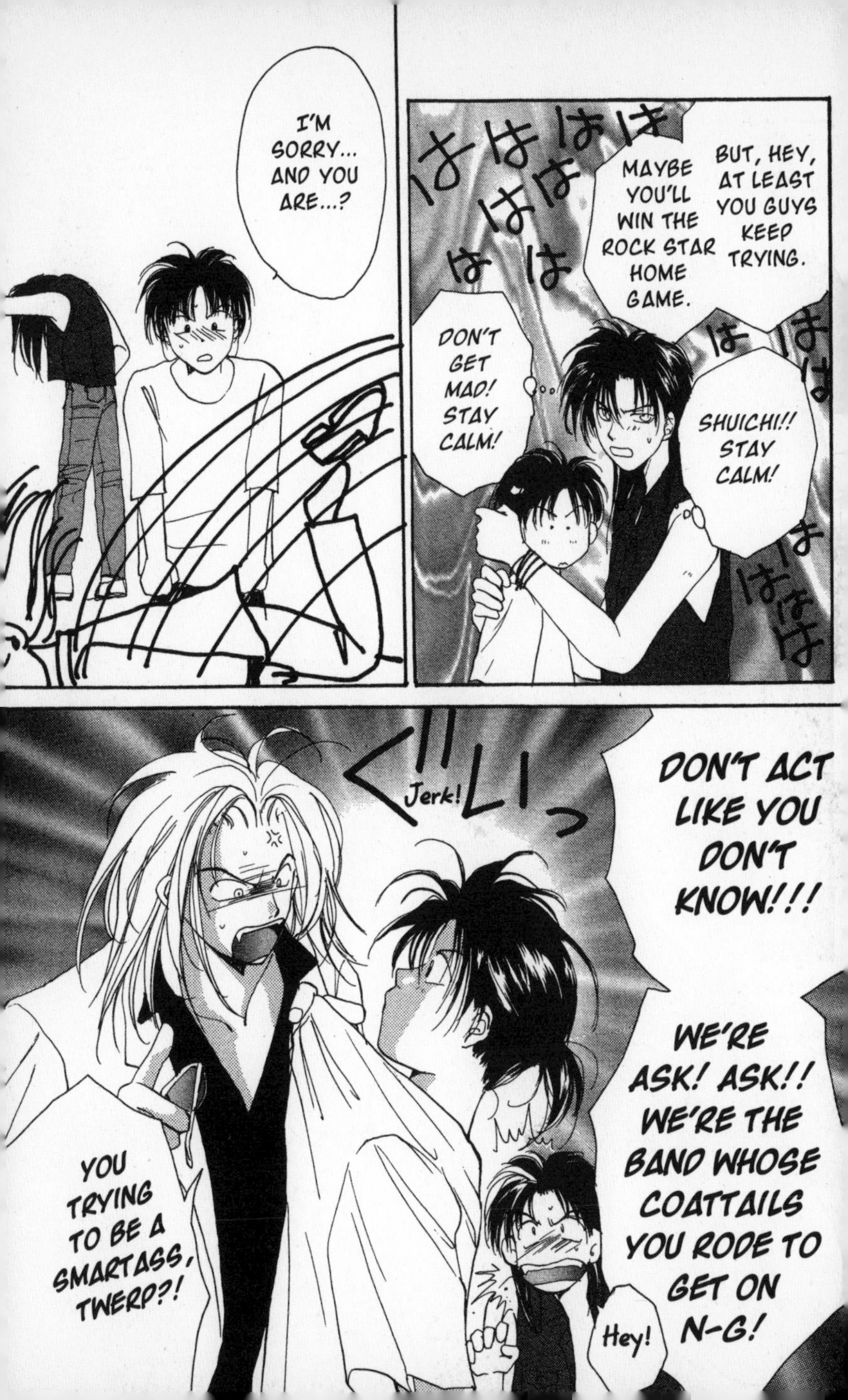
BUT, HEY, AT LEAST YOU GUYS KEEP TRYING.
MAYBE YOU'LL WIN THE ROCK STAR HOME GAME.
SHUICHI!! STAY CALM!
DON'T GET MAD! STAY CALM!
I'M SORRY... AND YOU ARE...?
DON'T ACT LIKE YOU DON'T KNOW!!!
ぐいっ
Jerk!
WE'RE ASK! ASK!! WE'RE THE BAND WHOSE COATTAILS YOU RODE TO GET ON N-G!
Hey!
YOU TRYING TO BE A SMARTASS, TWERP?!

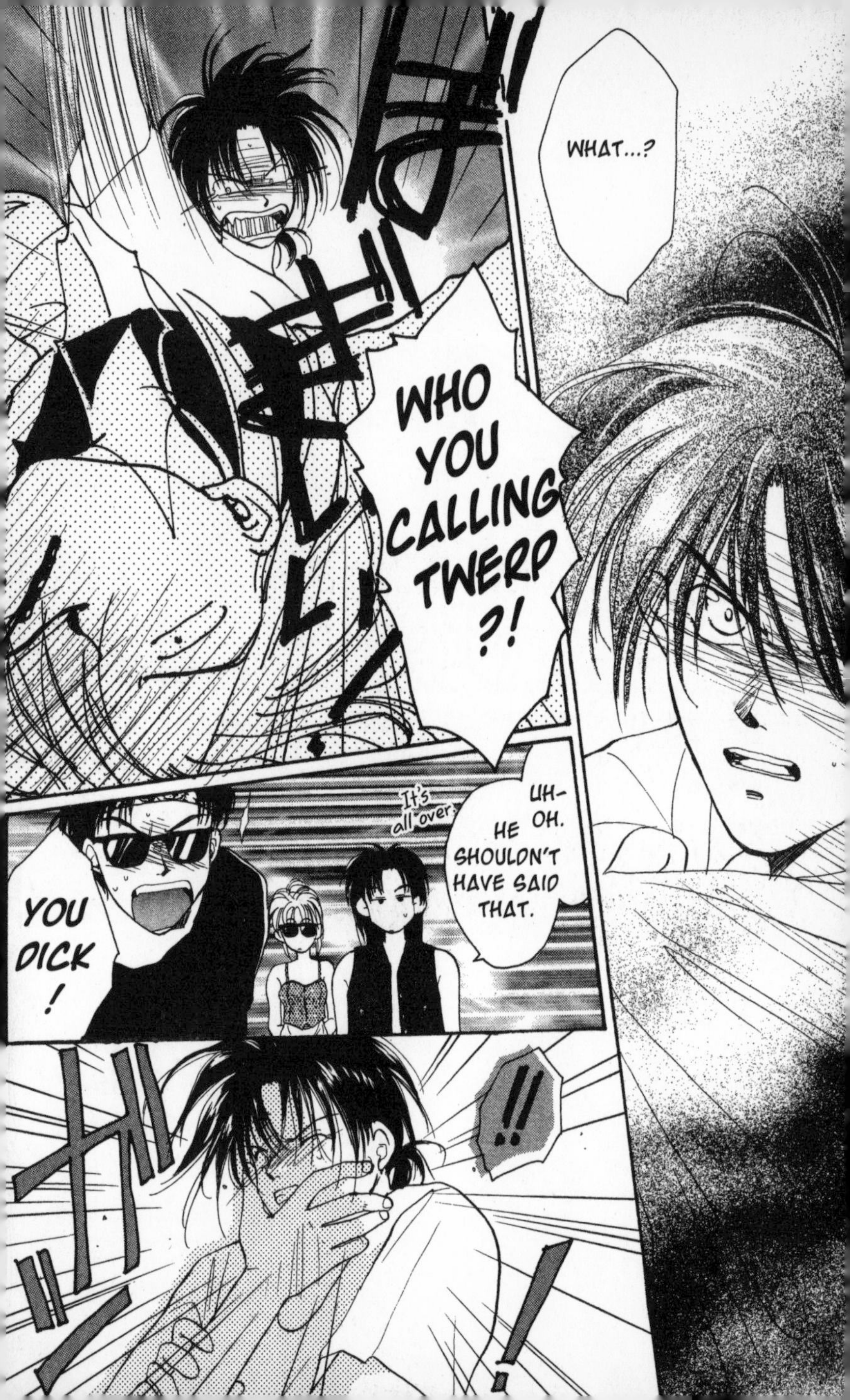
WHAT...?
WHO YOU CALLING TWERP?!
UH-OH. HE SHOULDN'T HAVE SAID THAT.
It's all over.
YOU DICK!
!!

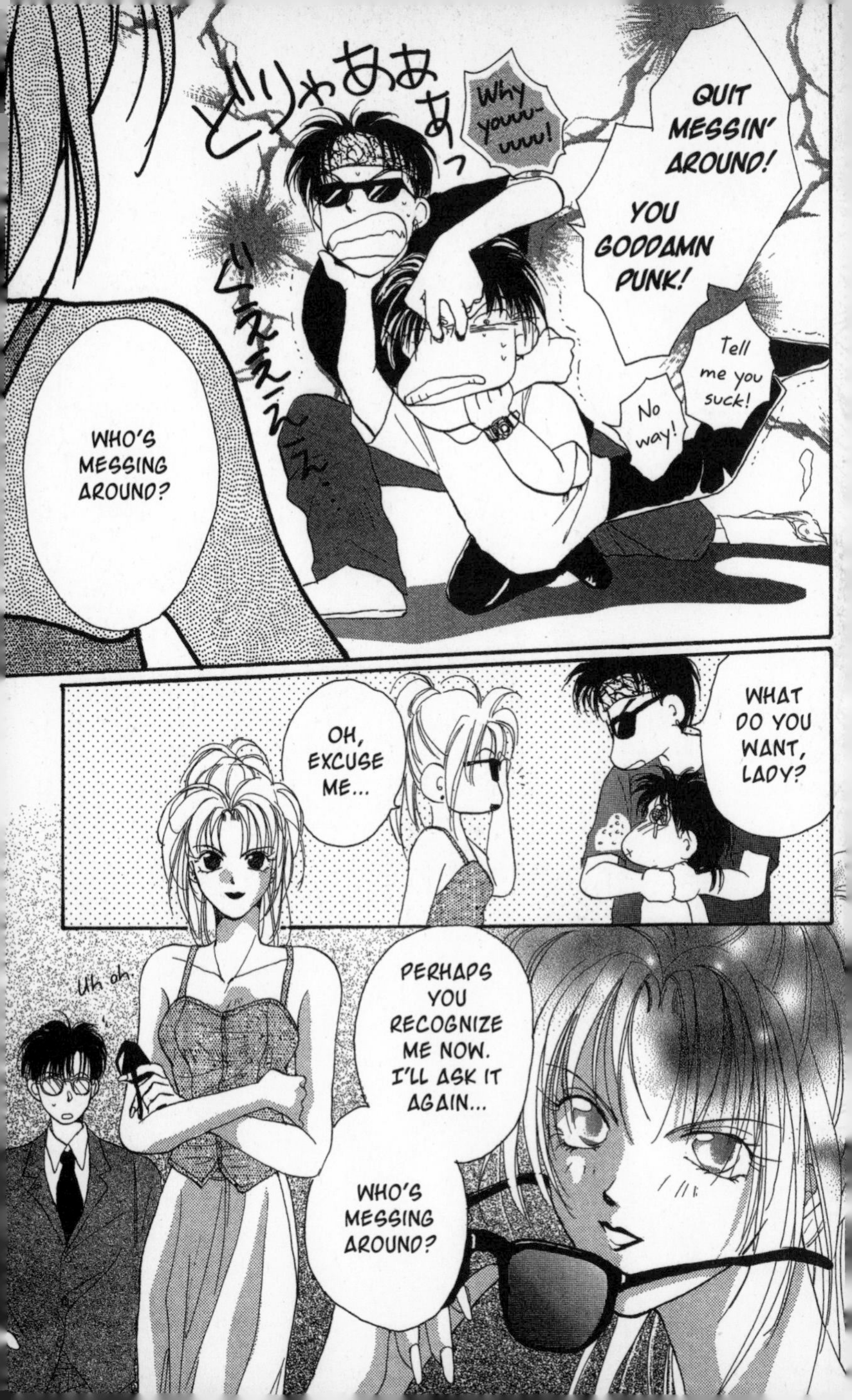
QUIT MESSIN' AROUND!
YOU GODDAMN PUNK!
Why youuu-uuuu!
どりゃあああっ
Tell me you suck!
No way!
WHO'S MESSING AROUND?
WHAT DO YOU WANT, LADY?
OH, EXCUSE ME...
PERHAPS YOU RECOGNIZE ME NOW. I'LL ASK IT AGAIN...
WHO'S MESSING AROUND?
Uh oh.

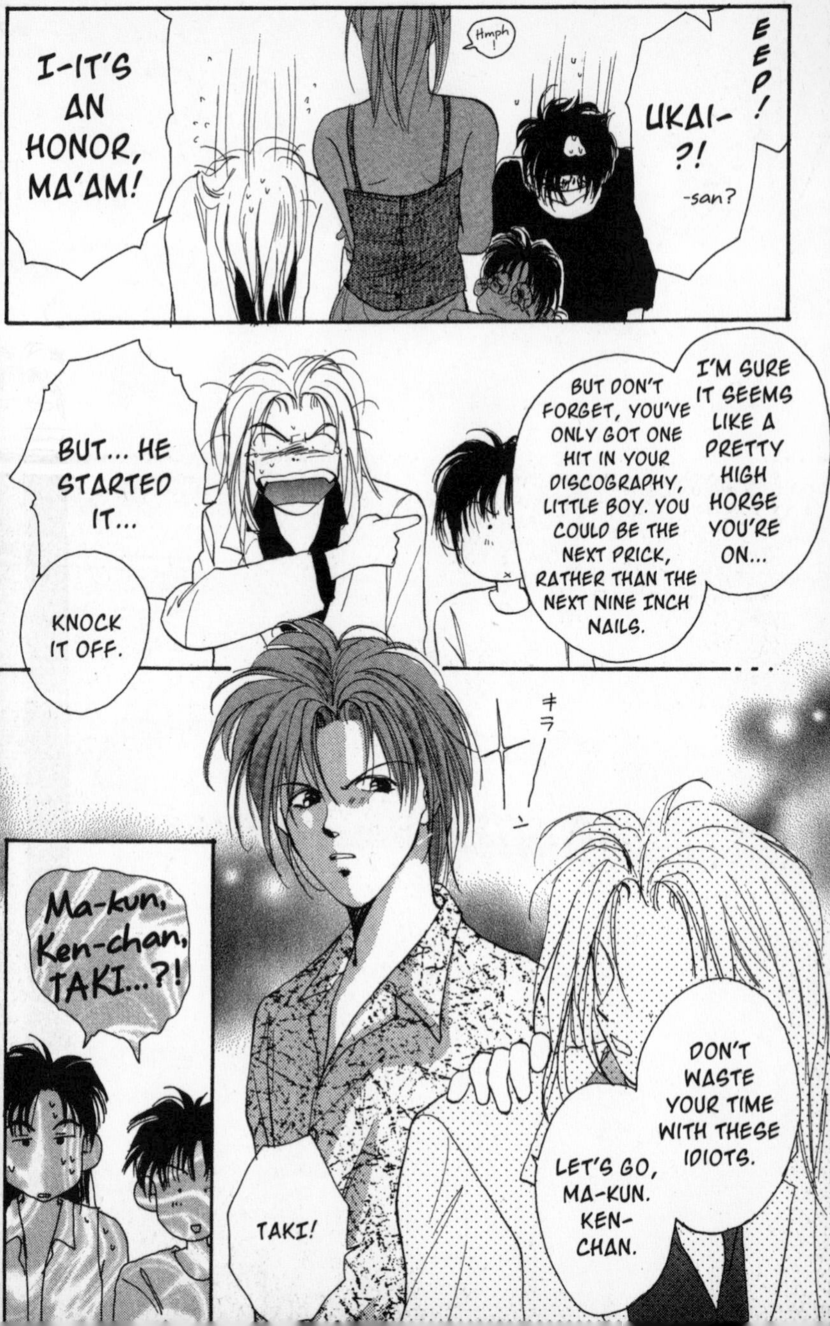
EEP!
UKAI-?!
-san?
Hmph!
I-IT'S AN HONOR, MA'AM!
I'M SURE IT SEEMS LIKE A PRETTY HIGH HORSE YOU'RE ON...
BUT DON'T FORGET, YOU'VE ONLY GOT ONE HIT IN YOUR DISCOGRAPHY, LITTLE BOY. YOU COULD BE THE NEXT PRICK, RATHER THAN THE NEXT NINE INCH NAILS.
BUT... HE STARTED IT...
KNOCK IT OFF.
キラ
DON'T WASTE YOUR TIME WITH THESE IDIOTS.
LET'S GO, MA-KUN. KEN-CHAN.
TAKI!
Ma-kun, Ken-chan, TAKI...?!

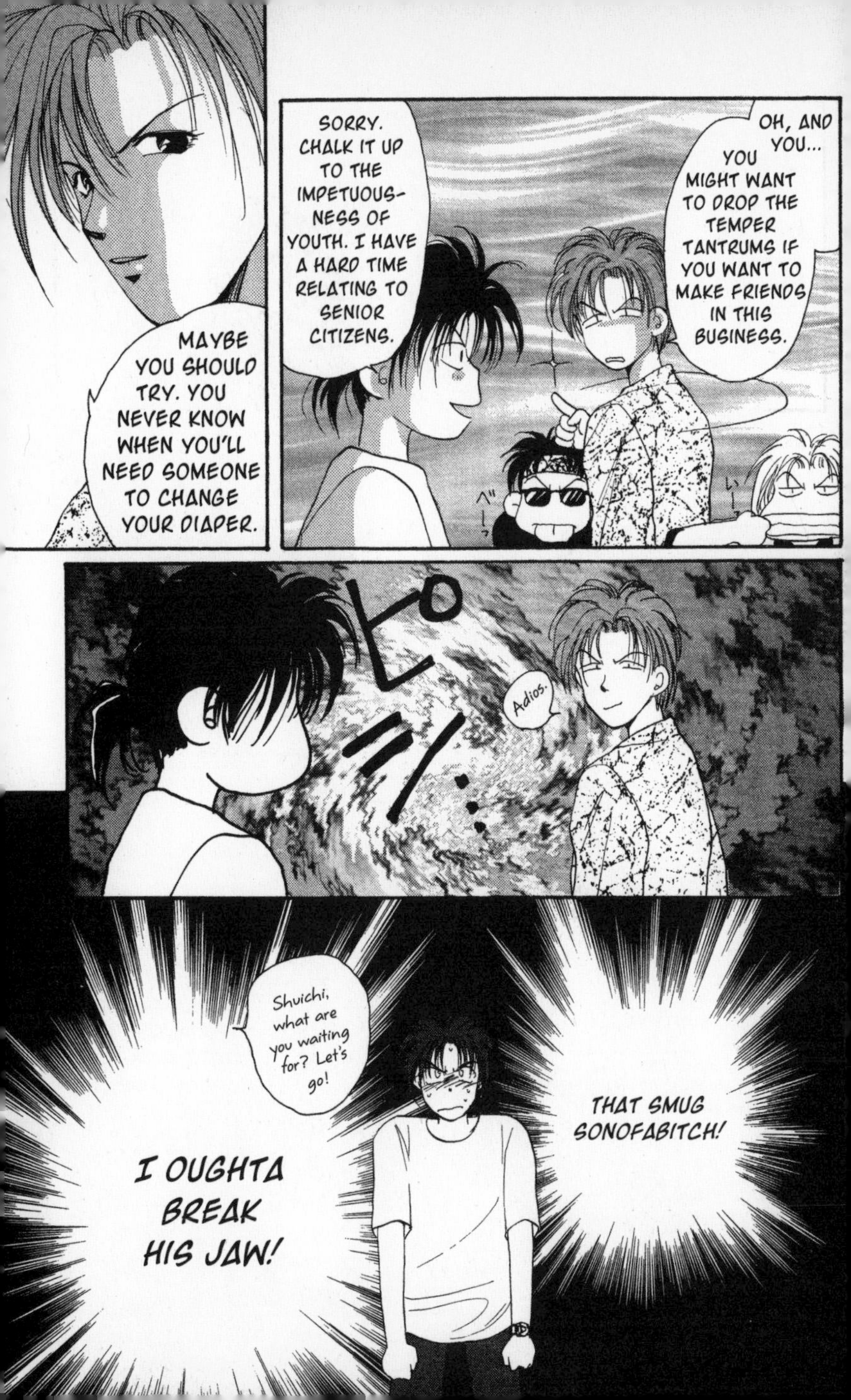
OH, AND YOU... YOU MIGHT WANT TO DROP THE TEMPER TANTRUMS IF YOU WANT TO MAKE FRIENDS IN THIS BUSINESS.
SORRY. CHALK IT UP TO THE IMPETUOUS-NESS OF YOUTH. I HAVE A HARD TIME RELATING TO SENIOR CITIZENS.
MAYBE YOU SHOULD TRY. YOU NEVER KNOW WHEN YOU'LL NEED SOMEONE TO CHANGE YOUR DIAPER.
Adios.
Shuichi, what are you waiting for? Let's go!
THAT SMUG SONOFABITCH!
I OUGHTA BREAK HIS JAW!

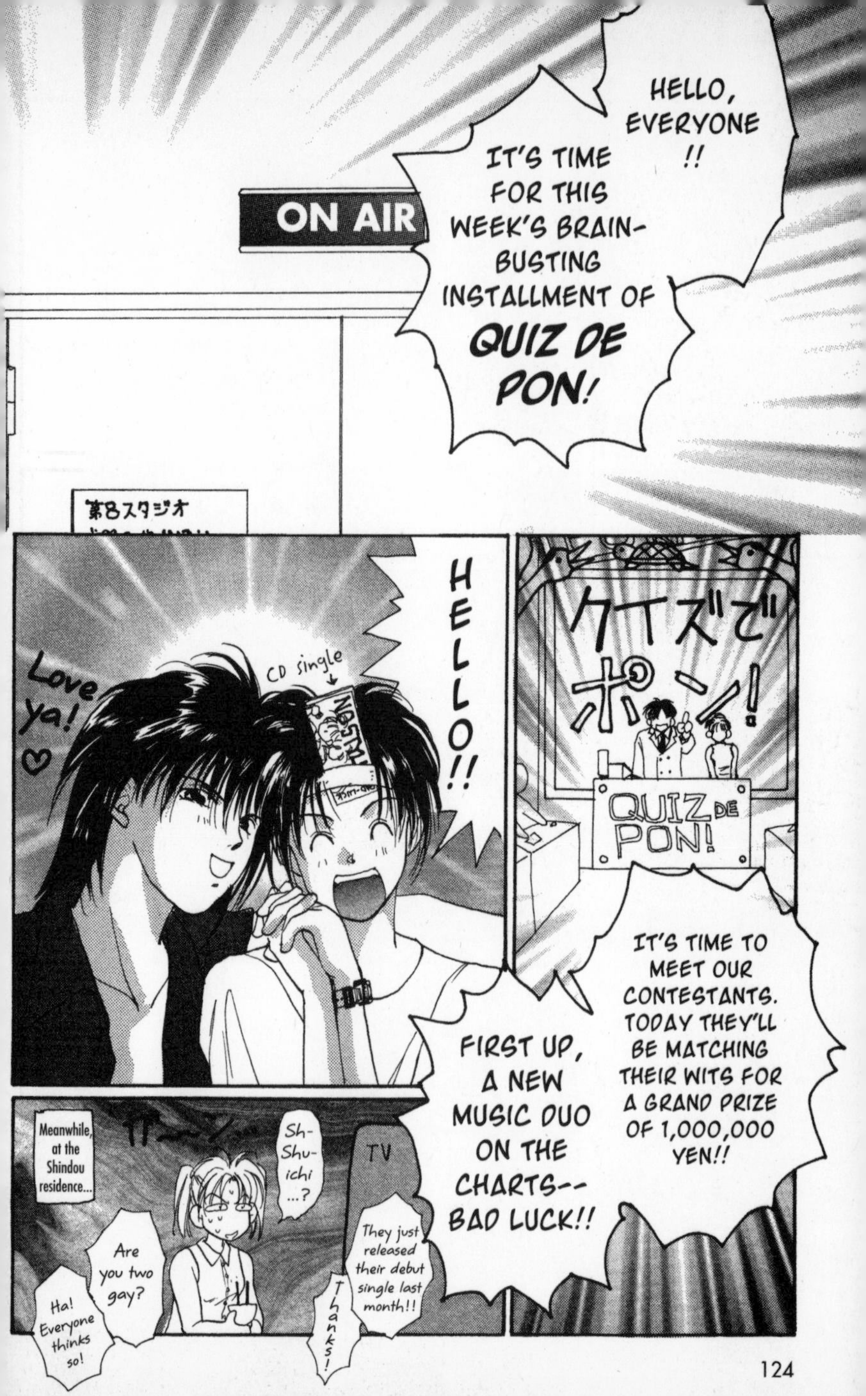
HELLO, EVERYONE!!
IT'S TIME FOR THIS WEEK'S BRAIN-BUSTING INSTALLMENT OF QUIZ DE PON!
ON AIR
第8スタジオ
クイズでポーン!
QUIZ DE PON!
IT'S TIME TO MEET OUR CONTESTANTS. TODAY THEY'LL BE MATCHING THEIR WITS FOR A GRAND PRIZE OF 1,000,000 YEN!!
HELLO!!
CD single
Love ya! ♡
FIRST UP, A NEW MUSIC DUO ON THE CHARTS--BAD LUCK!!
TV
They just released their debut single last month!!
Thanks!
Sh-Shu-ichi...?
Meanwhile, at the Shindou residence...
Are you two gay?
Ha! Everyone thinks so!

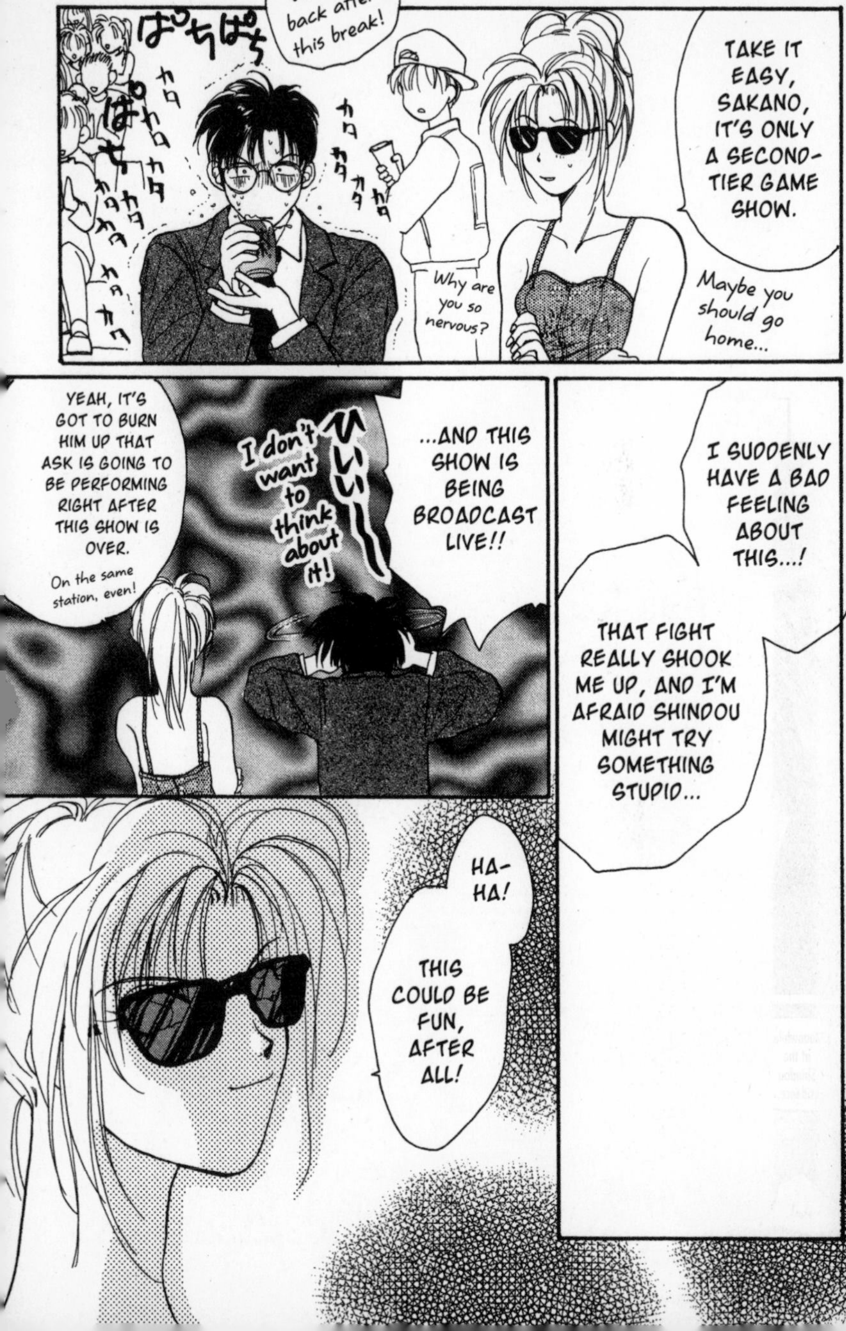
TAKE IT EASY, SAKANO, IT'S ONLY A SECOND-TIER GAME SHOW.
Maybe you should go home...
Why are you so nervous?
We'll be back after this break!
ぱちぱち
ぱち
カタカタ
I SUDDENLY HAVE A BAD FEELING ABOUT THIS...!
THAT FIGHT REALLY SHOOK ME UP, AND I'M AFRAID SHINDOU MIGHT TRY SOMETHING STUPID...
...AND THIS SHOW IS BEING BROADCAST LIVE!!
ひぃぃ——
I don't want to think about it!
YEAH, IT'S GOT TO BURN HIM UP THAT ASK IS GOING TO BE PERFORMING RIGHT AFTER THIS SHOW IS OVER.
On the same station, even!
HA-HA!
THIS COULD BE FUN, AFTER ALL!

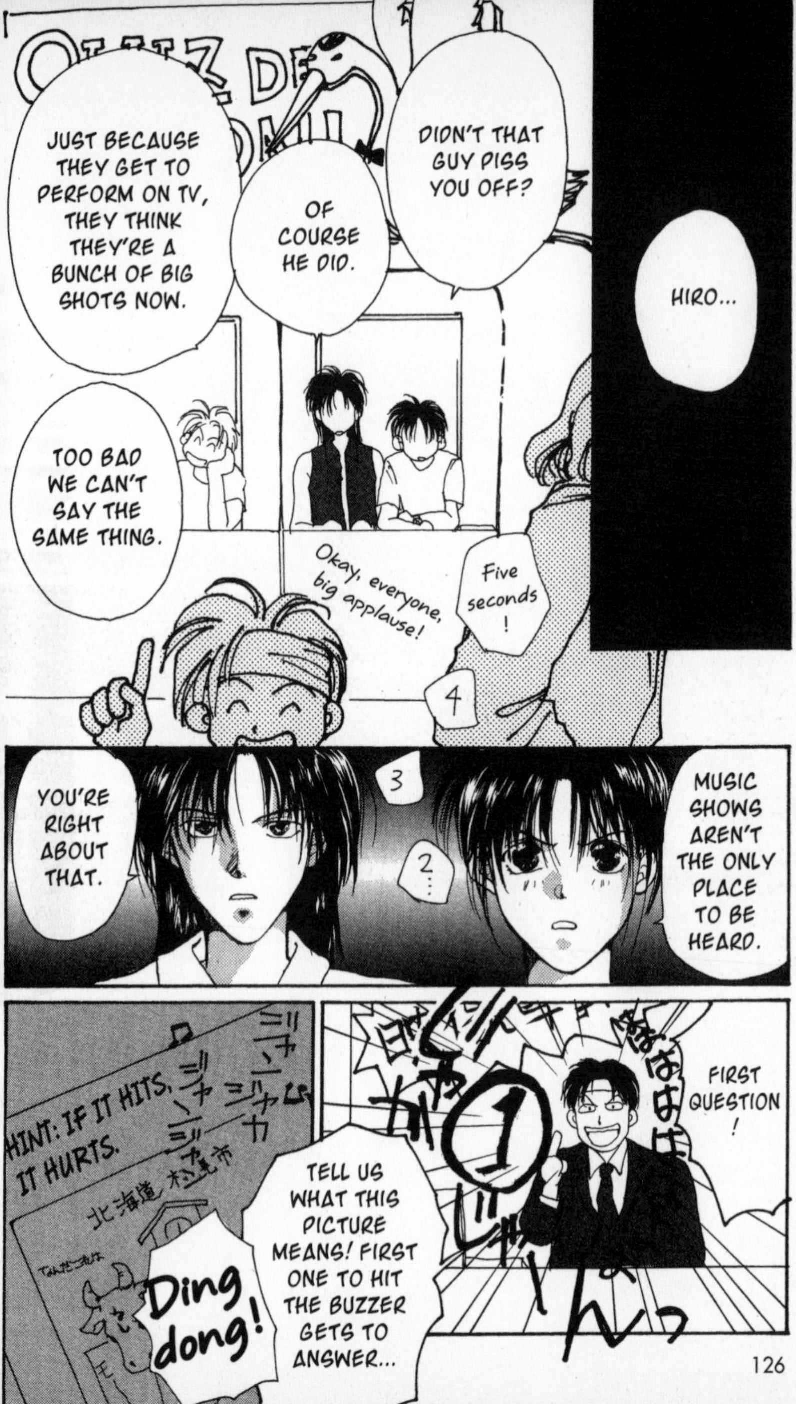
HIRO...
DIDN'T THAT GUY PISS YOU OFF?
OF COURSE HE DID.
JUST BECAUSE THEY GET TO PERFORM ON TV, THEY THINK THEY'RE A BUNCH OF BIG SHOTS NOW.
TOO BAD WE CAN'T SAY THE SAME THING.
Five seconds!
Okay, everyone, big applause!
4
MUSIC SHOWS AREN'T THE ONLY PLACE TO BE HEARD.
3
2...
YOU'RE RIGHT ABOUT THAT.
FIRST QUESTION!
TELL US WHAT THIS PICTURE MEANS! FIRST ONE TO HIT THE BUZZER GETS TO ANSWER...
HINT: IF IT HITS, IT HURTS.
北海道
Ding dong!

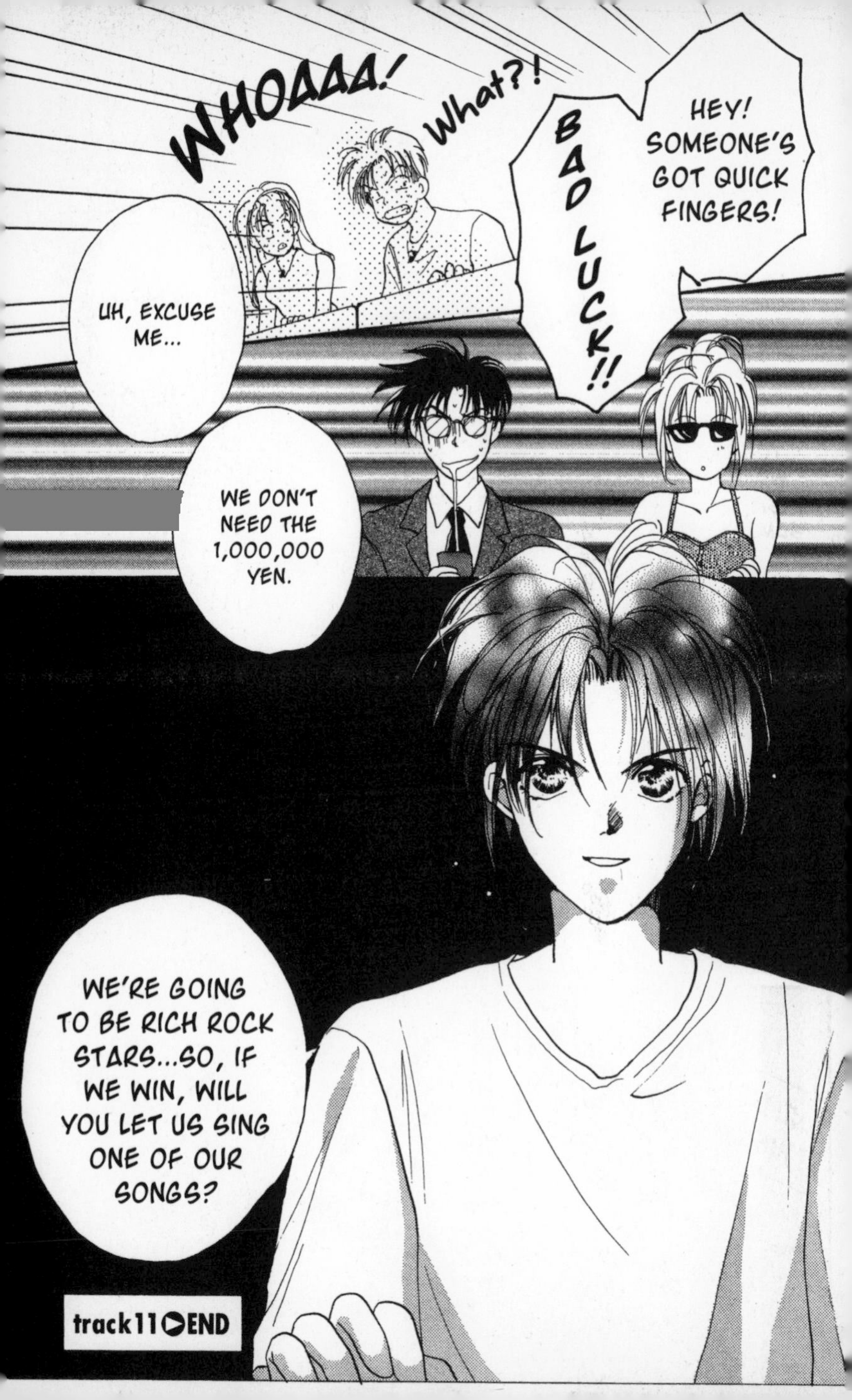
HEY! SOMEONE'S GOT QUICK FINGERS!
BAD LUCK!!
What?!
WHOAAA!
UH, EXCUSE ME...
WE DON'T NEED THE 1,000,000 YEN.
WE'RE GOING TO BE RICH ROCK STARS...SO, IF WE WIN, WILL YOU LET US SING ONE OF OUR SONGS?
track11 ▶END

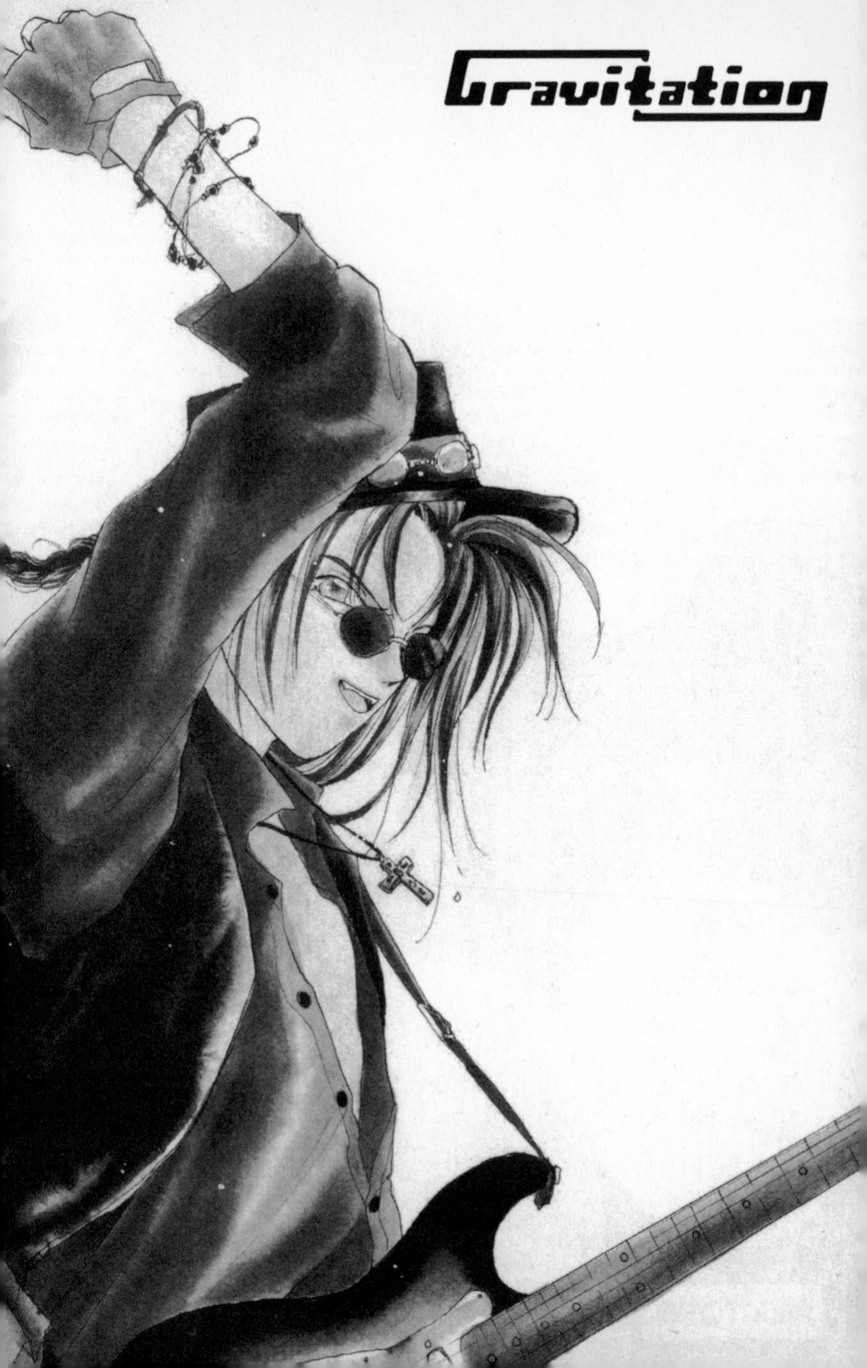
Gravitation

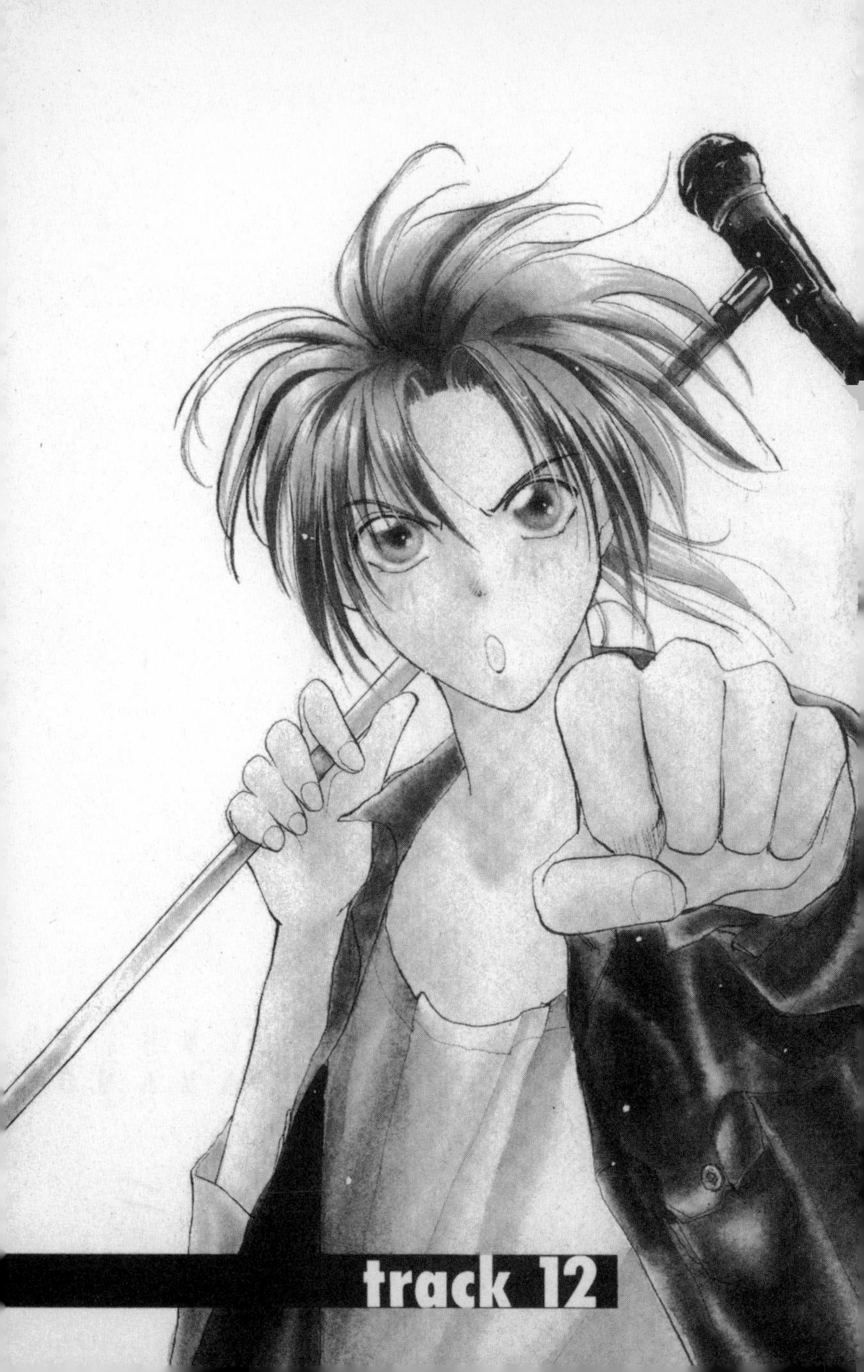

track 12

HIROSHI
NAKANO

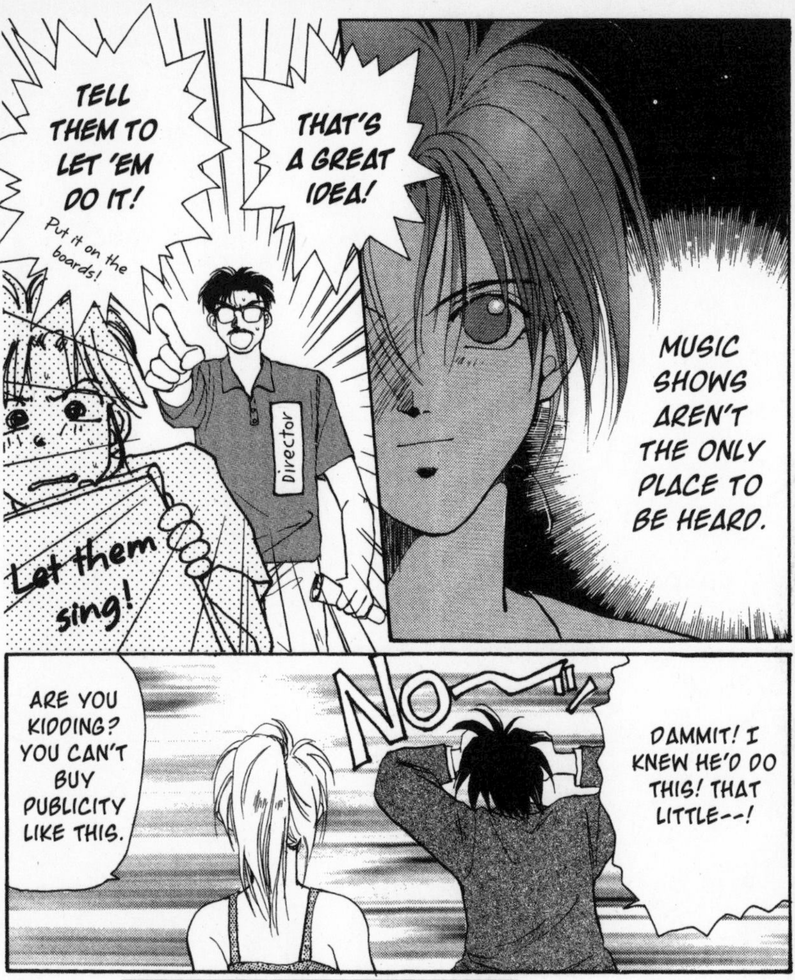
MUSIC SHOWS AREN'T THE ONLY PLACE TO BE HEARD.
THAT'S A GREAT IDEA!
TELL THEM TO LET 'EM DO IT!
Put it on the boards!
Director
Let them sing!
DAMMIT! I KNEW HE'D DO THIS! THAT LITTLE--!
No—!
ARE YOU KIDDING? YOU CAN'T BUY PUBLICITY LIKE THIS.

ABOUT GRAVITATION TRACK 12

Quiz de Pon...

Not exactly an inspiring name for a game show... But I guess I like the Japanese phrase, "de Pon!" I have a habit of sticking "de Pon!" at the end of my sentences. Sounds a little fishy, but it's actually rather simple. I like the way things sound when you add "de Pon" at the end. Track 12 is a pretty comedic episode—one of those "oh, come on now" kind of stories. Stop me before it turns into one of those gag mangas. Sorry.

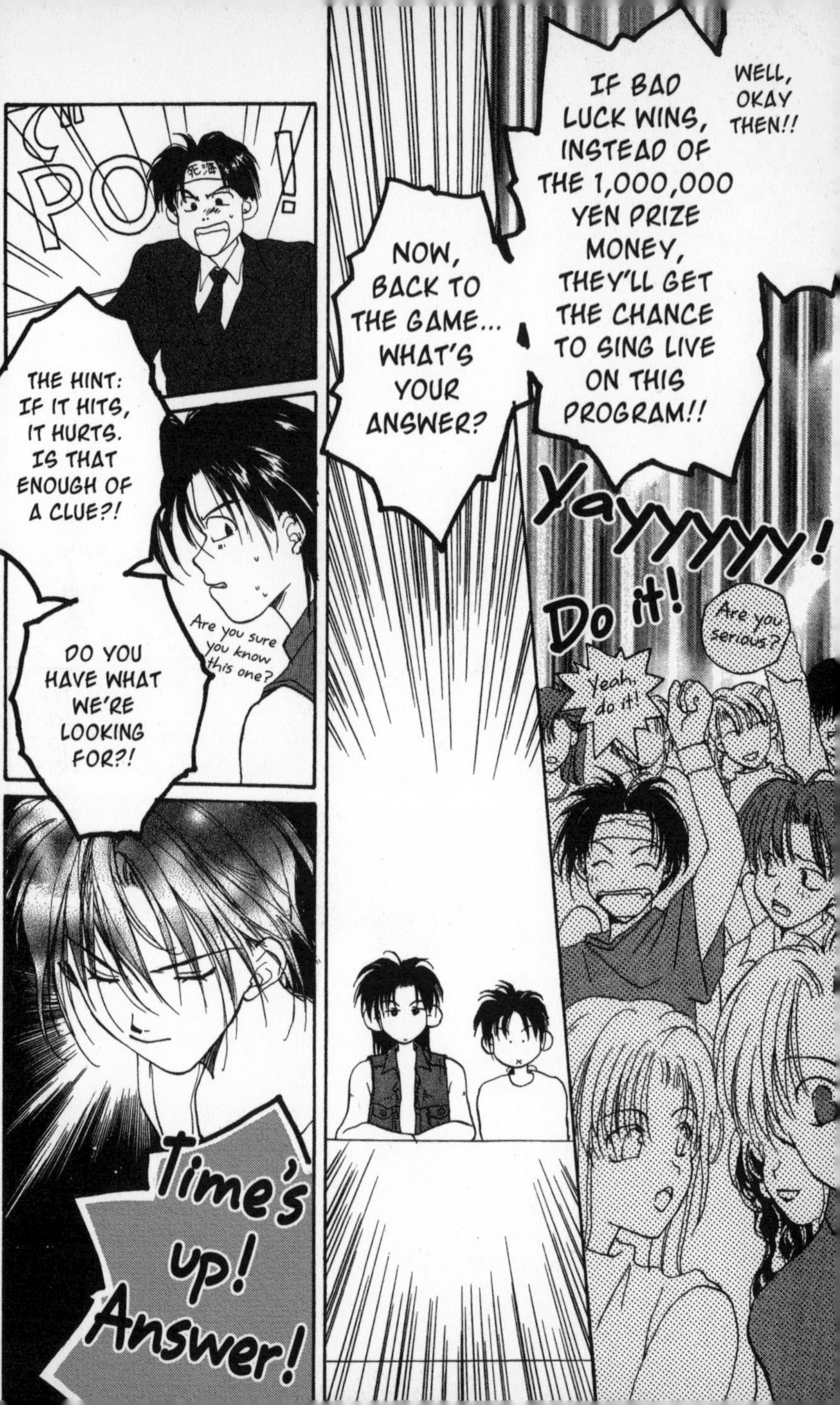
WELL, OKAY THEN!!
IF BAD LUCK WINS, INSTEAD OF THE 1,000,000 YEN PRIZE MONEY, THEY'LL GET THE CHANCE TO SING LIVE ON THIS PROGRAM!!
Yayyyyy!
Do it!
Are you serious?
Yeah, do it!
NOW, BACK TO THE GAME... WHAT'S YOUR ANSWER?
PO!
THE HINT: IF IT HITS, IT HURTS. IS THAT ENOUGH OF A CLUE?!
Are you sure you know this one?
DO YOU HAVE WHAT WE'RE LOOKING FOR?!
Time's up! Answer!

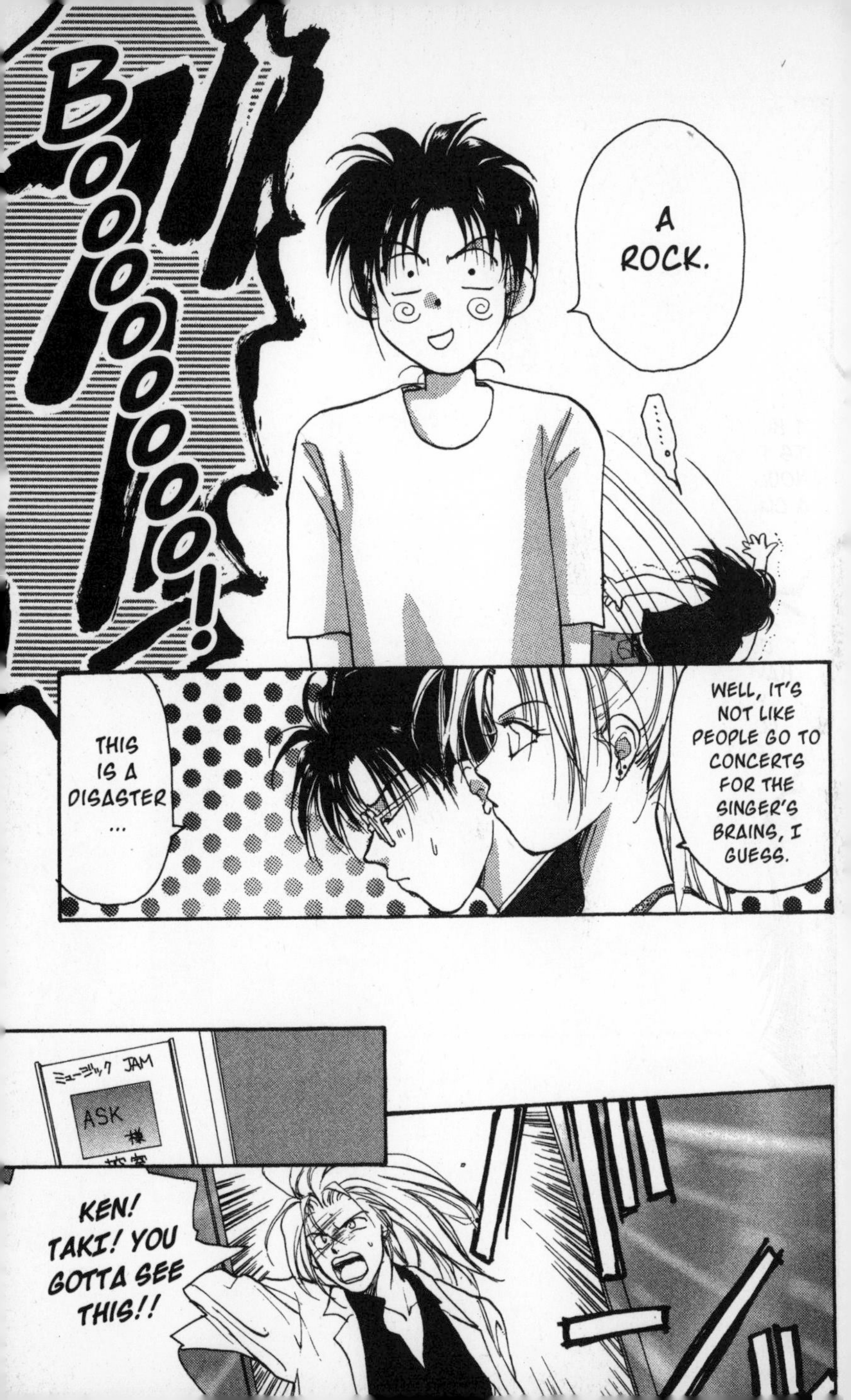
A ROCK.
...!
BOOOOOOOOOO!
WELL, IT'S NOT LIKE PEOPLE GO TO CONCERTS FOR THE SINGER'S BRAINS, I GUESS.
THIS IS A DISASTER ...
ミュージック JAM
ASK 様
KEN! TAKI! YOU GOTTA SEE THIS!!

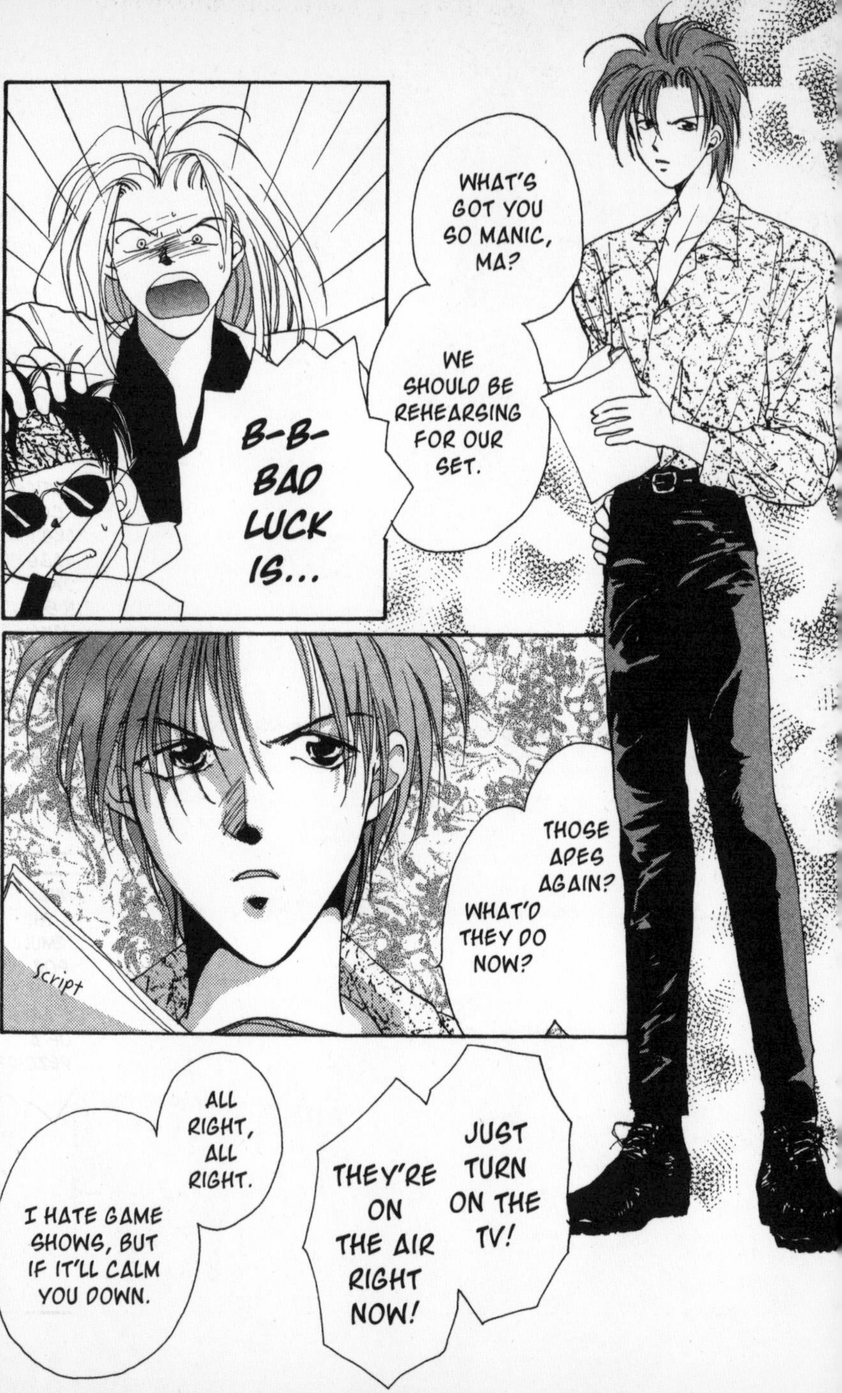
WHAT'S GOT YOU SO MANIC, MA?
WE SHOULD BE REHEARSING FOR OUR SET.
B-B-BAD LUCK IS...
THOSE APES AGAIN?
WHAT'D THEY DO NOW?
Script
JUST TURN ON THE TV!
THEY'RE ON THE AIR RIGHT NOW!
ALL RIGHT, ALL RIGHT.
I HATE GAME SHOWS, BUT IF IT'LL CALM YOU DOWN.

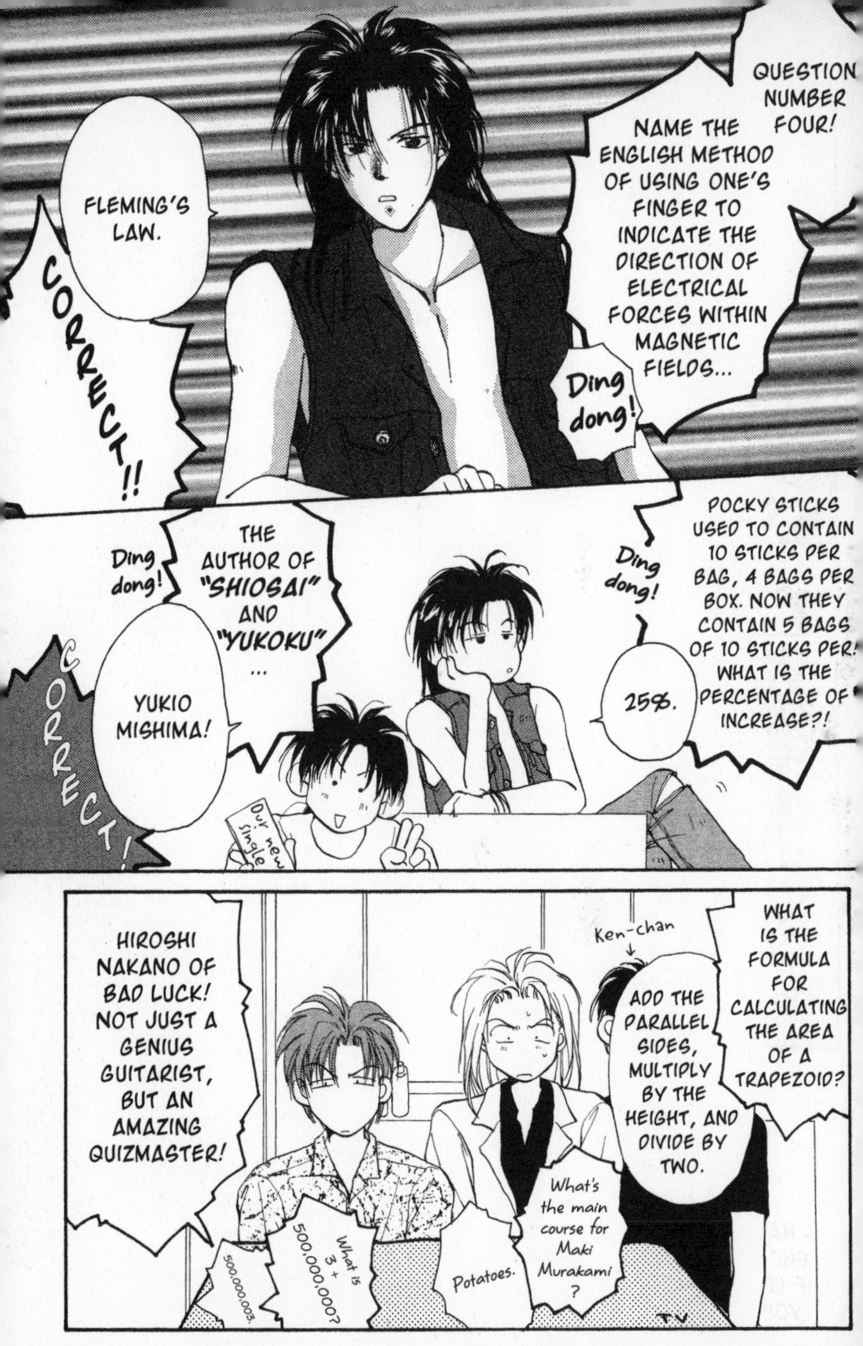
QUESTION NUMBER FOUR!
NAME THE ENGLISH METHOD OF USING ONE'S FINGER TO INDICATE THE DIRECTION OF ELECTRICAL FORCES WITHIN MAGNETIC FIELDS...
Ding dong!
FLEMING'S LAW.
CORRECT!!
POCKY STICKS USED TO CONTAIN 10 STICKS PER BAG, 4 BAGS PER BOX. NOW THEY CONTAIN 5 BAGS OF 10 STICKS PER! WHAT IS THE PERCENTAGE OF INCREASE?!
Ding dong!
25%.
THE AUTHOR OF "SHIOSAI" AND "YUKOKU" ...
Ding dong!
YUKIO MISHIMA!
CORRECT!
Our new single
WHAT IS THE FORMULA FOR CALCULATING THE AREA OF A TRAPEZOID?
Ken-chan
ADD THE PARALLEL SIDES, MULTIPLY BY THE HEIGHT, AND DIVIDE BY TWO.
HIROSHI NAKANO OF BAD LUCK! NOT JUST A GENIUS GUITARIST, BUT AN AMAZING QUIZMASTER!
What's the main course for Maki Murakami?
Potatoes.
What is 3 + 500,000,000?
500,000,003.

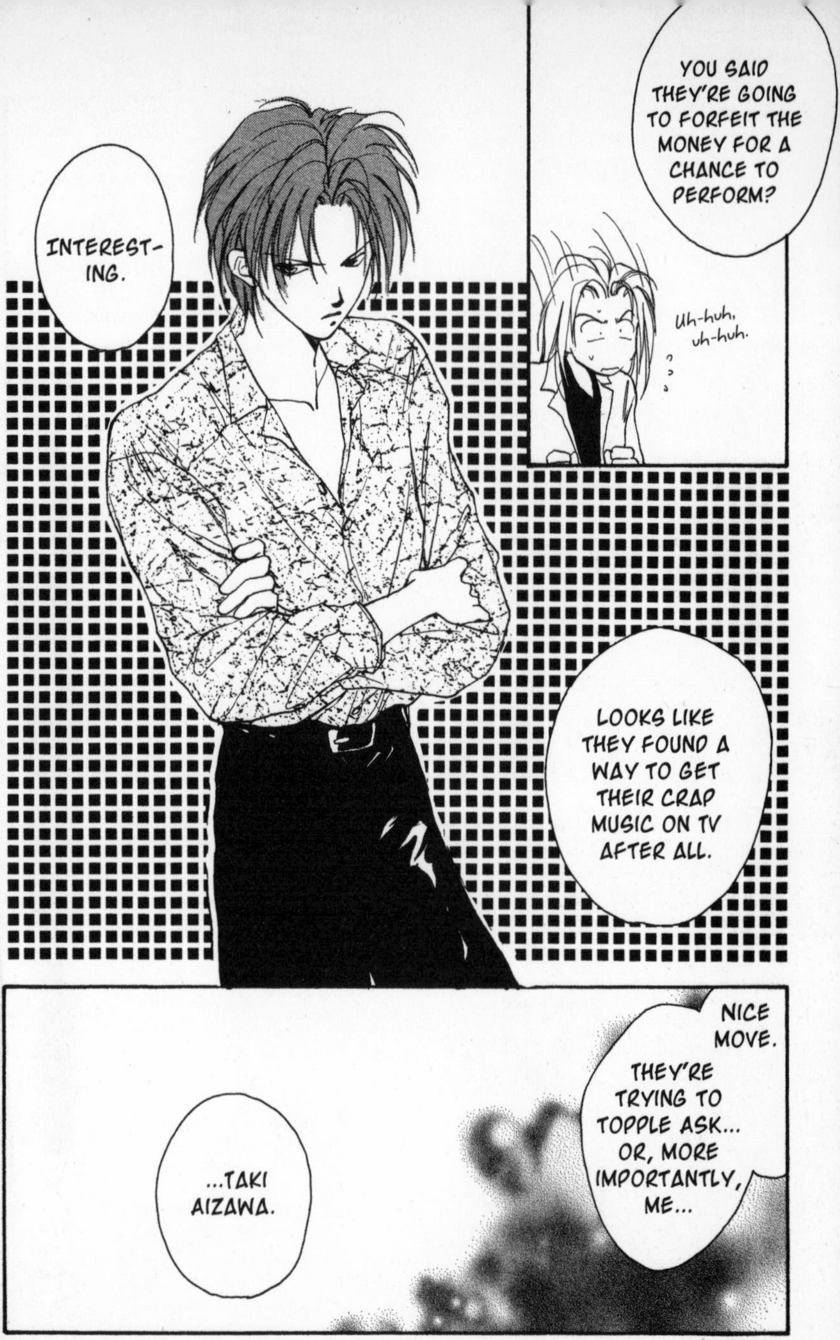
YOU SAID THEY'RE GOING TO FORFEIT THE MONEY FOR A CHANCE TO PERFORM?
Uh-huh, uh-huh.
INTEREST-ING.
LOOKS LIKE THEY FOUND A WAY TO GET THEIR CRAP MUSIC ON TV AFTER ALL.
NICE MOVE.
THEY'RE TRYING TO TOPPLE ASK... OR, MORE IMPORTANTLY, ME...
...TAKI AIZAWA.

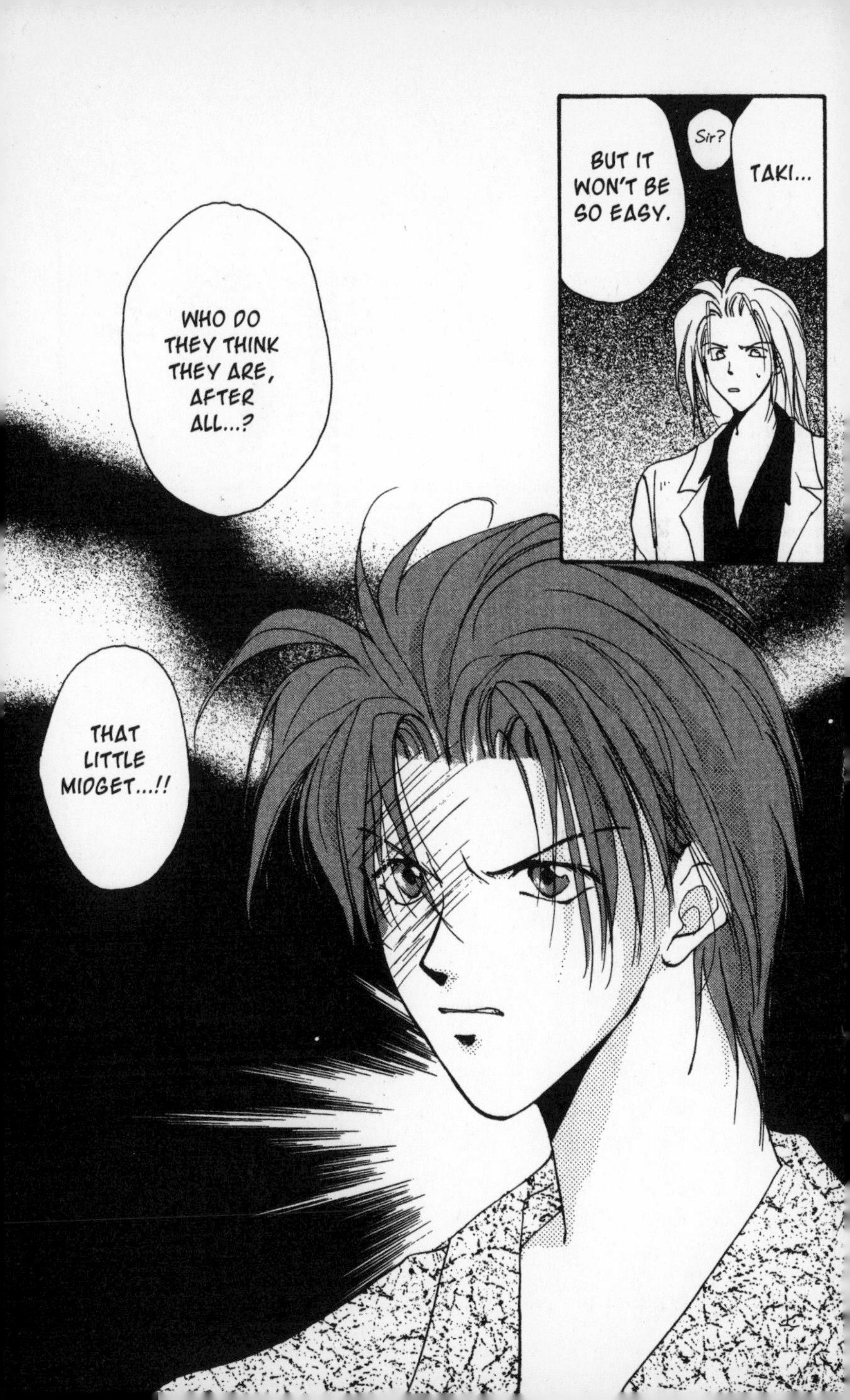
TAKI...
Sir?
BUT IT WON'T BE SO EASY.
WHO DO THEY THINK THEY ARE, AFTER ALL...?
THAT LITTLE MIDGET...!!

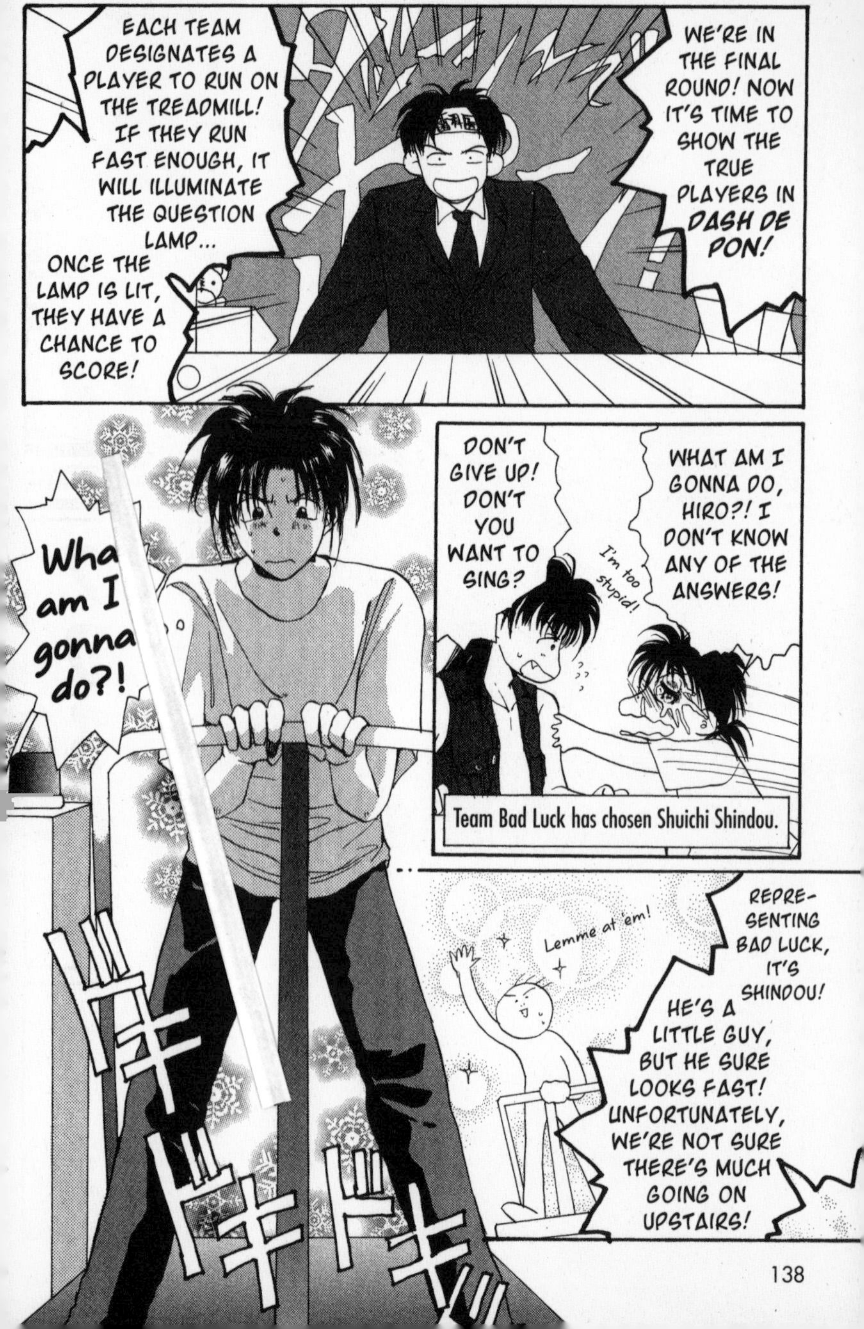
WE'RE IN THE FINAL ROUND! NOW IT'S TIME TO SHOW THE TRUE PLAYERS IN DASH DE PON!
EACH TEAM DESIGNATES A PLAYER TO RUN ON THE TREADMILL! IF THEY RUN FAST ENOUGH, IT WILL ILLUMINATE THE QUESTION LAMP...
ONCE THE LAMP IS LIT, THEY HAVE A CHANCE TO SCORE!
WHAT AM I GONNA DO, HIRO?! I DON'T KNOW ANY OF THE ANSWERS!
I'm too stupid!
DON'T GIVE UP! DON'T YOU WANT TO SING?
Team Bad Luck has chosen Shuichi Shindou.
REPRESENTING BAD LUCK, IT'S SHINDOU!
HE'S A LITTLE GUY, BUT HE SURE LOOKS FAST! UNFORTUNATELY, WE'RE NOT SURE THERE'S MUCH GOING ON UPSTAIRS!
Lemme at 'em!
What am I gonna do?!
ドキドキドキ

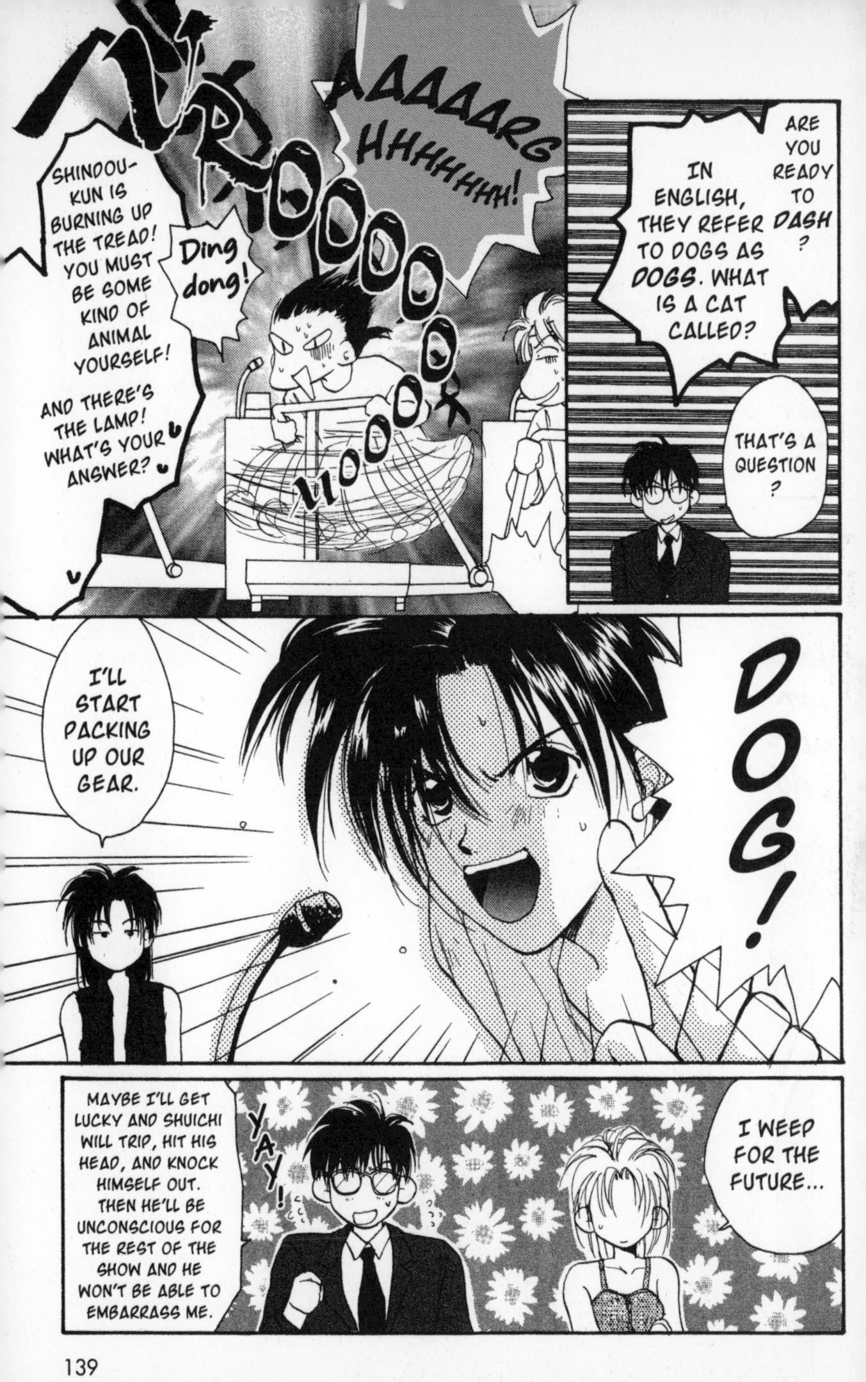
ARE YOU READY TO DASH?
IN ENGLISH, THEY REFER TO DOGS AS DOGS. WHAT IS A CAT CALLED?
THAT'S A QUESTION?
AAAAARGHHHHHH!
Ding dong!
SHINDOU-KUN IS BURNING UP THE TREAD! YOU MUST BE SOME KIND OF ANIMAL YOURSELF!
AND THERE'S THE LAMP! WHAT'S YOUR ANSWER?
DOG!
I'LL START PACKING UP OUR GEAR.
I WEEP FOR THE FUTURE...
YAY!
MAYBE I'LL GET LUCKY AND SHUICHI WILL TRIP, HIT HIS HEAD, AND KNOCK HIMSELF OUT. THEN HE'LL BE UNCONSCIOUS FOR THE REST OF THE SHOW AND HE WON'T BE ABLE TO EMBARRASS ME.

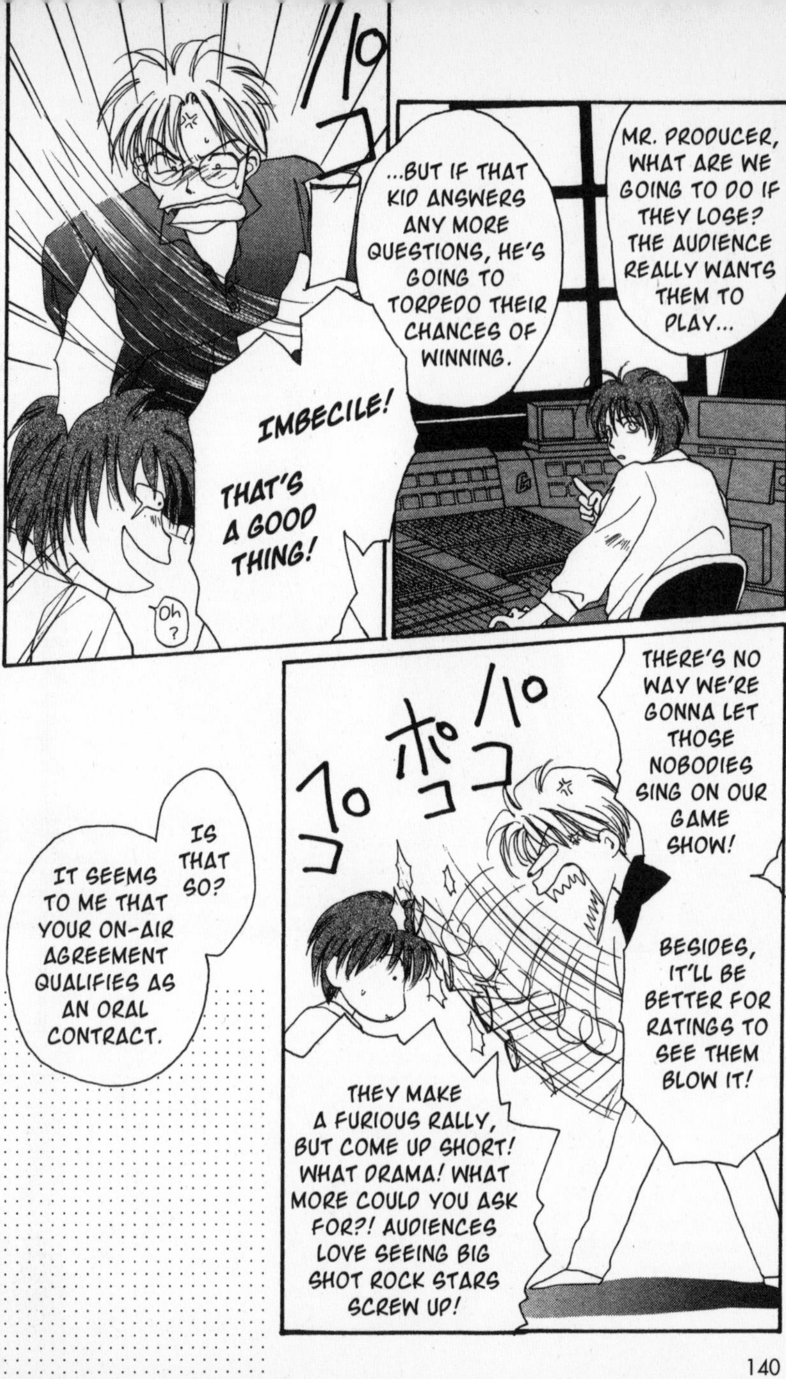
MR. PRODUCER, WHAT ARE WE GOING TO DO IF THEY LOSE? THE AUDIENCE REALLY WANTS THEM TO PLAY...
...BUT IF THAT KID ANSWERS ANY MORE QUESTIONS, HE'S GOING TO TORPEDO THEIR CHANCES OF WINNING.
IMBECILE!
THAT'S A GOOD THING!
Oh ?
THERE'S NO WAY WE'RE GONNA LET THOSE NOBODIES SING ON OUR GAME SHOW!
BESIDES, IT'LL BE BETTER FOR RATINGS TO SEE THEM BLOW IT!
THEY MAKE A FURIOUS RALLY, BUT COME UP SHORT! WHAT DRAMA! WHAT MORE COULD YOU ASK FOR?! AUDIENCES LOVE SEEING BIG SHOT ROCK STARS SCREW UP!
IS THAT SO?
IT SEEMS TO ME THAT YOUR ON-AIR AGREEMENT QUALIFIES AS AN ORAL CONTRACT.

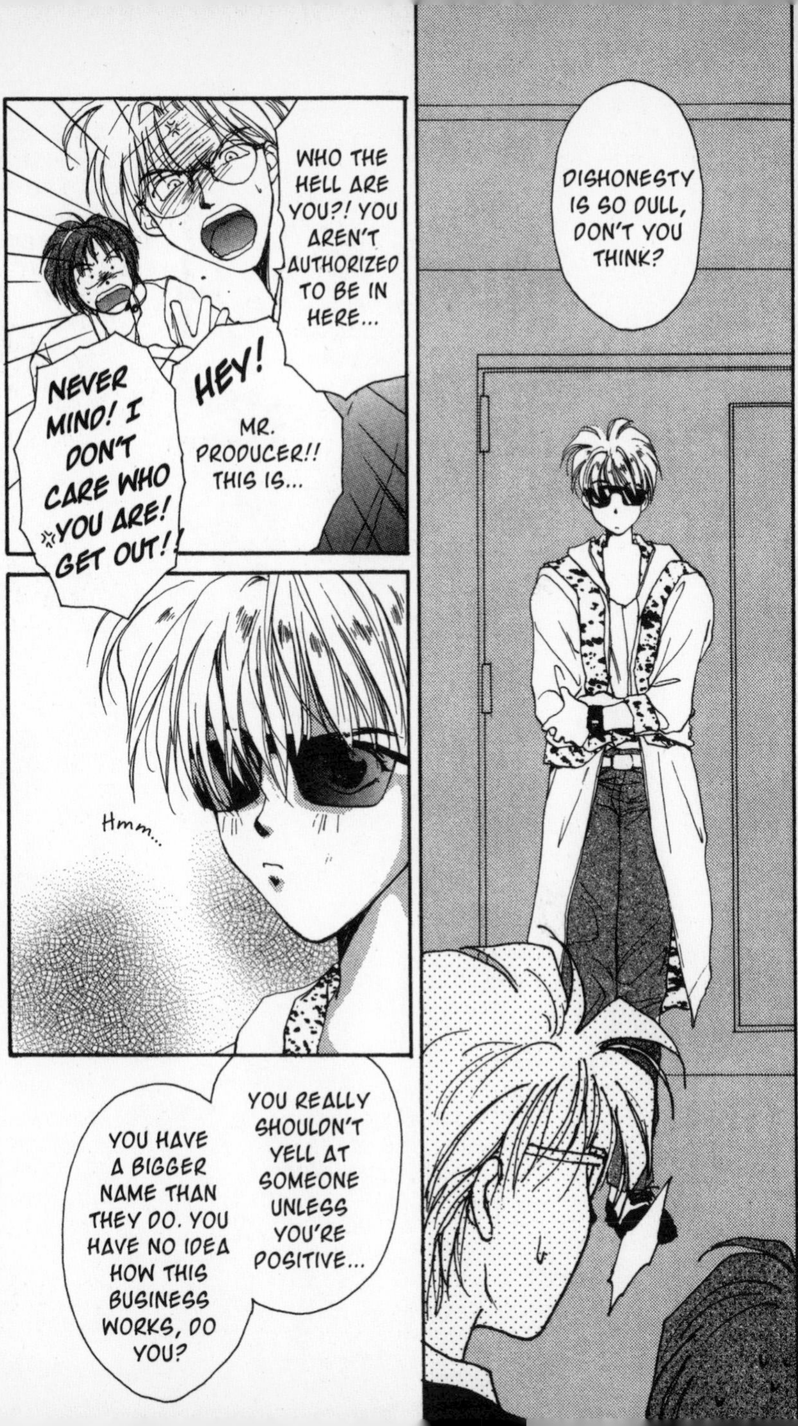
DISHONESTY IS SO DULL, DON'T YOU THINK?
WHO THE HELL ARE YOU?! YOU AREN'T AUTHORIZED TO BE IN HERE...
HEY!
MR. PRODUCER!! THIS IS...
NEVER MIND! I DON'T CARE WHO YOU ARE! GET OUT!!
Hmm...
YOU REALLY SHOULDN'T YELL AT SOMEONE UNLESS YOU'RE POSITIVE...
YOU HAVE A BIGGER NAME THAN THEY DO. YOU HAVE NO IDEA HOW THIS BUSINESS WORKS, DO YOU?

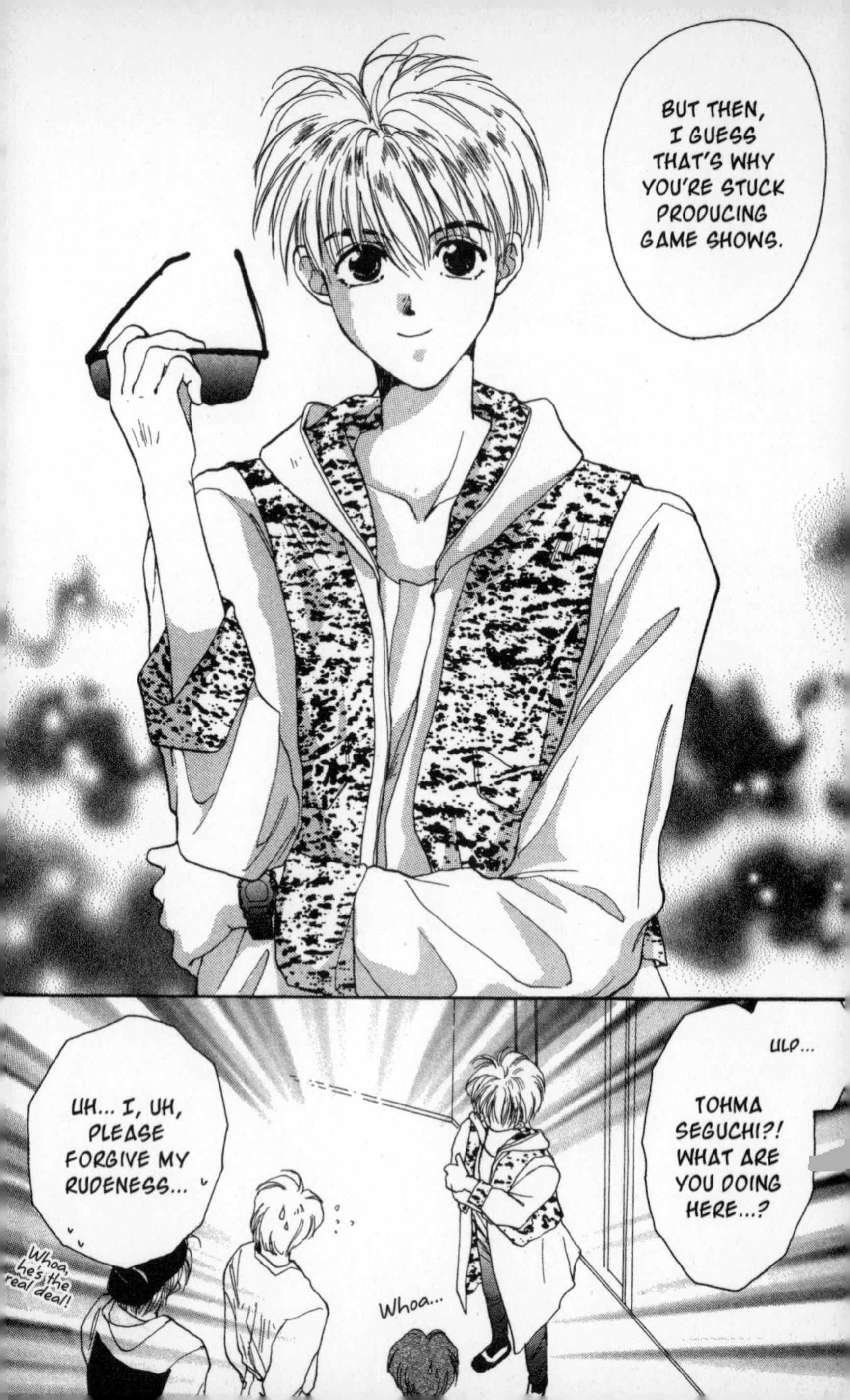
BUT THEN, I GUESS THAT'S WHY YOU'RE STUCK PRODUCING GAME SHOWS.
ULP...
TOHMA SEGUCHI?! WHAT ARE YOU DOING HERE...?
UH... I, UH, PLEASE FORGIVE MY RUDENESS...
Whoa, he's the real deal!
Whoa...

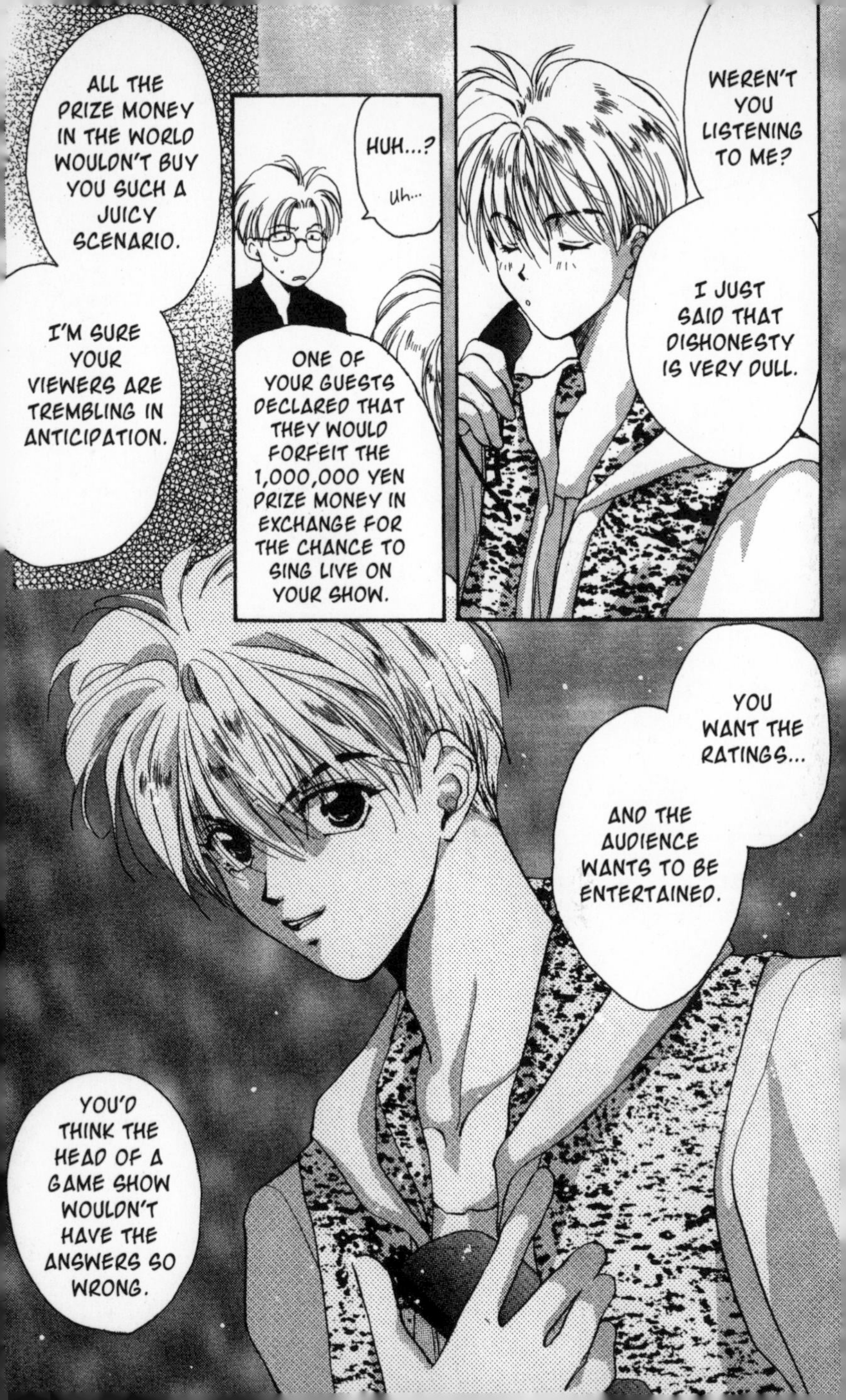
WEREN'T YOU LISTENING TO ME?
I JUST SAID THAT DISHONESTY IS VERY DULL.
HUH...?
Uh...
ONE OF YOUR GUESTS DECLARED THAT THEY WOULD FORFEIT THE 1,000,000 YEN PRIZE MONEY IN EXCHANGE FOR THE CHANCE TO SING LIVE ON YOUR SHOW.
ALL THE PRIZE MONEY IN THE WORLD WOULDN'T BUY YOU SUCH A JUICY SCENARIO.
I'M SURE YOUR VIEWERS ARE TREMBLING IN ANTICIPATION.
YOU WANT THE RATINGS...
AND THE AUDIENCE WANTS TO BE ENTERTAINED.
YOU'D THINK THE HEAD OF A GAME SHOW WOULDN'T HAVE THE ANSWERS SO WRONG.

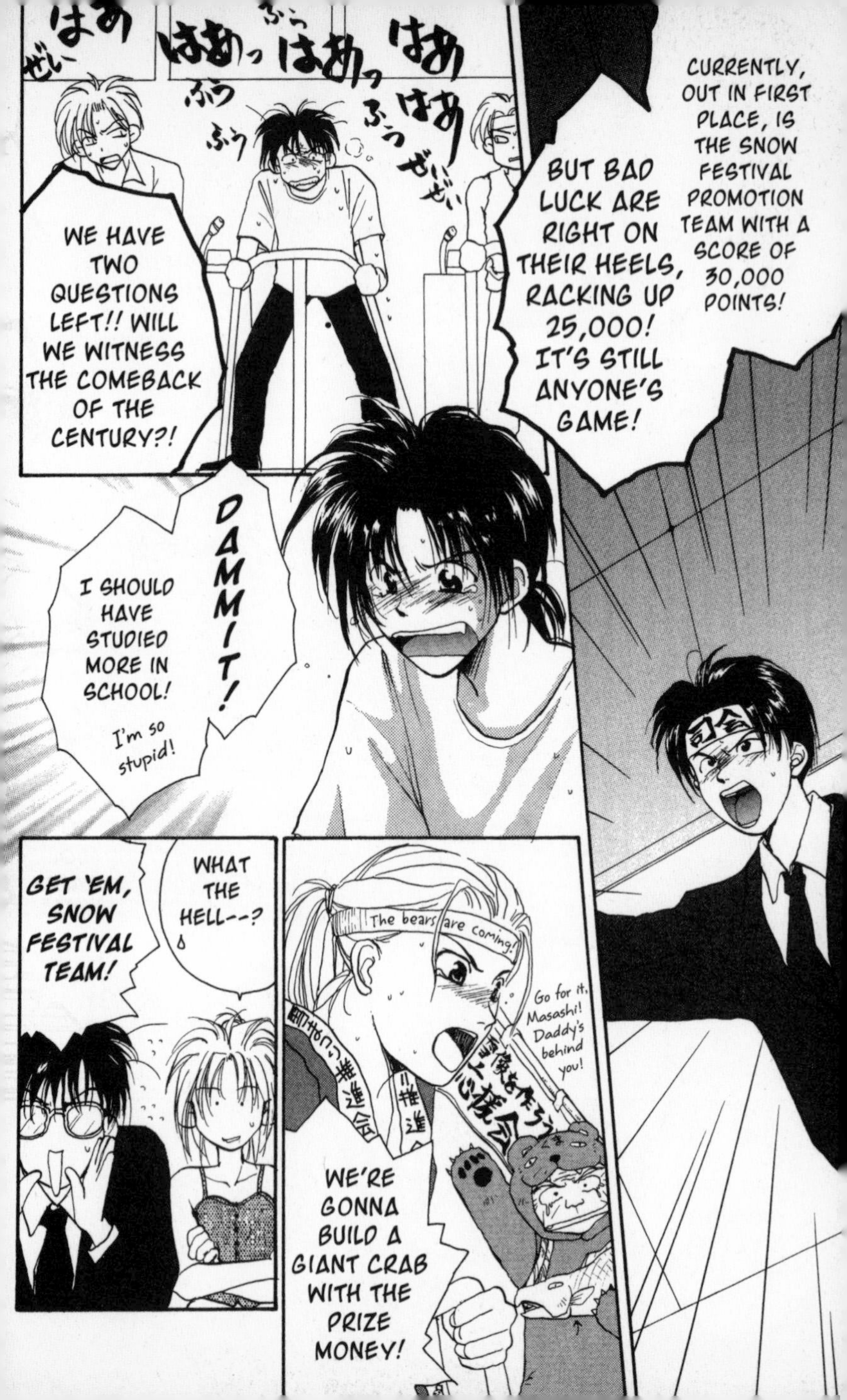
CURRENTLY, OUT IN FIRST PLACE, IS THE SNOW FESTIVAL PROMOTION TEAM WITH A SCORE OF 30,000 POINTS!
BUT BAD LUCK ARE RIGHT ON THEIR HEELS, RACKING UP 25,000! IT'S STILL ANYONE'S GAME!
はあ
ぜい
はあっ はあっ はあ
ふぅ
ふぅ
はあ
ふぅ
ぜいぜい
WE HAVE TWO QUESTIONS LEFT!! WILL WE WITNESS THE COMEBACK OF THE CENTURY?!
DAMMIT!
I SHOULD HAVE STUDIED MORE IN SCHOOL!
I'm so stupid!
The bears are coming!
Go for it, Masashi! Daddy's behind you!
WE'RE GONNA BUILD A GIANT CRAB WITH THE PRIZE MONEY!
GET 'EM, SNOW FESTIVAL TEAM!
WHAT THE HELL--?

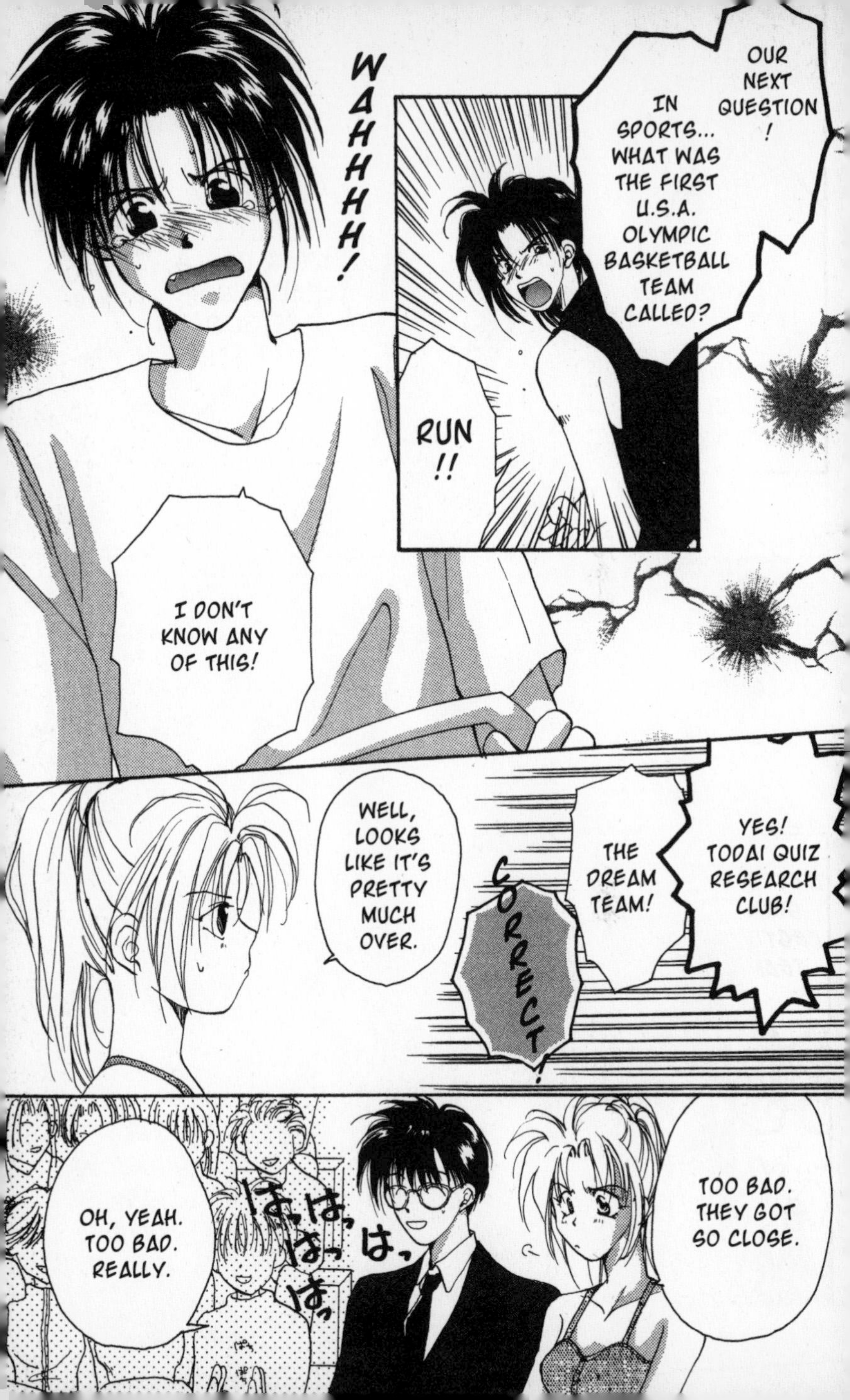
OUR NEXT QUESTION!
IN SPORTS... WHAT WAS THE FIRST U.S.A. OLYMPIC BASKETBALL TEAM CALLED?
RUN!!
WAHHHHHH!
I DON'T KNOW ANY OF THIS!
YES! TODAI QUIZ RESEARCH CLUB!
THE DREAM TEAM!
CORRECT!
WELL, LOOKS LIKE IT'S PRETTY MUCH OVER.
TOO BAD. THEY GOT SO CLOSE.
はっはっはっはっ
OH, YEAH. TOO BAD. REALLY.

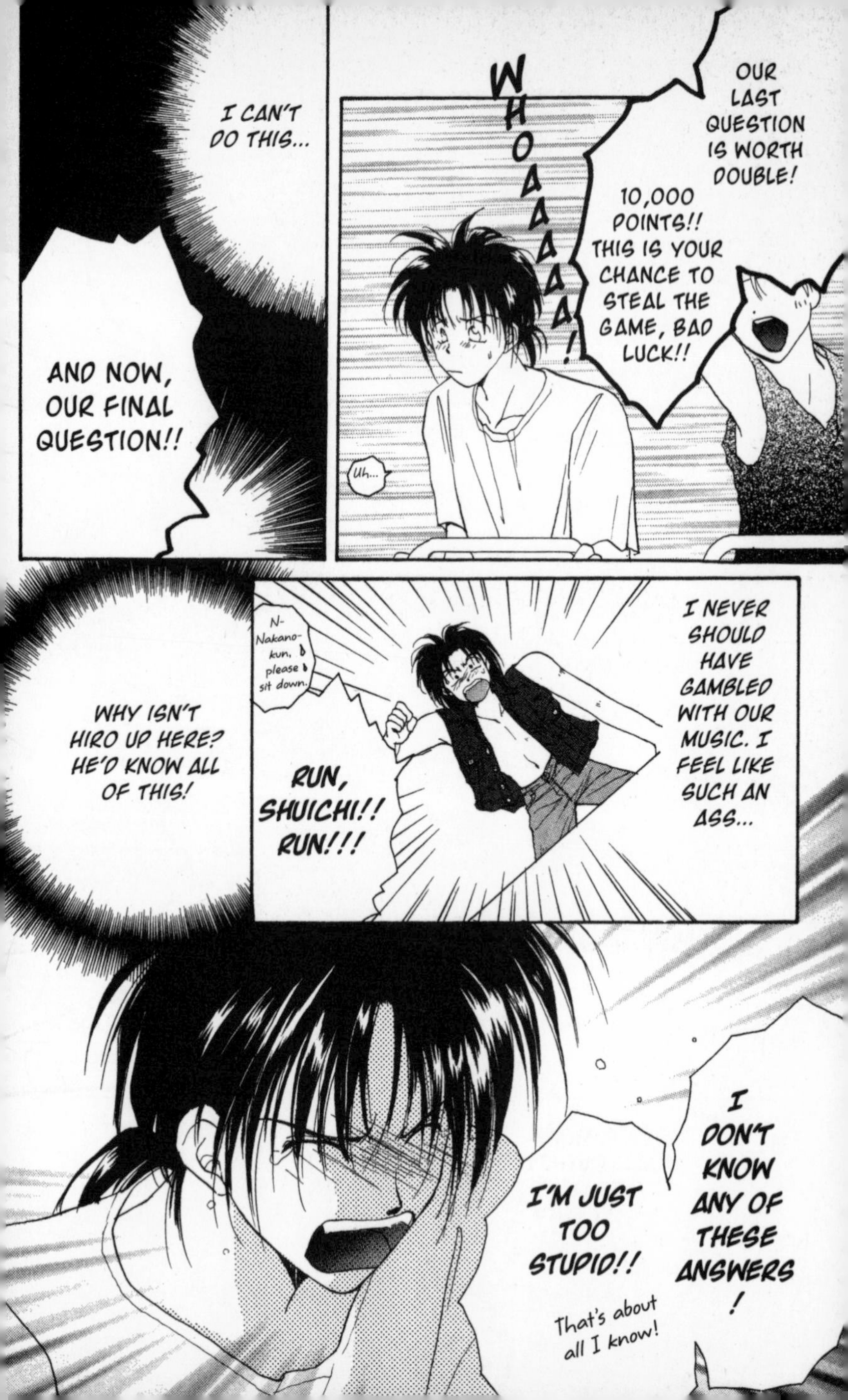
OUR LAST QUESTION IS WORTH DOUBLE!
10,000 POINTS!! THIS IS YOUR CHANCE TO STEAL THE GAME, BAD LUCK!!
WHOAAAAAAA!
Uh...
I CAN'T DO THIS...
AND NOW, OUR FINAL QUESTION!!
I NEVER SHOULD HAVE GAMBLED WITH OUR MUSIC. I FEEL LIKE SUCH AN ASS...
N-Nakano-kun, please sit down.
RUN, SHUICHI!! RUN!!!
WHY ISN'T HIRO UP HERE? HE'D KNOW ALL OF THIS!
I DON'T KNOW ANY OF THESE ANSWERS!
I'M JUST TOO STUPID!!
That's about all I know!

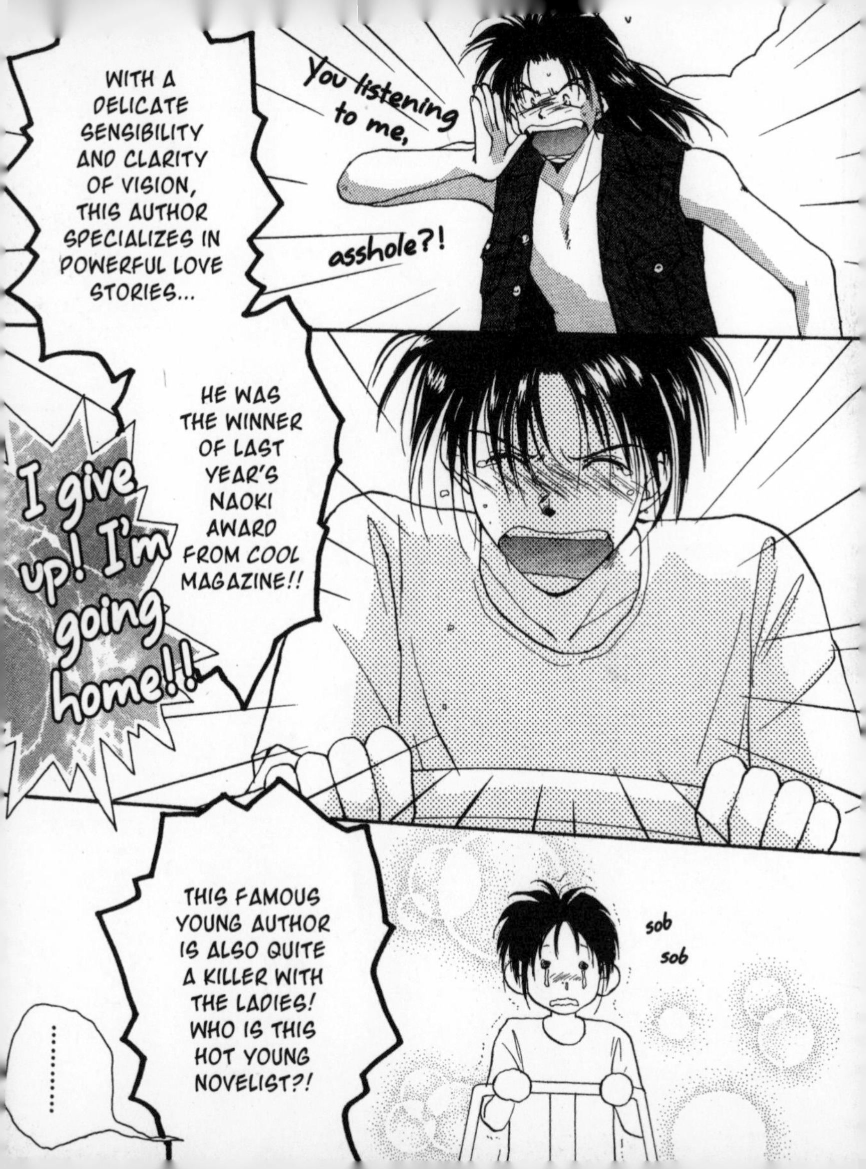
You listening to me, asshole?!
WITH A DELICATE SENSIBILITY AND CLARITY OF VISION, THIS AUTHOR SPECIALIZES IN POWERFUL LOVE STORIES...
HE WAS THE WINNER OF LAST YEAR'S NAOKI AWARD FROM COOL MAGAZINE!!
I give up! I'm going home!!
sob sob
THIS FAMOUS YOUNG AUTHOR IS ALSO QUITE A KILLER WITH THE LADIES! WHO IS THIS HOT YOUNG NOVELIST?!
....

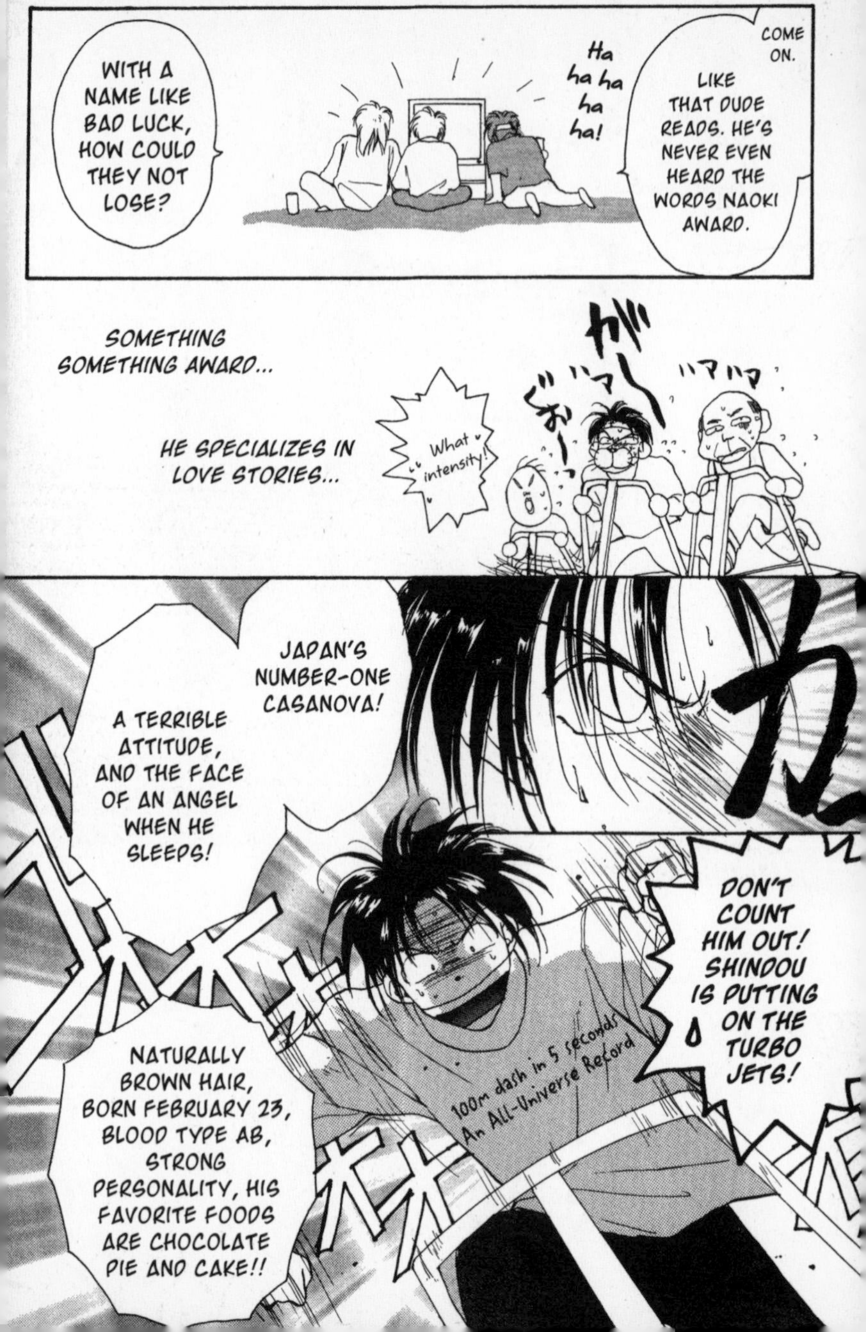
COME ON.
LIKE THAT DUDE READS. HE'S NEVER EVEN HEARD THE WORDS NAOKI AWARD.
Ha ha ha ha ha!
WITH A NAME LIKE BAD LUCK, HOW COULD THEY NOT LOSE?
What intensity!
HE SPECIALIZES IN LOVE STORIES...
SOMETHING SOMETHING AWARD...
JAPAN'S NUMBER-ONE CASANOVA!
A TERRIBLE ATTITUDE, AND THE FACE OF AN ANGEL WHEN HE SLEEPS!
DON'T COUNT HIM OUT! SHINDOU IS PUTTING ON THE TURBO JETS!
100m dash in 5 seconds An All-Universe Record
NATURALLY BROWN HAIR, BORN FEBRUARY 23, BLOOD TYPE AB, STRONG PERSONALITY, HIS FAVORITE FOODS ARE CHOCOLATE PIE AND CAKE!!

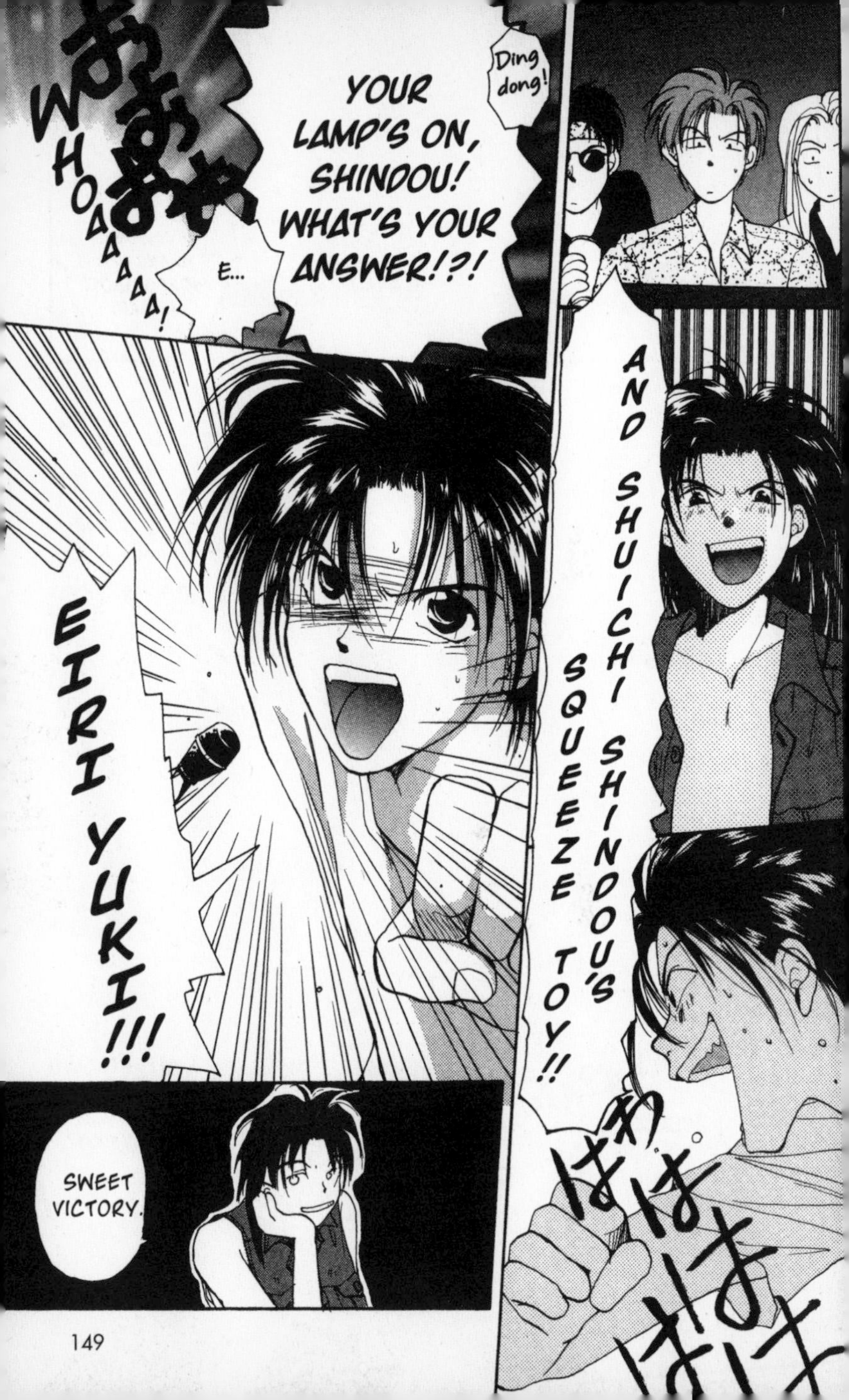
Ding dong!
YOUR LAMP'S ON, SHINDOU! WHAT'S YOUR ANSWER!?!
E...
WHOAAAAAA!
EIRI YUKI!!!
AND SHUICHI SHINDOU'S SQUEEZE TOY!!
SWEET VICTORY.

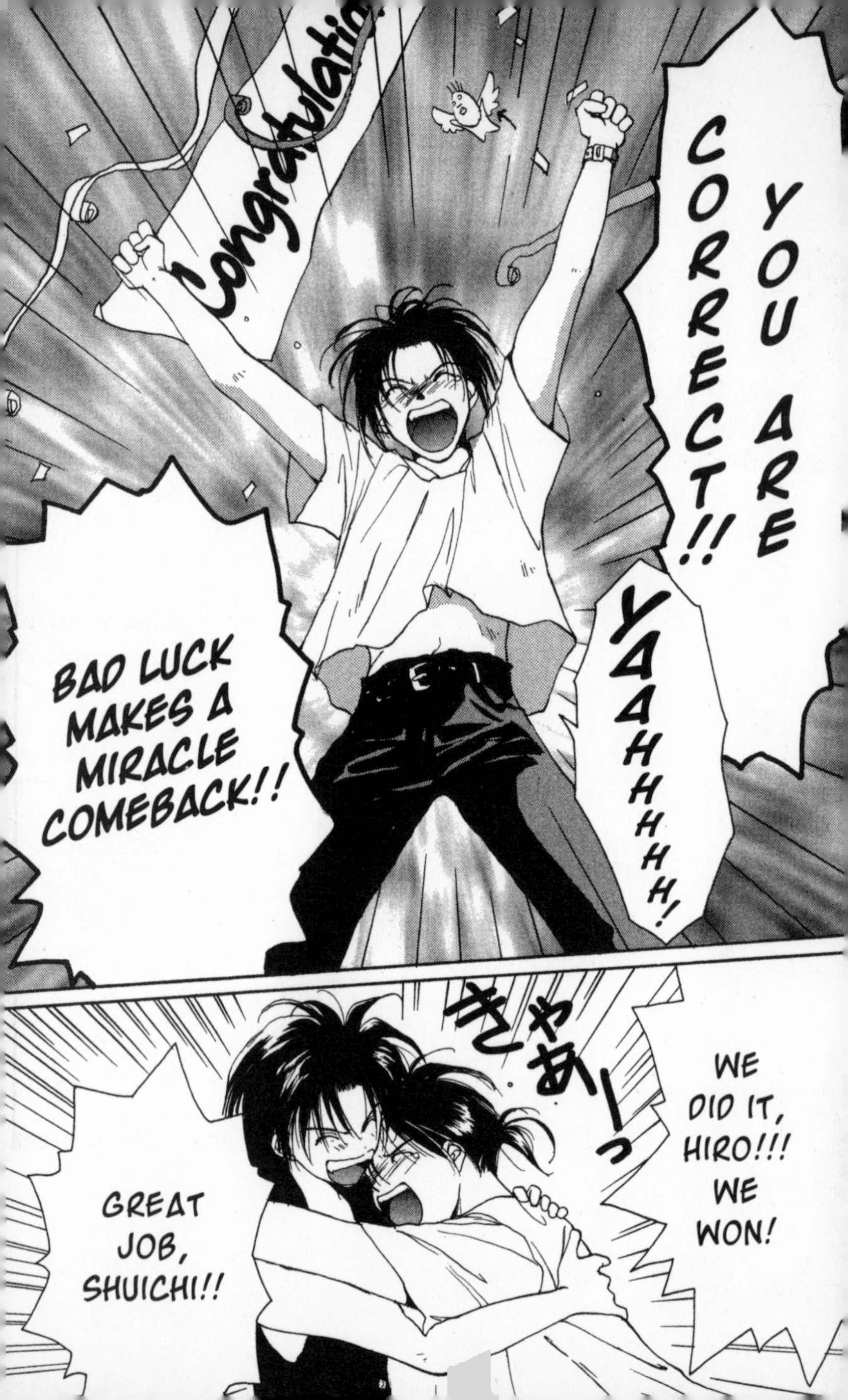
YOU ARE CORRECT!!
Congratulatio
YAAAHHHHHH!
BAD LUCK MAKES A MIRACLE COMEBACK!!
WE DID IT, HIRO!!! WE WON!
きゃあーっ
GREAT JOB, SHUICHI!!

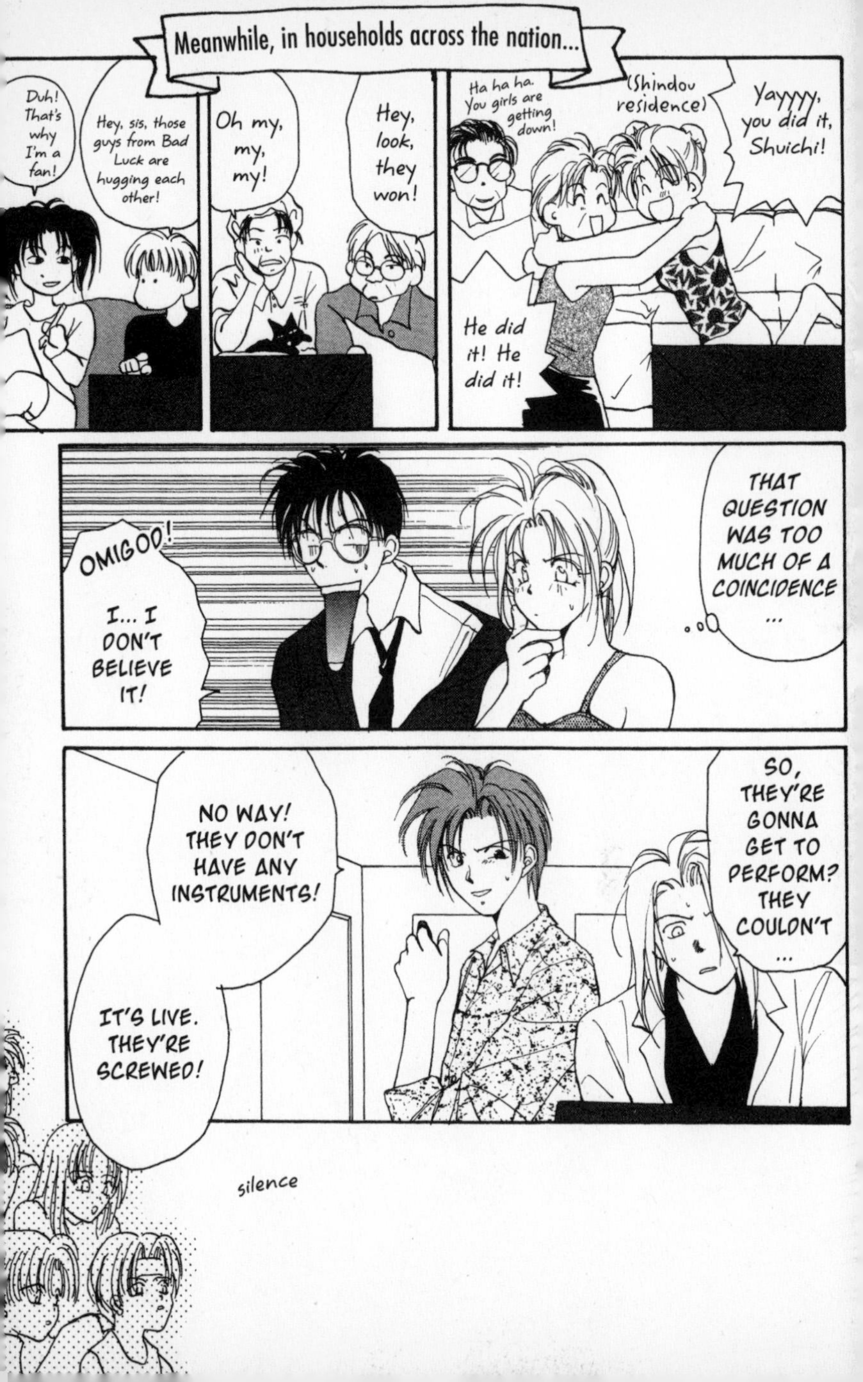
Meanwhile, in households across the nation...
(Shindou residence)
Yayyyy, you did it, Shuichi!
Ha ha ha. You girls are getting down!
He did it! He did it!
Hey, look, they won!
Oh my, my, my!
Hey, sis, those guys from Bad Luck are hugging each other!
Duh! That's why I'm a fan!
THAT QUESTION WAS TOO MUCH OF A COINCIDENCE ...
OMIGOD!
I... I DON'T BELIEVE IT!
SO, THEY'RE GONNA GET TO PERFORM? THEY COULDN'T ...
NO WAY! THEY DON'T HAVE ANY INSTRUMENTS!
IT'S LIVE. THEY'RE SCREWED!
silence

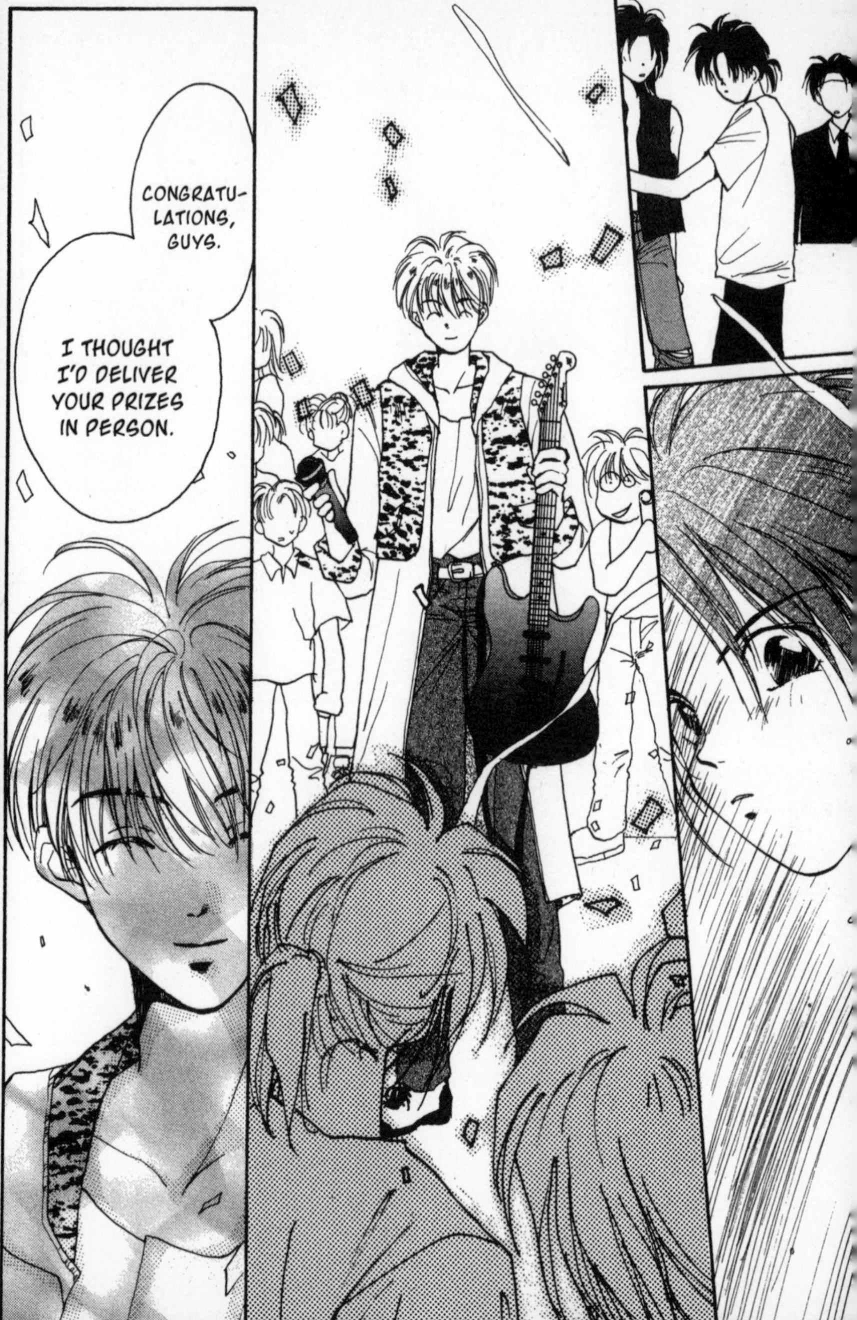
CONGRATULATIONS, GUYS.
I THOUGHT I'D DELIVER YOUR PRIZES IN PERSON.

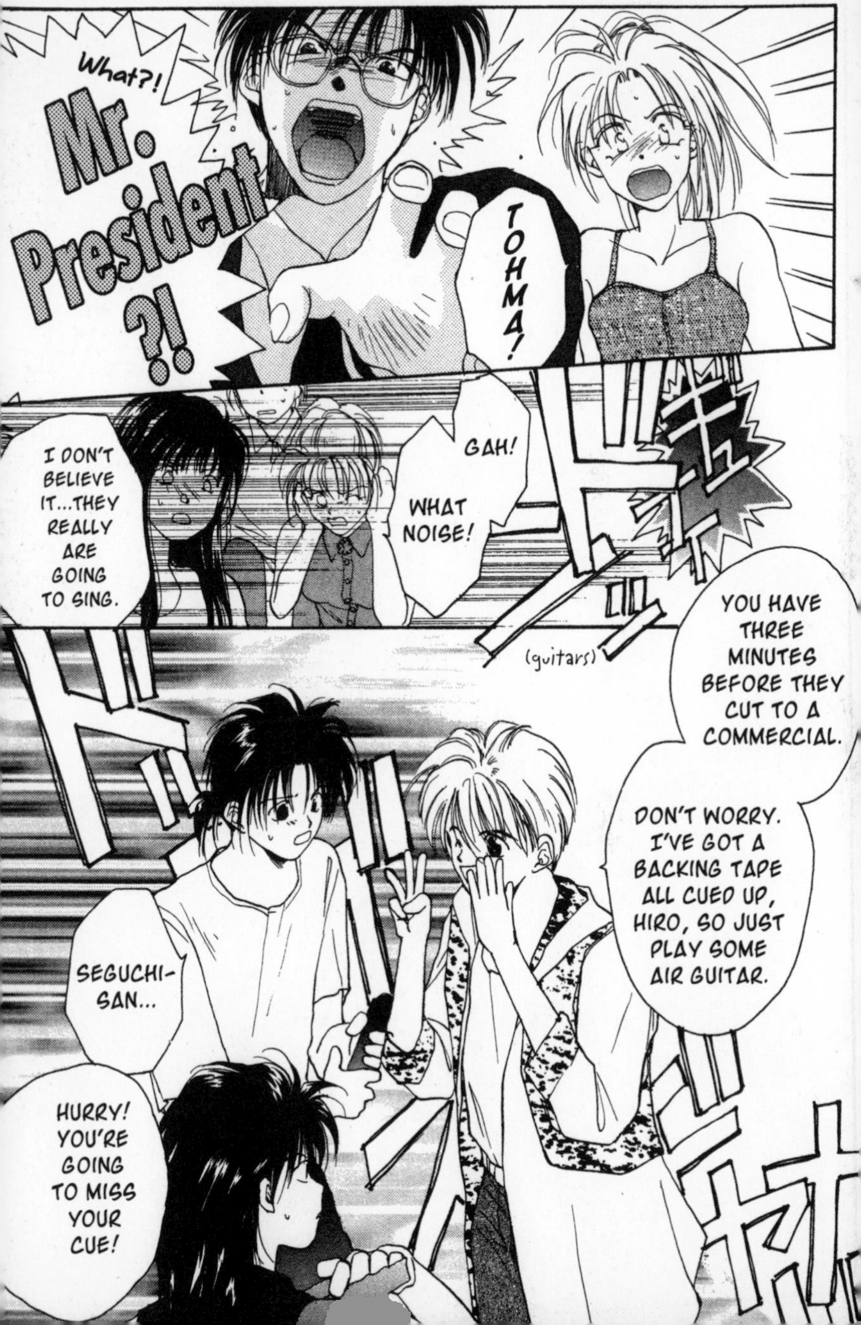
TOHMA!
What?!
Mr. President?!
(guitars)
GAH!
WHAT NOISE!
I DON'T BELIEVE IT...THEY REALLY ARE GOING TO SING.
YOU HAVE THREE MINUTES BEFORE THEY CUT TO A COMMERCIAL.
DON'T WORRY. I'VE GOT A BACKING TAPE ALL CUED UP, HIRO, SO JUST PLAY SOME AIR GUITAR.
SEGUCHI-SAN...
HURRY! YOU'RE GOING TO MISS YOUR CUE!

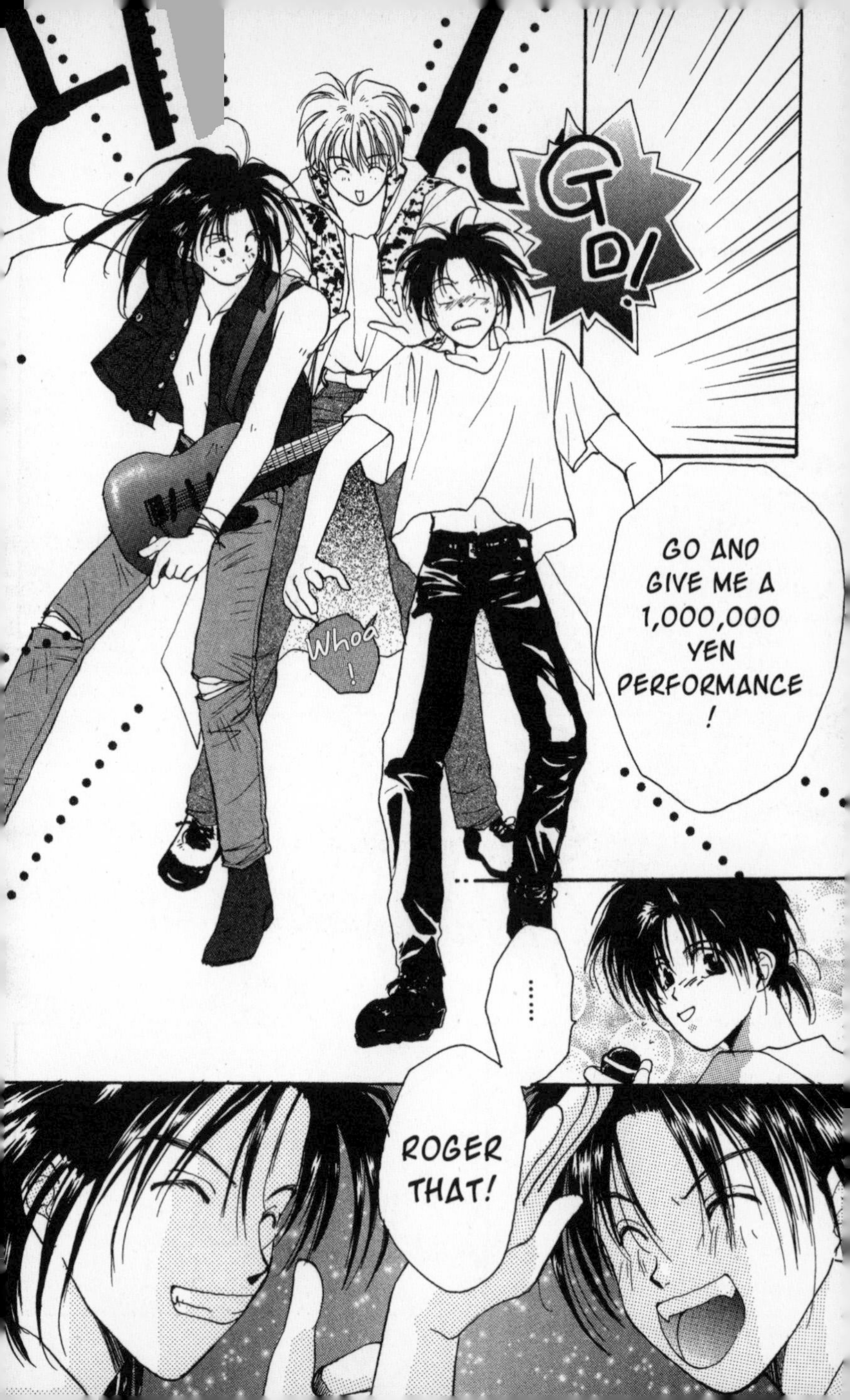
GD!
Whoa!
GO AND GIVE ME A 1,000,000 YEN PERFORMANCE!
......
ROGER THAT!

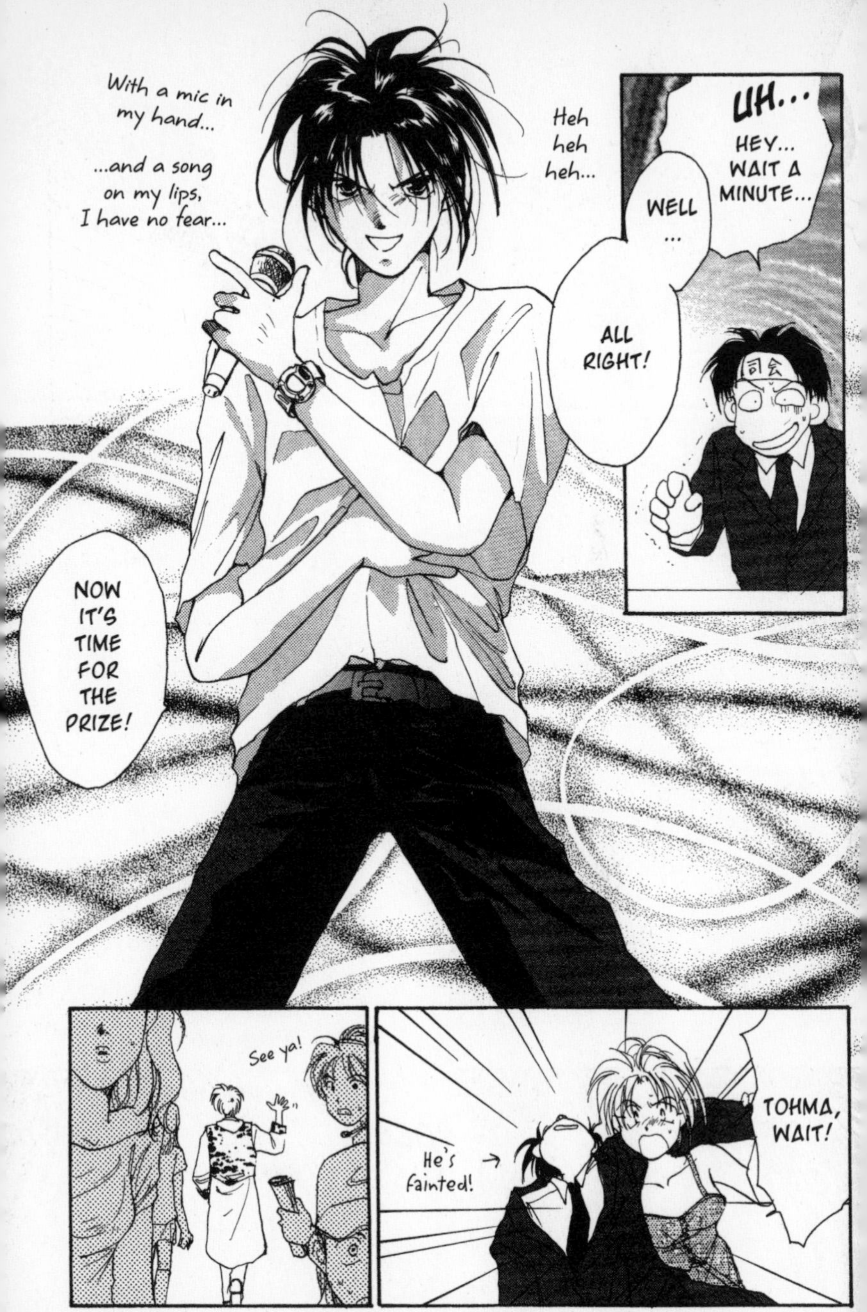

UH...
HEY... WAIT A MINUTE...
WELL ...
ALL RIGHT!
Heh heh heh...
With a mic in my hand...
...and a song on my lips, I have no fear...
NOW IT'S TIME FOR THE PRIZE!
TOHMA, WAIT!
He's fainted!
See ya!

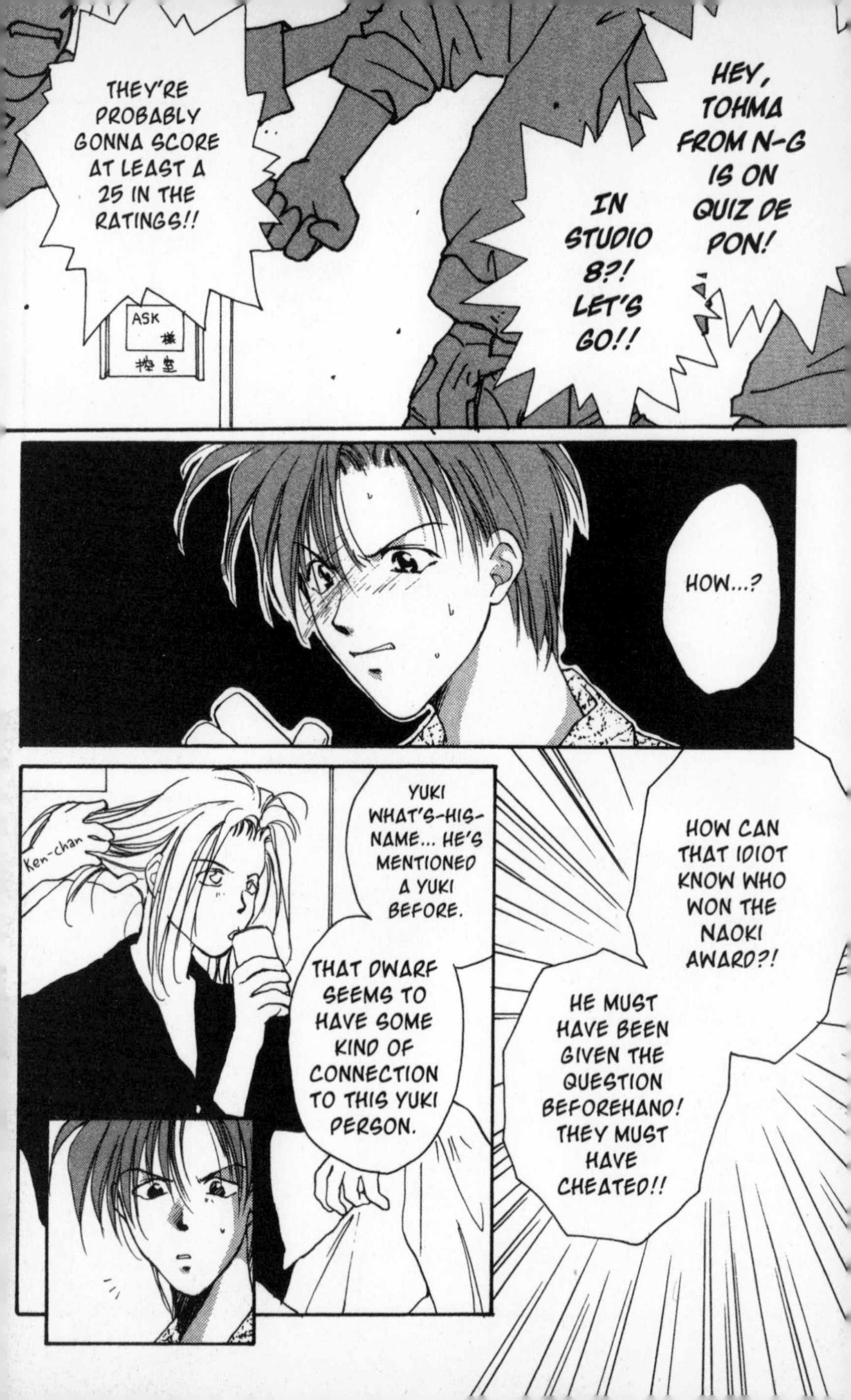
HEY, TOHMA FROM N-G IS ON QUIZ DE PON!
IN STUDIO 8?! LET'S GO!!
THEY'RE PROBABLY GONNA SCORE AT LEAST A 25 IN THE RATINGS!!
ASK
HOW...?
HOW CAN THAT IDIOT KNOW WHO WON THE NAOKI AWARD?!
HE MUST HAVE BEEN GIVEN THE QUESTION BEFOREHAND! THEY MUST HAVE CHEATED!!
YUKI WHAT'S-HIS-NAME... HE'S MENTIONED A YUKI BEFORE.
Ken-chan
THAT DWARF SEEMS TO HAVE SOME KIND OF CONNECTION TO THIS YUKI PERSON.

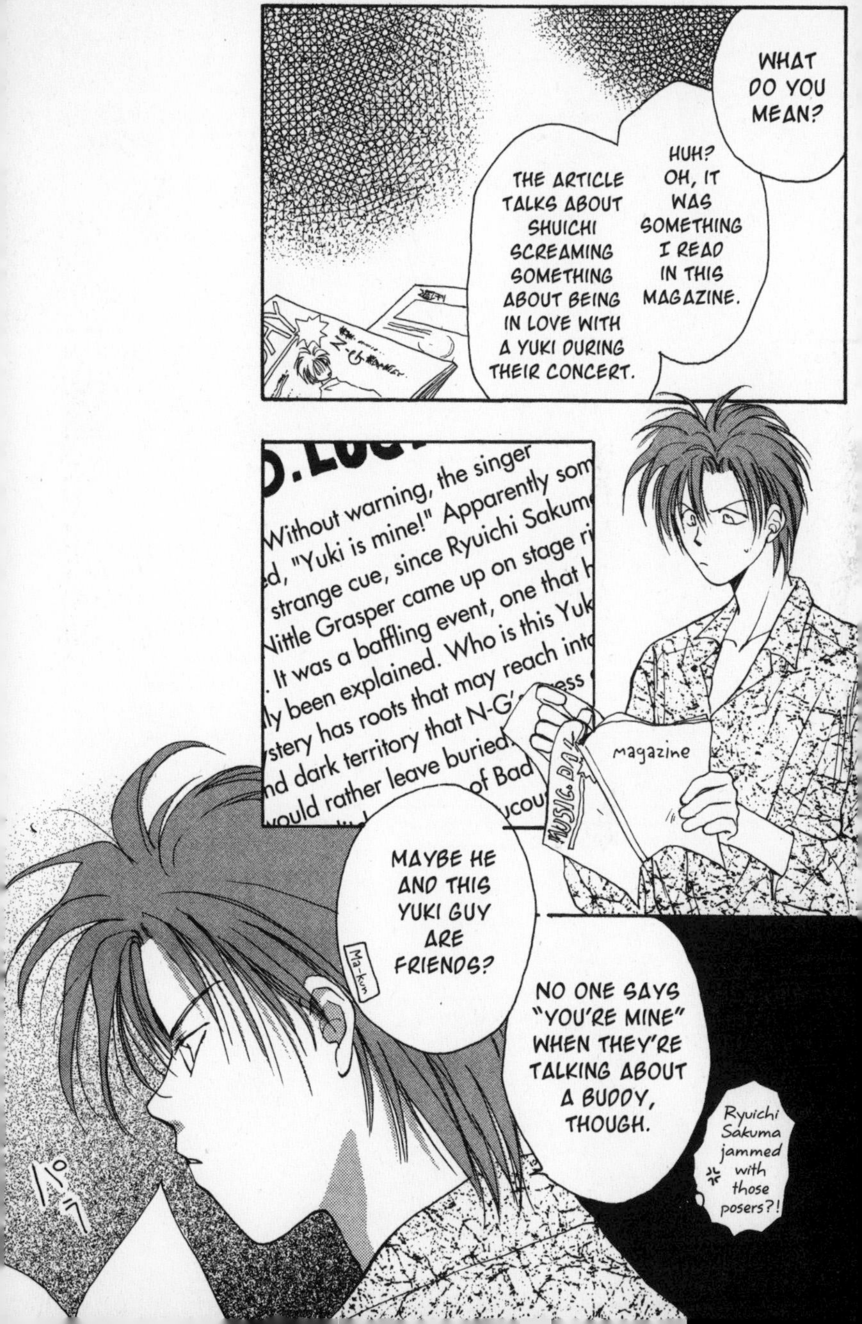

WHAT DO YOU MEAN?
HUH? OH, IT WAS SOMETHING I READ IN THIS MAGAZINE.
THE ARTICLE TALKS ABOUT SHUICHI SCREAMING SOMETHING ABOUT BEING IN LOVE WITH A YUKI DURING THEIR CONCERT.
magazine
Without warning, the singer
ed, "Yuki is mine!" Apparently som
strange cue, since Ryuichi Sakum
Nittle Grasper came up on stage ri
. It was a baffling event, one that h
lly been explained. Who is this Yuk
ystery has roots that may reach int
nd dark territory that N-G's
would rather leave buried.
MAYBE HE AND THIS YUKI GUY ARE FRIENDS?
Ma-kun
NO ONE SAYS "YOU'RE MINE" WHEN THEY'RE TALKING ABOUT A BUDDY, THOUGH.
Ryuichi Sakuma jammed with those posers?!

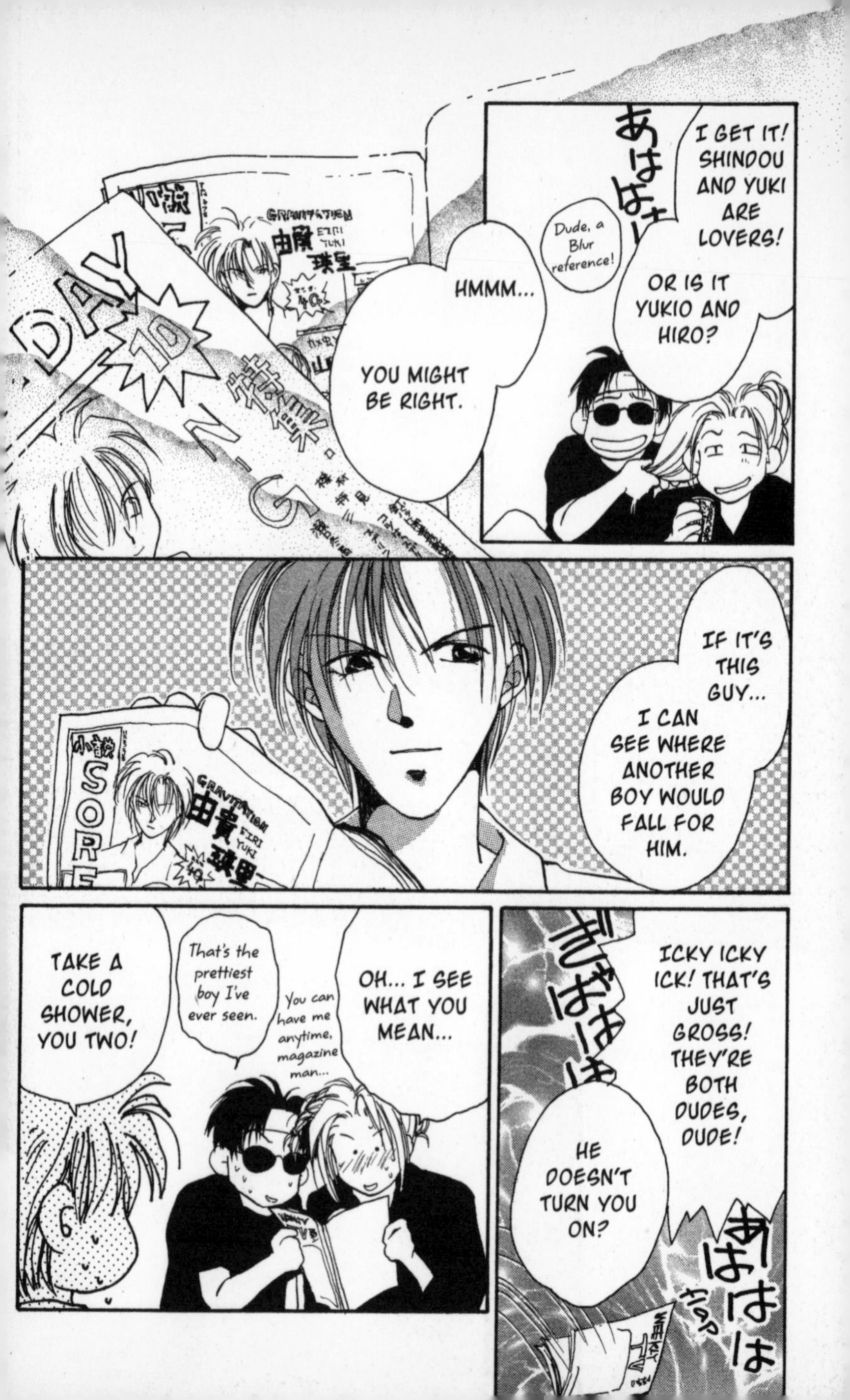
あはは
I GET IT! SHINDOU AND YUKI ARE LOVERS!
Dude, a Blur reference!
OR IS IT YUKIO AND HIRO?
HMMM...
YOU MIGHT BE RIGHT.
DAY
IF IT'S THIS GUY...
I CAN SEE WHERE ANOTHER BOY WOULD FALL FOR HIM.
ICKY ICKY ICK! THAT'S JUST GROSS! THEY'RE BOTH DUDES, DUDE!
HE DOESN'T TURN YOU ON?
あはは
OH... I SEE WHAT YOU MEAN...
You can have me anytime, magazine man...
That's the prettiest boy I've ever seen.
TAKE A COLD SHOWER, YOU TWO!

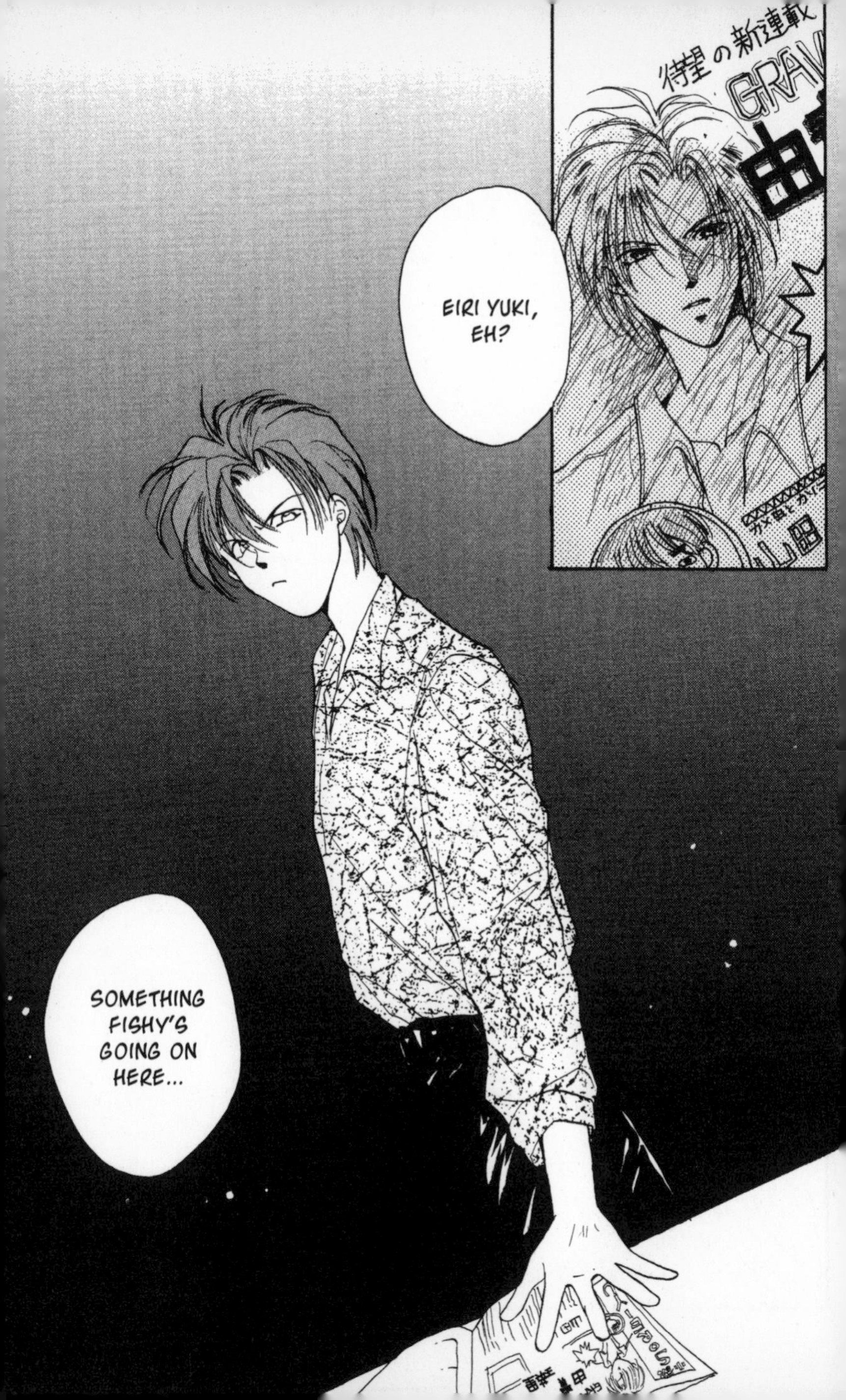
待望の新連載
EIRI YUKI, EH?
SOMETHING FISHY'S GOING ON HERE...

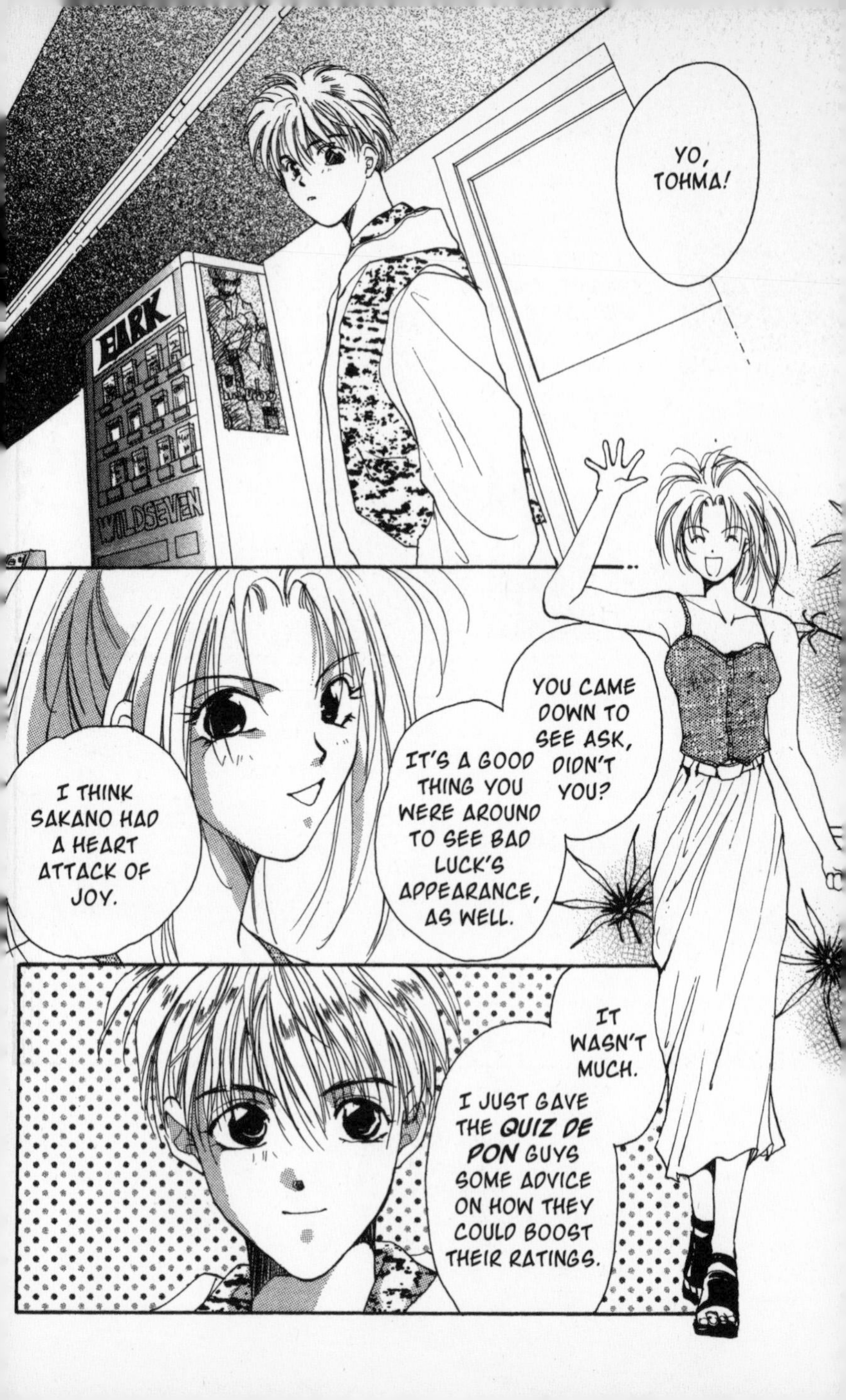
YO, TOHMA!
WILDSEVEN
YOU CAME DOWN TO SEE ASK, DIDN'T YOU?
IT'S A GOOD THING YOU WERE AROUND TO SEE BAD LUCK'S APPEARANCE, AS WELL.
I THINK SAKANO HAD A HEART ATTACK OF JOY.
IT WASN'T MUCH.
I JUST GAVE THE *QUIZ DE PON* GUYS SOME ADVICE ON HOW THEY COULD BOOST THEIR RATINGS.

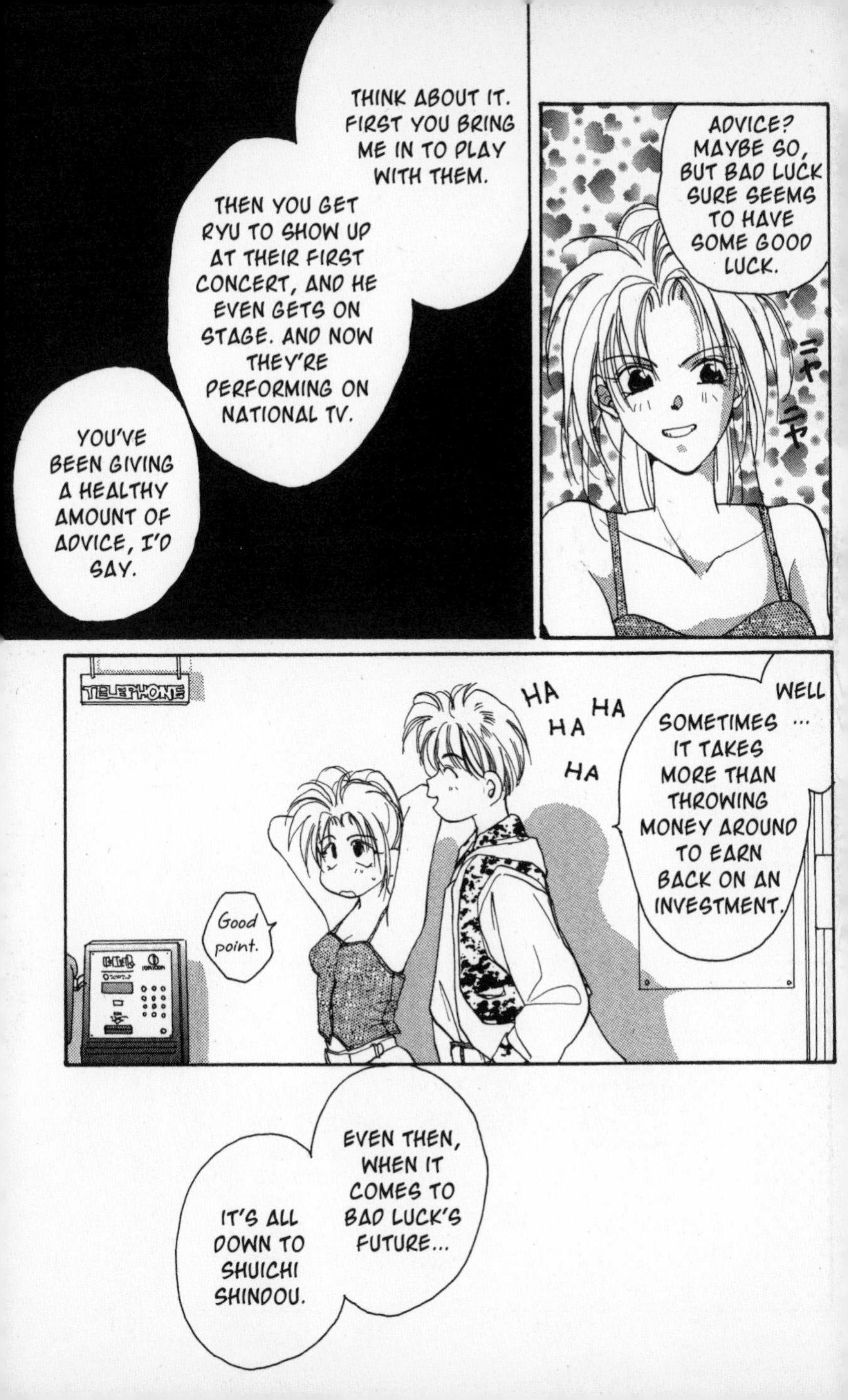
THINK ABOUT IT. FIRST YOU BRING ME IN TO PLAY WITH THEM.
THEN YOU GET RYU TO SHOW UP AT THEIR FIRST CONCERT, AND HE EVEN GETS ON STAGE. AND NOW THEY'RE PERFORMING ON NATIONAL TV.
YOU'VE BEEN GIVING A HEALTHY AMOUNT OF ADVICE, I'D SAY.
ADVICE? MAYBE SO, BUT BAD LUCK SURE SEEMS TO HAVE SOME GOOD LUCK.
ニヤ
ニヤ
TELEPHONE
WELL
SOMETIMES... IT TAKES MORE THAN THROWING MONEY AROUND TO EARN BACK ON AN INVESTMENT.
HA
HA
HA
HA
Good point.
EVEN THEN, WHEN IT COMES TO BAD LUCK'S FUTURE...
IT'S ALL DOWN TO SHUICHI SHINDOU.

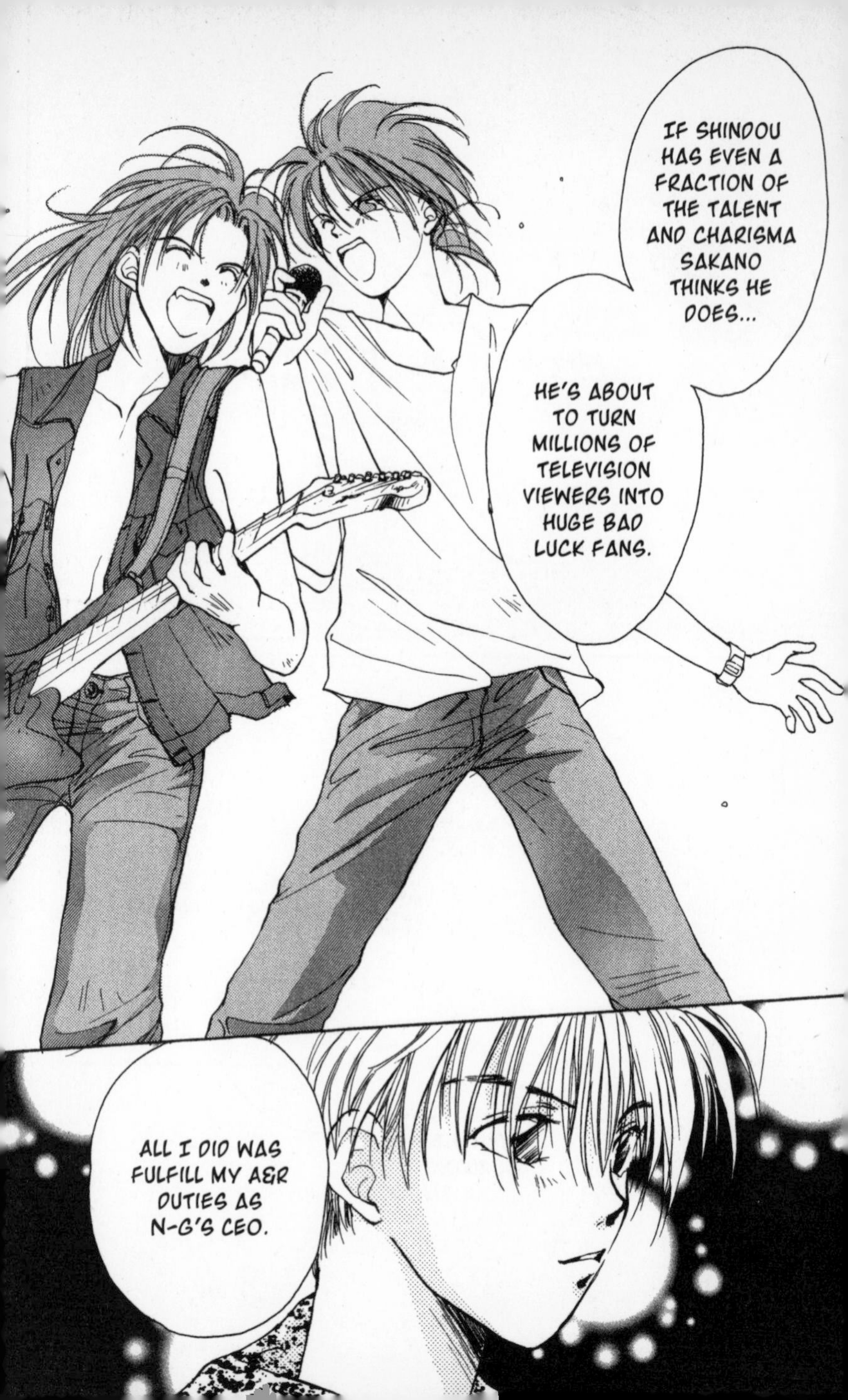
IF SHINDOU HAS EVEN A FRACTION OF THE TALENT AND CHARISMA SAKANO THINKS HE DOES...
HE'S ABOUT TO TURN MILLIONS OF TELEVISION VIEWERS INTO HUGE BAD LUCK FANS.
ALL I DID WAS FULFILL MY A&R DUTIES AS N-G'S CEO.

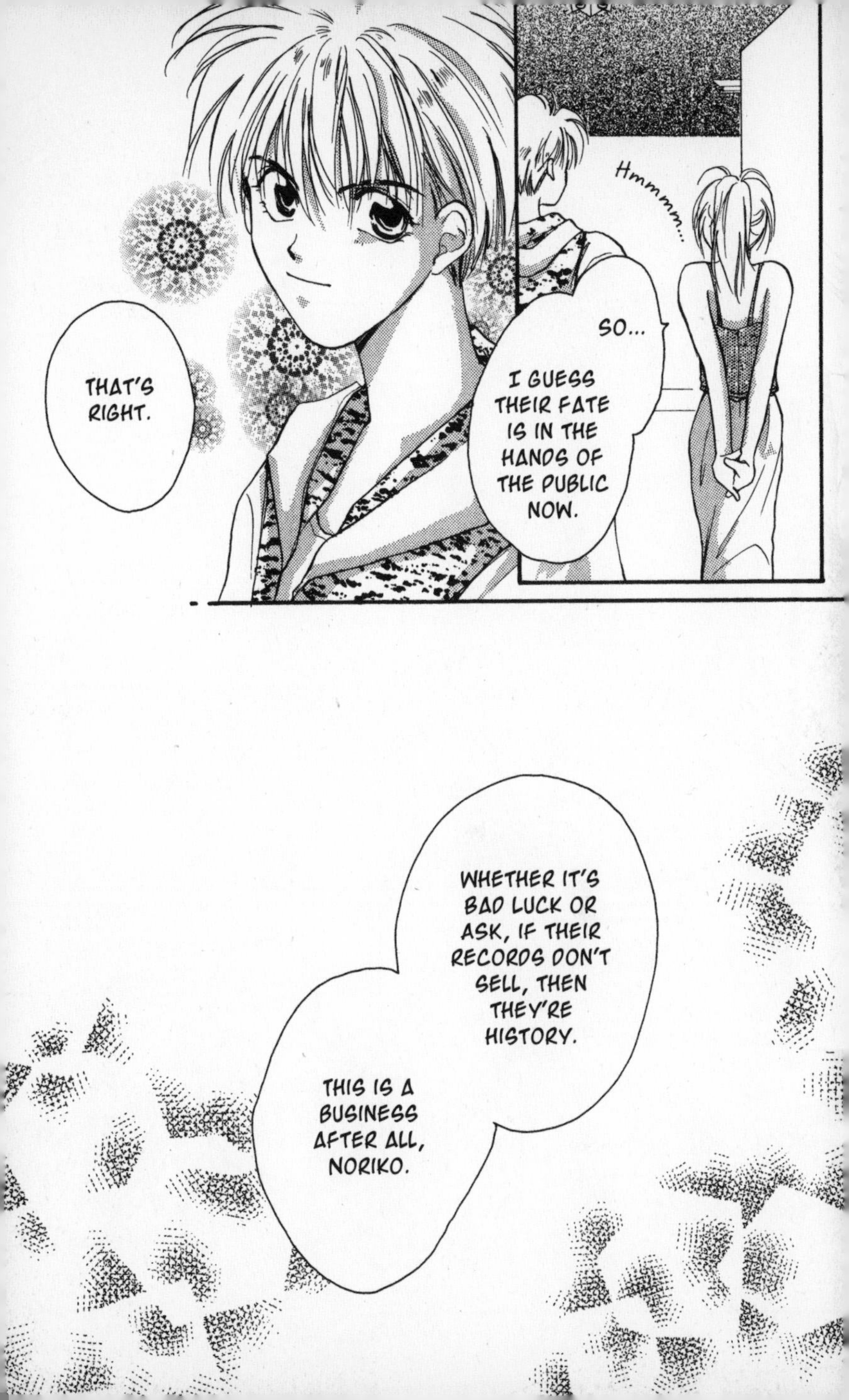
Hmmmm...
SO... I GUESS THEIR FATE IS IN THE HANDS OF THE PUBLIC NOW.
THAT'S RIGHT.
WHETHER IT'S BAD LUCK OR ASK, IF THEIR RECORDS DON'T SELL, THEN THEY'RE HISTORY.
THIS IS A BUSINESS AFTER ALL, NORIKO.

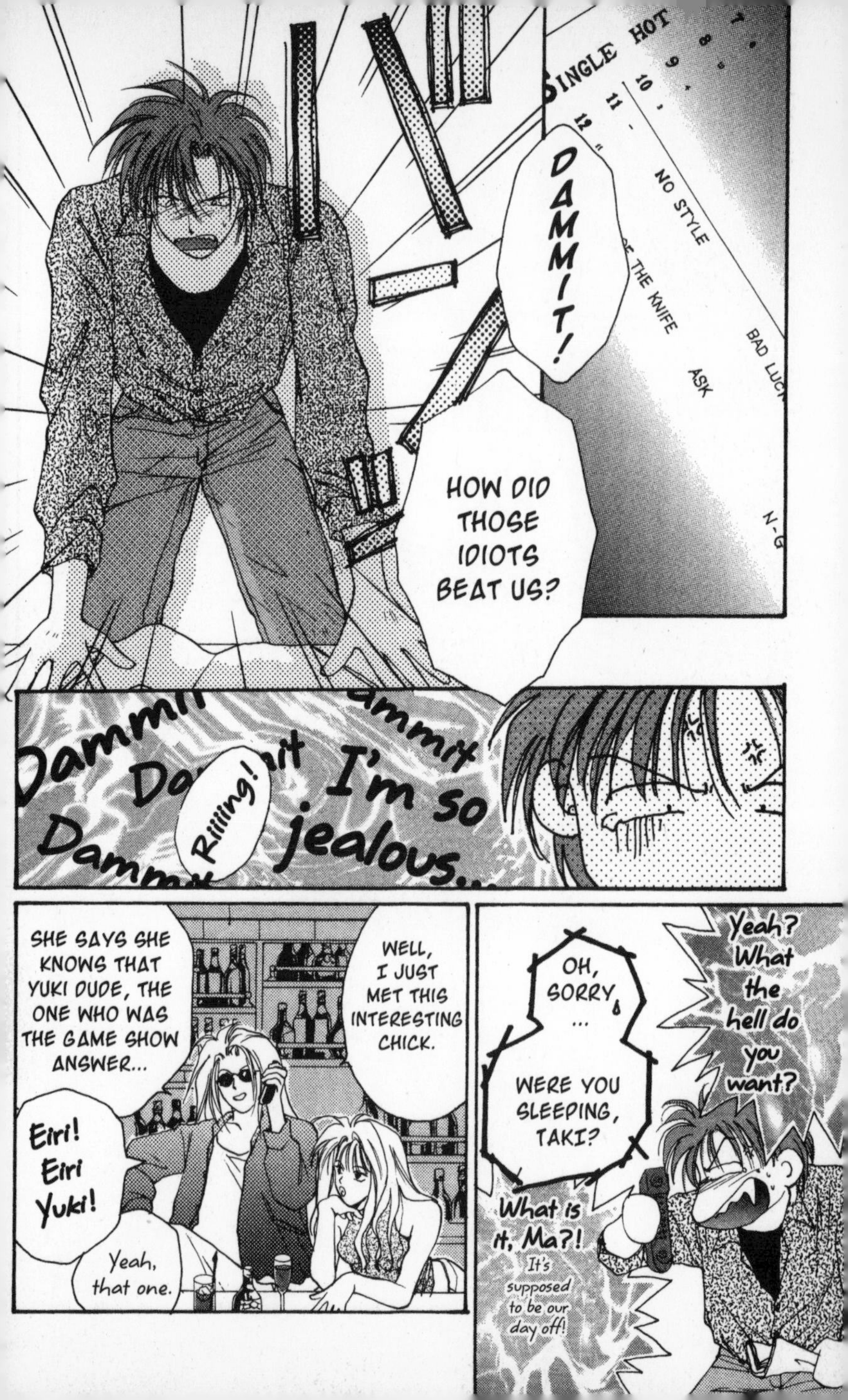
SINGLE HOT
NO STYLE
ASK
DAMMIT!
HOW DID THOSE IDIOTS BEAT US?
I'm so jealous...
Riiiing!
Yeah? What the hell do you want?
OH, SORRY, ... WERE YOU SLEEPING, TAKI?
What is it, Ma?! It's supposed to be our day off!
WELL, I JUST MET THIS INTERESTING CHICK.
SHE SAYS SHE KNOWS THAT YUKI DUDE, THE ONE WHO WAS THE GAME SHOW ANSWER...
Eiri! Eiri Yuki!
Yeah, that one.

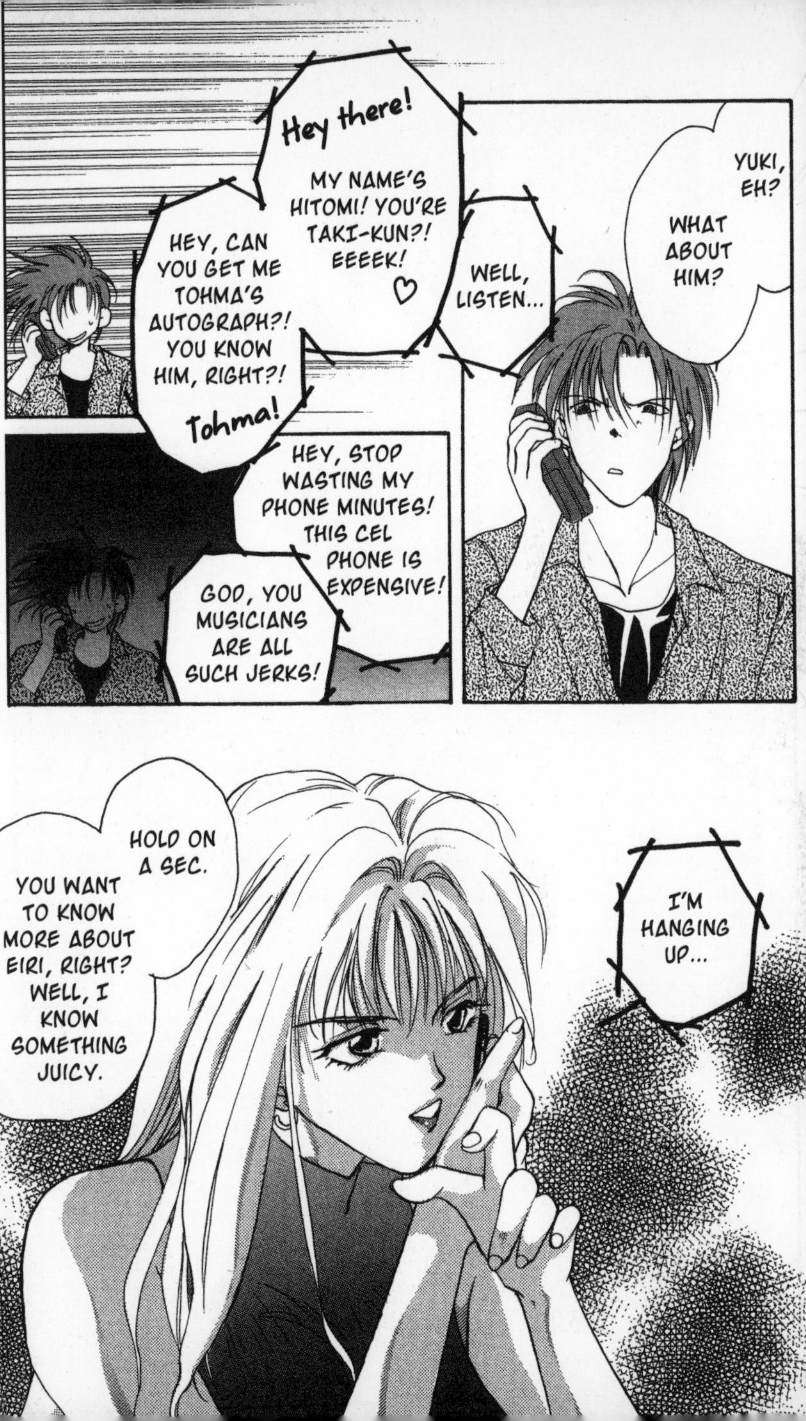

YUKI, EH? WHAT ABOUT HIM?
WELL, LISTEN...
Hey there! MY NAME'S HITOMI! YOU'RE TAKI-KUN?! EEEEK! ♡
HEY, CAN YOU GET ME TOHMA'S AUTOGRAPH?! YOU KNOW HIM, RIGHT?! Tohma!
HEY, STOP WASTING MY PHONE MINUTES! THIS CEL PHONE IS EXPENSIVE!
GOD, YOU MUSICIANS ARE ALL SUCH JERKS!
I'M HANGING UP...
HOLD ON A SEC. YOU WANT TO KNOW MORE ABOUT EIRI, RIGHT? WELL, I KNOW SOMETHING JUICY.

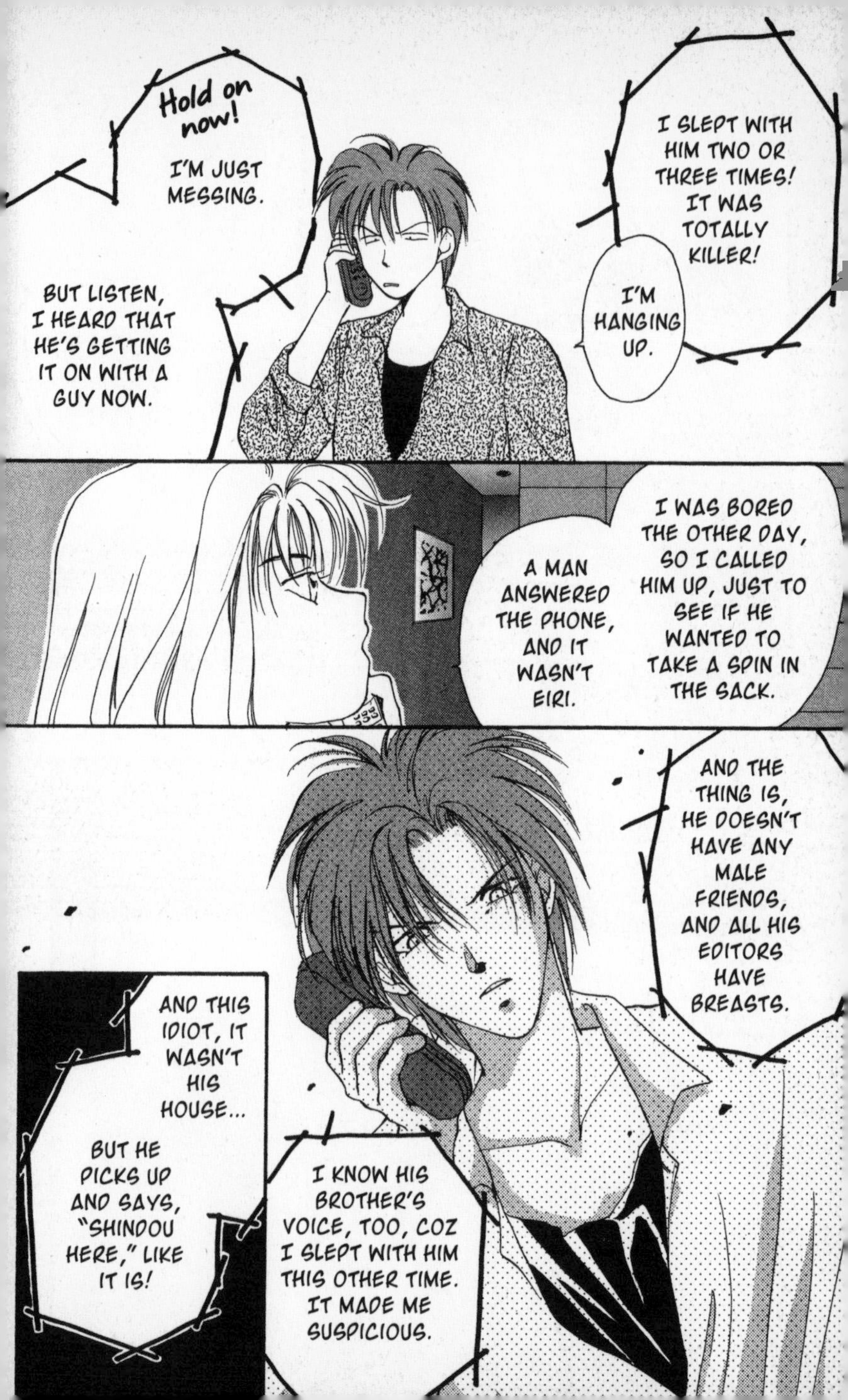
I SLEPT WITH HIM TWO OR THREE TIMES! IT WAS TOTALLY KILLER!
I'M HANGING UP.
Hold on now!
I'M JUST MESSING.
BUT LISTEN, I HEARD THAT HE'S GETTING IT ON WITH A GUY NOW.
I WAS BORED THE OTHER DAY, SO I CALLED HIM UP, JUST TO SEE IF HE WANTED TO TAKE A SPIN IN THE SACK.
A MAN ANSWERED THE PHONE, AND IT WASN'T EIRI.
AND THE THING IS, HE DOESN'T HAVE ANY MALE FRIENDS, AND ALL HIS EDITORS HAVE BREASTS.
AND THIS IDIOT, IT WASN'T HIS HOUSE...
BUT HE PICKS UP AND SAYS, "SHINDOU HERE," LIKE IT IS!
I KNOW HIS BROTHER'S VOICE, TOO, COZ I SLEPT WITH HIM THIS OTHER TIME. IT MADE ME SUSPICIOUS.

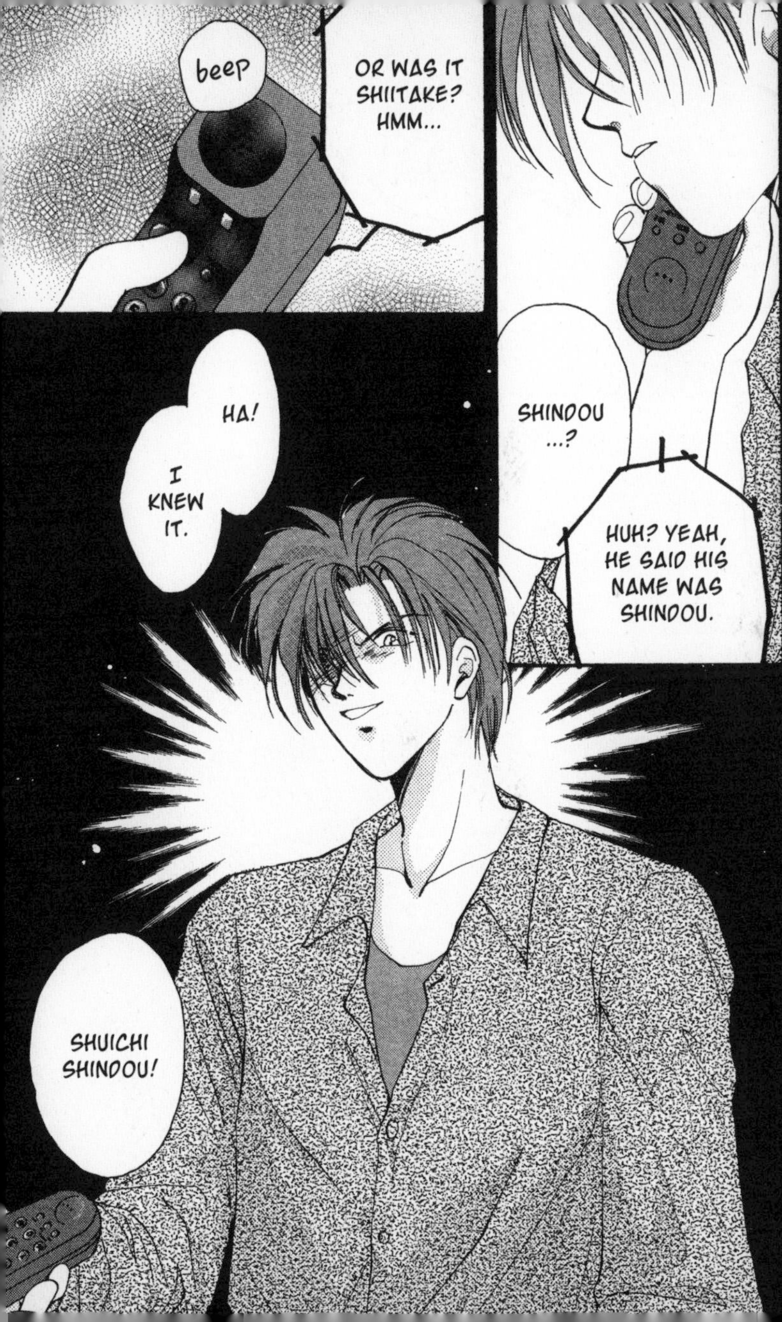
SHINDOU ...?
HUH? YEAH, HE SAID HIS NAME WAS SHINDOU.
OR WAS IT SHIITAKE? HMM...
beep
HA!
I KNEW IT.
SHUICHI SHINDOU!

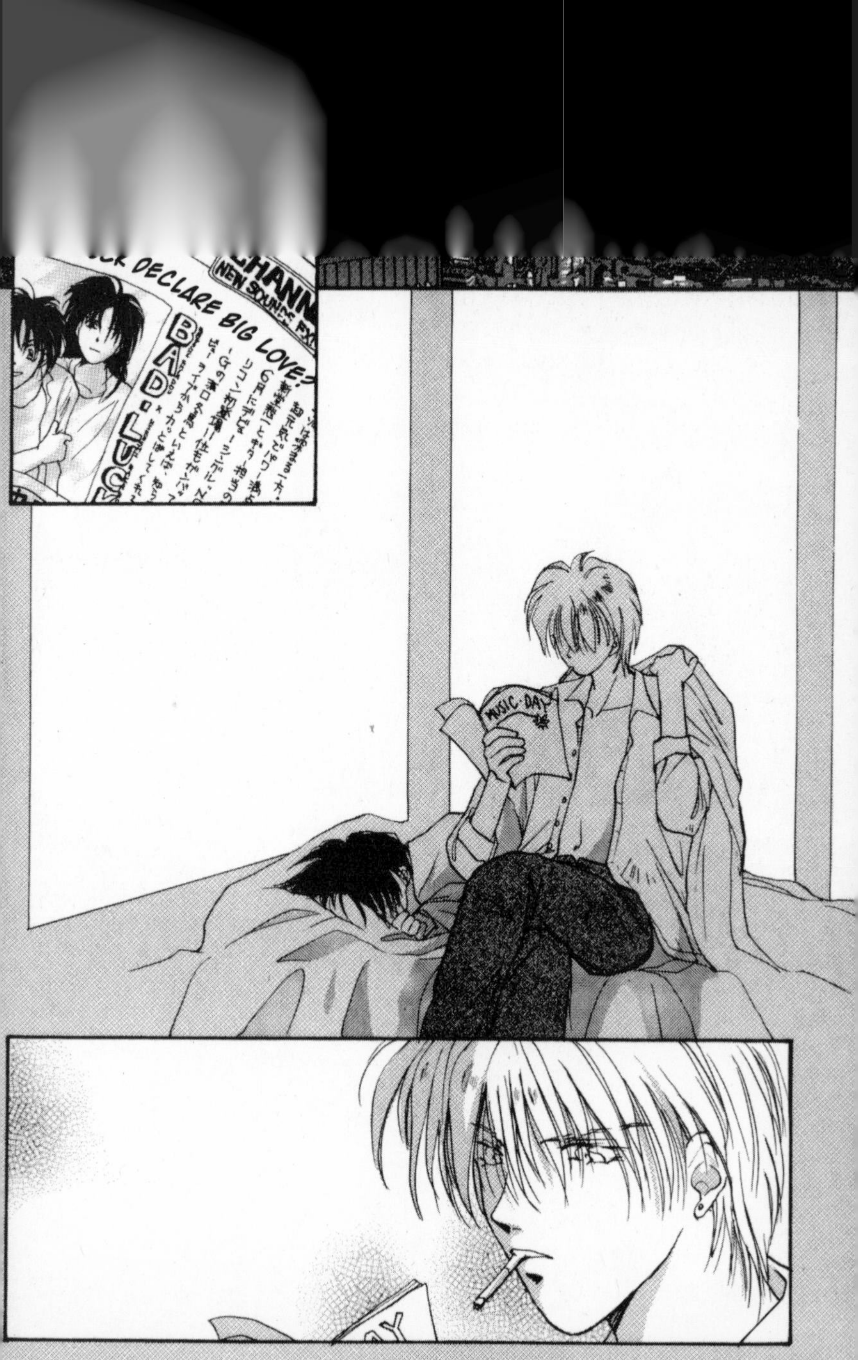

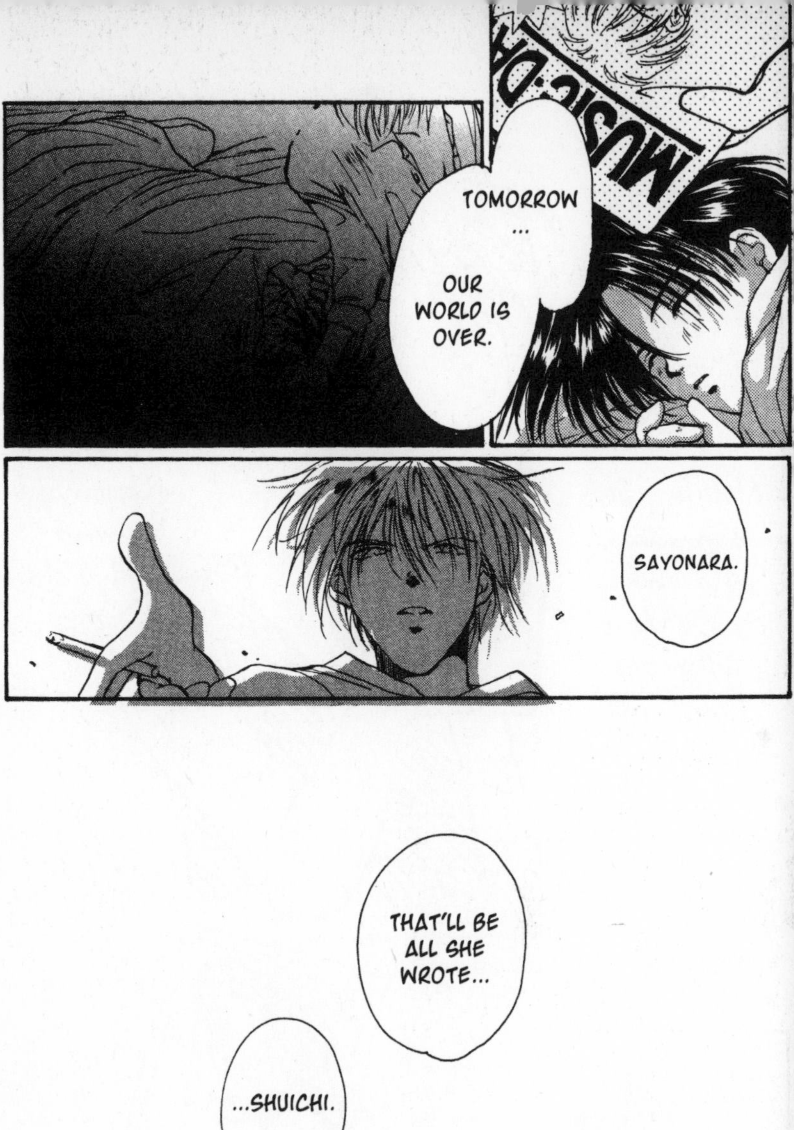
TOMORROW ... OUR WORLD IS OVER.
SAYONARA.
THAT'LL BE ALL SHE WROTE...
...SHUICHI.

track12 ▶ END

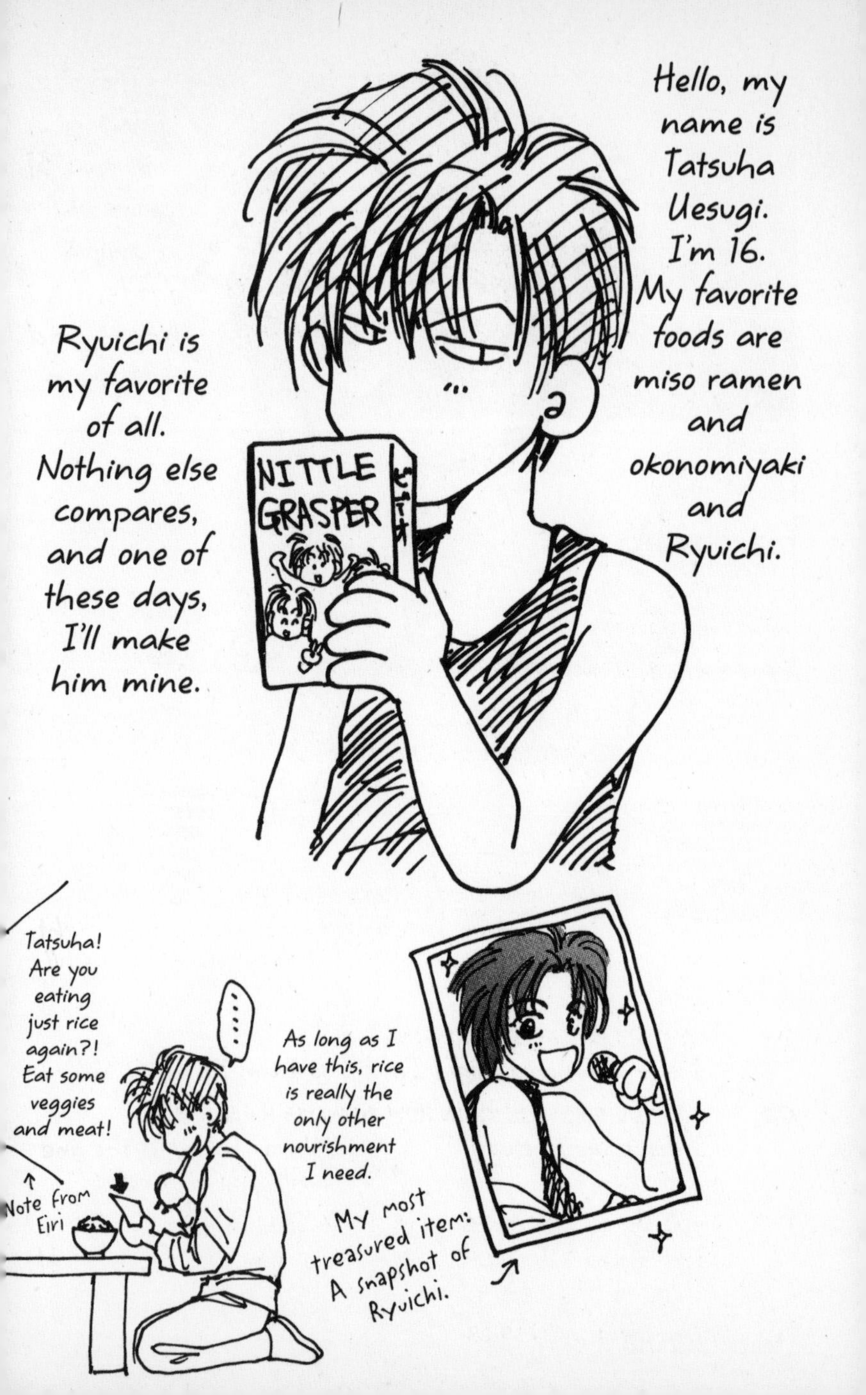
Hello, my name is Tatsuha Uesugi. I'm 16. My favorite foods are miso ramen and okonomiyaki and Ryuichi.
...
NITTLE GRASPER
Ryuichi is my favorite of all. Nothing else compares, and one of these days, I'll make him mine.
My most treasured item: A snapshot of Ryuichi.
As long as I have this, rice is really the only other nourishment I need.
.....
Tatsuha! Are you eating just rice again?! Eat some veggies and meat!
Note from Eiri

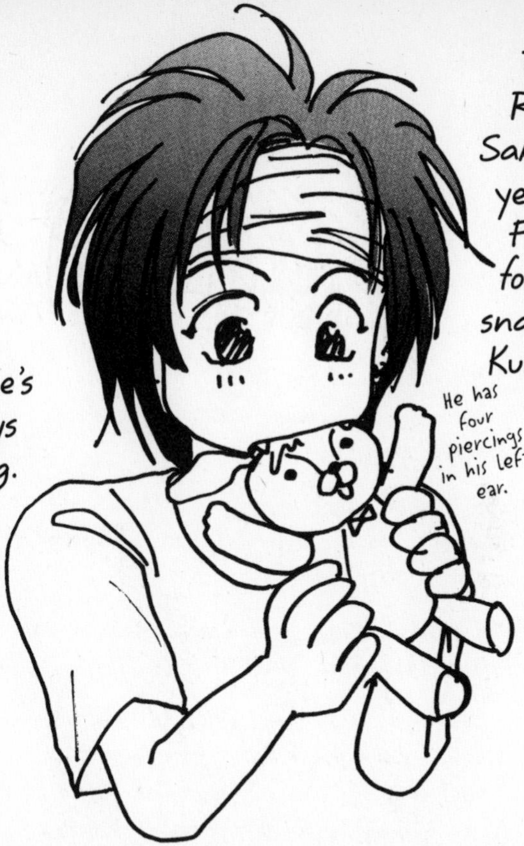
This is Ryuichi Sakuma. 31 years old. Favorite foods are snacks and Kumagoro-kun.
He has four piercings in his left ear.
And he's always eating.

Q1 WHAT DO YOU THINK OF TATSUHA UESUGI-SAN?

Tatsuha-kun is a fun kid, and that makes him all right by me. He'd be cooler if he didn't keep touching me all the time.

Q2 ARE YOU REALLY 31 YEARS OLD?

I sure am. Tohma said I'm 31, so I am 31.

Q3 ARE YOU SURE YOU KNOW HOW TO WRITE HIRAGANA?

I don't like to study. 馬 (Uma (horse) is the one kanji that he knows.)

Q4 YOU LIVE OVERSEAS NOW, BUT HOW'S YOUR ENGLISH?

I can speak English fairly well, so I'm fine. I'm good at it, actually.

THANK YOU VERY MUCH.

The manga beginning on the next page is called "Pretty Dynamite."

It's not one of my favorites amongst my stories, but I wonder what you readers might think?

It probably isn't important to know, but when I did this manga, I was working at a pretty fast rate.

Honestly, it was unreal how speedy I was. But that was a long time ago.

Getting back to the subject, let me tell you why I don't particularly like this manga that much. I think it's too conservative. I like the absurdity of the story, but the overall feeling of it seems kind of blasé to me. I like the idea behind it, though. And I like the punch lines, too.

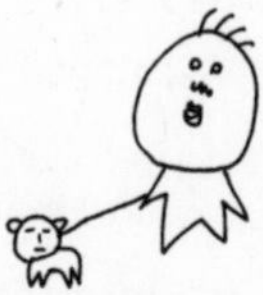

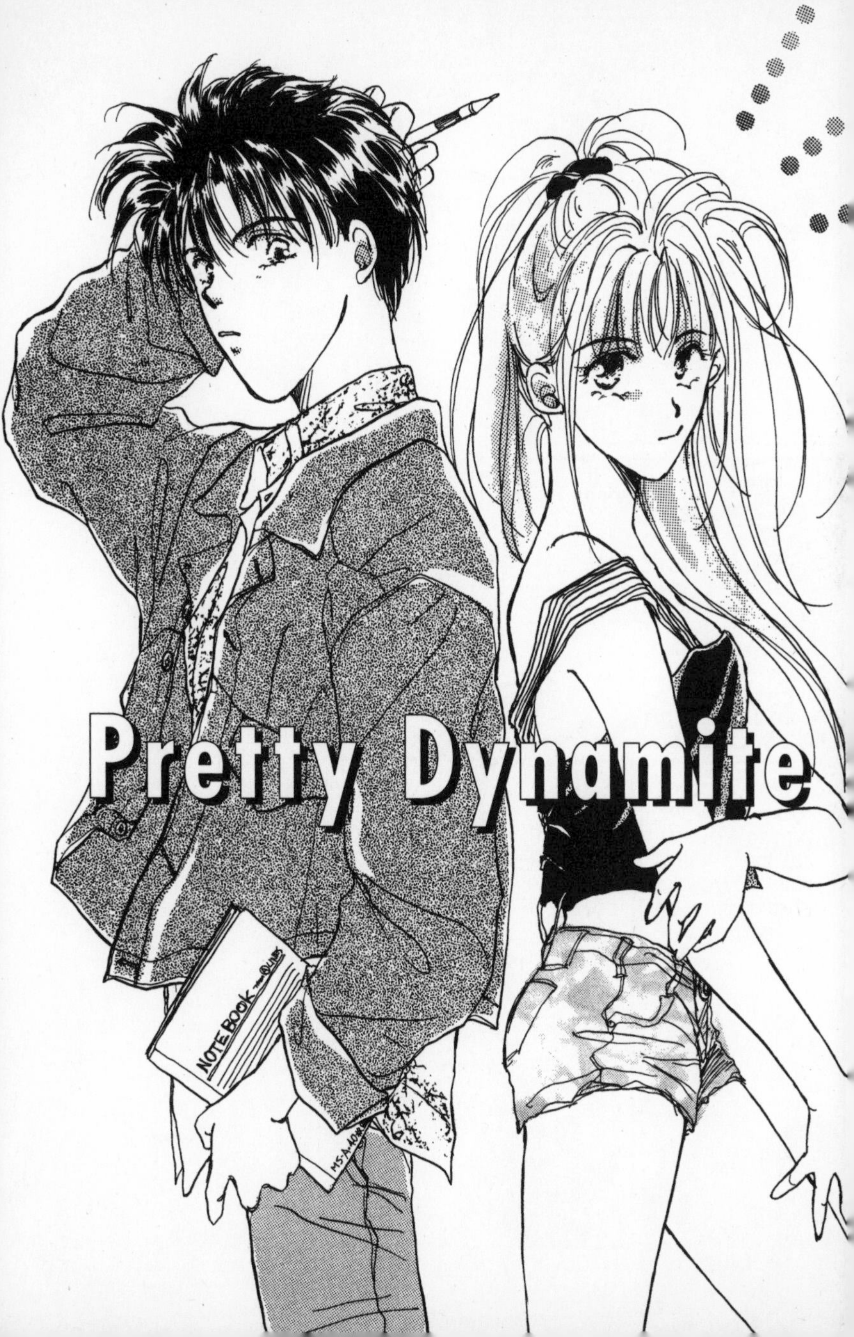
Pretty Dynamite
NOTE BOOK

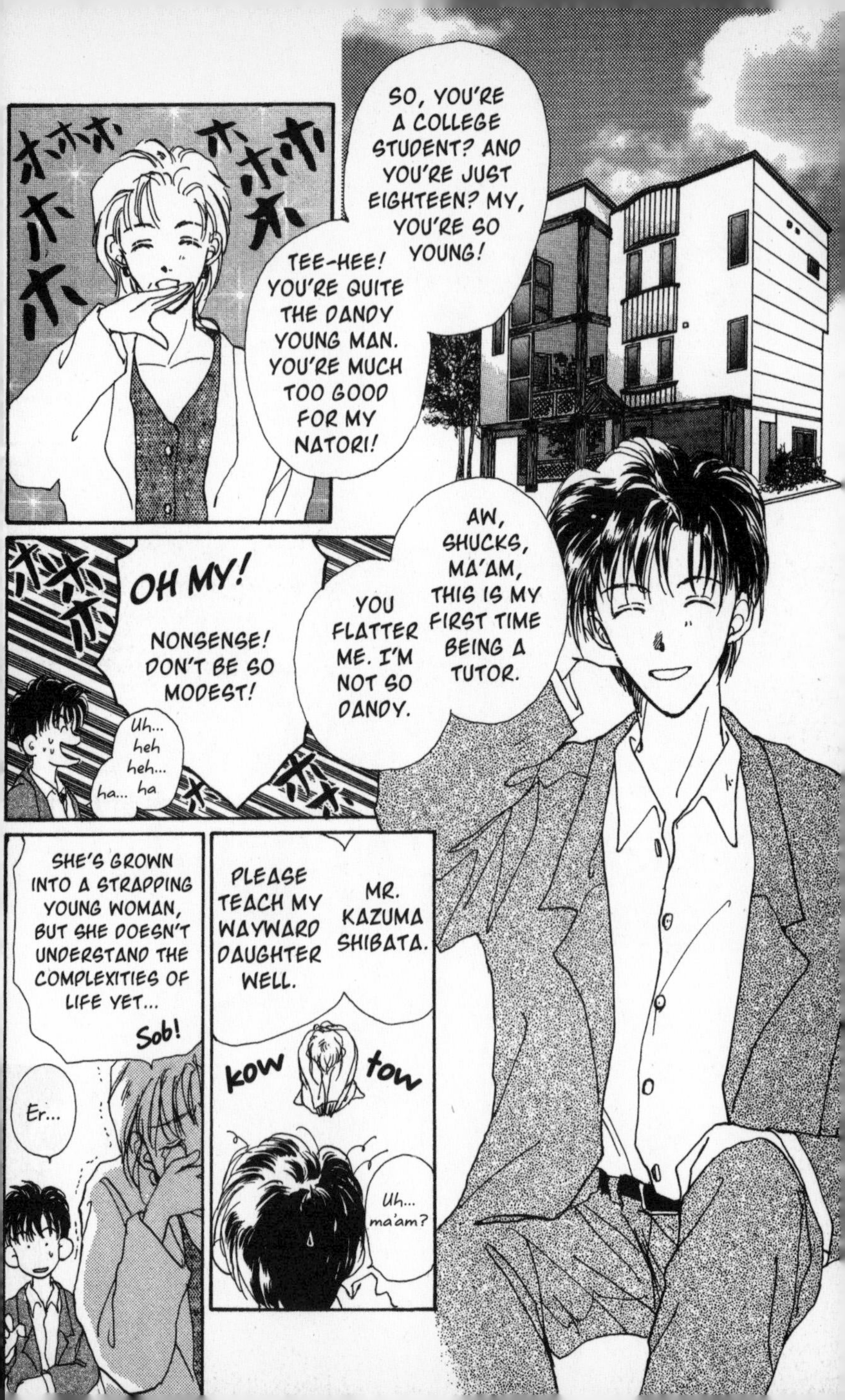

SO, YOU'RE A COLLEGE STUDENT? AND YOU'RE JUST EIGHTEEN? MY, YOU'RE SO YOUNG!
TEE-HEE! YOU'RE QUITE THE DANDY YOUNG MAN. YOU'RE MUCH TOO GOOD FOR MY NATORI!
AW, SHUCKS, MA'AM, THIS IS MY FIRST TIME BEING A TUTOR.
YOU FLATTER ME. I'M NOT SO DANDY.
OH MY!
NONSENSE! DON'T BE SO MODEST!
Uh... heh heh... ha... ha
MR. KAZUMA SHIBATA.
PLEASE TEACH MY WAYWARD DAUGHTER WELL.
kow tow
Uh... ma'am?
SHE'S GROWN INTO A STRAPPING YOUNG WOMAN, BUT SHE DOESN'T UNDERSTAND THE COMPLEXITIES OF LIFE YET...
Sob!
Er...

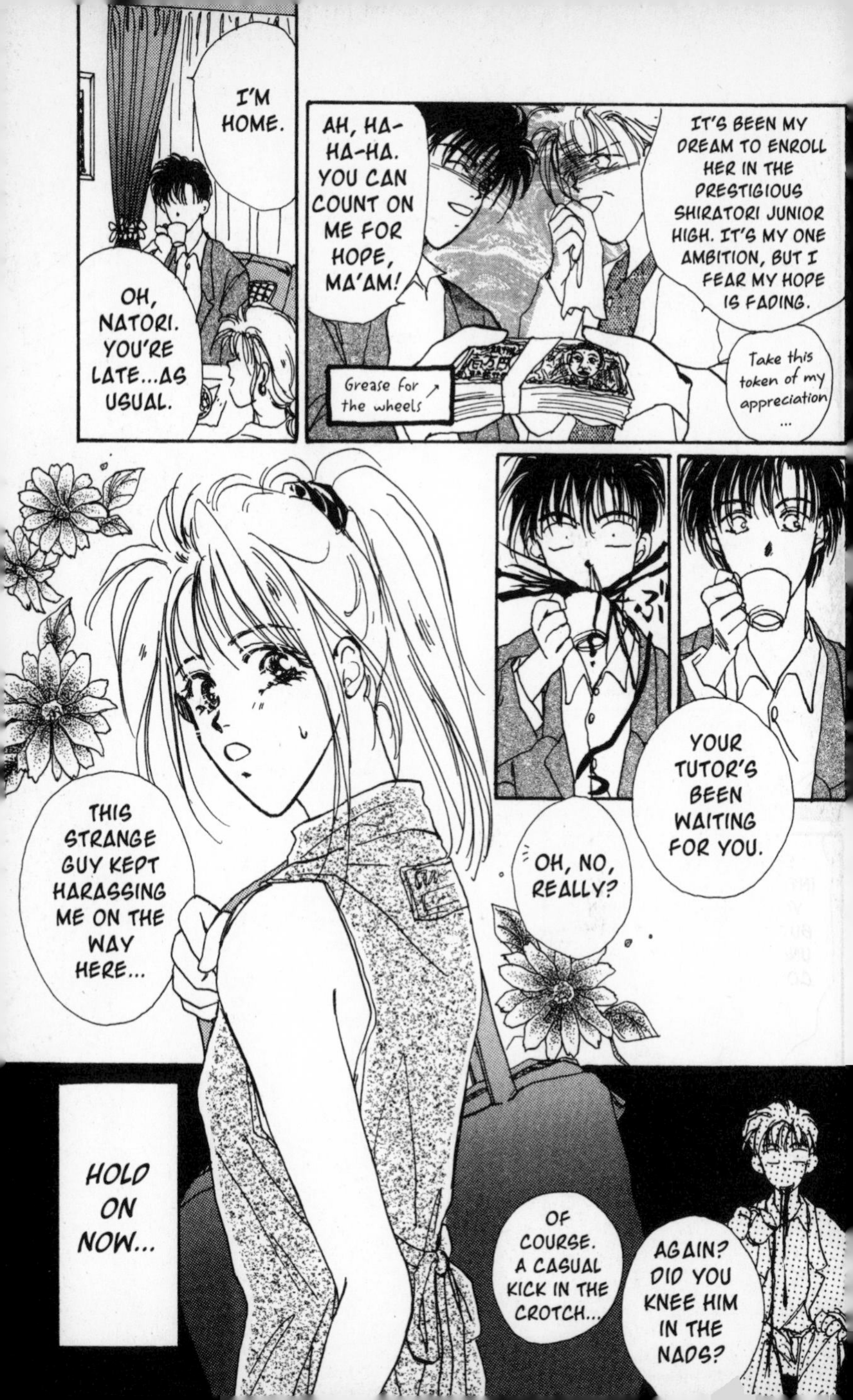
IT'S BEEN MY DREAM TO ENROLL HER IN THE PRESTIGIOUS SHIRATORI JUNIOR HIGH. IT'S MY ONE AMBITION, BUT I FEAR MY HOPE IS FADING.
Take this token of my appreciation...
AH, HA-HA-HA. YOU CAN COUNT ON ME FOR HOPE, MA'AM!
Grease for the wheels
I'M HOME.
OH, NATORI. YOU'RE LATE...AS USUAL.
YOUR TUTOR'S BEEN WAITING FOR YOU.
ぶ
THIS STRANGE GUY KEPT HARASSING ME ON THE WAY HERE...
OH, NO, REALLY?
AGAIN? DID YOU KNEE HIM IN THE NADS?
OF COURSE. A CASUAL KICK IN THE CROTCH...
HOLD ON NOW...

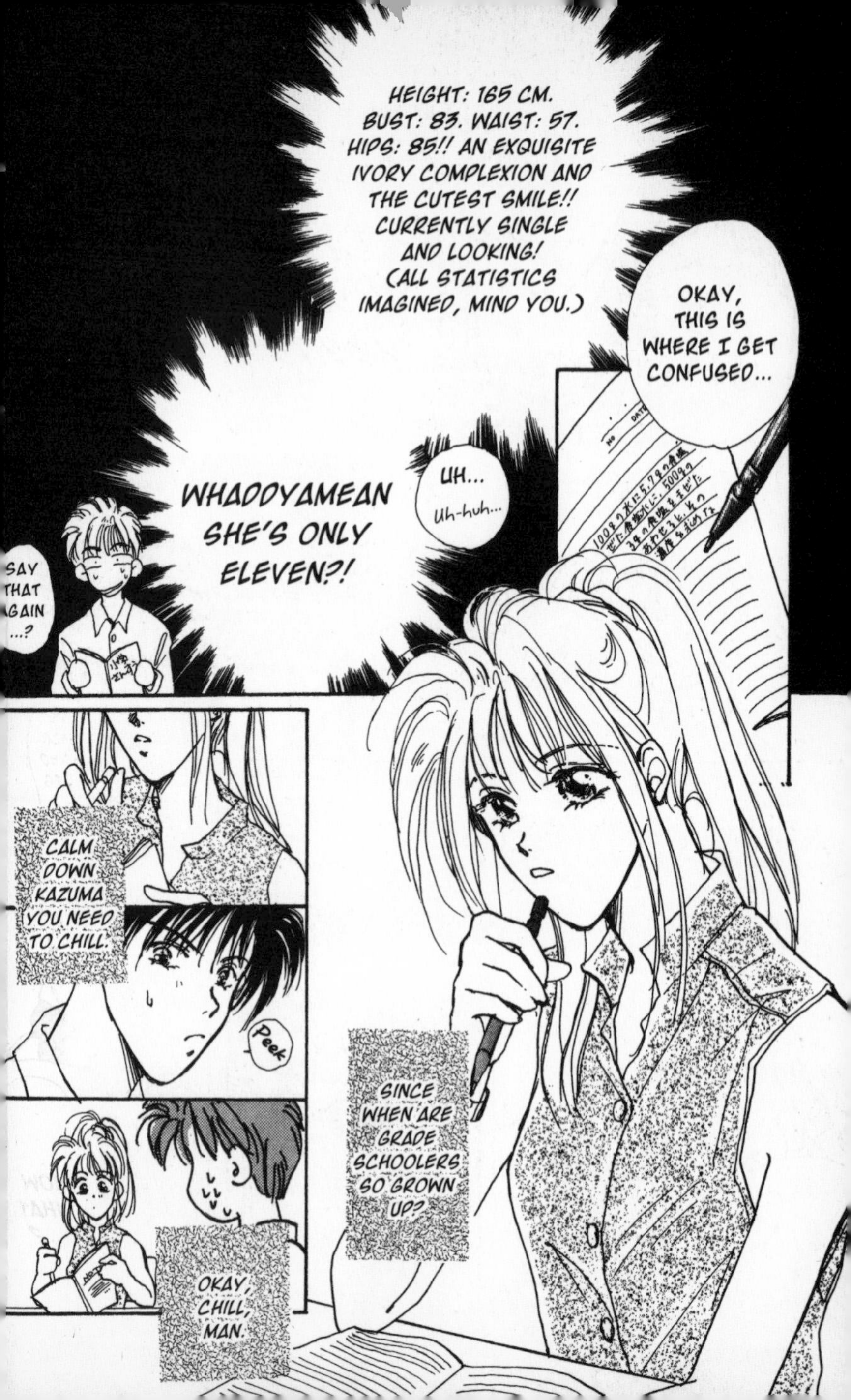
HEIGHT: 165 CM. BUST: 83. WAIST: 57. HIPS: 85!! AN EXQUISITE IVORY COMPLEXION AND THE CUTEST SMILE!! CURRENTLY SINGLE AND LOOKING! (ALL STATISTICS IMAGINED, MIND YOU.)
OKAY, THIS IS WHERE I GET CONFUSED...
UH... Uh-huh...
WHADDYAMEAN SHE'S ONLY ELEVEN?!
SAY THAT GAIN ...?
SINCE WHEN ARE GRADE SCHOOLERS SO GROWN UP?
CALM DOWN KAZUMA YOU NEED TO CHILL.
Peek
OKAY, CHILL, MAN.

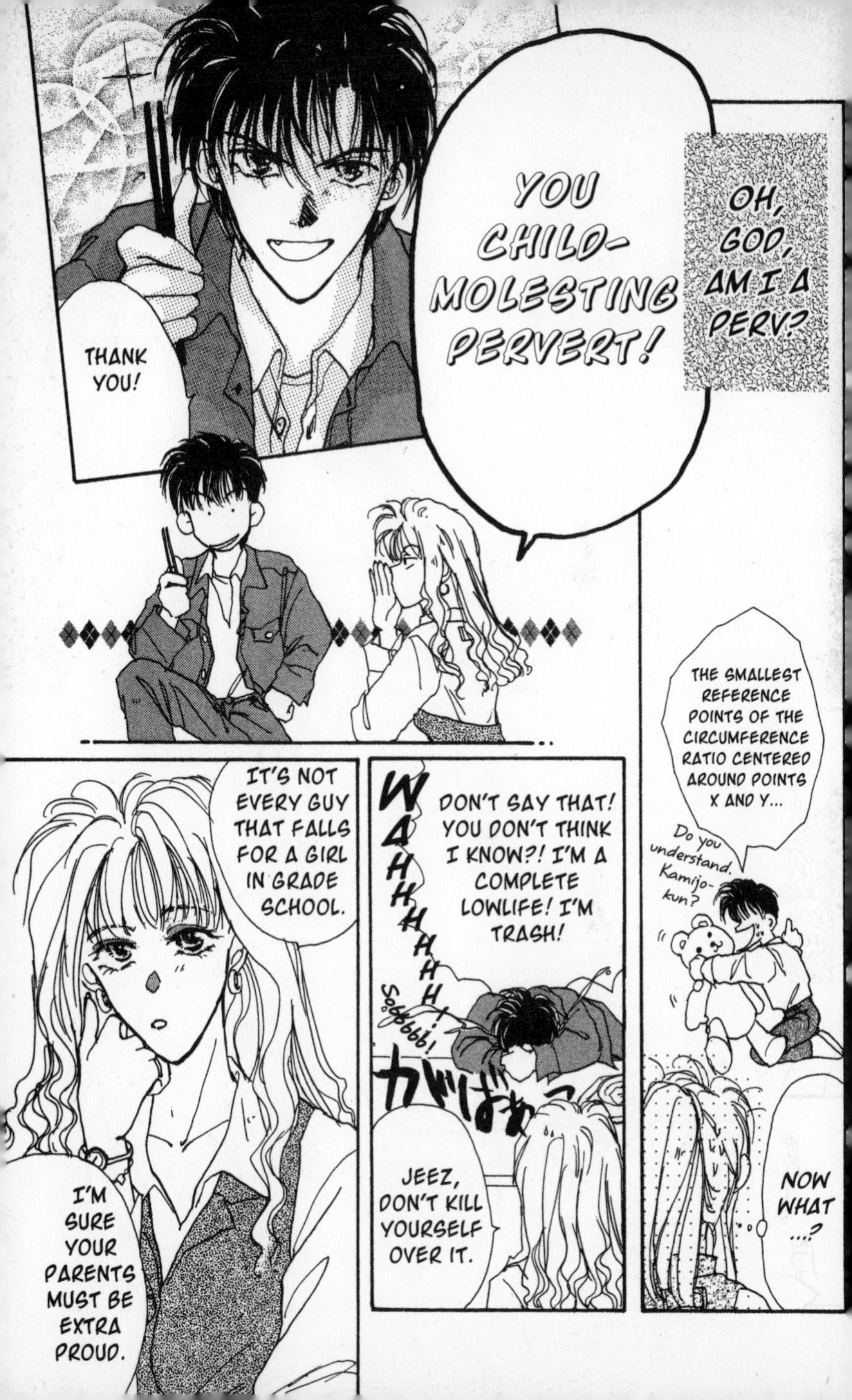
THANK YOU!
YOU CHILD-MOLESTING PERVERT!
OH, GOD, AM I A PERV?
IT'S NOT EVERY GUY THAT FALLS FOR A GIRL IN GRADE SCHOOL.
I'M SURE YOUR PARENTS MUST BE EXTRA PROUD.
WAHHHHHHHH!
DON'T SAY THAT! YOU DON'T THINK I KNOW?! I'M A COMPLETE LOWLIFE! I'M TRASH!
Sobbbbb!
JEEZ, DON'T KILL YOURSELF OVER IT.
THE SMALLEST REFERENCE POINTS OF THE CIRCUMFERENCE RATIO CENTERED AROUND POINTS X AND Y...
Do you understand. Kamijo-kun?
NOW WHAT ...?

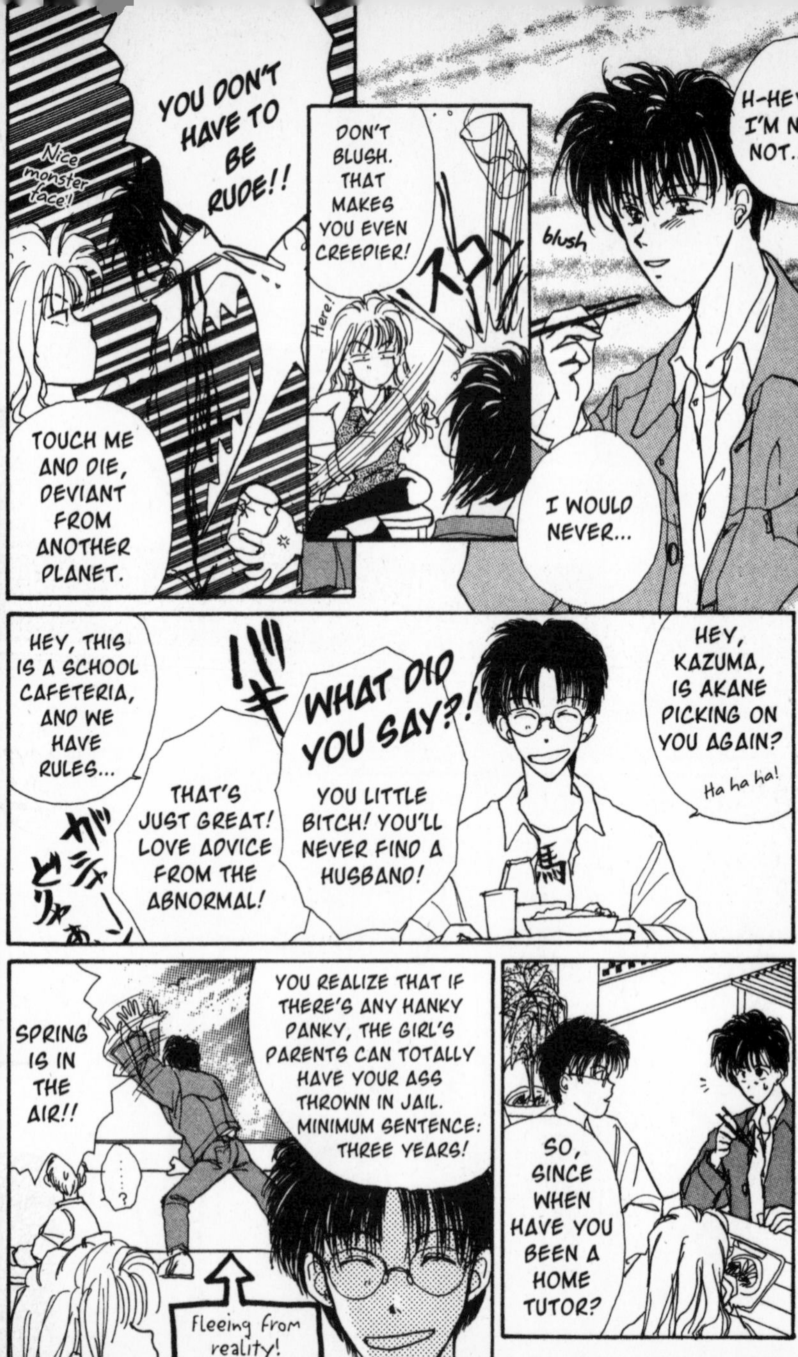
H-HEY, I'M N-NOT...
blush
I WOULD NEVER...
DON'T BLUSH. THAT MAKES YOU EVEN CREEPIER!
Here!
YOU DON'T HAVE TO BE RUDE!!
Nice monster face!
TOUCH ME AND DIE, DEVIANT FROM ANOTHER PLANET.
HEY, KAZUMA, IS AKANE PICKING ON YOU AGAIN?
Ha ha ha!
WHAT DID YOU SAY?!
YOU LITTLE BITCH! YOU'LL NEVER FIND A HUSBAND!
THAT'S JUST GREAT! LOVE ADVICE FROM THE ABNORMAL!
HEY, THIS IS A SCHOOL CAFETERIA, AND WE HAVE RULES...
SO, SINCE WHEN HAVE YOU BEEN A HOME TUTOR?
YOU REALIZE THAT IF THERE'S ANY HANKY PANKY, THE GIRL'S PARENTS CAN TOTALLY HAVE YOUR ASS THROWN IN JAIL. MINIMUM SENTENCE: THREE YEARS!
SPRING IS IN THE AIR!!
......?
Fleeing from reality!

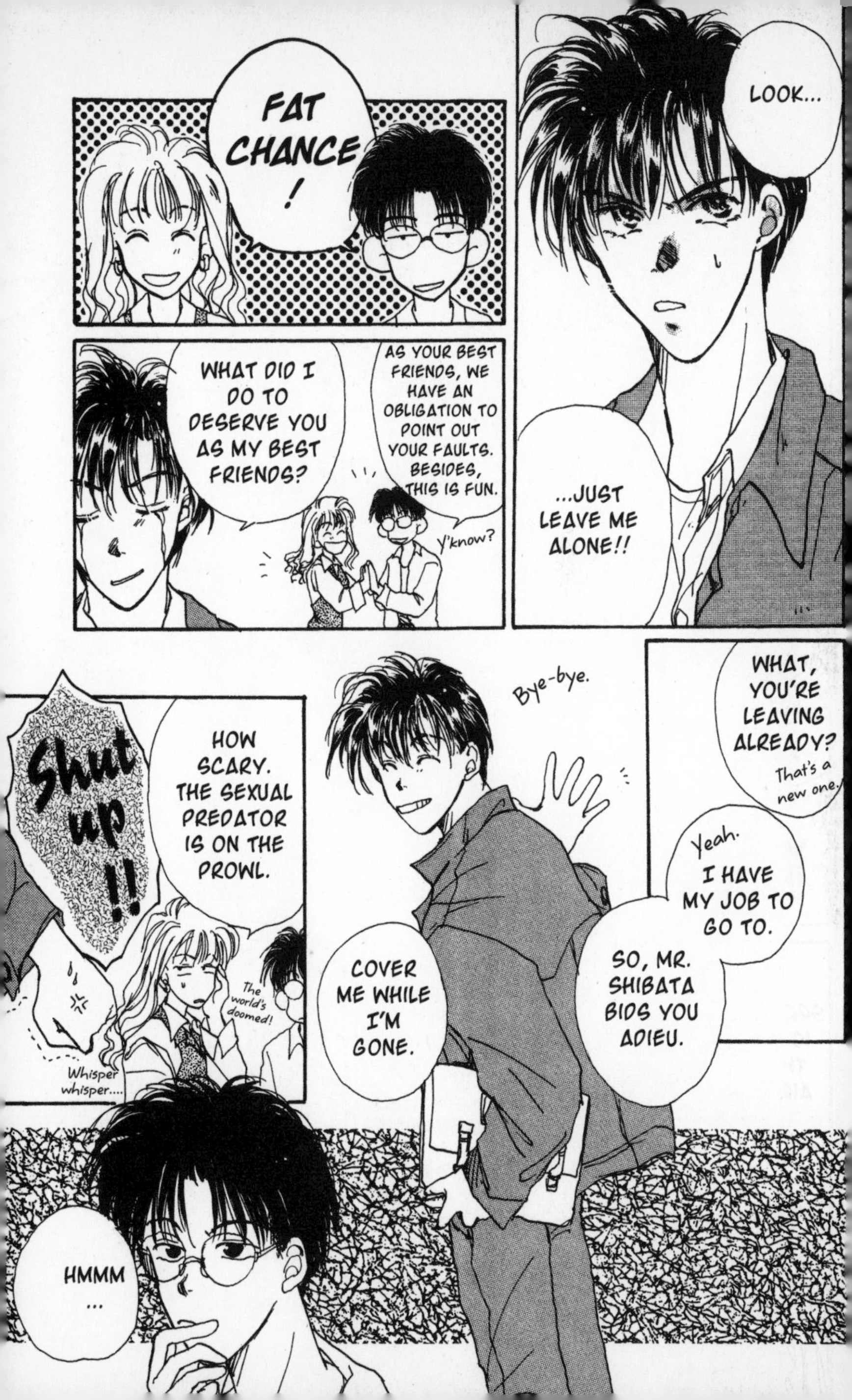
LOOK...
...JUST LEAVE ME ALONE!!
FAT CHANCE!
AS YOUR BEST FRIENDS, WE HAVE AN OBLIGATION TO POINT OUT YOUR FAULTS. BESIDES, THIS IS FUN.
WHAT DID I DO TO DESERVE YOU AS MY BEST FRIENDS?
Y'know?
WHAT, YOU'RE LEAVING ALREADY?
That's a new one.
Yeah.
I HAVE MY JOB TO GO TO.
SO, MR. SHIBATA BIDS YOU ADIEU.
Bye-bye.
COVER ME WHILE I'M GONE.
HOW SCARY. THE SEXUAL PREDATOR IS ON THE PROWL.
Shut up!!
The world's doomed!
Whisper whisper....
HMMM...

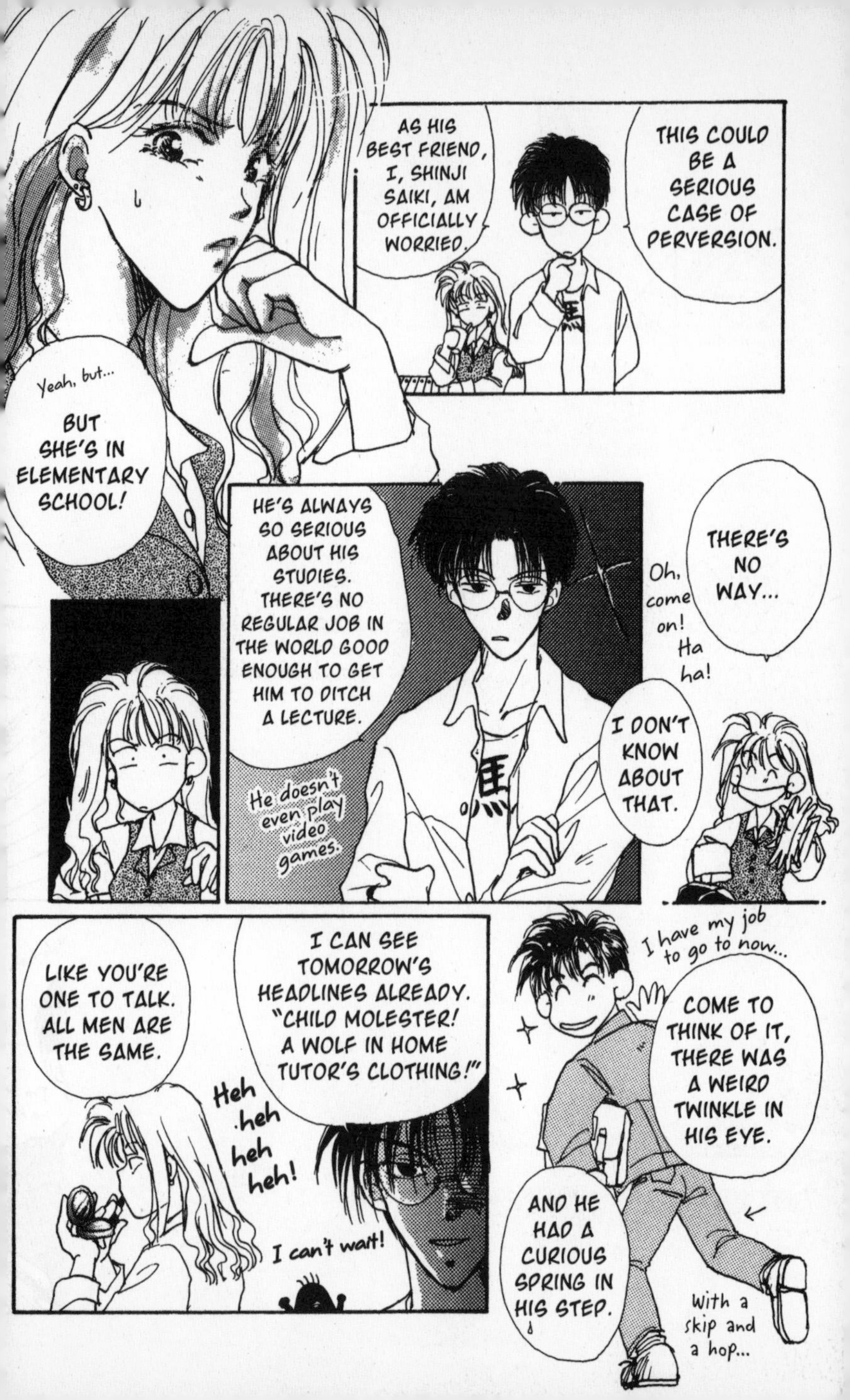
THIS COULD BE A SERIOUS CASE OF PERVERSION.
AS HIS BEST FRIEND, I, SHINJI SAIKI, AM OFFICIALLY WORRIED.
Yeah, but...
BUT SHE'S IN ELEMENTARY SCHOOL!
THERE'S NO WAY...
Oh, come on! Ha ha!
I DON'T KNOW ABOUT THAT.
HE'S ALWAYS SO SERIOUS ABOUT HIS STUDIES. THERE'S NO REGULAR JOB IN THE WORLD GOOD ENOUGH TO GET HIM TO DITCH A LECTURE.
He doesn't even play video games.
I have my job to go to now...
COME TO THINK OF IT, THERE WAS A WEIRD TWINKLE IN HIS EYE.
AND HE HAD A CURIOUS SPRING IN HIS STEP.
With a skip and a hop...
I CAN SEE TOMORROW'S HEADLINES ALREADY. "CHILD MOLESTER! A WOLF IN HOME TUTOR'S CLOTHING!"
LIKE YOU'RE ONE TO TALK. ALL MEN ARE THE SAME.
Heh heh heh heh!
I can't wait!

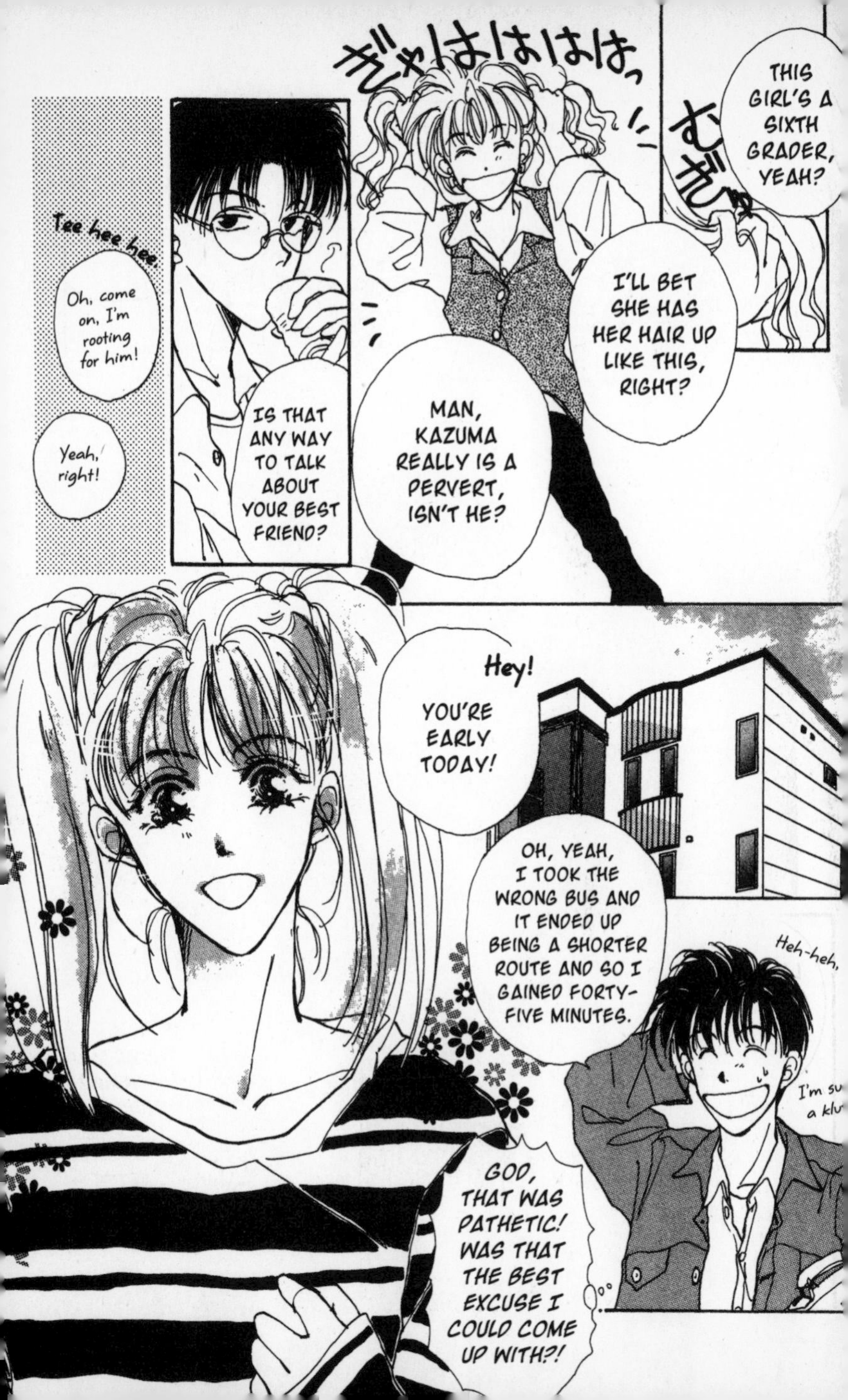
THIS GIRL'S A SIXTH GRADER, YEAH?
むぎゅ
ぎゃははははっ
I'LL BET SHE HAS HER HAIR UP LIKE THIS, RIGHT?
MAN, KAZUMA REALLY IS A PERVERT, ISN'T HE?
IS THAT ANY WAY TO TALK ABOUT YOUR BEST FRIEND?
Tee hee hee.
Oh, come on, I'm rooting for him!
Yeah, right!
Hey!
YOU'RE EARLY TODAY!
OH, YEAH, I TOOK THE WRONG BUS AND IT ENDED UP BEING A SHORTER ROUTE AND SO I GAINED FORTY-FIVE MINUTES.
Heh-heh,
GOD, THAT WAS PATHETIC! WAS THAT THE BEST EXCUSE I COULD COME UP WITH?!

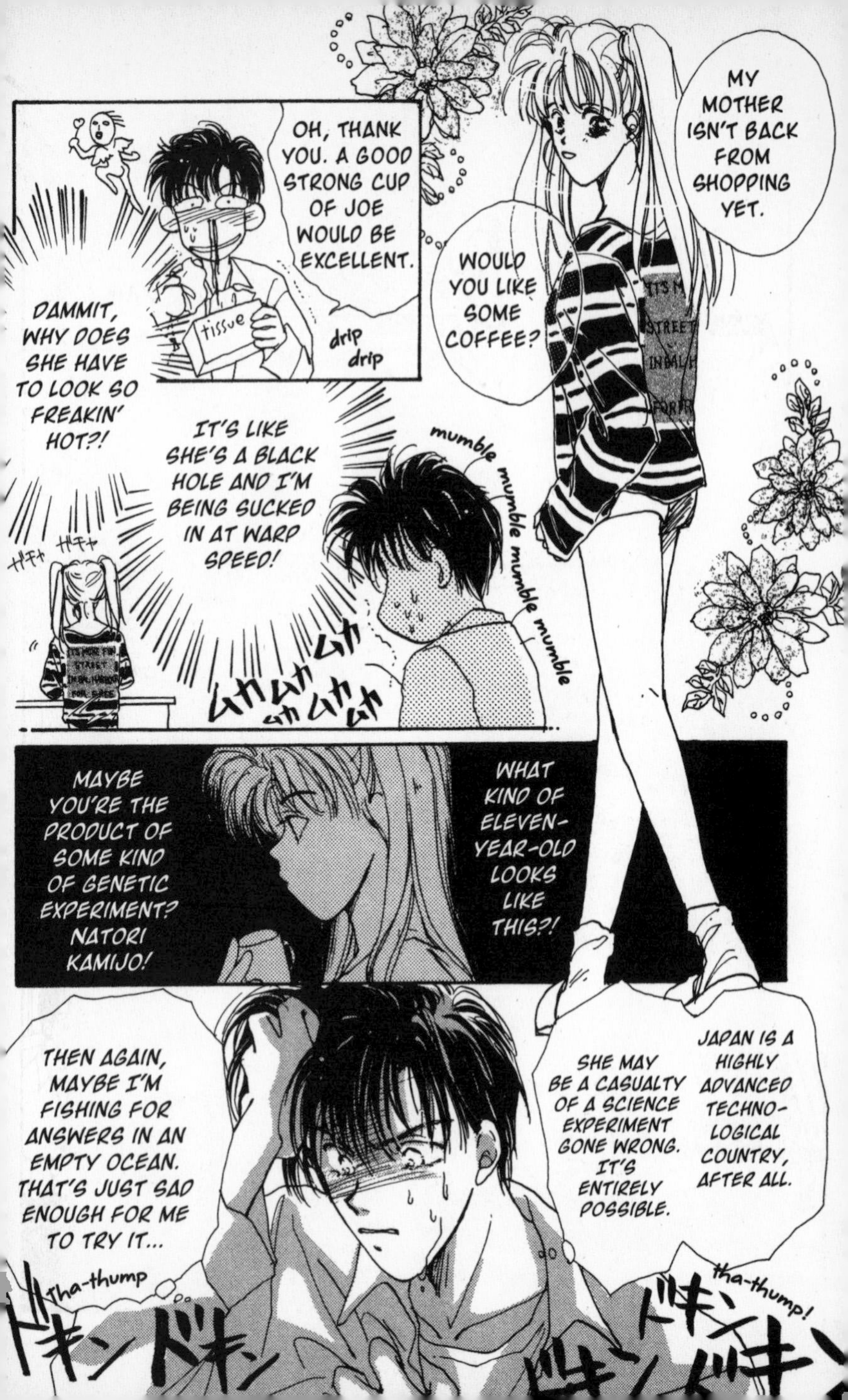
MY MOTHER ISN'T BACK FROM SHOPPING YET.
WOULD YOU LIKE SOME COFFEE?
OH, THANK YOU. A GOOD STRONG CUP OF JOE WOULD BE EXCELLENT.
tissue
drip drip
DAMMIT, WHY DOES SHE HAVE TO LOOK SO FREAKIN' HOT?!
mumble mumble mumble mumble
IT'S LIKE SHE'S A BLACK HOLE AND I'M BEING SUCKED IN AT WARP SPEED!
WHAT KIND OF ELEVEN-YEAR-OLD LOOKS LIKE THIS?!
MAYBE YOU'RE THE PRODUCT OF SOME KIND OF GENETIC EXPERIMENT? NATORI KAMIJO!
JAPAN IS A HIGHLY ADVANCED TECHNO-LOGICAL COUNTRY, AFTER ALL.
SHE MAY BE A CASUALTY OF A SCIENCE EXPERIMENT GONE WRONG. IT'S ENTIRELY POSSIBLE.
THEN AGAIN, MAYBE I'M FISHING FOR ANSWERS IN AN EMPTY OCEAN. THAT'S JUST SAD ENOUGH FOR ME TO TRY IT...
tha-thump!
tha-thump

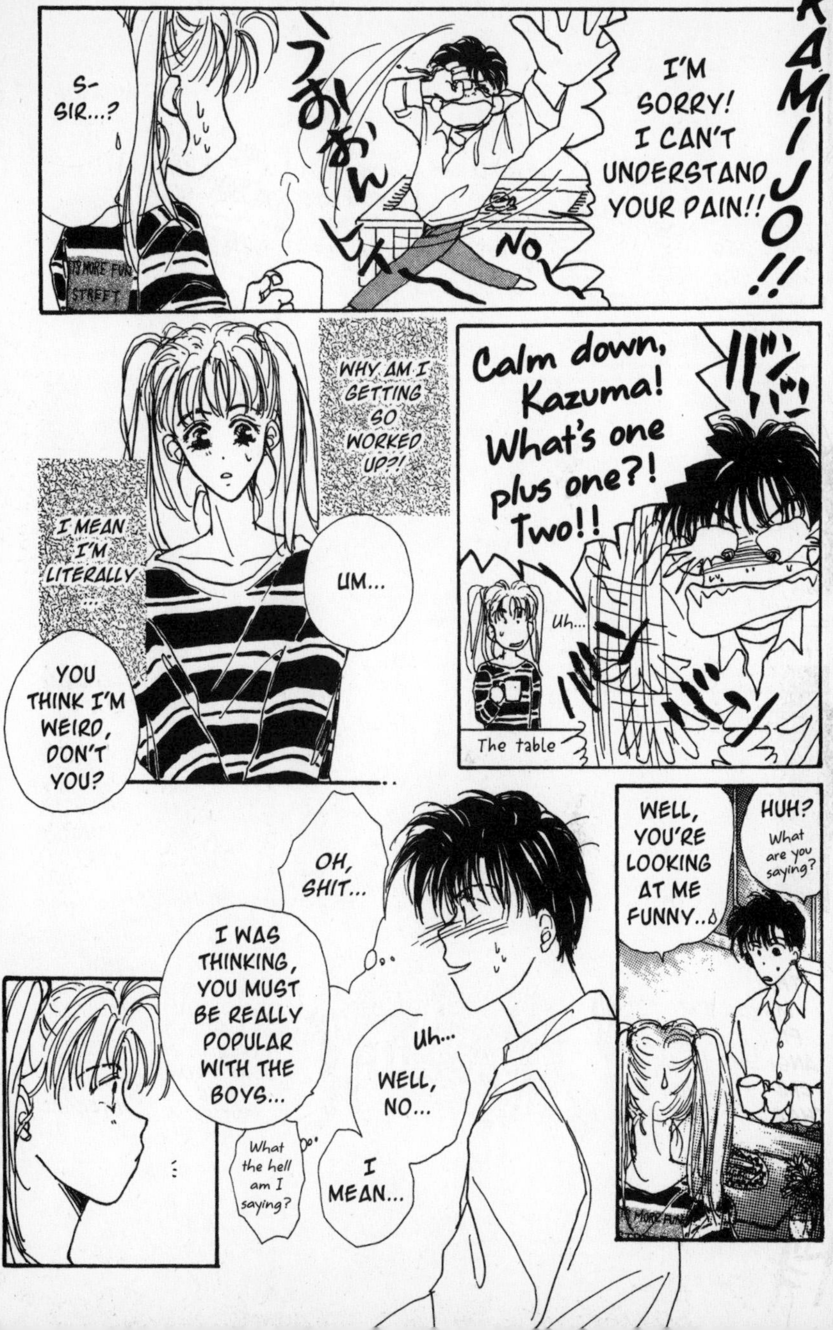
KAMIJO!!
I'M SORRY! I CAN'T UNDERSTAND YOUR PAIN!!
NO...
うおおん
S-SIR...?
Calm down, Kazuma! What's one plus one?! Two!!
Uh...
The table
WHY AM I GETTING SO WORKED UP?!
I MEAN I'M LITERALLY...
UM...
YOU THINK I'M WEIRD, DON'T YOU?
HUH? What are you saying?
WELL, YOU'RE LOOKING AT ME FUNNY..
OH, SHIT...
I WAS THINKING, YOU MUST BE REALLY POPULAR WITH THE BOYS...
Uh... WELL, NO...
I MEAN...
What the hell am I saying?
...

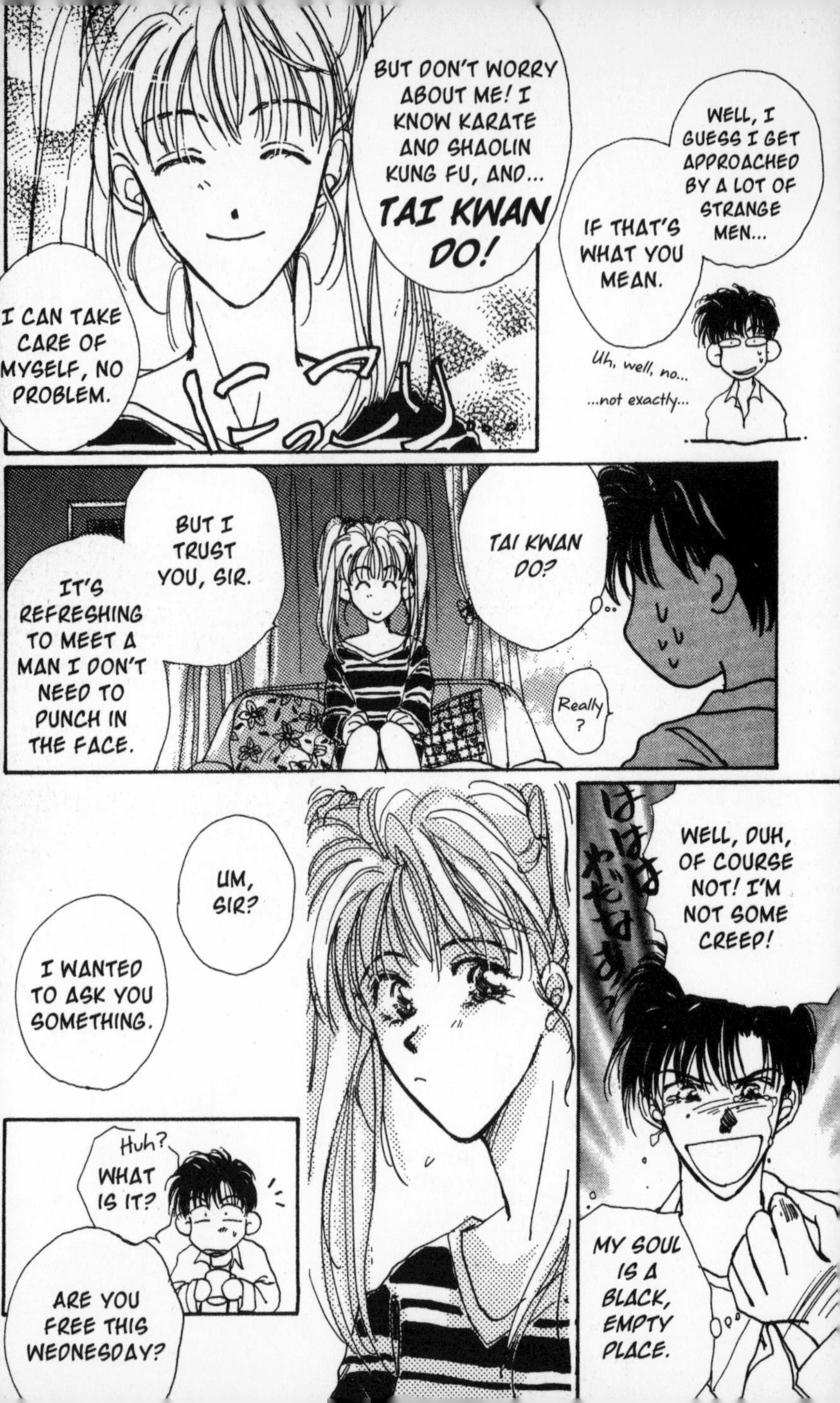
WELL, I GUESS I GET APPROACHED BY A LOT OF STRANGE MEN...
IF THAT'S WHAT YOU MEAN.
Uh, well, no...
...not exactly...
BUT DON'T WORRY ABOUT ME! I KNOW KARATE AND SHAOLIN KUNG FU, AND... TAI KWAN DO!
I CAN TAKE CARE OF MYSELF, NO PROBLEM.
TAI KWAN DO?
Really?
BUT I TRUST YOU, SIR.
IT'S REFRESHING TO MEET A MAN I DON'T NEED TO PUNCH IN THE FACE.
ははは
WELL, DUH, OF COURSE NOT! I'M NOT SOME CREEP!
MY SOUL IS A BLACK, EMPTY PLACE.
UM, SIR?
I WANTED TO ASK YOU SOMETHING.
Huh? WHAT IS IT?
ARE YOU FREE THIS WEDNESDAY?

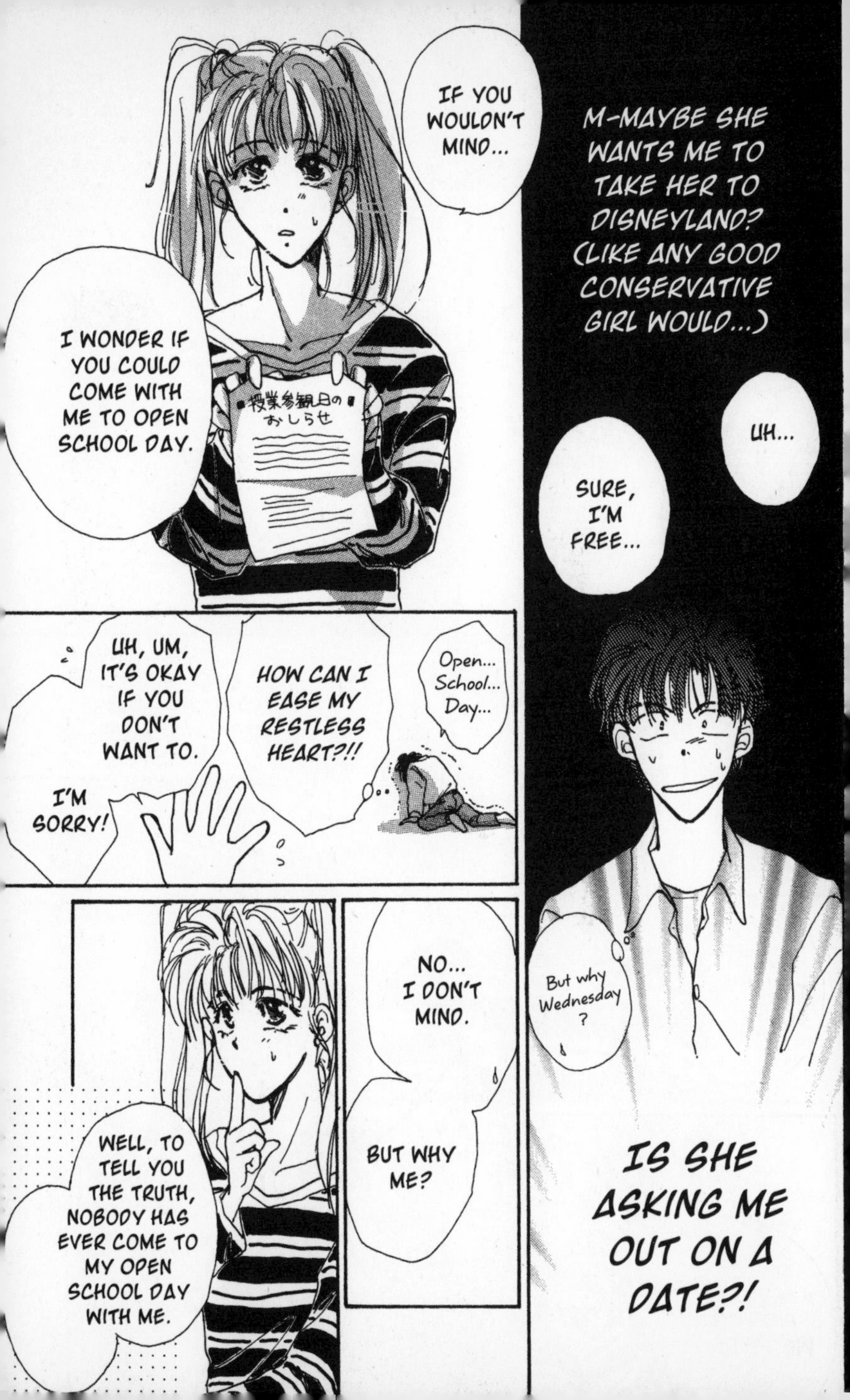
M-MAYBE SHE WANTS ME TO TAKE HER TO DISNEYLAND? (LIKE ANY GOOD CONSERVATIVE GIRL WOULD...)
UH...
SURE, I'M FREE...
But why Wednesday ?
IS SHE ASKING ME OUT ON A DATE?!
IF YOU WOULDN'T MIND...
I WONDER IF YOU COULD COME WITH ME TO OPEN SCHOOL DAY.
■授業参観日の■
おしらせ
Open... School... Day...
HOW CAN I EASE MY RESTLESS HEART?!!
UH, UM, IT'S OKAY IF YOU DON'T WANT TO.
I'M SORRY!
NO... I DON'T MIND.
BUT WHY ME?
WELL, TO TELL YOU THE TRUTH, NOBODY HAS EVER COME TO MY OPEN SCHOOL DAY WITH ME.

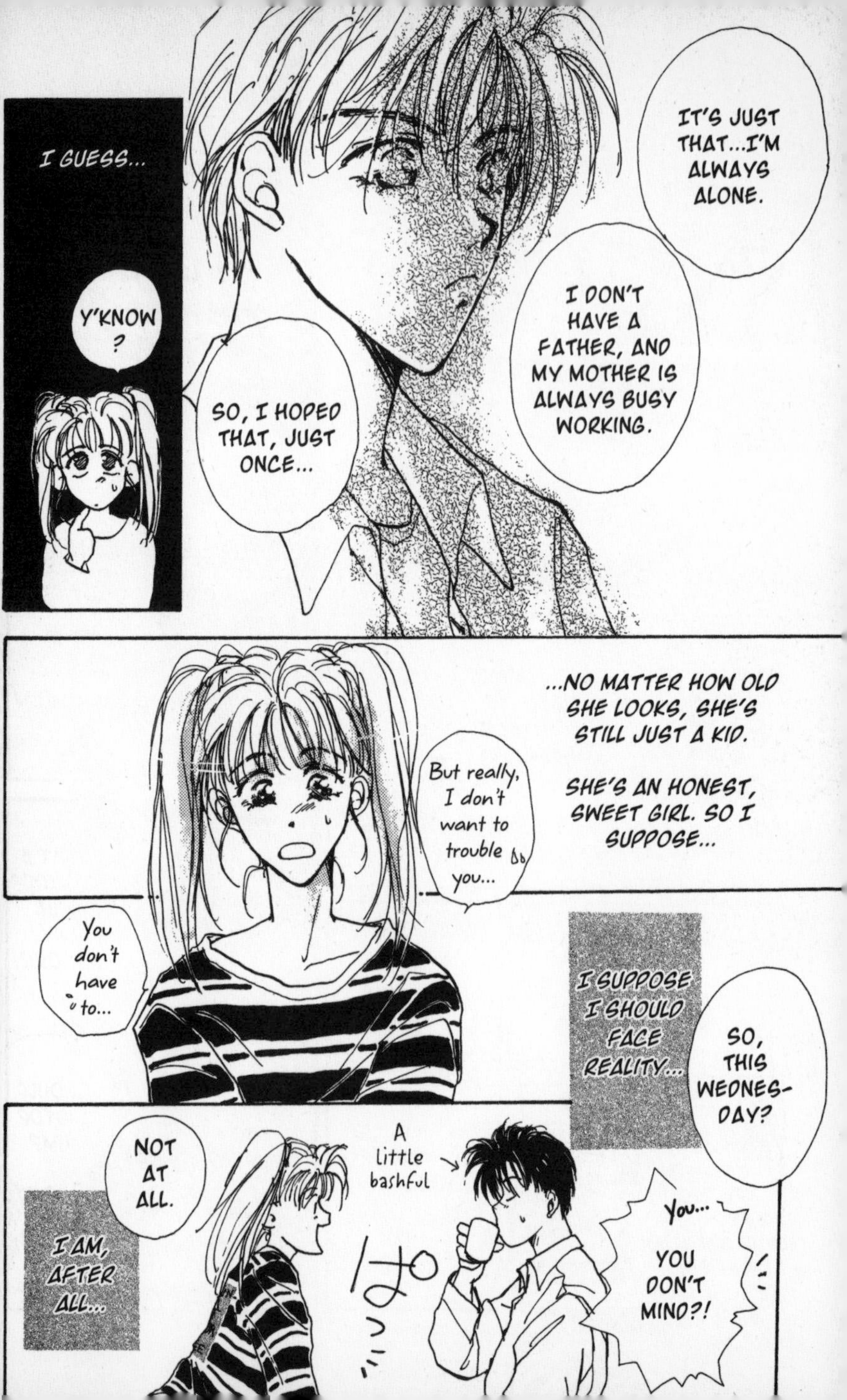

IT'S JUST THAT...I'M ALWAYS ALONE.
I DON'T HAVE A FATHER, AND MY MOTHER IS ALWAYS BUSY WORKING.
SO, I HOPED THAT, JUST ONCE...
I GUESS...
Y'KNOW?
...NO MATTER HOW OLD SHE LOOKS, SHE'S STILL JUST A KID.
SHE'S AN HONEST, SWEET GIRL. SO I SUPPOSE...
But really, I don't want to trouble you...
You don't have to...
I SUPPOSE I SHOULD FACE REALITY...
SO, THIS WEDNESDAY?
You...
YOU DON'T MIND?!
A little bashful
はっ
NOT AT ALL.
I AM, AFTER ALL...

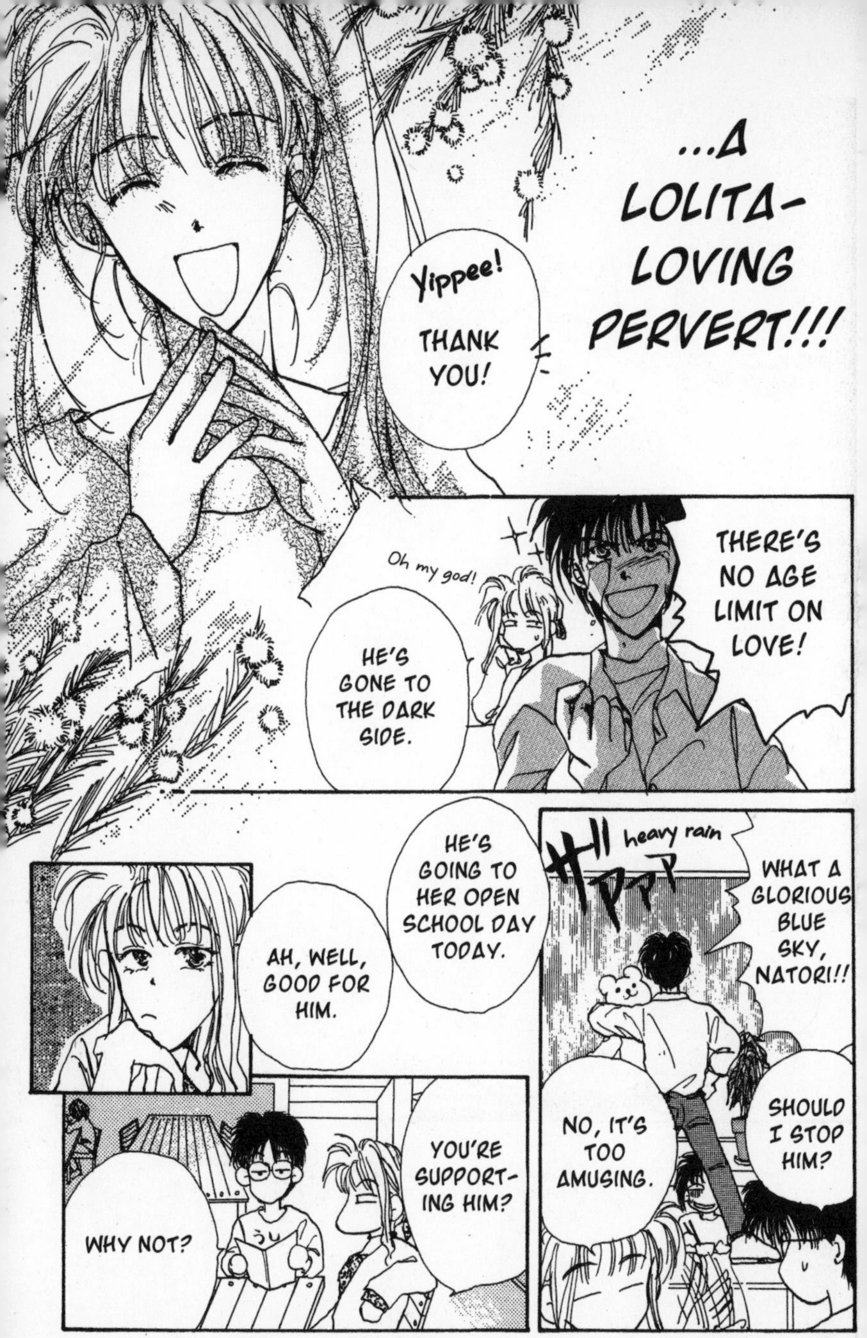

...A LOLITA-LOVING PERVERT!!!
Yippee! THANK YOU!
THERE'S NO AGE LIMIT ON LOVE!
Oh my god!
HE'S GONE TO THE DARK SIDE.
heavy rain
WHAT A GLORIOUS BLUE SKY, NATORI!!!
SHOULD I STOP HIM?
NO, IT'S TOO AMUSING.
HE'S GOING TO HER OPEN SCHOOL DAY TODAY.
AH, WELL, GOOD FOR HIM.
YOU'RE SUPPORT-ING HIM?
WHY NOT?

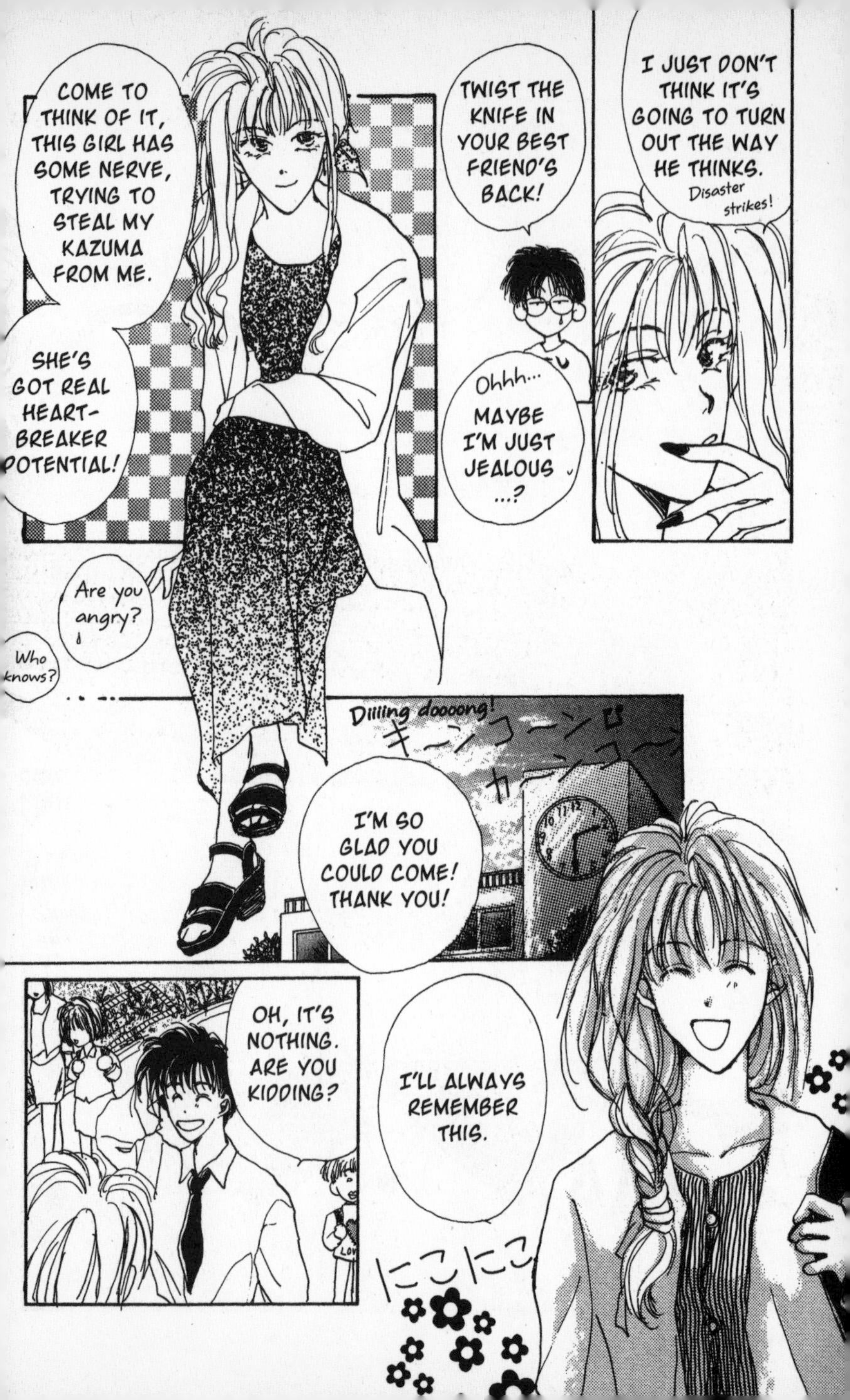
I JUST DON'T THINK IT'S GOING TO TURN OUT THE WAY HE THINKS.
Disaster strikes!
TWIST THE KNIFE IN YOUR BEST FRIEND'S BACK!
Ohhh... MAYBE I'M JUST JEALOUS ...?
COME TO THINK OF IT, THIS GIRL HAS SOME NERVE, TRYING TO STEAL MY KAZUMA FROM ME.
SHE'S GOT REAL HEART-BREAKER POTENTIAL!
Are you angry?
Who knows?
Diiling doooong!
キ〜ンコ〜ン
カ〜ンコ〜ン
I'M SO GLAD YOU COULD COME! THANK YOU!
I'LL ALWAYS REMEMBER THIS.
にこにこ
OH, IT'S NOTHING. ARE YOU KIDDING?

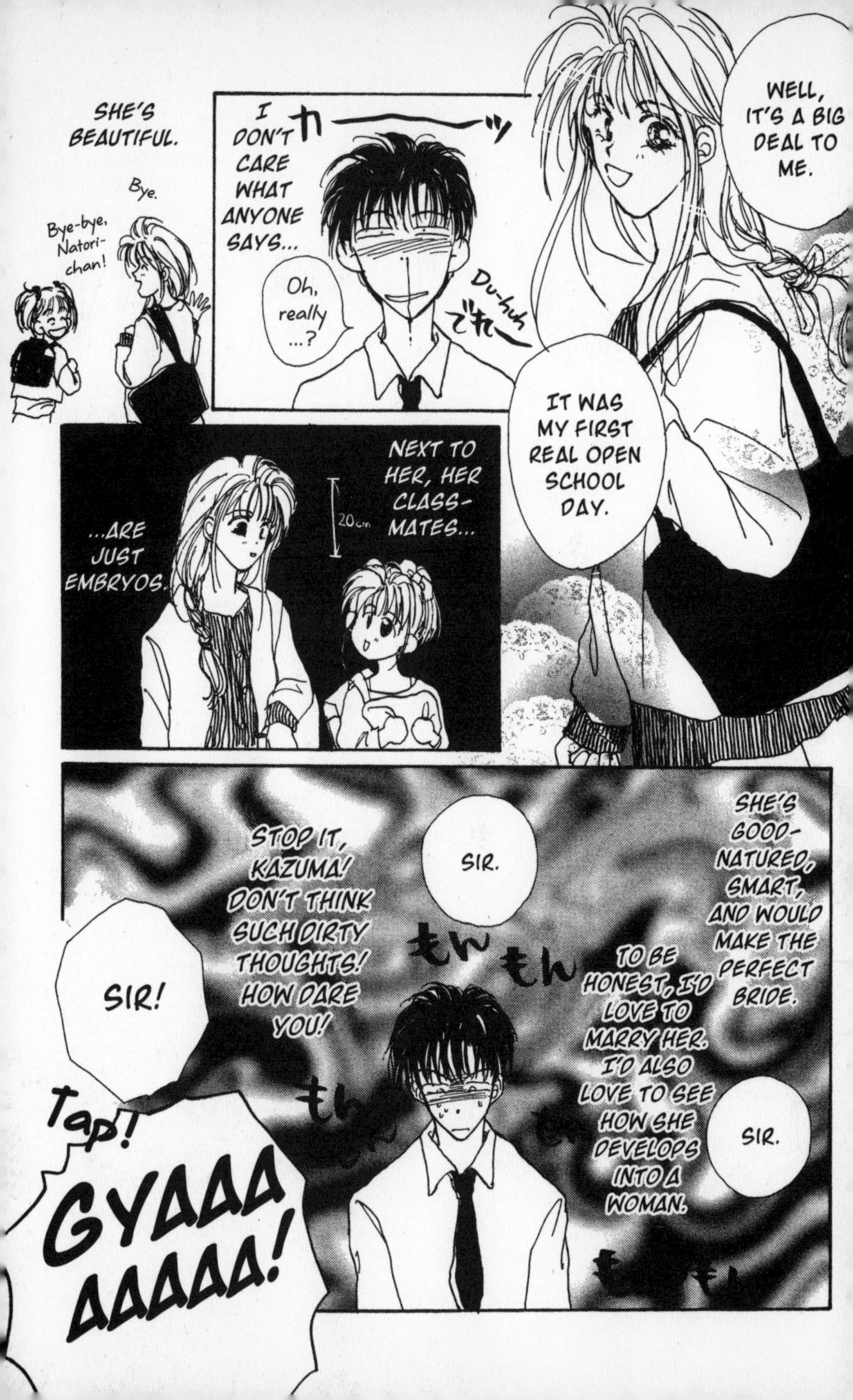
WELL, IT'S A BIG DEAL TO ME.
IT WAS MY FIRST REAL OPEN SCHOOL DAY.
カーーーッ
I DON'T CARE WHAT ANYONE SAYS...
Oh, really ...?
Du-huh
でれー
SHE'S BEAUTIFUL.
Bye.
Bye-bye, Natori-chan!
NEXT TO HER, HER CLASSMATES...
20cm
...ARE JUST EMBRYOS.
SHE'S GOOD-NATURED, SMART, AND WOULD MAKE THE PERFECT BRIDE.
SIR.
TO BE HONEST, I'D LOVE TO MARRY HER. I'D ALSO LOVE TO SEE HOW SHE DEVELOPS INTO A WOMAN.
SIR.
もんもん
STOP IT, KAZUMA! DON'T THINK SUCH DIRTY THOUGHTS! HOW DARE YOU!
SIR!
Tap!
GYAAAA AAAAA!

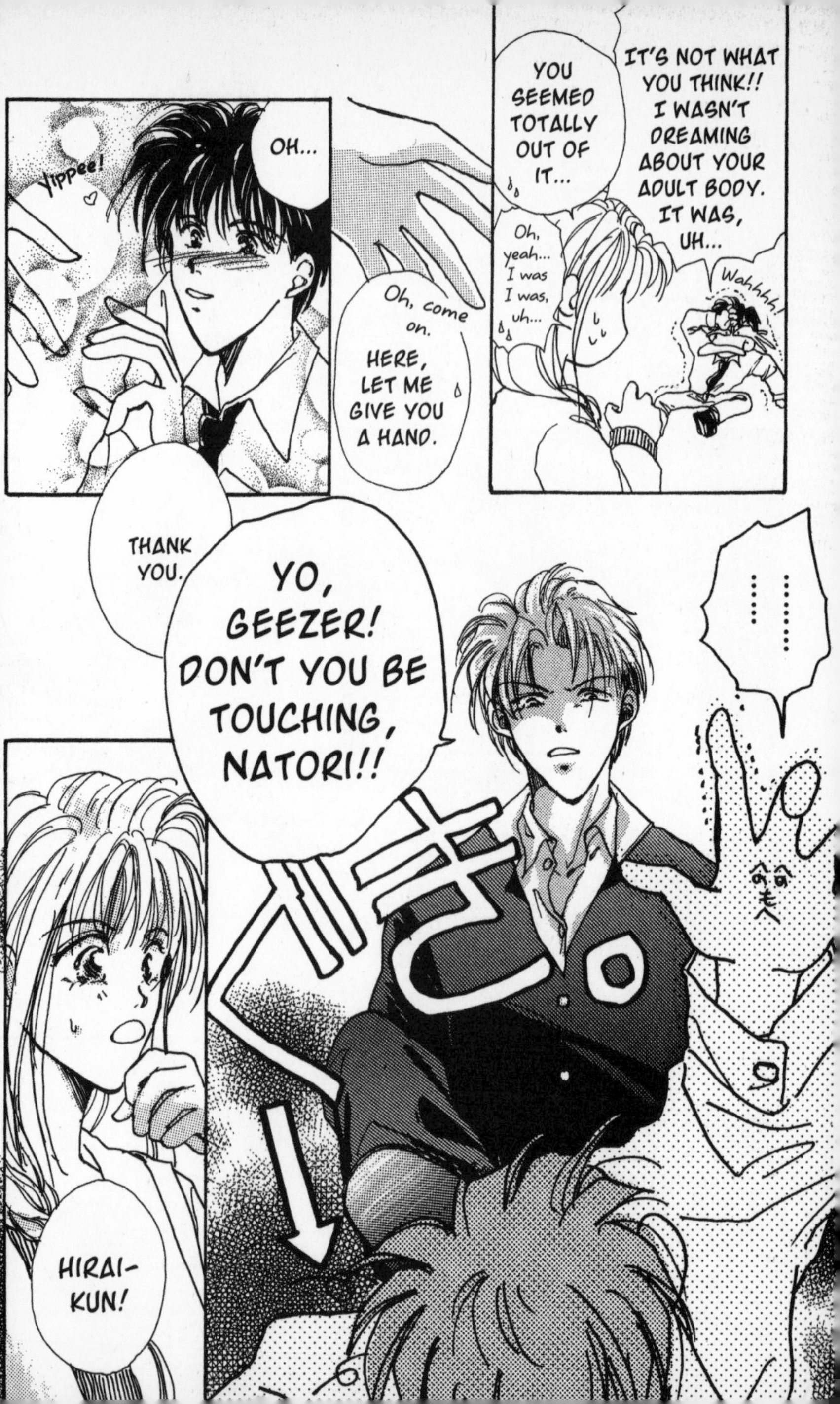
IT'S NOT WHAT YOU THINK!! I WASN'T DREAMING ABOUT YOUR ADULT BODY. IT WAS, UH...
YOU SEEMED TOTALLY OUT OF IT...
Wahhhh!
Oh, yeah... I was I was, uh...
Oh, come on.
HERE, LET ME GIVE YOU A HAND.
OH...
Yippee!
THANK YOU.
......
YO, GEEZER! DON'T YOU BE TOUCHING, NATORI!!
HIRAI-KUN!

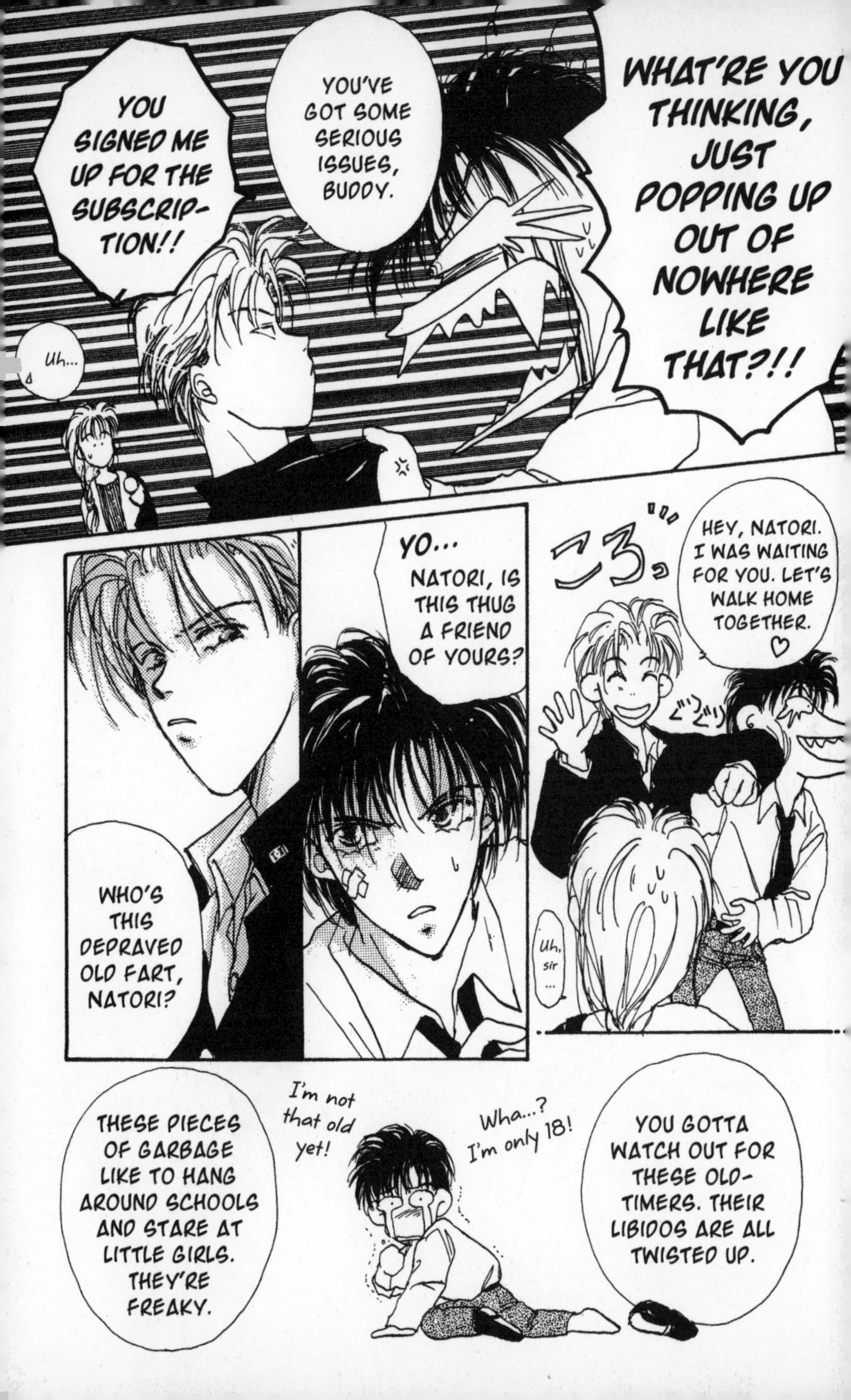
WHAT'RE YOU THINKING, JUST POPPING UP OUT OF NOWHERE LIKE THAT?!!
YOU'VE GOT SOME SERIOUS ISSUES, BUDDY.
YOU SIGNED ME UP FOR THE SUBSCRIP-TION!!
Uh...
ごろっ
HEY, NATORI. I WAS WAITING FOR YOU. LET'S WALK HOME TOGETHER. ♡
ぐりぐり
Uh, sir ...
YO... NATORI, IS THIS THUG A FRIEND OF YOURS?
WHO'S THIS DEPRAVED OLD FART, NATORI?
YOU GOTTA WATCH OUT FOR THESE OLD-TIMERS. THEIR LIBIDOS ARE ALL TWISTED UP.
Wha...? I'm only 18!
I'm not that old yet!
THESE PIECES OF GARBAGE LIKE TO HANG AROUND SCHOOLS AND STARE AT LITTLE GIRLS. THEY'RE FREAKY.

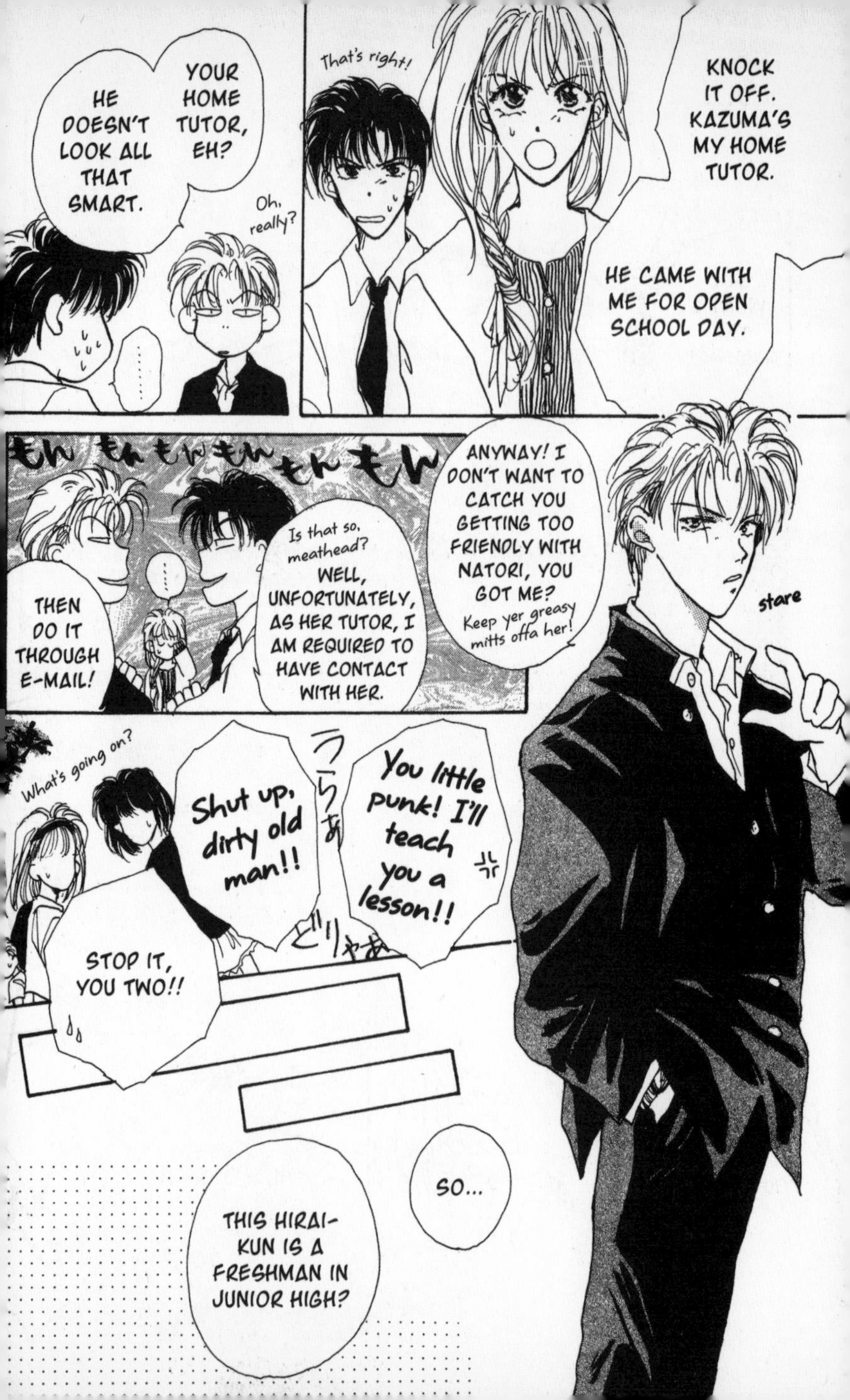
KNOCK IT OFF. KAZUMA'S MY HOME TUTOR.
That's right!
HE CAME WITH ME FOR OPEN SCHOOL DAY.
YOUR HOME TUTOR, EH?
HE DOESN'T LOOK ALL THAT SMART.
Oh, really?
......
ANYWAY! I DON'T WANT TO CATCH YOU GETTING TOO FRIENDLY WITH NATORI, YOU GOT ME?
Keep yer greasy mitts offa her!
stare
Is that so, meathead?
WELL, UNFORTUNATELY, AS HER TUTOR, I AM REQUIRED TO HAVE CONTACT WITH HER.
THEN DO IT THROUGH E-MAIL!
......
You little punk! I'll teach you a lesson!!
Shut up, dirty old man!!
What's going on?
STOP IT, YOU TWO!!
SO...
THIS HIRAI-KUN IS A FRESHMAN IN JUNIOR HIGH?

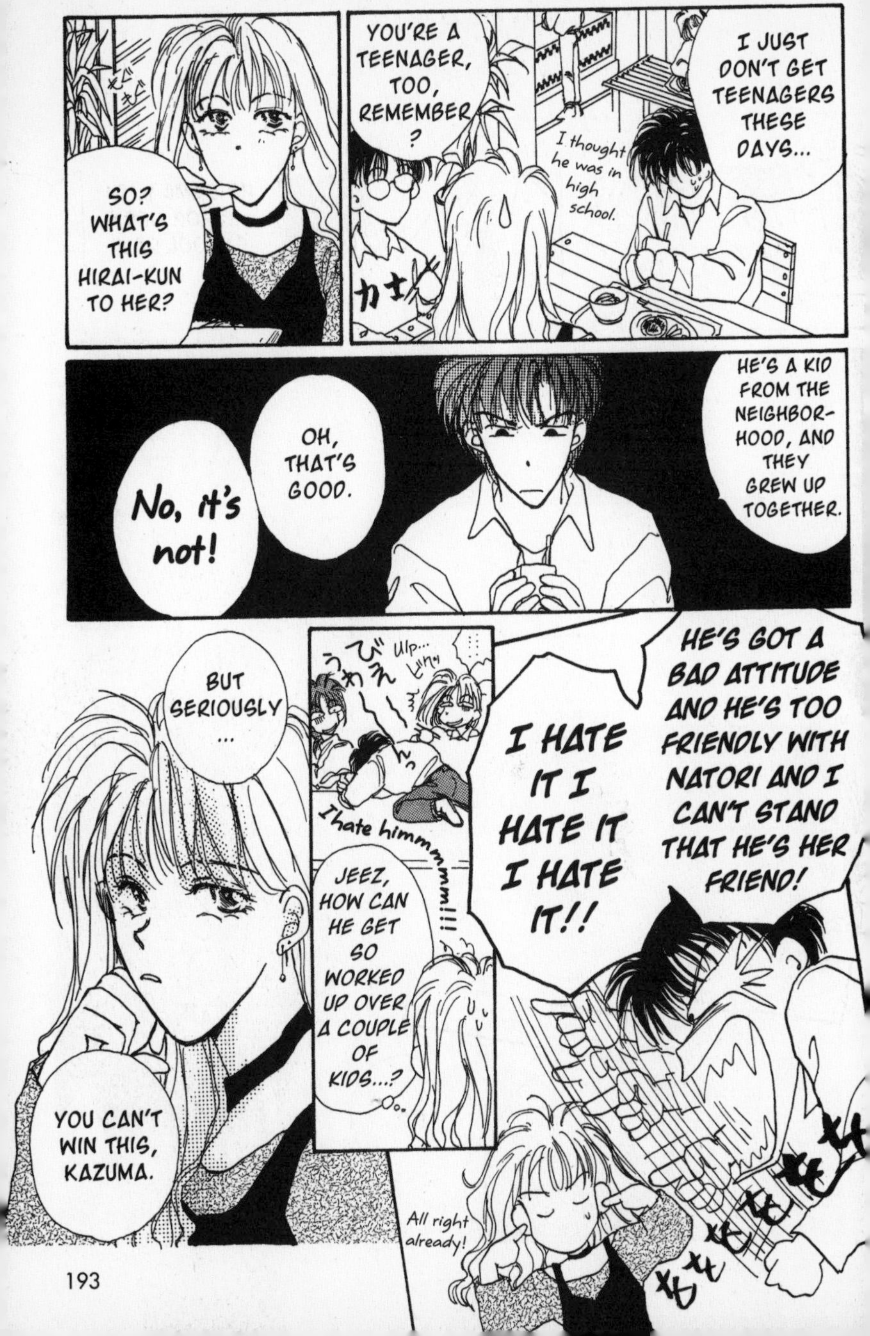
I JUST DON'T GET TEENAGERS THESE DAYS...
I thought he was in high school.
YOU'RE A TEENAGER, TOO, REMEMBER?
SO? WHAT'S THIS HIRAI-KUN TO HER?
HE'S A KID FROM THE NEIGHBORHOOD, AND THEY GREW UP TOGETHER.
OH, THAT'S GOOD.
No, it's not!
HE'S GOT A BAD ATTITUDE AND HE'S TOO FRIENDLY WITH NATORI AND I CAN'T STAND THAT HE'S HER FRIEND!
I HATE IT I HATE IT I HATE IT!!
Ulp...
I hate himmmmm!!!
JEEZ, HOW CAN HE GET SO WORKED UP OVER A COUPLE OF KIDS...?
All right already!
BUT SERIOUSLY...
YOU CAN'T WIN THIS, KAZUMA.

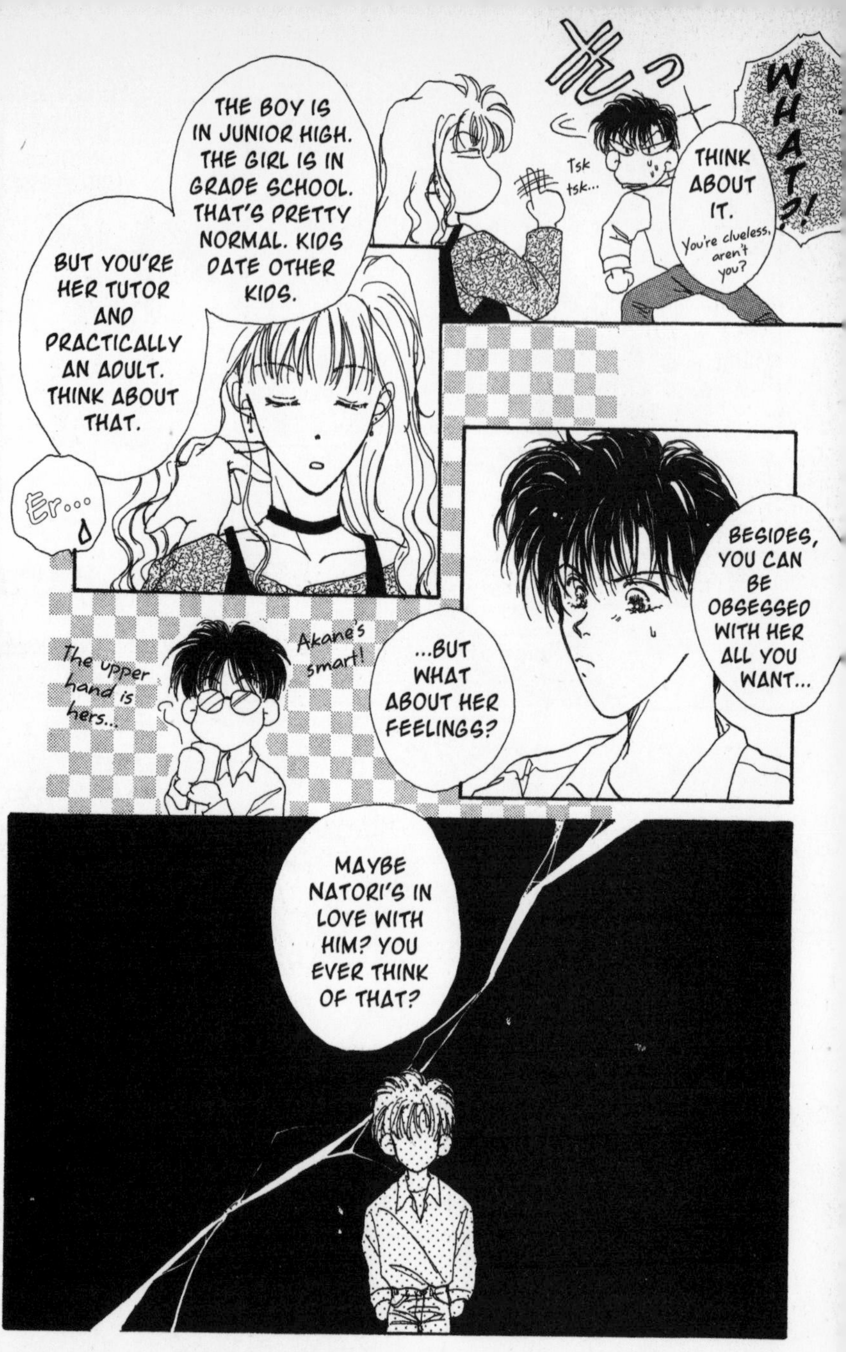
THE BOY IS IN JUNIOR HIGH. THE GIRL IS IN GRADE SCHOOL. THAT'S PRETTY NORMAL. KIDS DATE OTHER KIDS.
WHAT?!
Tsk tsk...
THINK ABOUT IT.
You're clueless, aren't you?
BUT YOU'RE HER TUTOR AND PRACTICALLY AN ADULT. THINK ABOUT THAT.
Er...
BESIDES, YOU CAN BE OBSESSED WITH HER ALL YOU WANT...
...BUT WHAT ABOUT HER FEELINGS?
Akane's smart!
The upper hand is hers...
MAYBE NATORI'S IN LOVE WITH HIM? YOU EVER THINK OF THAT?

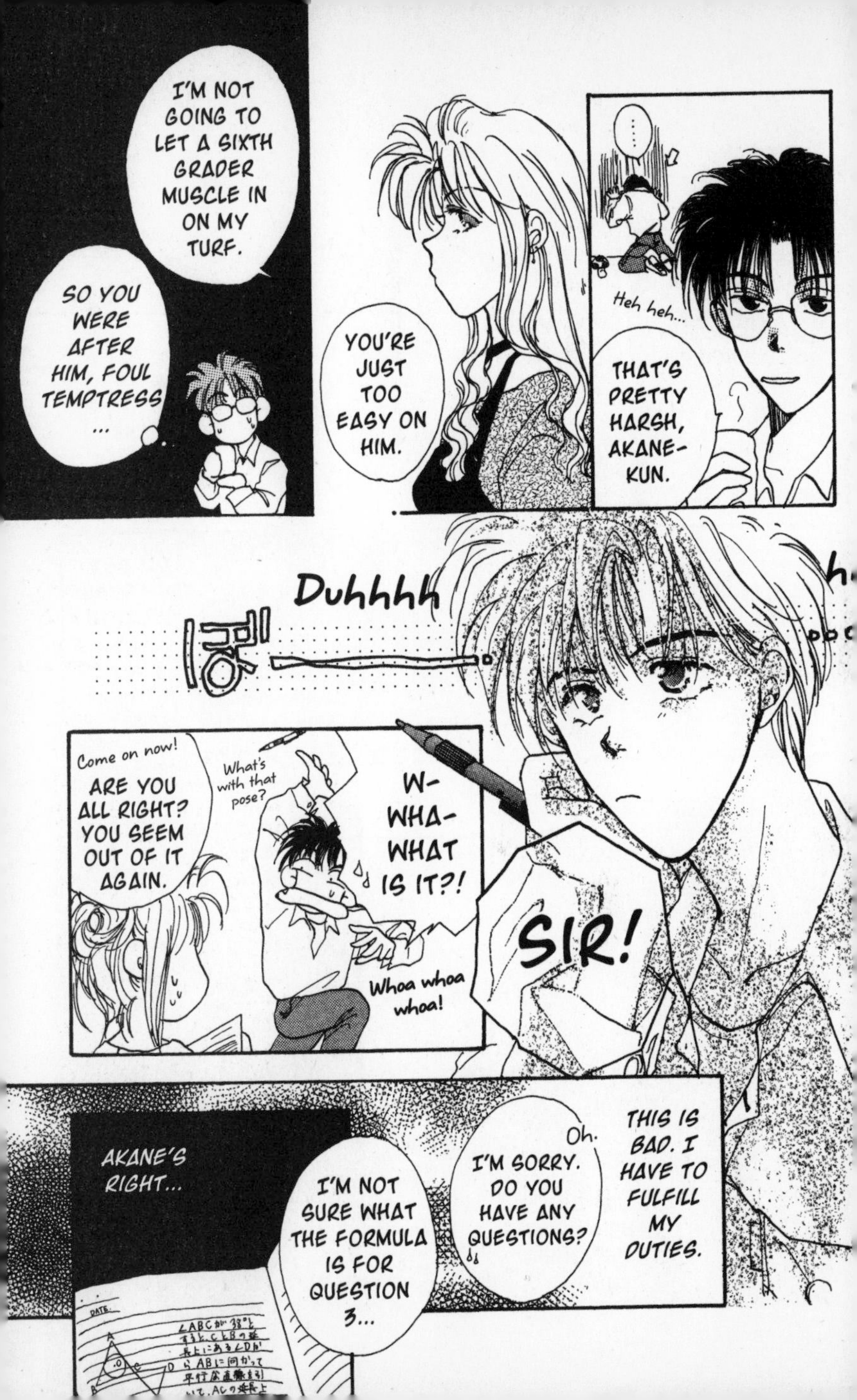
...
Heh heh...
THAT'S PRETTY HARSH, AKANE-KUN.
YOU'RE JUST TOO EASY ON HIM.
I'M NOT GOING TO LET A SIXTH GRADER MUSCLE IN ON MY TURF.
SO YOU WERE AFTER HIM, FOUL TEMPTRESS...
Duhhhh
SIR!
W-WHA-WHAT IS IT?!
What's with that pose?
Come on now!
ARE YOU ALL RIGHT? YOU SEEM OUT OF IT AGAIN.
Whoa whoa whoa!
THIS IS BAD. I HAVE TO FULFILL MY DUTIES.
Oh.
I'M SORRY. DO YOU HAVE ANY QUESTIONS?
I'M NOT SURE WHAT THE FORMULA IS FOR QUESTION 3...
AKANE'S RIGHT...

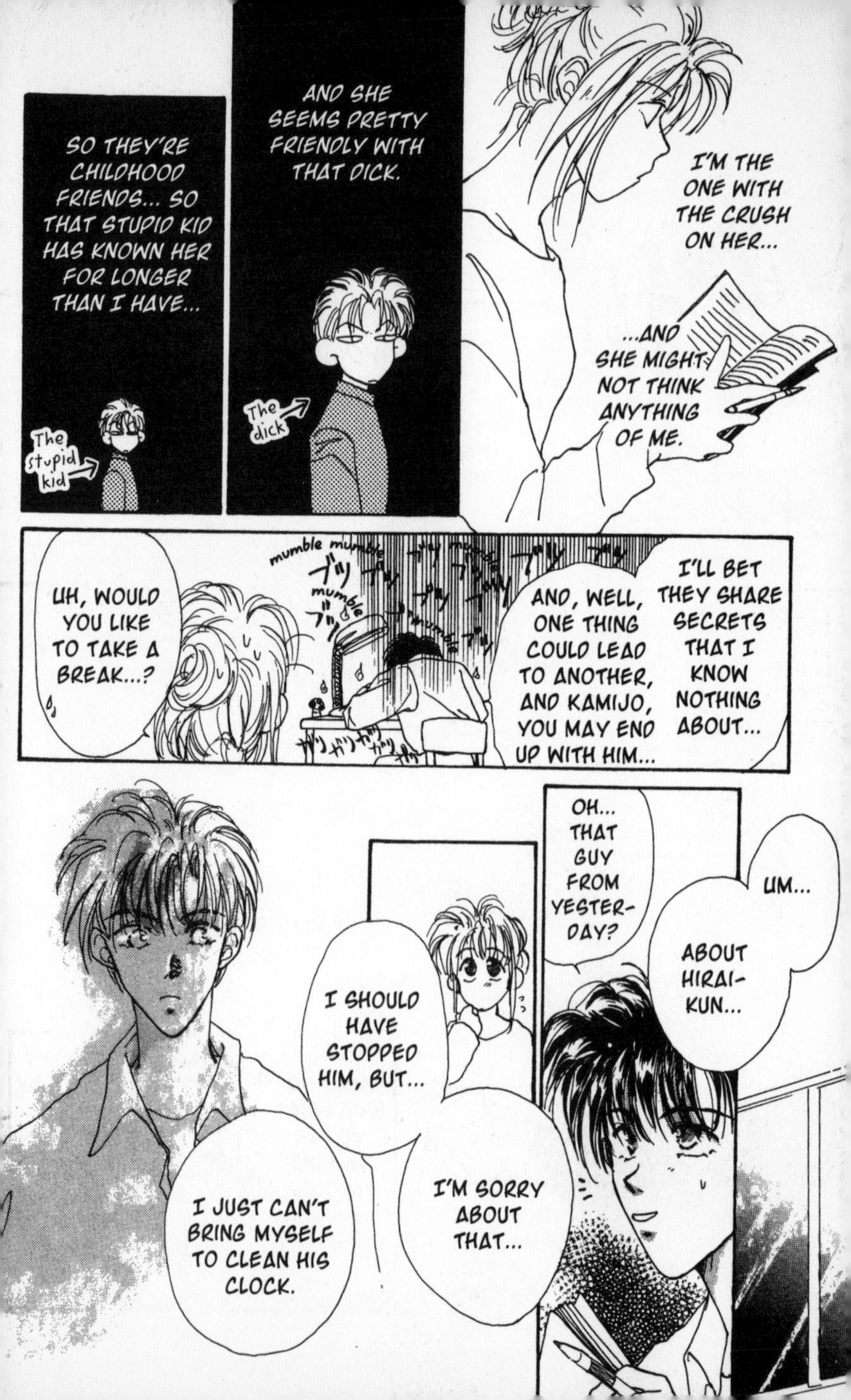
I'M THE ONE WITH THE CRUSH ON HER...
...AND SHE MIGHT NOT THINK ANYTHING OF ME.
AND SHE SEEMS PRETTY FRIENDLY WITH THAT DICK.
The dick
SO THEY'RE CHILDHOOD FRIENDS... SO THAT STUPID KID HAS KNOWN HER FOR LONGER THAN I HAVE...
The stupid kid
I'LL BET THEY SHARE SECRETS THAT I KNOW NOTHING ABOUT...
AND, WELL, ONE THING COULD LEAD TO ANOTHER, AND KAMIJO, YOU MAY END UP WITH HIM...
mumble mumble
mumble
UH, WOULD YOU LIKE TO TAKE A BREAK...?
UM...
ABOUT HIRAI-KUN...
OH... THAT GUY FROM YESTERDAY?
I'M SORRY ABOUT THAT...
I SHOULD HAVE STOPPED HIM, BUT...
I JUST CAN'T BRING MYSELF TO CLEAN HIS CLOCK.

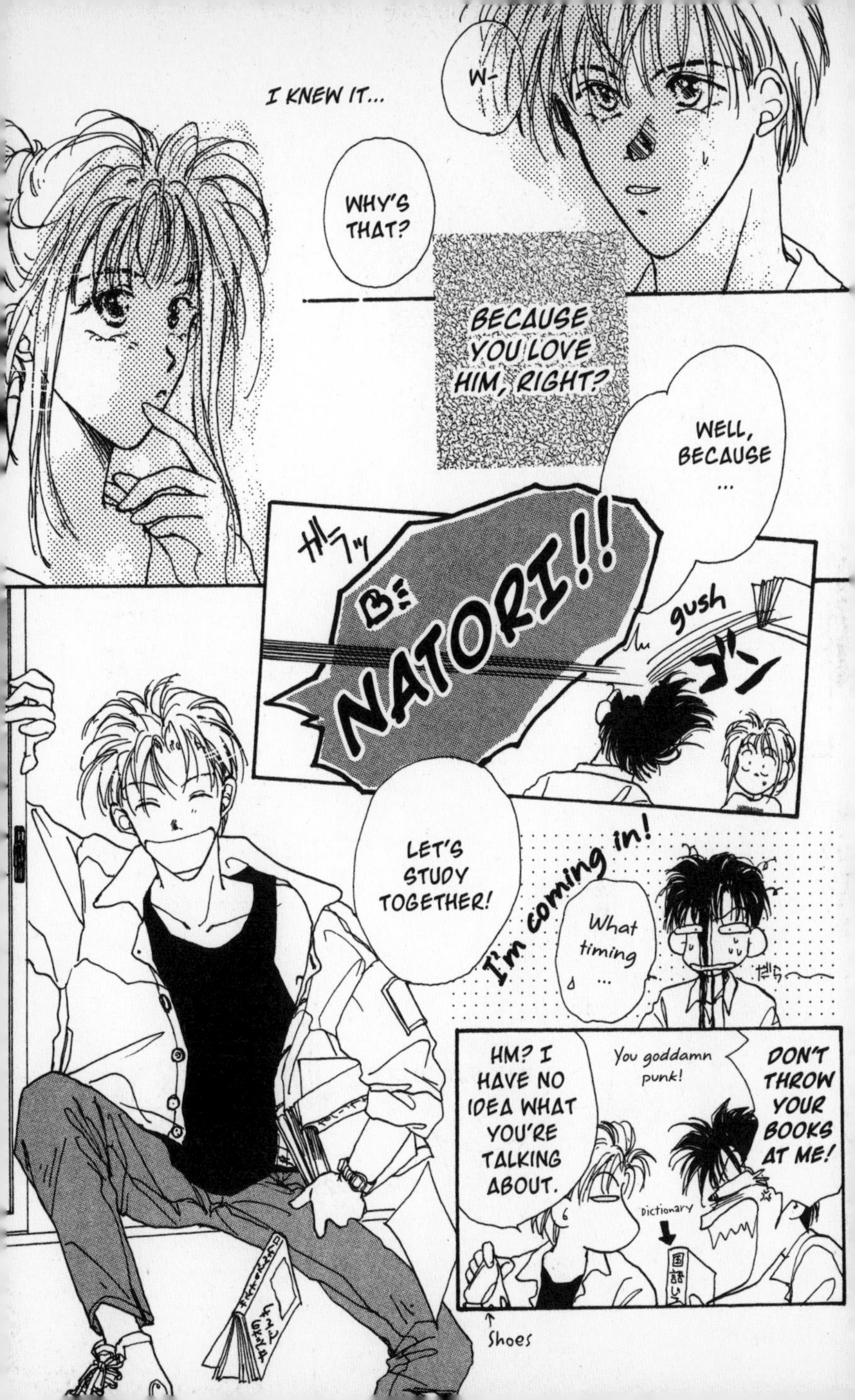
W-
WHY'S THAT?
I KNEW IT...
BECAUSE YOU LOVE HIM, RIGHT?
WELL, BECAUSE ...
gush
B: NATORI!!
I'm coming in!
What timing ...
DON'T THROW YOUR BOOKS AT ME!
You goddamn punk!
HM? I HAVE NO IDEA WHAT YOU'RE TALKING ABOUT.
Dictionary
Shoes
LET'S STUDY TOGETHER!

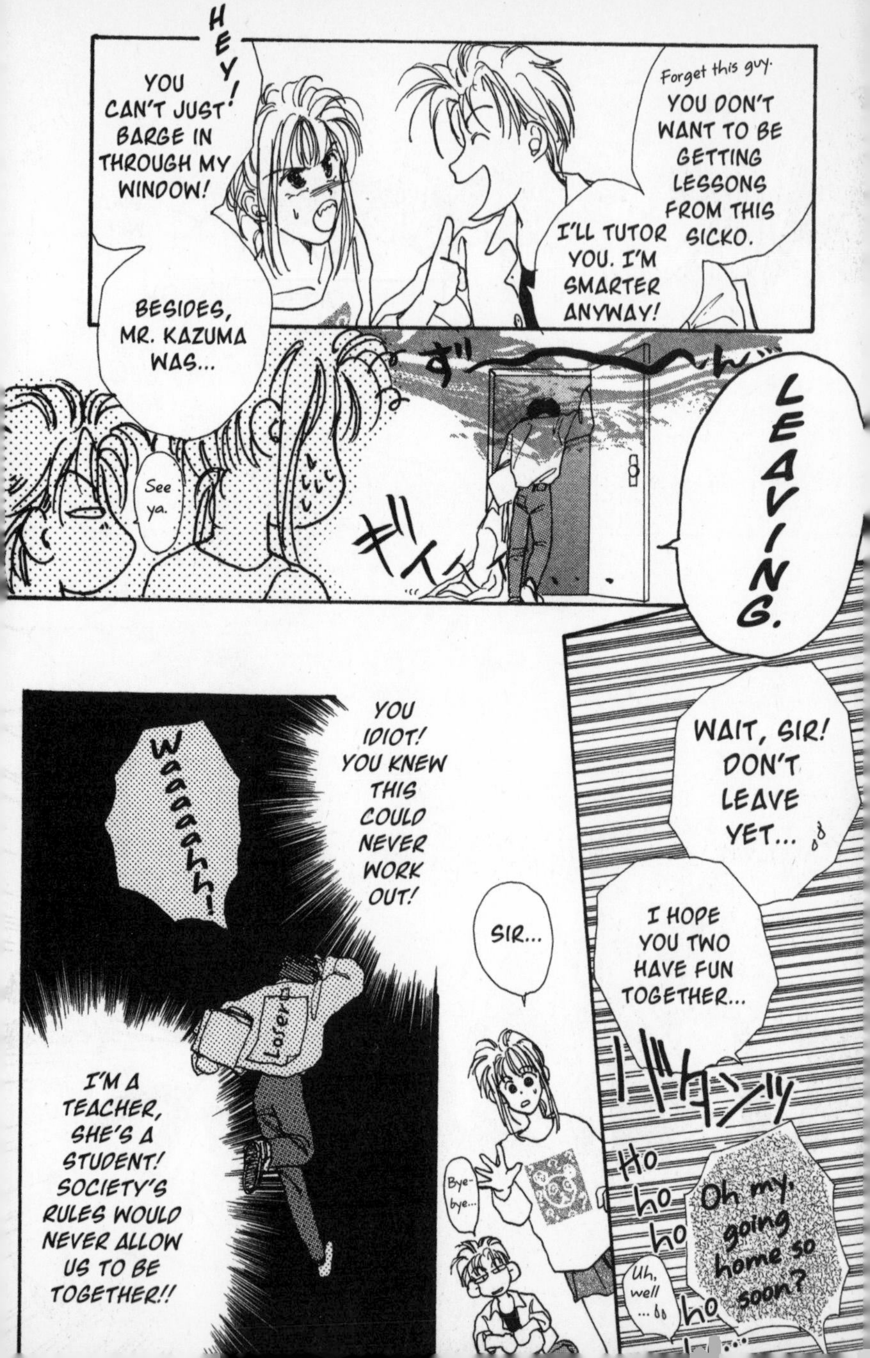
Forget this guy.
YOU DON'T WANT TO BE GETTING LESSONS FROM THIS SICKO.
I'LL TUTOR YOU. I'M SMARTER ANYWAY!
HEY!
YOU CAN'T JUST BARGE IN THROUGH MY WINDOW!
BESIDES, MR. KAZUMA WAS...
LEAVING.
ずーん
ギィ
See ya.
WAIT, SIR! DON'T LEAVE YET...
I HOPE YOU TWO HAVE FUN TOGETHER...
Ho ho ho ho
Oh my, going home so soon?
Uh, well...
Bye-bye...
SIR...
YOU IDIOT! YOU KNEW THIS COULD NEVER WORK OUT!
Waaaaahh!
Loser
I'M A TEACHER, SHE'S A STUDENT! SOCIETY'S RULES WOULD NEVER ALLOW US TO BE TOGETHER!!

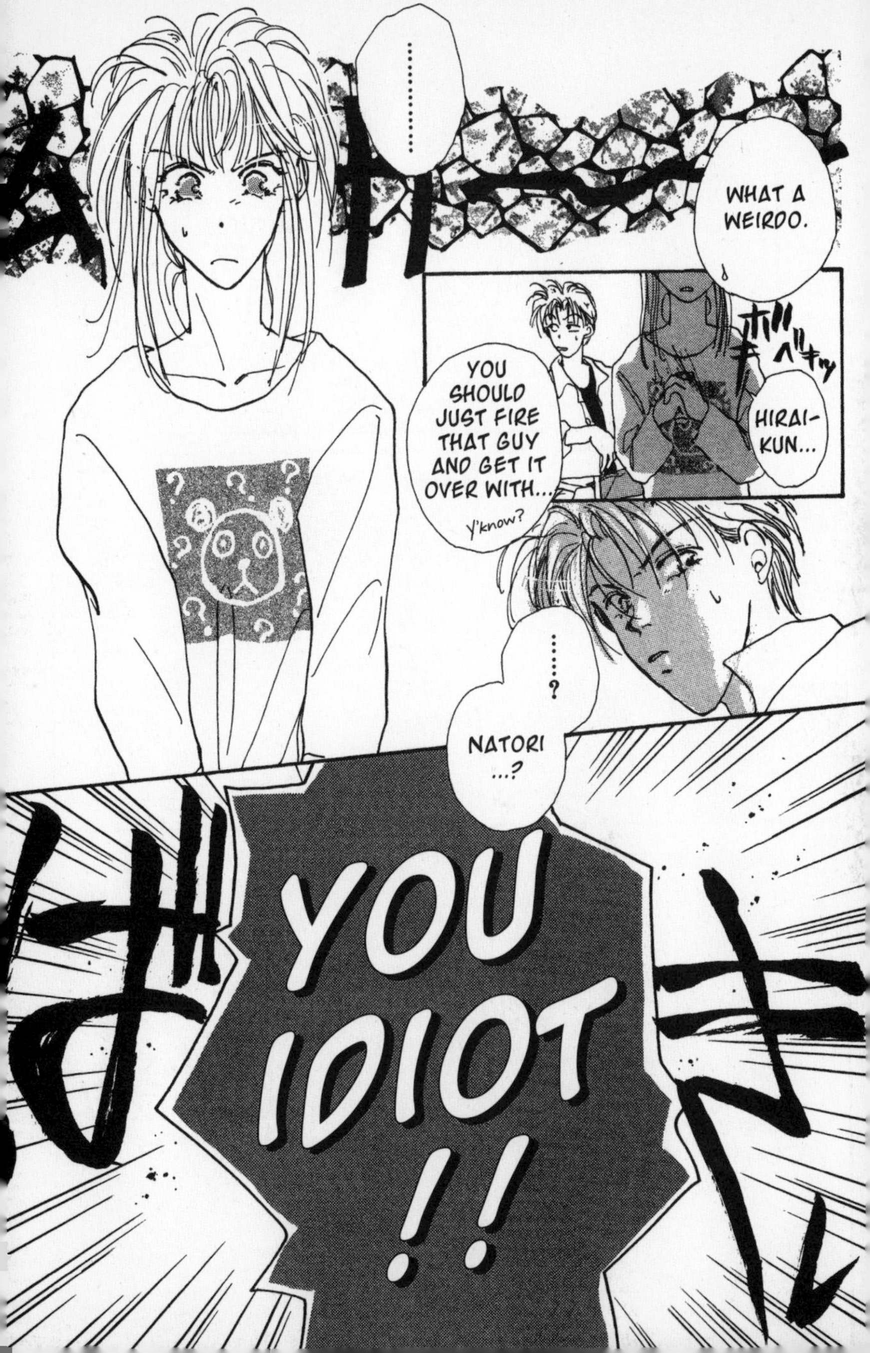
WHAT A WEIRDO.
HIRAI-KUN...
YOU SHOULD JUST FIRE THAT GUY AND GET IT OVER WITH...
Y'know?
......?
NATORI ...?
......
YOU IDIOT !!

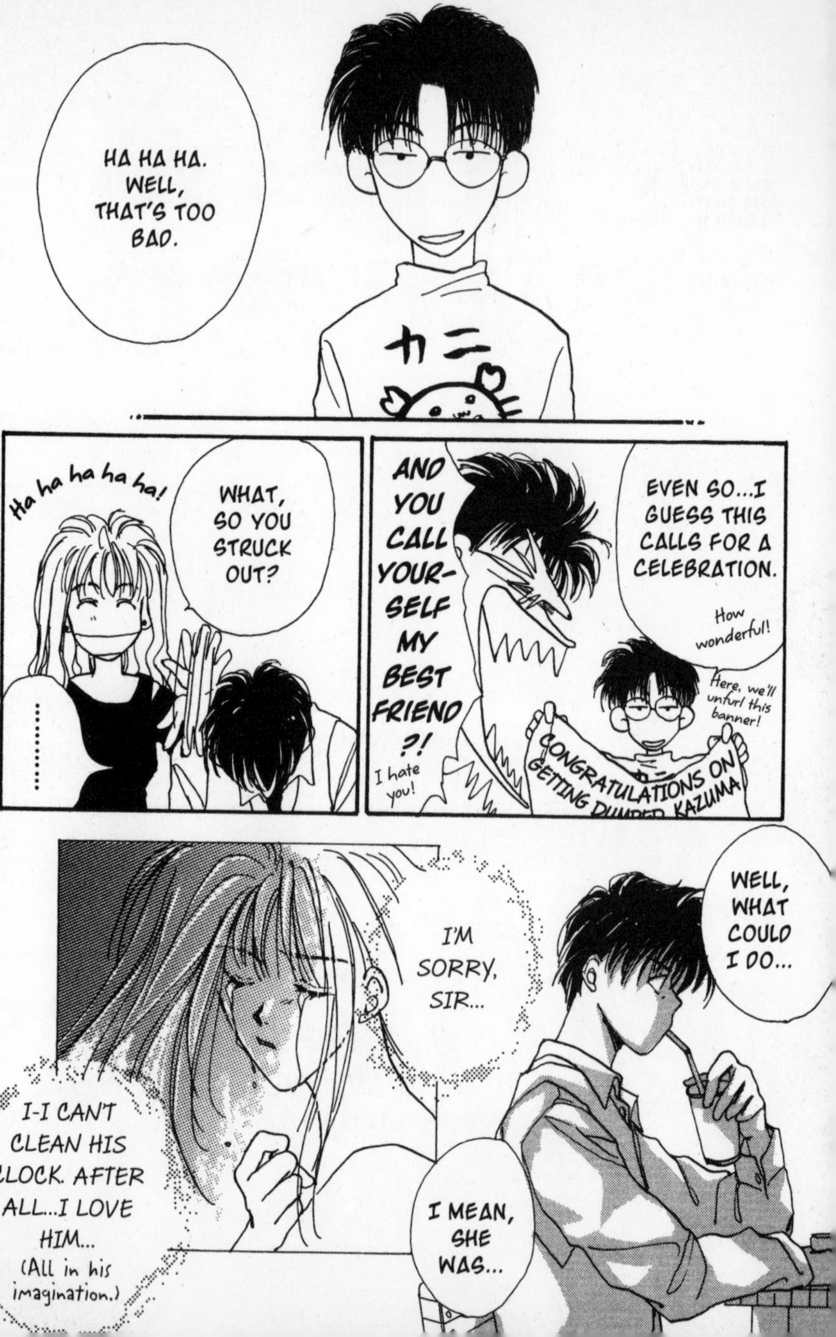
HA HA HA. WELL, THAT'S TOO BAD.
カニ
EVEN SO...I GUESS THIS CALLS FOR A CELEBRATION.
How wonderful!
Here, we'll unfurl this banner!
CONGRATULATIONS ON GETTING DUMPED KAZUMA
AND YOU CALL YOURSELF MY BEST FRIEND?!
I hate you!
WHAT, SO YOU STRUCK OUT?
Ha ha ha ha ha!
....
WELL, WHAT COULD I DO...
I'M SORRY, SIR...
I MEAN, SHE WAS...
I-I CAN'T CLEAN HIS CLOCK. AFTER ALL...I LOVE HIM...
(All in his imagination.)

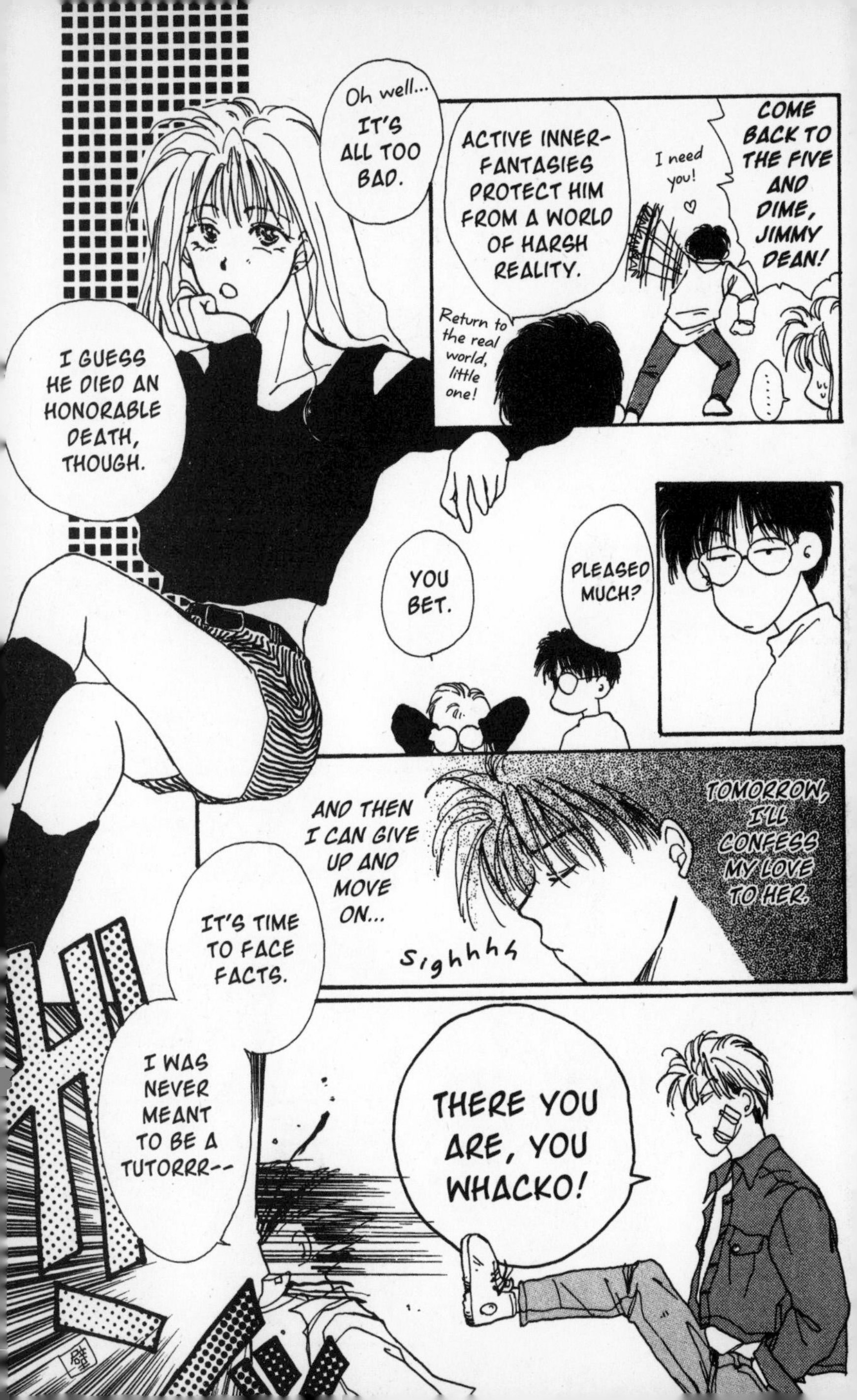
COME BACK TO THE FIVE AND DIME, JIMMY DEAN!
I need you!
ACTIVE INNER-FANTASIES PROTECT HIM FROM A WORLD OF HARSH REALITY.
Return to the real world, little one!
......
Oh well... IT'S ALL TOO BAD.
I GUESS HE DIED AN HONORABLE DEATH, THOUGH.
PLEASED MUCH?
YOU BET.
TOMORROW, I'LL CONFESS MY LOVE TO HER.
AND THEN I CAN GIVE UP AND MOVE ON...
Sighhhh
IT'S TIME TO FACE FACTS.
I WAS NEVER MEANT TO BE A TUTORRR--
THERE YOU ARE, YOU WHACKO!

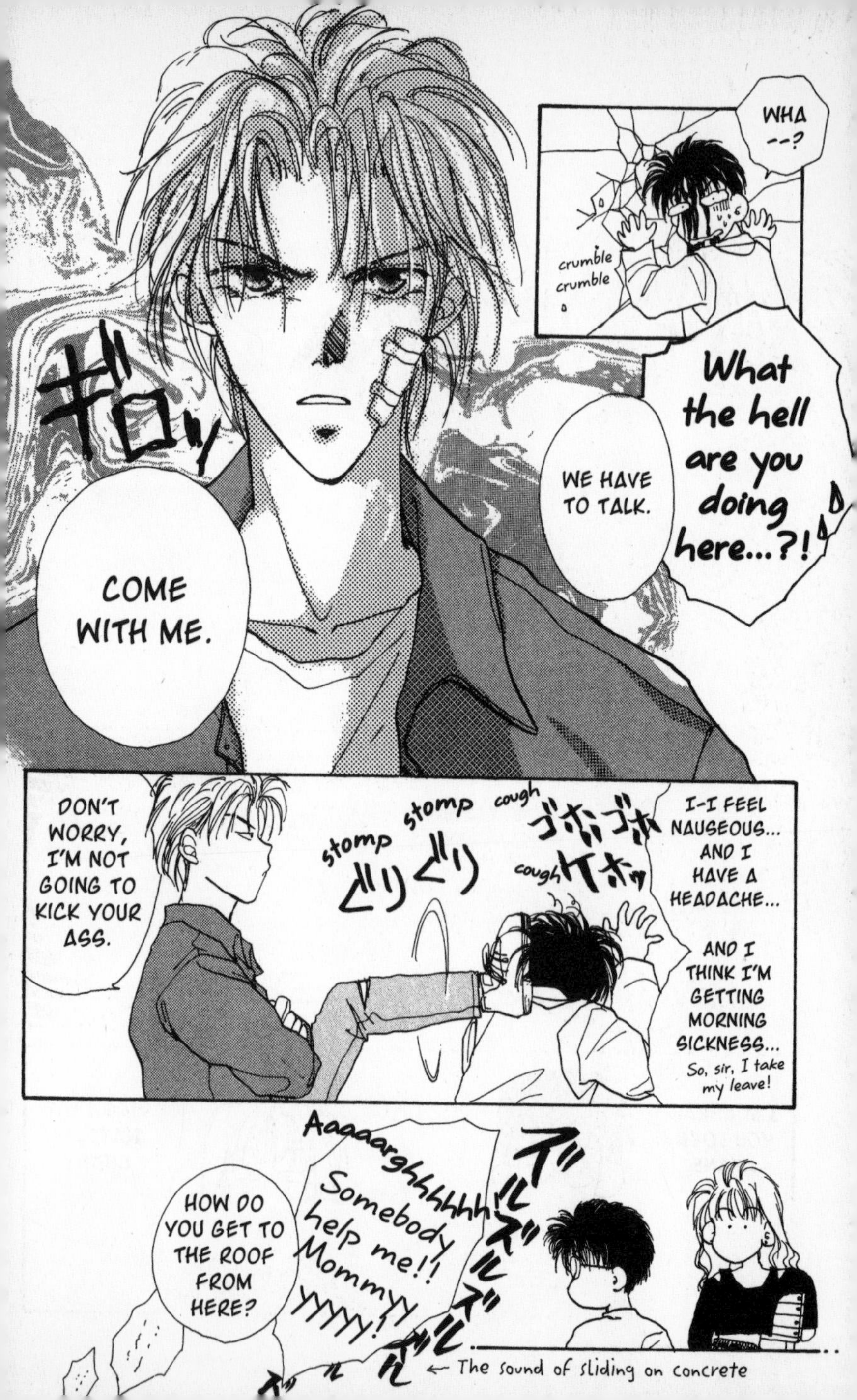
WHA--?
crumble crumble
What the hell are you doing here...?!
WE HAVE TO TALK.
ギロッ
COME WITH ME.
I-I FEEL NAUSEOUS... AND I HAVE A HEADACHE...
AND I THINK I'M GETTING MORNING SICKNESS... So, sir, I take my leave!
cough ゴホゴホ
cough ケホッ
stomp ごり
stomp ごり
DON'T WORRY, I'M NOT GOING TO KICK YOUR ASS.
← The sound of sliding on concrete
ズルズルズルズル
Aaaaarghhhhhh Somebody help me!! Mommyyyyyyy!
HOW DO YOU GET TO THE ROOF FROM HERE?

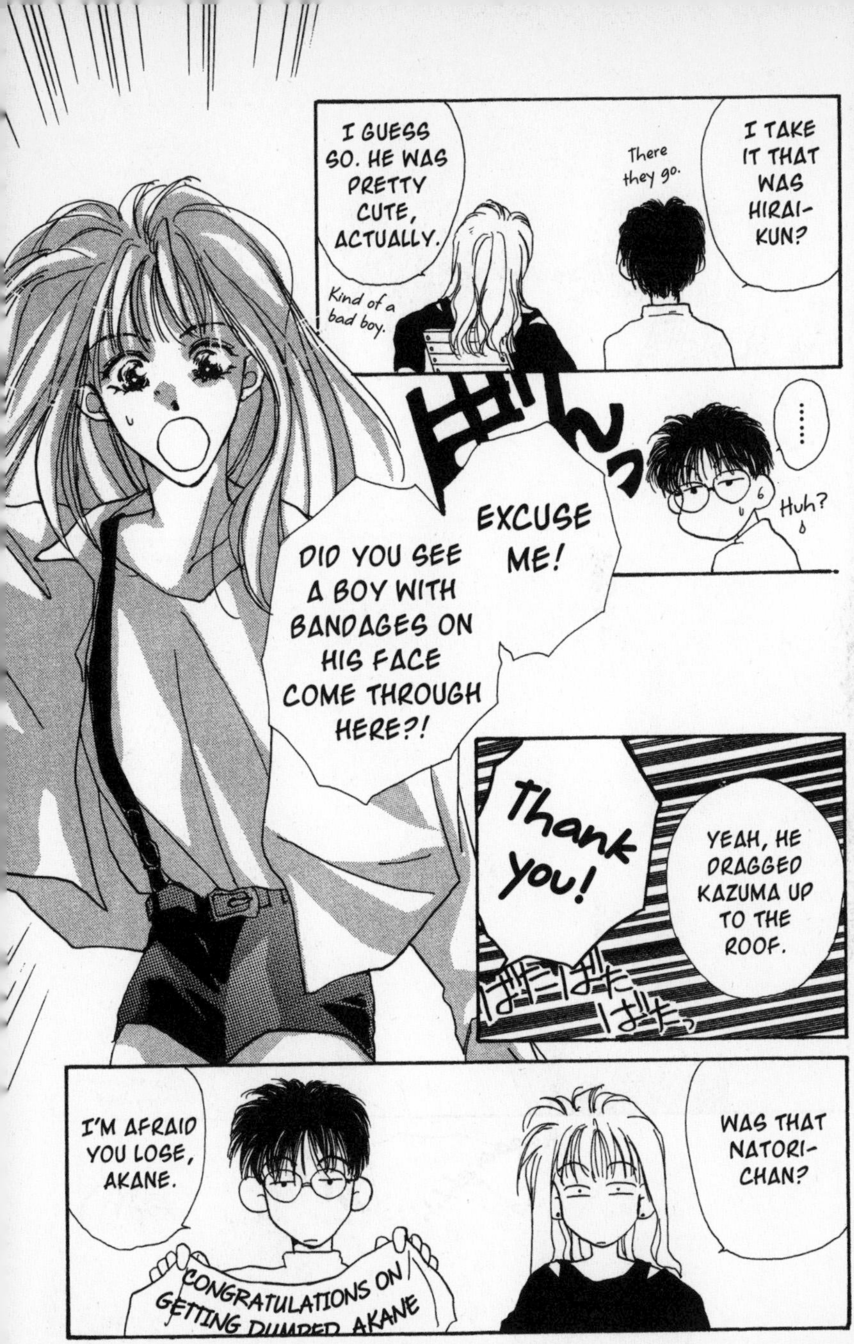
I TAKE IT THAT WAS HIRAI-KUN?
There they go.
I GUESS SO. HE WAS PRETTY CUTE, ACTUALLY.
Kind of a bad boy.
......
Huh?
EXCUSE ME!
DID YOU SEE A BOY WITH BANDAGES ON HIS FACE COME THROUGH HERE?!
Thank you!
YEAH, HE DRAGGED KAZUMA UP TO THE ROOF.
ぱたぱた ぱたっ
WAS THAT NATORI-CHAN?
I'M AFRAID YOU LOSE, AKANE.
CONGRATULATIONS ON GETTING DUMPED AKANE

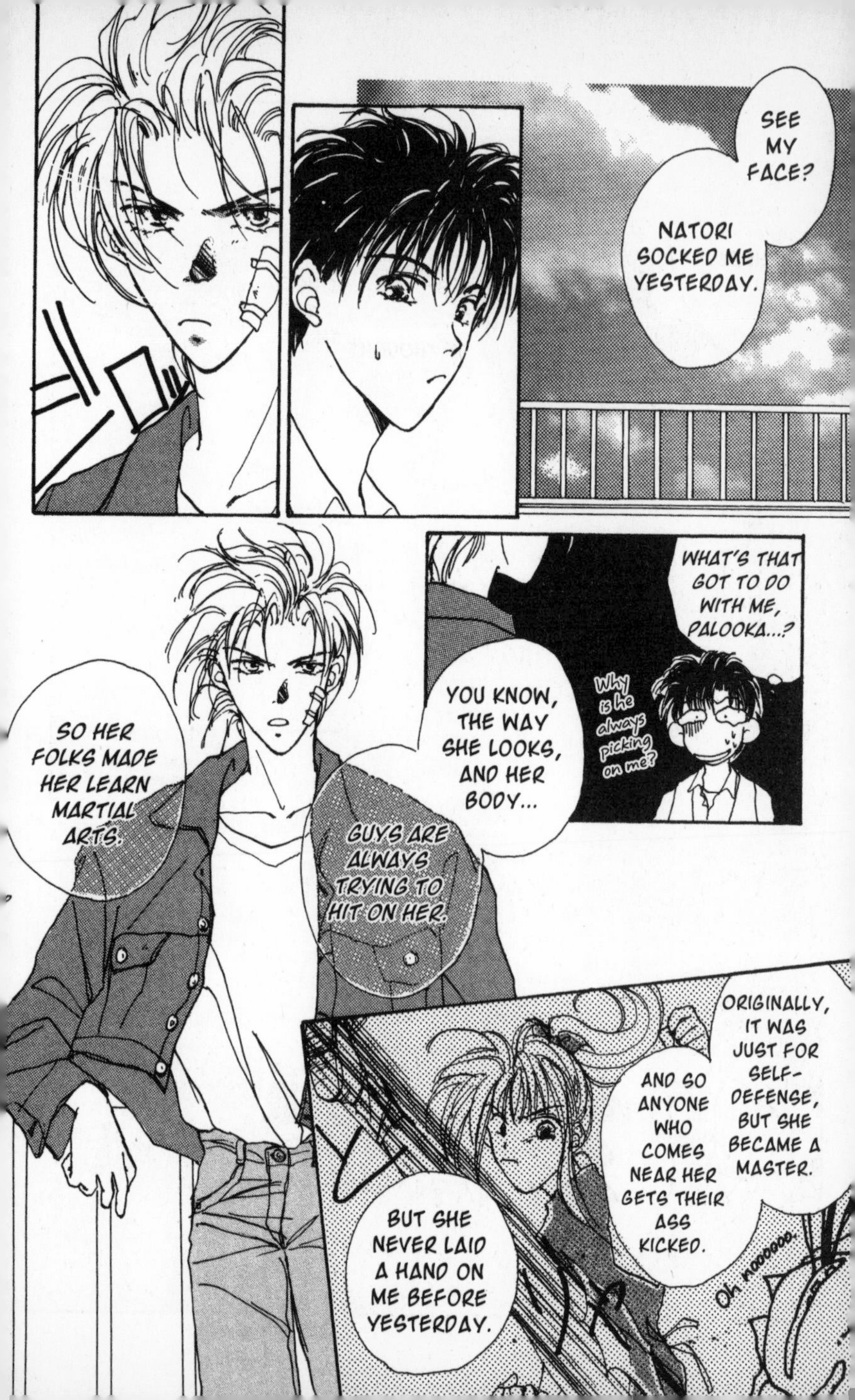
SEE MY FACE?
NATORI SOCKED ME YESTERDAY.
WHAT'S THAT GOT TO DO WITH ME, PALOOKA...?
Why is he always picking on me?
YOU KNOW, THE WAY SHE LOOKS, AND HER BODY...
GUYS ARE ALWAYS TRYING TO HIT ON HER.
SO HER FOLKS MADE HER LEARN MARTIAL ARTS.
ORIGINALLY, IT WAS JUST FOR SELF-DEFENSE, BUT SHE BECAME A MASTER.
AND SO ANYONE WHO COMES NEAR HER GETS THEIR ASS KICKED.
Oh nooooooo.
BUT SHE NEVER LAID A HAND ON ME BEFORE YESTERDAY.

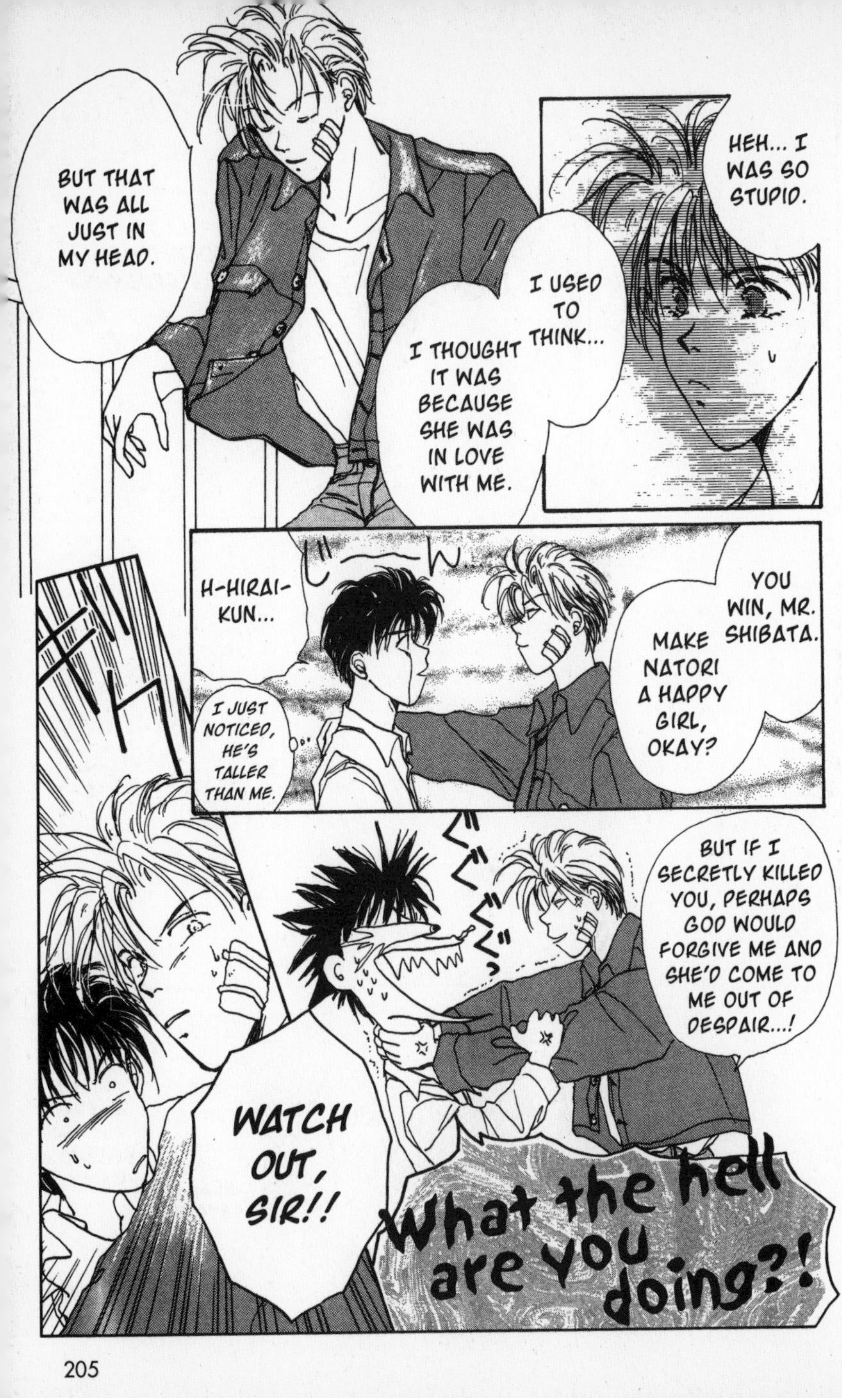
HEH... I WAS SO STUPID.
I USED TO THINK...
I THOUGHT IT WAS BECAUSE SHE WAS IN LOVE WITH ME.
BUT THAT WAS ALL JUST IN MY HEAD.
YOU WIN, MR. SHIBATA.
MAKE NATORI A HAPPY GIRL, OKAY?
H-HIRAI-KUN...
I JUST NOTICED, HE'S TALLER THAN ME.
BUT IF I SECRETLY KILLED YOU, PERHAPS GOD WOULD FORGIVE ME AND SHE'D COME TO ME OUT OF DESPAIR...!
What the hell are you doing?!
WATCH OUT, SIR!!

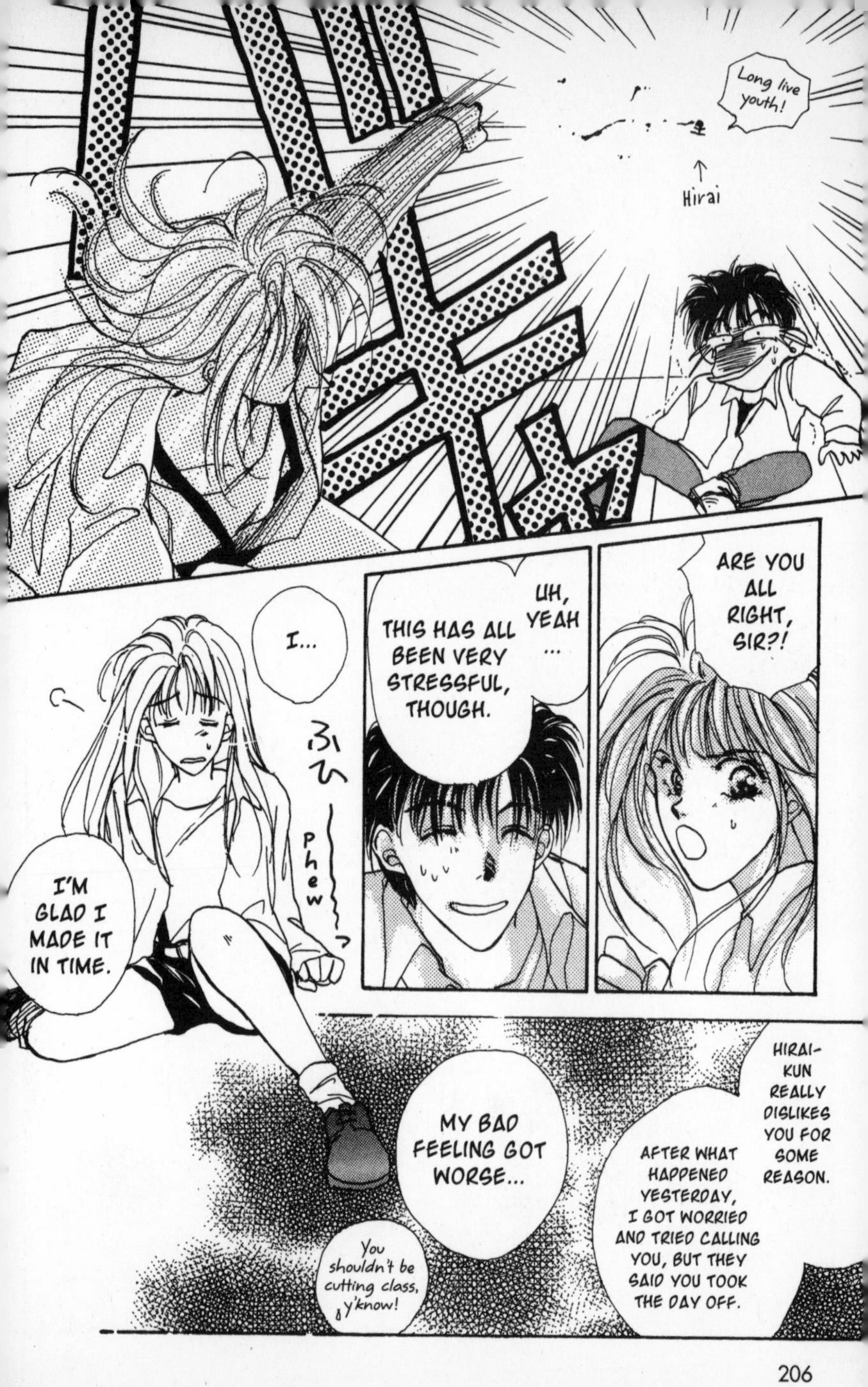
Long live youth!
Hirai
ARE YOU ALL RIGHT, SIR?!
UH, YEAH ...
THIS HAS ALL BEEN VERY STRESSFUL, THOUGH.
I...
Phew
I'M GLAD I MADE IT IN TIME.
HIRAI-KUN REALLY DISLIKES YOU FOR SOME REASON.
AFTER WHAT HAPPENED YESTERDAY, I GOT WORRIED AND TRIED CALLING YOU, BUT THEY SAID YOU TOOK THE DAY OFF.
MY BAD FEELING GOT WORSE...
You shouldn't be cutting class, y'know!

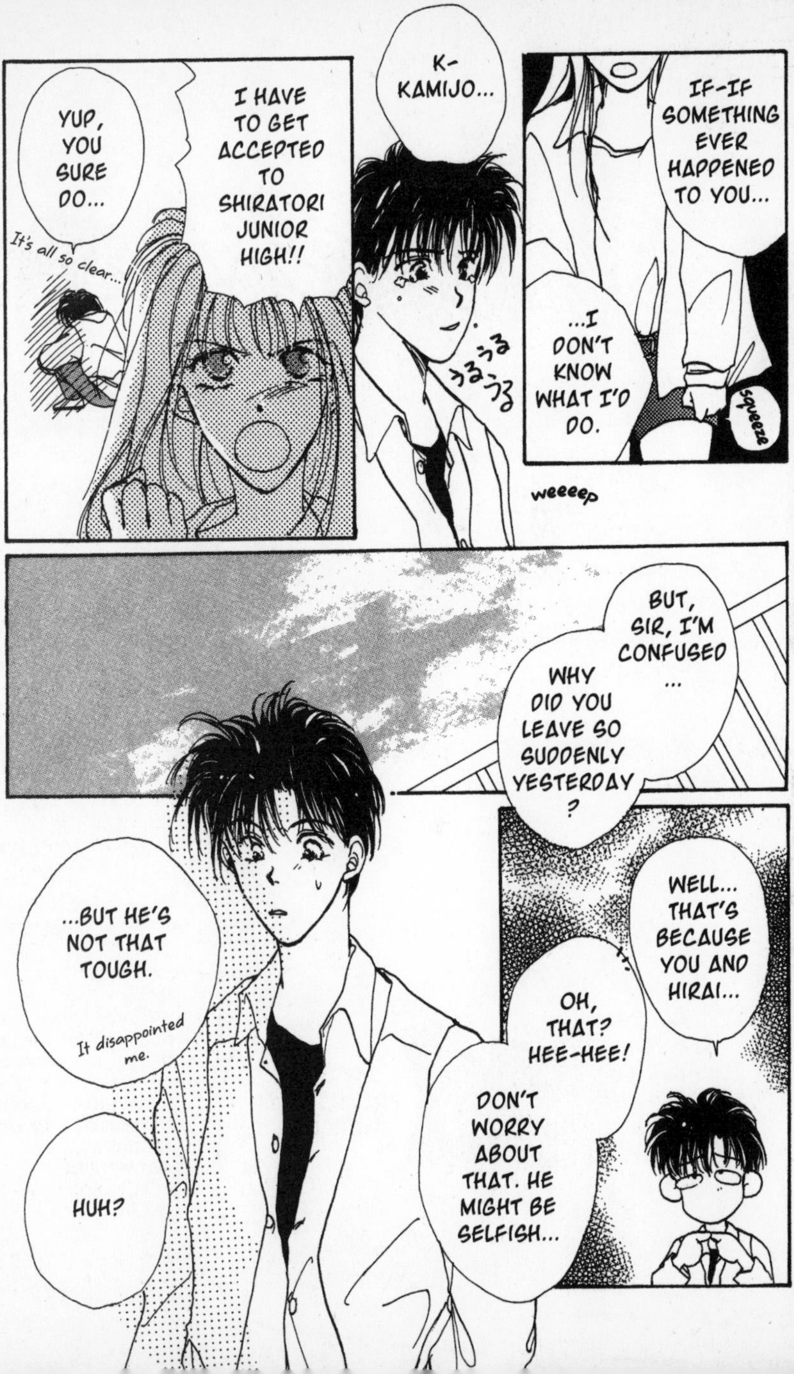
IF-IF SOMETHING EVER HAPPENED TO YOU...
...I DON'T KNOW WHAT I'D DO.
squeeze
K-KAMIJO...
うるうる うるうる
weeeep
I HAVE TO GET ACCEPTED TO SHIRATORI JUNIOR HIGH!!
YUP, YOU SURE DO...
It's all so clear...
BUT, SIR, I'M CONFUSED...
WHY DID YOU LEAVE SO SUDDENLY YESTERDAY?
WELL... THAT'S BECAUSE YOU AND HIRAI...
OH, THAT? HEE-HEE!
DON'T WORRY ABOUT THAT. HE MIGHT BE SELFISH...
...BUT HE'S NOT THAT TOUGH.
It disappointed me.
HUH?

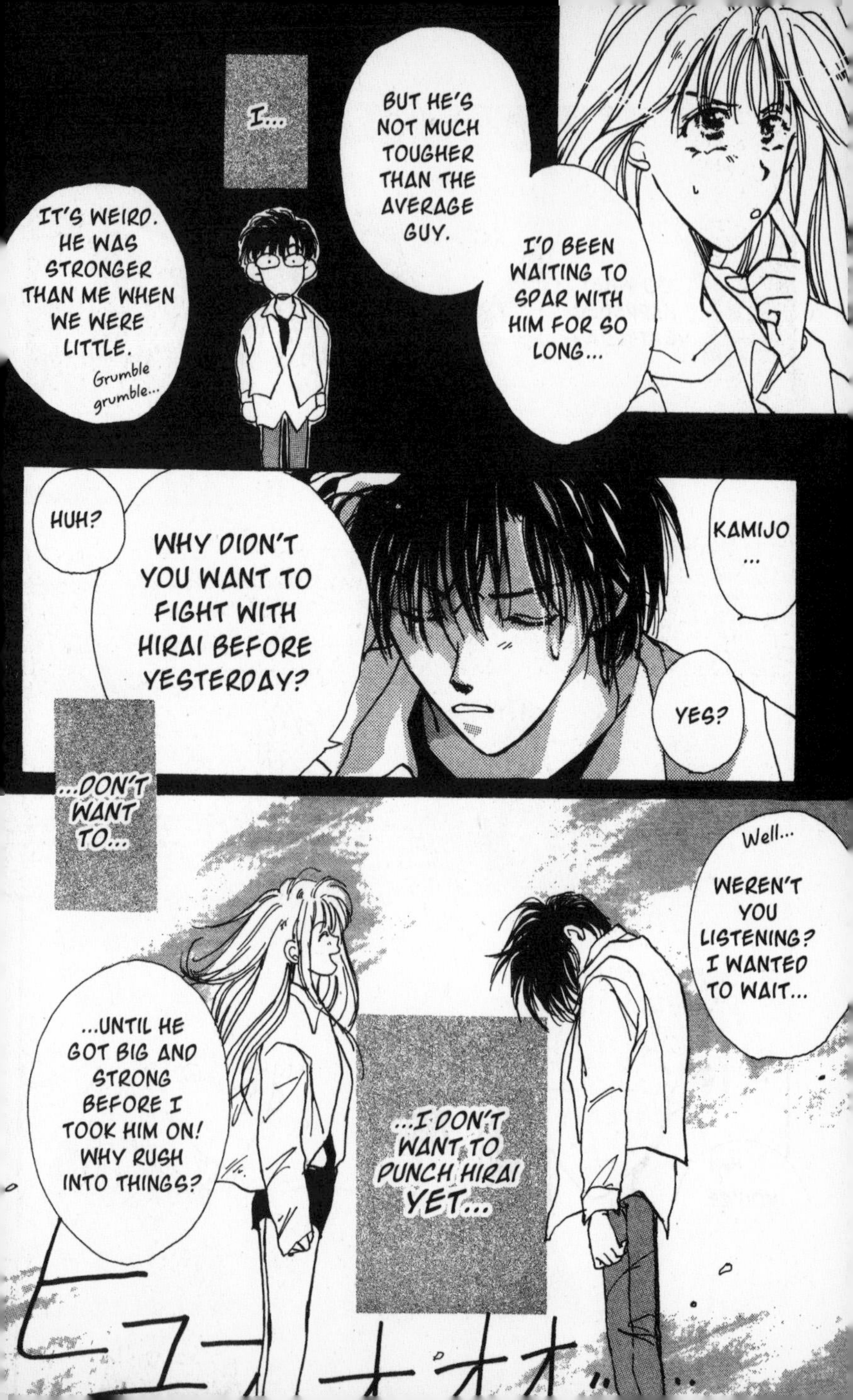
BUT HE'S NOT MUCH TOUGHER THAN THE AVERAGE GUY.
I'D BEEN WAITING TO SPAR WITH HIM FOR SO LONG...
I...
IT'S WEIRD. HE WAS STRONGER THAN ME WHEN WE WERE LITTLE.
Grumble grumble...
KAMIJO...
YES?
WHY DIDN'T YOU WANT TO FIGHT WITH HIRAI BEFORE YESTERDAY?
HUH?
...DON'T WANT TO...
Well...
WEREN'T YOU LISTENING? I WANTED TO WAIT...
...I DON'T WANT TO PUNCH HIRAI YET...
...UNTIL HE GOT BIG AND STRONG BEFORE I TOOK HIM ON! WHY RUSH INTO THINGS?
ヒューーオオオ…

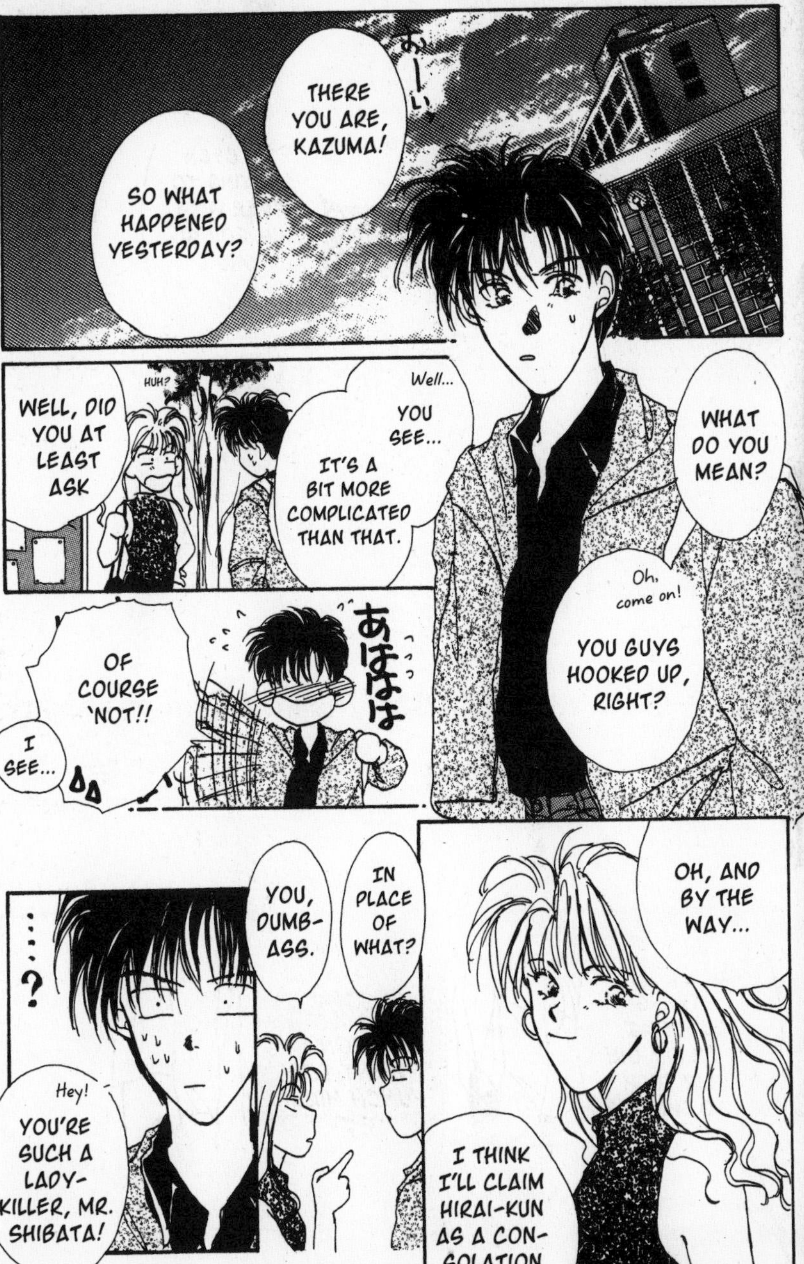
おーい
THERE YOU ARE, KAZUMA!
SO WHAT HAPPENED YESTERDAY?
WHAT DO YOU MEAN?
Oh, come on!
YOU GUYS HOOKED UP, RIGHT?
Well...
YOU SEE...
IT'S A BIT MORE COMPLICATED THAN THAT.
HUH?
WELL, DID YOU AT LEAST ASK
あははは
OF COURSE 'NOT!!
I SEE...
OH, AND BY THE WAY...
I THINK I'LL CLAIM HIRAI-KUN AS A CON-SOLATION PRIZE.
IN PLACE OF WHAT?
YOU, DUMB-ASS.
...?
Hey!
YOU'RE SUCH A LADY-KILLER, MR. SHIBATA!

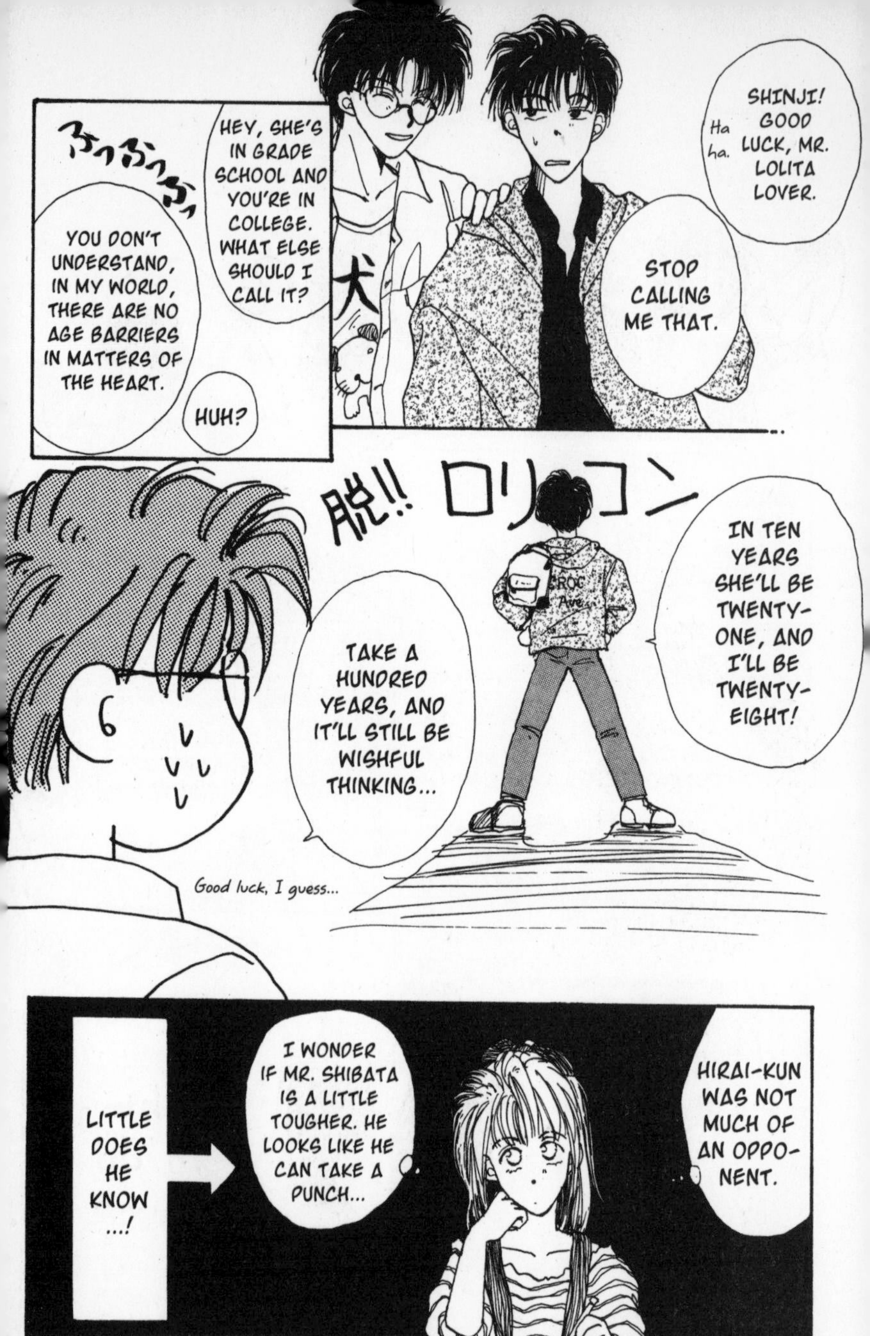

SHINJI! GOOD LUCK, MR. LOLITA LOVER.
Ha ha.
STOP CALLING ME THAT.
HEY, SHE'S IN GRADE SCHOOL AND YOU'RE IN COLLEGE. WHAT ELSE SHOULD I CALL IT?
ふっふっふっ
YOU DON'T UNDERSTAND, IN MY WORLD, THERE ARE NO AGE BARRIERS IN MATTERS OF THE HEART.
HUH?
脱!! ロリコン
IN TEN YEARS SHE'LL BE TWENTY-ONE, AND I'LL BE TWENTY-EIGHT!
TAKE A HUNDRED YEARS, AND IT'LL STILL BE WISHFUL THINKING...
Good luck, I guess...
HIRAI-KUN WAS NOT MUCH OF AN OPPO-NENT.
I WONDER IF MR. SHIBATA IS A LITTLE TOUGHER. HE LOOKS LIKE HE CAN TAKE A PUNCH...
LITTLE DOES HE KNOW ...!

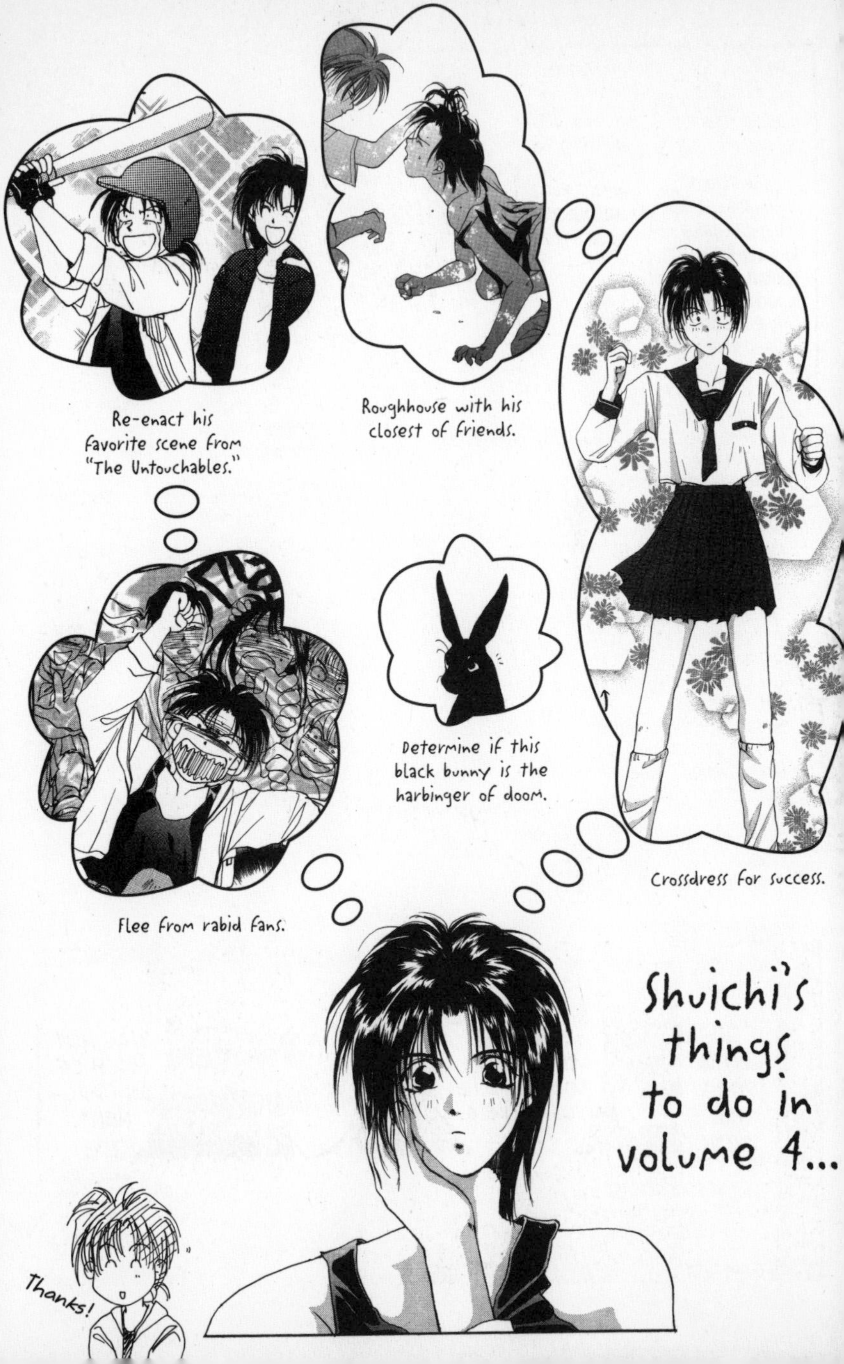
Shuichi's things to do in volume 4...
Crossdress for success.
Roughhouse with his closest of friends.
Re-enact his favorite scene from "The Untouchables."
Determine if this black bunny is the harbinger of doom.
Flee from rabid fans.
Thanks!

ALSO AVAILABLE FROM TOKYOPOP®

**For more
information visit
www.TOKYOPOP.com**

10103

ALSO AVAILABLE FROM ☺TOKYOPOP®

MANGA

.HACK//LEGEND OF THE TWILIGHT
@LARGE
A.I. LOVE YOU February 2004
AI YORI AOSHI January 2004
ANGELIC LAYER
BABY BIRTH
BATTLE ROYALE
BATTLE VIXENS April 2004
BIRTH May 2004
BRAIN POWERED
BRIGADOON
B'TX January 2004
CARDCAPTOR SAKURA
CARDCAPTOR SAKURA - MASTER OF THE CLOW
CARDCAPTOR SAKURA: BOXED SET COLLECTION 1
CARDCAPTOR SAKURA: BOXED SET COLLECTION 2
    March 2004
CHOBITS
CHRONICLES OF THE CURSED SWORD
CLAMP SCHOOL DETECTIVES
CLOVER
COMIC PARTY June 2004
CONFIDENTIAL CONFESSIONS
CORRECTOR YUI
COWBOY BEBOP: BOXED SET THE COMPLETE
    COLLECTION
CRESCENT MOON May 2004
CREST OF THE STARS June 2004
CYBORG 009
DEMON DIARY
DIGIMON
DIGIMON SERIES 3 April 2004
DIGIMON ZERO TWO February 2004
DNANGEL April 2004
DOLL May 2004
DRAGON HUNTER
DRAGON KNIGHTS
DUKLYON: CLAMP SCHOOL DEFENDERS:
DV June 2004
ERICA SAKURAZAWA
FAERIES' LANDING January 2004
FAKE
FLCL
FORBIDDEN DANCE
FRUITS BASKET February 2004
G GUNDAM
GATEKEEPERS
GETBACKERS February 2004
GHOST! March 2004
GIRL GOT GAME January 2004
GRAVITATION
GTO

GUNDAM WING
GUNDAM WING: BATTLEFIELD OF PACIFISTS
GUNDAM WING: ENDLESS WALTZ
GUNDAM WING: THE LAST OUTPOST
HAPPY MANIA
HARLEM BEAT
I.N.V.U.
INITIAL D
ISLAND
JING: KING OF BANDITS
JULINE
JUROR 13 March 2004
KARE KANO
KILL ME, KISS ME February 2004
KINDAICHI CASE FILES, THE
KING OF HELL
KODOCHA: SANA'S STAGE
LAMENT OF THE LAMB May 2004
LES BIJOUX February 2004
LIZZIE MCGUIRE
LOVE HINA
LUPIN III
LUPIN III SERIES 2
MAGIC KNIGHT RAYEARTH I
MAGIC KNIGHT RAYEARTH II February 2004
MAHOROMATIC: AUTOMATIC MAIDEN May 2004
MAN OF MANY FACES
MARMALADE BOY
MARS
METEOR METHUSELA June 2004
METROID June 2004
MINK April 2004
MIRACLE GIRLS
MIYUKI-CHAN IN WONDERLAND
MODEL May 2004
NELLY MUSIC MANGA April 2004
ONE April 2004
PARADISE KISS
PARASYTE
PEACH GIRL
PEACH GIRL CHANGE OF HEART
PEACH GIRL RELAUNCH BOX SET
PET SHOP OF HORRORS
PITA-TEN January 2004
PLANET LADDER February 2004
PLANETES
PRIEST
PRINCESS AI April 2004
PSYCHIC ACADEMY March 2004
RAGNAROK
RAGNAROK: BOXED SET COLLECTION 1
RAVE MASTER
RAVE MASTER: BOXED SET March 2004

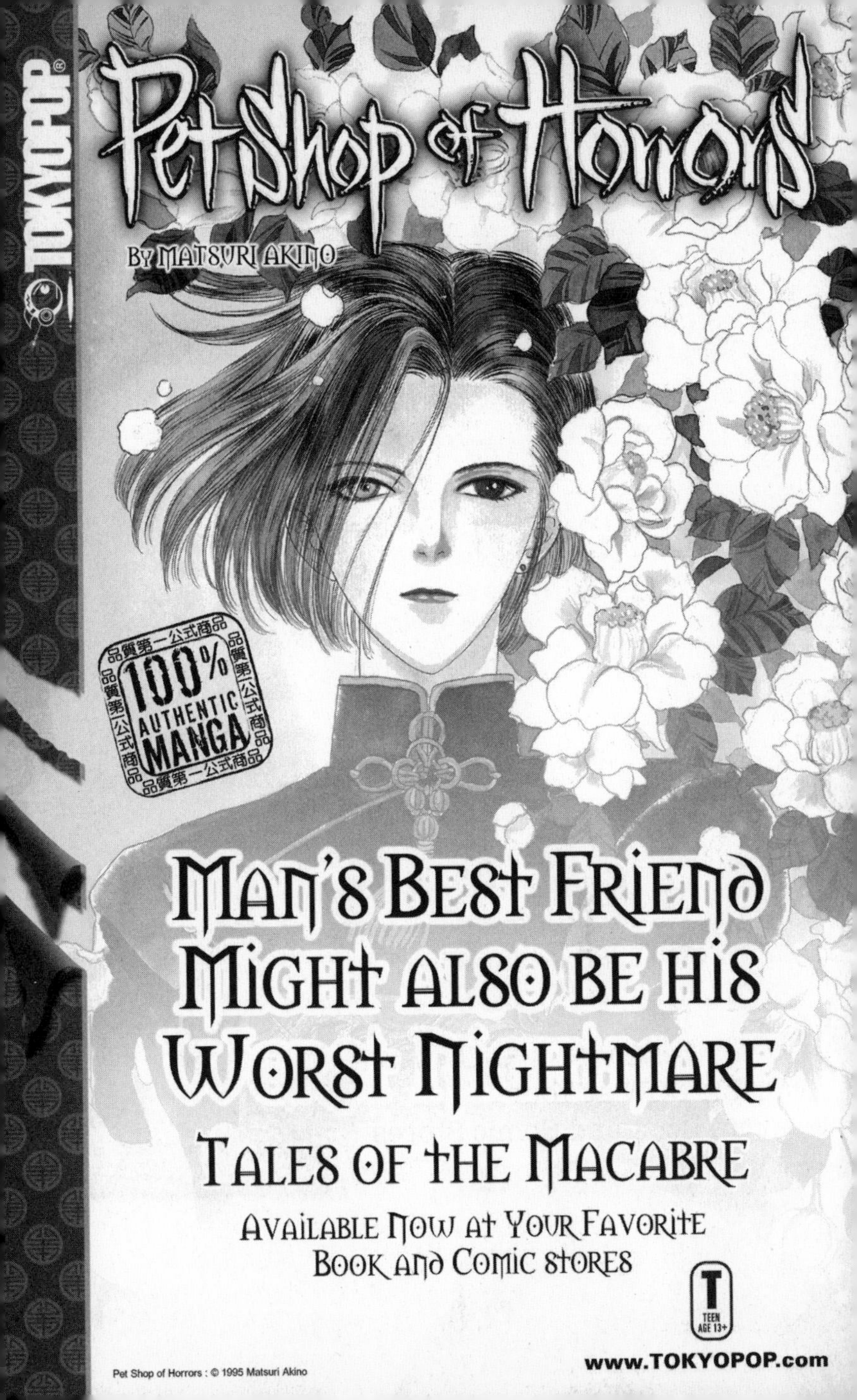
TOKYOPOP
Pet Shop of Horrors
BY MATSURI AKINO
100% AUTHENTIC MANGA
品質第一公式商品
MAN'S BEST FRIEND MIGHT ALSO BE HIS WORST NIGHTMARE
TALES OF THE MACABRE
AVAILABLE NOW AT YOUR FAVORITE BOOK AND COMIC STORES
T TEEN AGE 13+
www.TOKYOPOP.com
Pet Shop of Horrors : © 1995 Matsuri Akino

STOP!

This is the back of the book.
You wouldn't want to spoil a great ending!

This book is printed "manga-style," in the authentic Japanese right-to-left format. Since none of the artwork has been flipped or altered, readers get to experience the story just as the creator intended. You've been asking for it, so TOKYOPOP® delivered: authentic, hot-off-the-press, and far more fun!

DIRECTIONS

If this is your first time reading manga-style, here's a quick guide to help you understand how it works.

It's easy... just start in the top right panel and follow the numbers. Have fun, and look for more 100% authentic manga from TOKYOPOP®!